Understanding Jewish History

Texts and Commentaries

Understanding Jewish History

TEXTS AND COMMENTARIES

by

Steven Bayme

KTAV Publishing House, Inc.

in association with

The American Jewish Committee

Library of Congress Cataloging-in-Publication Data

Understanding Jewish history : texts and commentaries / [edited] by Steven Bayme.
p. cm.
Includes bibliographical references and index.
ISBN 0-88125-581-5 (hc)
1.Jews—History—Sources 2. Judaism—History—Sources. I. Bayme, Steven.
DS102.U53 1997
909'.04924—DC21 97-6196
CIP
r97

Manufactured in the United States of America

Funds for this volume were made available by a grant
from the Susan and Jack Lapin Fund for Jewish Continuity.

Contents

	Acknowledgments	ix
	Introduction	xiii
I	Creation, Covenant, Redemption	1
II	Monarchy and Political Centralization	12
III	Prophecy and Biblical Religion	24
IV	Destruction and Exile	35
V	Athens and Jerusalem	50
VI	Jewish Sectarianism	63
VII	Rome and Jerusalem	74
VIII	Destruction and Renewal	89
IX	Origins of Christianity	103
X	The Church and the Jews	115
XI	Jewry and Islam	126
XII	Jewish Messianism and Sectarianism	140
XIII	Medieval Jewish Philosophy and Mysticism	152
XIV	The Crusades and the Jews	164
XV	Islamic Jewish Culture	176
XVI	Jews and Christian Spain	188
XVII	Renaissance and Reformation	198
XVIII	The Marrano Phenomenon	212
XIX	East European Jewry	223
XX	Sabbetianism and its Aftermath	233
XXI	Hasidism	245

XXII	Decline of the Medieval Kehilla	258
XXIII	Jewish Emancipation in France	269
XXIV	Reform Judaism	279
XXV	Neo-Orthodoxy	295
XXVI	Modern Anti-Semitism	307
XXVII	Reaction in Eastern Europe	321
XXVIII	Modern Zionism	332
XXIX	Jewish Settlement in America	346
XXX	Conservative Judaism and Reconstructionism	359
XXXI	Jewry and the Soviet Union	370
XXXII	The Holocaust	383
XXXIII	Israel and World Jewry	403
XXXIV	Where Are We?	422
	Index	431

Acknowledgments

I thank the following publishers for granting permission to reproduce the following material. While every effort has been made to trace and to acknowledge all copyright holders, I would like to apologize for any omissions.

Elie Wiesel, "The Death Train," Copyright ©1956 by Elie Wiesel. Reprinted by permission of Georges Borchardt, Inc.

———. *The Jewish War,* Book 7, Chapters 8–9, from *Flavius Josephus, Selections from his Works,* edited by Abraham Wasserstein, pp. 296–305. Used by permission of the B'nai Brith Commission on Continuing Jewish Education.

Augustine, *City of God,* pp. 543–545, The Catholic University of America Press, Fathers of the Church series, Washington, DC.

Isaac Metzger, ed., *A Bintel Brief,* selections. Used by permission of Doubleday & Co. and the estate of the editor.

Samson Rafael Hirsch, *The Nineteen Letters of Ben Uziel,* letter 15, Joseph Elias, trans. Copyright by the translator. Used by permission of Feldheim Publishers.

Bernard Lewis, ed., *Islam: From the Prophet Muhammad to the Capture of Constantinople,* vol. 2, pp. 22–219, Copyright ©1974 by Bernard Lewis. Reprinted by permission of HarperCollins Publishers, Inc.

Lucy Dawidowicz, *The Golden Tradition: Jewish Life and Thought in Eastern Europe,* Copyright ©1967 by the author. Reprinted by permission of Henry Holt and Co., Inc.

Genesis I:1–5, 24–31; IX:1–17, XV:7-18; Judges I:1-8, 19–21; II Samuel XII:1–14; Isaiah I; Jeremiah XXIX:1–10, LII; Esther I; Ecclesiastes I, from *The Tanakh: The New JPS Translation According to the Traditional Hebrew Text,* Copyright ©1985; Arie (Ben Ami) Eliav, *Between Hammer and Sickle,* pp. 76–79, Copyright ©1967; Jacob R. Marcus, *The Jew in the Medieval World,* pp. 227–228; Moses Maimonides, "Epistle to Yemen," in Abraham Halkin and David Hartman, eds., *Crisis and Leadership: The Epistles of Maimonides,* pp. 114–115, and "The Epistle on Martyrdom," pp. 30–31, Copyright ©1985; *Three Jewish Philosophers,* Saadya Gaon section, ed. by Alexander Altmann, pp. 178–179; Arthur Hertzberg, *The Zionist Idea,* pp. 186–188, 198. Used by permission of the Jewish Publication Society.

Frank Talmage, ed., *Disputation and Dialogue,* pp. 82–84, KTAV Publishing House, 1975.

Hans Kohn, ed., *Nationalism: Its Meaning and History,* pp. 165–166, with the permission of Immanuel Kohn.

Karl Marx, *Early Writings,* excerpts. Used by permission of McGraw-Hill Companies.

Paul Mendes-Flohr and Jehuda Reinharz, eds., *The Jew in the Modern World.* Copyright ©1980 by the editors; *The Oxford Annotated Bible.* Used by permission of Oxford University Press.

Flavius Josephus, *Antiquities,* Book 18, Chapter 1, from *The Second Jewish Commonwealth,* edited by Nahum N. Glatzer. Copyright ©1971 by Schocken Books, Inc.; Gershom Scholem, ed., *The Zohar: Book of Splendor,* pp. 79–81. Copyright ©1949, renewed 1977 by Schocken Books, Inc. Published by Pantheon Books, a divison of Random House, Inc. Reprinted by permission.

Eusebius, *The History of the Church,* trans. G. A. Williamson, Penguin Classics, 1965. Copyright ©1965 by the translator.

The Koran, N. J. Dawood, trans., Penguin Classics, 1956. Copyright ©1956, 1959, 1960, and 1966 by the translator.

James Pritchard, *The Ancient Near East: An Anthology of Texts,* Copyright ©1958 by Princeton University Press. Used by permission.

Emet V'Emunah, pp. 56–57, Copyright by The Jewish Theological Seminary of America, the Rabbinical Assembly and the United Synagogue of America; I Maccabees: Chapter I reprinted from

Megillat Hanukkah, edited by Arthur A. Chiel, Copyright ©1980 by the Rabbinical Assembly, 1980. Used by permission.

Robert Chazan, *European Jewry and the First Crusade,* pp. 254–256, ©1987, The Regents of the University of California.

Solomon Grayzel, *The Church and the Jews in the Thirteenth Century,* pp. 93–95, reprinted by permission of Sepher-Hermon Press, Inc., Copyright ©1966 by the estate of the author.

Tractate Sanhedrin 93b, *Tractate Gittin* 55b–56a, from the *Babylonian Talmud,* translated by I. Epstein, The Soncino Press.

Michael Meyer, ed. *Ideas of Jewish History,* pp. 135–137, Wayne State University Press, 1987, reprinted with permission of Wayne State University Press.

Gunther Plaut, ed., *The Growth of Reform Judaism,* pp. 33–34, 96–99, copyright by World Union for Progressive Judaism.

Leon Nemoy, ed., *Karaite Anthology,* pp. 17–18, Yale University Press. Used by permission.

Elkan Adler, *Jewish Travellers,* pp. 292–295; Benedict Spinoza, *Theological-Political Treatise,* pp. 122–124; Oscar Janowsky, *Foundations of Israel,* p. 135, in the public domain.

Introduction

This book constitutes an invitation to a unique adventure—a *tour d' horizon* of the Jewish experience from ancient through modern times. Organized in 34 units, the volume is effectively a guide to all facets of Jewish historical experience—cultural, religious, political, and social. If there is a message contained here concerning Jewish identity, it is that to be a Jew today means ongoing contact and dialogue with Jewish tradition.

The volume is aimed at the general reader desiring a core course covering the main contours of Jewish history. Based upon my two decades of teaching college students and adult education, this book assumes that most American Jews have attained a relatively high level of secular education but only rarely have applied the same level of rigor and expertise to the study of the Jewish experience. To address this gap, this book has been conceived of as a thinking person's teaching volume.

Its particular objectives include an understanding of the primary historical experiences of the Jews, the distinctive ideas which Jews and Judaism have advocated, and some exposure to the classical texts of the Judaic heritage. It is unrealistic, of course, to attempt to cover everything that has ever happened in Jewish history. Rather, this book's teaching goals address broad currents, seeing where Judaism has differed, and attaining a basic literacy in reading classical Jewish literature. Each unit will be accompanied by textual readings, questions for discussion, and additional bibliography.

Given the limitations of scope, this volume is shaped by several assumptions about Jewish experience: continuity rather than discontinuity, salience rather than irrelevance, and the value of honest and informed confrontation with Jewish sources.

Continuity: There are no radical breaks in the course of Jewish history. Change, although significant, occurs only over prolonged periods. Jewish emancipation did not take place overnight, nor did the exile begin with the destruction of the Second Temple. Although events such as these were doubtless significant, they developed in the context of long pre-existing conditions. Therefore, in speaking of continuity in history, the evolutionary nature of change suggests continued common ground with past generations. The contemporary Jewish condition comprises an outgrowth of the sum of Jewish experience. Understanding contemporary Jewish life, therefore, presupposes understanding how the Jews have evolved as a people.

Salience: The relevance of the past does *not* mean there are particular lessons to be applied to contemporary experience. All too often, individuals seeking to "learn" from history develop facile instructions for state leaders based upon historical experience. Human nature and development, however, are far more diverse and complicated. Conditions are rarely equivalent, and human behaviors cannot so easily be predicted.

Rarely, therefore, can history provide unequivocal instruction in particular decision-making. The value in studying history, and its continued salience, lie elsewhere. Contemporary issues and problems do not exist in a vacuum. The origins, development, and contemporary context are all rooted in the past. To approach issues from a strictly present-day perspective will blur complexities and limit understanding. The Middle East conflict is a good case in point.

It did not begin with the Intifada nor, for that matter, with the 1967 Six-Day War. The root causes of the conflict lie in Arab rejection of Jewish nationalism as an alien and intrusive force within the region. From this historical perspective, statecraft requires recognition that peace will come, not by signing a treaty, but only through fundamental changes in the perceptions of Zionism in Arab consciousness, underscored by extensive efforts at public education to signal that the Jewish State is now, indeed, welcome in the Middle East.

Jews are heirs to a unique and rich tradition. Dialogue with the past enables, not current decision-making, but rather understanding the context of contemporary life. Study of Jewish tradition, in this view, is not the study of an obsolete body of teachings, but rather an attempt to understand Jewish civilization through the prism of teachings that have guided, subject to development, Jewish life for millennia.

Jewish sources: There are three ways to read Jewish texts: Initially, students read primarily for information—to understand what is inside the text. On a secondary level, individuals may read texts as documents from the time in which they were written—voices from the past providing a record of the society, its values, and the culture of the times. This is known as the historical reading of texts. It requires some distancing between the reader and the text, asking questions of what the text meant in its own time period. On a third level, we ask what this text says to me personally and existentially. All too often, unfortunately, readers become stuck on the first level of reading and fail to ask the necessary questions concerning what a document meant in its own time, much less what it means today.

This course will utilize all three levels of reading. Jewish sources, to come alive for the reader, must speak on multiple levels. It is not enough to know Bible stories in terms of what happened. Far more significant is to utilize sources to provide a snapshot of the culture in which they were written and, subsequently, to be able to ask whether these sources can address the existential dilemmas of being Jewish in the twentieth century. Although these three levels apply to virtually any text, the course will begin by utilizing a number of biblical texts and then progress through rabbinic, medieval, and ultimately modern source materials.

Goals: Given these three assumptions of continuity, salience, and value in reading texts, what can a course in Jewish history accomplish? The course will operate on diverse levels: On one level, the aim is to nurture understanding of how the Jews evolved as a people. Accumulating data and bits of information is insufficient. Rather, the questions must concern what historical events mean in shaping the evolution of the Jews as a people.

On yet another level, the goal is to ensure confrontation with Jewish texts and enhance Judaic literacy. Each unit is therefore followed by guided readings taken exclusively from primary source materials. The student is encouraged to study the text in question after reviewing the historical background and context contained in the study unit. In this way, the text acts not only as a repository of information, but as a voice calling to us from the historical past.

Beyond information-gathering and textual literacy, the distinctiveness of this volume lies in its emphasis upon Jewish ideas and their continued salience to the modern Jew. On this level, readers will be asked not only to understand which ideas were distinctive Judaically and how they developed, but to continue the process of dialogue and questioning of these ideas to determine whether, how, and should these ideas affect contemporary Jewish living.

This work would not have been possible without the ongoing cooperation, encouragement, and assistance of numerous individuals. At the American Jewish Committee, David Harris, AJC Executive Director, has stimulated the broad expansion of Judaic literacy initiatives and seminars. I am grateful both to him and to Shula Bahat, AJC Associate Director, for encouraging this project and for granting me a sabbatical to complete it. Moreover, I have been privileged over many years to work with AJC's lay leadership. In many ways, this book is an outgrowth of the forums we have run at AJC chapter and national events. Robert S. Rifkind, AJC National President, Alfred Moses, his immediate predecessor, and Jack Lapin, Chair of the Committee's National Council, have served as a constant inspiration for my labors through their dedication to Jewish continuity and the future of the Jewish people.

The idea for the volume itself originated, as have so many good ideas, from a Shabbat luncheon with my dear friends Jack and Mierle Ukeles and Ezra and Batya Levin. Their encouragement helped transform a dim vision into reality.

Over the years I have been privileged to study with some of the outstanding teachers in contemporary Jewish life. The late Yehuda Rosenman initially invited me to work at the American Jewish Committee and served as my direct supervisor. Under Yehuda's close supervision, we developed the idea for an adult curriculum in Jewish history. Bert Gold, then AJC's executive director, appointed me to succeed Yehuda and gave me the opportunity to help transmit Yehuda's love for Jewish learning. At Yeshiva University, I was privileged to study with Dr. Irving Greenberg, currently President of the National Jewish Center for Learning and Leadership (CLAL). He first articulated for me the excitement in relating Jewish tradition to modern values and contexts. He has since served as mentor and role model for me in more ways than I can count. Professor David Berger, then at Yeshiva University, first introduced me to the value for all Jews in a core survey course in Jewish history. Subsequently, I was privileged to study at Columbia University with Profs. Zvi Ankori, Lloyd Gartner, Arthur Hertzberg, Paula Hyman, and Ismar Schorsch. Dr. Norman Lamm, President of Yeshiva University, first exposed me to the beauties of Jewish philosophy. He subsequently invited me to develop and teach courses in Jewish history at Yeshiva on both undergraduate and graduate levels. Professors David Berger and Jonathan Sarna read drafts of numerous chapters and provided many useful suggestions and corrections. The influence of these people, both individually and collectively, is reflected on virtually every one of the following pages. They are, of course, in no way responsible for my errors.

Partial funding for this volume was made possible through the American Jewish Committee's Susan and Jack Lapin Fund for Jewish Continuity and by a fellowship from the Memorial Foundation for Jewish Culture. I thank Dr. Jerry Hochbaum of the Memorial Foundation for his assistance and constant friendship.

It has been my pleasure to work with Bernard Scharfstein of KTAV Publishing House on this and other projects. Roselyn Bell expertly edited the final manuscript and offered many helpful suggestions for improving it.

Last and by no means least, the volume would not have been possible without the constant love and support of my family. My three children, Ilana, Eytan, and Yehuda, participated in regular Friday evening lectures on Jewish history (over raspberries), while my wife Edith has been a guiding and inspirational presence since graduate school. It is to them that I lovingly dedicate this volume.

Steven Bayme
January, 1997

Unit I

Creation, Covenant, Redemption

The Hebrew Bible is divided into three components: the Pentateuch, or the Five Books of Moses, detail narratives of the patriarchs Abraham, Isaac, and Jacob, the formation of Israel as a nation via exodus from slavery, and its wanderings in the desert for 40 years before entering the Promised Land of Canaan. However, the essential meaning of the word Torah is instruction. In that context, the Pentateuch is by no means a history book, although it contains much historical information. Its primary purpose is to instruct the Jews in the distinctive legal codes of the Jews governing personal, familial, and societal behaviors. The Prophetic Writings contain both historical accounts of the settlement of the Jews in Canaan (Joshua, Judges, Samuel, and Kings) as well as the moral exhortations of the literary prophets (Isaiah, Jeremiah, Ezekiel, and Minor Prophets). The Hagiographa, or Holy Writings, contain religious, historical, and wisdom literature, often in the form of parables or stories, which offer good advice on how to lead one's day-to-day life. A fourth body of writings, the Apocrypha, consists of uncanonized books that relate primarily to Jewish life in Second Commonwealth times. These writings were preserved in the Christian Bible as intertestamental literature, meaning literature composed between the Hebrew Bible and the Christian New Testament.

Judaism begins distinctively as a religion of law. What sets the Jews apart as a people are the distinctive laws governing Jewish practice. In some respects, these laws are moral in nature, governing human relations. In other respects, the laws are ritualistic in nature, binding the Jews together as a people through their distinctive practices. Genesis, in particular the patriarchal narratives, communicates the essential origins of Judaism as a religion. Like other religions, Judaism begins with the question of how we came here. How did this world come into existence?

Classical religions originate with mythological tales of stories of the gods. The essence of ancient paganism lay in the reality that forces of nature governed day-to-day human activities. Ancient men and women looked around themselves and saw their lives regulated by many forces over which they had no control—thunder, lightning, rain, and sunshine. It was natural to assume that each of these forces represented a godly presence. In that sense paganism begins in the context of pluralism—namely, that there are many forces at work in the universe and none can claim exclusive power or truth. Ancient tales of creation, such as the Sumerian or Enuma Elish epic, posit creation as a result of struggle for supremacy among the deities.

Judaism rejected this paganism. The origins of Judaism as a religion lie in a struggle with paganism, in which Judaism posits a moral order and Divine Creator. Precisely because creation arose not by chance or struggle of the gods, but rather because of a Divine mind imposing order on the universe, Judaism articulated the principle of unity rather than pluralism and moral order rather than chaos. Genesis, therefore, begins with the statement "In the beginning God created heaven and earth"—meaning that creation occurred in time and through a Divine plan and purpose. Similarly, the second verse of Genesis states that the earth was chaotic; the process of creation imposed order amidst the chaos. Lastly, just as creation imposes a natural order on reality, the creation of human beings imposes a moral order in which the purpose of human existence is to build society and to shape it toward purposeful and moral ends. Man and woman, standing at the apex of creation, in effect become elevated into Divine partners. Just as God created nature, the message of Genesis to human beings is to build society for constructive and moral purposes.

The creation story gives humanity a past and an origin. The story of covenant suggests an ongoing presence. Several covenants dot the biblical narratives. The initial covenant is by no means designated as such. Rather it is simply assumed that humanity will carry on the work of creation. The record of humanity, however, is by no means that benign. Genesis records the story of the great flood as a Divine reaction to human corruption, i.e. to humanity's failure to fulfill the ongoing work of creation. The flood narrative is both similar and dissimilar to the Sumerian Epic of Gilgamesh. Most distinctively, Genesis emphasizes moral responsibility and culminates in the first formal covenant between God and humanity symbolized by the rainbow. This covenant with Noah we might refer to today as a covenant of natural law. God promises that nature will never overwhelm humanity again as happened in the flood. Conversely, Noah assumes the responsibility of fulfilling the moral code to respect human life. The symbolism of the rainbow is significant—a statement of beauty that the forces of nature, while powerful, are ultimately preservative of humanity. Only humanity has the capacity to effect its own self-destruction. Nature, as terrible as its actions may be, ultimately culminates in the rainbow—a symbol of peace and safety. Human actions, by contrast, contain no built-in guarantee and are, in fact, unpredictable.

This initial covenant is a universal one. God promises all of humanity that never again will nature overwhelm society. The responsibilities of natural law are incumbent upon all men and women. This universal covenant, however, is transcended by yet a third covenant between God and Abraham, applying strictly to the Jews. This covenant is symbolized by circumcision, suggesting that sexual prowess must be restrained by human responsibilities and obligations. More particularly, precisely because the Canaanites had been guilty of sexual abominations, they will forfeit the land of Canaan. The Jewish promise of a land of their own is directly conditioned upon whether the Jews will fulfill the obligations of covenant. To the extent that the Jews will adhere to the moral and legal imperatives of Torah, their presence in the land of Israel is secured. But there are no guarantees. If the covenant of Torah is not fulfilled, Jewish presence and security are jeopardized. To be sure, although the promise of covenant is eternal, implementation will require human activity.

This covenant with Abraham, binding upon all future generations of Jews, is ultimately translated as a concept of the chosen people—perhaps the most difficult concept to grasp in the entire corpus of Jewish literature. To be sure, the rabbis were troubled by the notion of why God would choose one people to the exclusion of all others. Their answer was that only the Jews accepted voluntarily the moral code of Torah. Similarly, the covenant with the Jews was by no means a racial covenant. It was available also to all born outside the covenant but who chose to join it.

In historical terms, moreover, the concept of the chosen people is indeed understandable. Virtually every nation has assigned itself a sense of distinctive mission and national purpose. Certainly the American doctrine of nationhood articulates American distinctiveness and even American exceptionalism. John F. Kennedy's inaugural address in 1961 proclaiming the New Frontier clearly articulated that American distinctiveness. The phrase, "The sun never sets on the British empire" similarly assigns a distinctive status to England. The Jewish concept of chosenness is by no means unique. Every nation wishes to see itself as pursuing a distinctive purpose and national dream.

Similarly, the idea of chosenness does speak to us on theological levels. It does not suggest that other peoples are less favored by God. Rather, it suggests that being a Jew is a heavy burden. It imposes specific responsibilities and obligations upon individual Jews and upon the Jews as a collective people. Elie Wiesel, for one, has gone so far as to argue that the price of the covenant with the Jews has simply been too heavy. Because the Jews were a chosen people, they were singled out for the most unique and destructive genocide known to human history. Others argue that the idea of chosenness articulates Jewish responsibility to the world at large. This was the famous "mission theory," first articulated by the prophet Isaiah and later emphasized heavily in Reform Judaism, as well as in German neo-Orthodoxy. Zionist theoreticians, particularly Ahad Ha'am and Martin Buber, have underscored the moral responsibility of the Jewish State to be a light unto the gentiles.

Common to these ideas of chosenness is the Jewish concept of holiness. The terms of the covenant dictate the Jews become a holy people, whose content forms Jewish distinctiveness. Holiness means separateness—the Jews are set apart from the nations of the world by their adherence to the Divine covenant. The Jews as a people must communicate distinctive content and national purpose in accord with the terms of covenant and chosen peoplehood. It is this sense of holiness and separateness that, in some respects, is most endangered today, when the boundary line between Jew and gentile has become so fluid in contemporary America.

Yet the idea of covenant remains salient. For minorities to survive in a democratic majority culture, they require distinctiveness, separateness and borders. The minority can and should open itself up to those who wish to join it—but not at the surrender of distinctive purpose and national content. For these reasons, Jews are enjoined not to intermarry with the surrounding gentile population. To be a Jew means to assert the covenant, to share it with others who wish to enter, but, at the same time, to recognize that it cannot mean all things to all people. The language of inclusiveness, so politically popular in our own day, must recognize that Jewish continuity presupposes some level of corporate distinctiveness that will be exclusionary to those who do not enter. Although that language of exclusivity may often seem harsh or insensitive, the very idea of a distinctive covenant with the Jews presupposes that it is not a covenant with all of humanity. The covenant with humanity at large remains, as symbolized by the rainbow, but the distinctive covenant with the Jews applies only to those who enter the *brit* of Abraham.

One other consequence of this covenant applies to monotheistic religions as a whole. Monotheistic faiths, particularly the Western ones, have been known for their religious intolerance rather than tolerance. In fact, it was the Jews who introduced the abominable concept of forced conversion to Western history in the time of the Maccabees. Needless to add, the Catholic Inquisition, the Moslem *jihad,* and the Protestant wars of religion all contained features of religious intolerance.

The concept of covenant to some extent explains why religious intolerance has been a feature of monotheistic faiths. The claim of monotheism is its possession of truth. By definition, that excludes those who do not share those truths. Taken to excess, this concept can and has been translated into violence against the infidel or those who do not share the truths of that monotheistic faith. Paganism, by contrast, precisely because of its pluralism, suggests that you can have your deity while we have ours. Deities are different, but by no means superior or inferior. In fact, there are even echoes of this pluralism within biblical references to ancient pagan cults. For example, in the Book of Judges, the judge Jephthah, on a diplomatic mission to the Ammonites, suggests to them that whatever their god Chemosh has given to them is theirs and whatever the God of the Jews has given to the Jews belongs to the Jews as a people. Although this may be dismissed as diplomatic parlance, the statement reflects the basic values of pagan pluralism—namely, a plurality of deities in which no deity can claim exclusive truths. Consequently, while pagan religions have often featured many unsavory practices, including witchcraft and human sacrifice, they have been relatively free of the religious intolerance that has characterized monotheistic faiths. Judaism, offended by contemporary pagan sexual and sacrificial practices, mounted a permanent protest against the essence of paganism. In effect, the message of the Jewish covenant was to fly in the face of reality—to assert the principles of ethics and monotheism in a world in which the reality of pluralism held sway.

Moreover, the idea of the covenant undergoes further development in later Jewish history. For Abraham, the covenant is primarily theological and territorial—belief in God rewarded by possession of land. The Mosaic code extends the covenant to a broad array of legal practices, the corpus of which defines the Jews as a moral people. At yet a later stage, David centralizes the covenant in the particular locality of Jerusalem, suggesting that while its terms apply to Jews everywhere, the sanctity of Jerusalem symbolizes a central address that will claim the passions, energies, and attention of Jews throughout the ages. Some of the prophets went a step further in suggesting that the covenant will remain binding until the end of days, at which time it will be replaced by a new covenant. This statement, originating in Jeremiah, became the basis for the Christian reading of the covenant that the New Testament supersedes the Old Testament, that the covenant of law applicable to the Jews gives way to a covenant of grace applicable to all humanity. Paul was the first to articulate this doctrine of supersessionism, that the covenant of law granted to the Jews was simply inadequate to work out human salvation. Paul stated that "the just shall live by faith alone," meaning that God became man to bestow the gift of faith in Him and make it available to all of humanity. For much of later Christian thought, Judaism was an obsolete faith—a covenant which had gone unfulfilled because human beings were incapable of working out their own salvation. Jews, of course, understood Jeremiah's "new covenant" as essentially a reaffirmation of the traditional covenant.

In more recent years, Jewish theologians have been perplexed by the reality of the Holocaust and have asked how the covenant could remain binding if the Jews had fallen victim to the worst genocide in history. Elie Wiesel, Irving Greenberg, and David Hartman, in particular, have emphasized human responsibility for the covenant in the aftermath of Auschwitz. Wiesel has articulated this theme most brilliantly through his novels, which portray an exchange of roles between God and man. As history has progressed, human beings have increasingly had to take the responsibility for their destiny and for the fulfillment of the covenant. The Holocaust, in that context, suggests the reality of human power to affect history toward ends that are clearly demonic. The Jews cannot rely upon a Divine promise. They can rely only upon their own power, tempered, to be sure, by covenantal concepts of justice. Irving Greenberg has, therefore, described Auschwitz as shattering the traditional covenant and replacing it with a voluntary covenant in which Jews assume the burdens of their destiny and history.

Although the terms of the covenant may have been altered by the reality of the Holocaust, most Jewish thinkers would agree that its ultimate promise remains that of Redemption. In that sense, if creation suggests a past from which we stem, and covenant suggests a present reality in which we live, redemption suggests the promise of a future in which the world will be better. This idea of redemption stands at the very root of the Jewish optimistic reading of history. Unlike Paul, the Jew is never overwhelmed by the reality of contemporary history. The idea of redemption offers a promise that no matter how dark individual moments in history may be, its overall direction is progressive. Although Jewish thinkers always attempted to marginalize messianic drives because they could be so destructive of contemporary reality, they did not marginalize the messianic idea or the dream of a future redemption. In their day-to-day lives, Jews are exhorted to live by the covenant in the present reality and to reject messianic activity as destructive. Yet at the same time, Jews pray every day for an ultimate arrival of the Messiah, who will fulfill their dreams of a national restoration and of universal peace among the nations.

These central ideas of creation, covenant, and redemption form the building blocks of Judaic distinctiveness. The books of the Jews transmit their historical memories—of being born as a nation in bondage, of being liberated, and of being granted their Promised Land. These historical narratives are not valued as history per se. The Bible makes no claim to offer a straight historical sequence.

Rather, it provides us with a wealth of information to articulate the distinctive Jewish ideas of creation, covenant, and redemption. The Jewish "story" reveals how these ideas not only preserved the Jews as a people, but provided them with the essential content of what being a Jew meant. In subsequent units of this study course, we will look at the particular historical experiences of the Jews and ask how these seminal ideas of Judaism developed under the impetus of concrete historical circumstances.

Readings: Genesis I: 1–5, 24–31; IX: 1–17; XV: 7–18

The Book of Genesis serves as a "pre-history" for the Jewish people. The patriarchal narratives of Genesis trace the family dynamics within the clans of Abraham, Isaac, and Jacob. Genesis, in effect, implies that before the Jews could become a people, they had to learn how to build family by resolving conflicts. The selections from Genesis detail the nature of covenant. Note in particular the differences between the universal or Noahide covenant, symbolized by the rainbow, and the Abrahamic covenant, uniquely with the Jewish people, symbolized by circumcision.

Chapter One

[1]When God began to create heaven and earth—[2]the earth being unformed and void, with darkness over the surface of the deep and a wind from God sweeping over the water—[3] God said, "Let there be light"; and there was light. [4]God saw that the light was good, and God separated the light from the darkness. [5]God called the light Day, and the darkness He called Night. And there was evening and there was morning, a first day . . .

[24]God said, "Let the earth bring forth every kind of living creature: cattle, creeping things, and wild beasts of every kind." And it was so. [25]God made wild beasts of every kind and cattle of every kind, and all kinds of creeping things of the earth. And God saw that this was good. [26]And God said, "Let us make man in our image, after our likeness. They shall rule the fish of the sea, the birds of the sky, the cattle, the whole earth, and all the creeping things that creep on earth." [27]And God created man in His image, in the image of God He created

him; male and female He created them. [28]God blessed them and God said to them, "Be fertile and increase, fill the earth and master it; and rule the fish of the sea, the birds of the sky, and all the living things that creep on earth."

[29]God said, "See, I give you every seed-bearing plant that is upon all the earth, and every tree that has seed-bearing fruit; they shall be yours for food. [30]And to all the animals on land, to all the birds of the sky, and to everything that creeps on earth, in which there is the breath of life, [I give] all the green plants for food." And it was so. [31]And God saw all that He had made, and found it very good. And there was evening and there was morning, the sixth day.

Chapter Nine

[1]God blessed Noah and his sons, and said to them, "Be fertile and increase, and fill the earth. [2]The fear and the dread of you shall be upon all the beasts of the earth and upon all the birds of the sky—everything with which the earth is astir—and upon all the fish of the sea; they are given into your hand. [3]Every creature that lives shall be yours to eat; as with the green grasses, I give you all these. [4]You must not, however, eat flesh with its life-blood in it. [5]But for your own life-blood I will require a reckoning: I will require it of every beast; of man, too, will I require a reckoning for human life, of every man for that of his fellow man!

[6]Whoever sheds the blood of man, by man shall his blood be shed;
For in His image did God make man.

[7]Be fertile, then, and increase; abound on the earth and increase on it."

[8]And God said to Noah and to his sons with him, [9]"I now establish My covenant with you and your offspring to come, [10]and with every living thing that is with you—birds, cattle, and every wild beast as well—all that have come out of the ark, every living thing on earth. [11]I will maintain My covenant with you: never again shall all flesh be cut off by the waters of a flood, and never again shall there be a flood to destroy the earth."

[12]God further said, "This is the sign that I set for the covenant between Me and you, and every living creature with you, for

all ages to come. [13]I have set My bow in the clouds, and it shall serve as a sign of the covenant between Me and the earth. [14]When I bring clouds over the earth, and the bow appears in the clouds, [15]I will remember My covenant between Me and you and every living creature among all flesh, so that the waters shall never again become a flood to destroy all flesh. [16]When the bow is in the clouds, I will see it and remember the everlasting covenant between God and all living creatures, all flesh that is on earth. [17]That," God said to Noah, "shall be the sign of the covenant that I have established between Me and all flesh that is on earth."

Chapter Fifteen

[7]Then He said to him, "I am the Lord who brought you out from Ur of the Chaldeans to assign this land to you as a possession." [8]And he said, "O Lord God, how shall I know that I am to possess it?" [9]He answered, "Bring Me a three-year-old heifer, a three-year-old she-goat, a three-year-old ram, a turtledove, and a young bird." [10]He brought Him all these and cut them in two, placing each half opposite the other; but he did not cut up the bird. [11]Birds of prey came down upon the carcasses, and Abram drove them away. [12]As the sun was about to set, a deep sleep fell upon Abram, and a great dark dread descended upon him. [13]And He said to Abram, "Know well that your offspring shall be strangers in a land not theirs, and they shall be enslaved and oppressed four hundred years; [14]but I will execute judgment on the nation they shall serve, and in the end they shall go free with great wealth. [15]As for you,

You shall go to your fathers in peace;
You shall be buried at a ripe old age.

[16]And they shall return here in the fourth generation, for the iniquity of the Amorites is not yet complete."

[17]When the sun set and it was very dark, there appeared a smoking oven, and a flaming torch which passed between those pieces. [18]On that day the Lord made a covenant with Abram, saying, "To your offspring I assign this land, from the river of Egypt to the great river, the river Euphrates: [19]the Kenites, the Kenizzites, the Kadmonites, [20]the Hittites, the Per-

izzites, the Rephaim, [21]the Amorites, the Canaanites, the Girgashites, and the Jebusites."

Bibliography for Further Reading

Alter, Robert. *The Art of Biblical Narrative,* (Jewish Publication Society/Basic Books), 1983

Fackenheim, Emil. *What Is Judaism?* (Schocken Books), 1987

Friedman, Richard. *Who Wrote the Bible?* (Harper and Rowe), 1989

Greenberg, Irving. *Voluntary Covenant* (CLAL [National Jewish Center for Learning and Leadership]), 1982

Holtz, Barry, ed. *Back to the Sources* (Summit Books), 1986

Sarna, Nahum. *Understanding Genesis* (Jewish Publication Society), 1966

———, general editor. *JPS Torah Commentary, Genesis* (Jewish Publication Society), 1989

Plaut, W. Gunther. *The Torah: A Modern Commentary* (UAHC), 1981

Zornberg, Aviva. *Genesis: The Beginning of Desire* (Jewish Publication Society), 1995

Unit II

Monarchy and Political Centralization

Slavery and Exodus

The memory of bondage in the Land of Egypt followed by an exodus to the Promised Land serves as the central orientating image binding the Jews together as a people. This is the essential meaning behind the Passover Seder ritual every year—namely, that every individual should see himself or herself as having been personally liberated from Egypt. The memory of historical slavery functioned as the critical formative ingredient cementing the Jews as a people with a common past and aspirations for a glorious future.

It is very difficult to explain the Exodus historically and with chronological precision. Although historians greatly debate the exact date of the Exodus, in recent years a consensus has arisen, albeit with some dissent, that the Exodus took place in the latter part of the thirteenth century B.C.E. under the reign of Pharaoh Merneptah. The reason for this dating relates primarily to the recently discovered Merneptah Stele, which records a victory over Israel around the year 1220 B.C.E. This is the earliest extra-biblical reference to Israel as a people. Moreover, the context of the stele seems to suggest that Israel was not yet a settled people, perhaps had yet to establish a centralized government and nation-state. This thirteenth century dating would then place Rameses II (1290–1224 B.C.E.) as the Pharaoh of the oppression who enslaved Israel.

Certainly his reign was one of the longest and most powerful in Egyptian history. The archeological record confirms that he built cities of storage, one of whom was named Rameses, a record paralleled in Exodus I:11. If Rameses II was indeed the Pharaoh of the oppression, then the Exodus itself occurred under his son Merneptah, for Exodus records that prior to Moses's initiating the call for freedom from bondage, "The king of Egypt died" (Exodus III:23).

Moreover, this thirteenth-century dating of the Exodus accords with the general eclipse of Egypt and the Hittite Empire from positions of influence in ancient Canaan. More particularly, as the Sea Peoples invaded the ancient Near East from the Greek islands—the most famous of these being the Philistines, who would subsequently plague Israel as well—Egypt was forced to attend to needs closer to home. That Israel became established as an independent nation-state, given the eclipse of her more powerful neighbors, suggests a basic theme of Jewish political history: Jewish independence and sovereignty in Israel have often been a function of superpower disinterest or eclipse from the area. Superpower intervention—at least in ancient, if not in modern times—generally led to a loss of sovereignty and independence.

Finally, the Ten Plagues themselves are interesting because they point up the contrast between Judaism and magic. Pharaoh relied upon his magicians, who were said to be able to accomplish wonders. Moses, however, rejects magic. He appeals to a God who rules nature, beside whom there can be no forces of magic or superstition. This rejection of magic, of course, is paralleled by the issuing of the Ten Commandments, a statement of moral order. In effect, the battle with paganism is extended to a denial of magic and identification of a single principle of unity and moral order in the cosmos, who is responsible for all of creation.

Conquest

The conquest of Canaan itself is described in two sharply contrasting ways by the biblical record. The Book of Joshua suggests a unified conquest in which massive destruction of Canaanite cities took place. The Book of Judges, by contrast, suggests a lengthened period of gradual infiltration in which Jews and Canaanites struggled over a period of generations, oftentimes living together in close proximity and hostility.

To some extent, both versions are correct. The archeological record does suggest that there was significant destruction of Canaanite towns. Conversely, it should be no surprise that the Israelites experienced long-term resistance on the part of the native inhabitants and certainly were unable to dislodge them in the brief span of one generation. Historians point to elements already within Canaan who effectively linked up with the invading Israelites. Certainly the biblical record suggests that the Jews attracted a number of "fellow travelers" who welcomed them into Canaan, and, to the extent that their allegiance proved vital, the conquest could be seen as an "inside job."

Moreover, the Jews were by no means a united people during the period of conquest. The twelve tribes were distinct entities with little more than a loose alliance existing among them. The experiences of the tribes were in many ways different from one another. The so-called northern tribes, grouped around Ephraim, or the sons of Rachel, seemed to have experienced greater success in conquering central Palestine. The southern tribes, grouped around Judah or the sons of Leah, tended to focus on southern Palestine and experienced greater difficulty in dislodging the native inhabitants.

Of course, the critical question regarding the conquest relates to the moral imperative. In ancient no less than in modern times, Jews were accused of robbing Canaan from its native inhabitants. The earliest reference to such a dispute can be found in the period of the Judges, when Jephtah justifies the conquest as simply being the rights of victory. Rabbinic tradition was troubled by this moral score. The rabbis offered several different explanations, none of them completely satisfying. First, the rabbis underscored the biblical rationale for the conquest. The Canaanites had sinned grievously. Their sins related primarily to sexual abominations culminating in child sacrifice. For these reasons, the land of Israel effectively "threw out" its native inhabitants because of their abominations. To be sure, the archeological record, to some extent, does justify this charge against the Canaanites. The Canaanites were the historical Phoenicians. We find their records scattered, as a seafaring people, across the Mediterranean. They may even have reached the Western Hemisphere. We know that in Carthage, where the Phoenician deity Moloch was worshipped, child sacrifice was by no means uncommon. To the extent that Judaism regarded child sacrifice as a moral abomination, it justified the conquest of Canaan as appropriate punishment to the Canaanites for their transgressions.

Secondly, the rabbis emphasized their tradition that the Canaanites were by no means the original inhabitants of the land of Canaan. An earlier people had once ruled there known as the "Rephaites," a legendary people of giants. The Canaanites had dislodged the Rephaites and, therefore, their title to the land of Canaan was limited in scope. The Canaanites had invaded the possession of others, and so their own property rights were tainted.

Although neither of these explanations are satisfactory, they do suggest that the rabbis were troubled by the moral question of Jewish rights to the land of Canaan. It should be no surprise that contemporary Palestinian Arab propaganda often tries to link up with the Canaanites of old—a proposition historically without foundation, but which makes for effective propaganda. The only historical explanation is one that can be articulated only with the critical distance that history provides us: namely, that conquests and depopulations were far from unusual in ancient times. The very people who accused the Jews of usurping the land of Canaan were guilty of similar depopulations in other periods and contexts. In contemporary times, as Israeli spokesmen have often pointed out at the United Nations, there are few national entities able to claim rights to land that are not based upon the rights of conquest.

Lastly, rabbinic tradition also historicized the moral issues regarding conquest. The rabbis noted that the command to eliminate the seven nations of Canaan was limited to one generation only. In subsequent years, Jews and Canaanites lived together in relative degrees of both amity and hostility. More pointedly, when David conquered the city of Jerusalem, the biblical text states explicitly that the native inhabitants, the Jebusites, were permitted to live in peace with the Israelites. These efforts to historicize the conflict by no means obliterate the moral problem, but do enable us to see the conquest as relative to a particular time and suggest a degree of moral discomfort with the problem of the Canaanites.

The Monarchy and Centralization

The conquest itself, as noted, took several generations, perhaps as long as two hundred years. During these years, the so-called period of the Judges, Jewish political life was sporadic and decentralized. The constant refrain of the latter half of the Book of Judges is that "in those days there was no king in Israel; each person did whatever was right in his eyes." Moreover, the Bible suggests that the Jews desired a strong monarch precisely because the rule of the Judges was too weak and sporadic, failing to provide either internal stability or defense against external stress.

Yet creation of a centralized monarchy ran counter to the tribal and separatist traditions of the Jews. David, who founded the continuous line of Jewish monarchy around 1000 B.C.E., established his legitimacy through unification of the country and through religious and political centralization in Jerusalem, an extra-tribal center beyond the boundaries of any particular Jewish tribe.

David's detractors cite his adultery with Bathsheba and his order that her husband, Uriah, be given an assignment likely to insure his death in battle. The biblical record, however, is remarkable not only in making no efforts at covering up or apologizing for David's sins, but in invoking the prophet Nathan as the moral conscience of the monarchy. When Nathan confronts David by saying "you are the man" who has engaged in oppression and tyranny, the extraordinary conclusion is David's confession of his sin. The Bible thereby suggests a very limited form of monarchy in which the sovereign could never be above the moral law. The encounter of Nathan and David must stand as an incredible instance of the moral power of the prophet prevailing over the political power of the monarch—an event probably otherwise unknown in the annals of ancient Near Eastern monarchies.

In creating a unified central monarchy, David and his son Solomon weakened some of the traditional centers of power in the Israelite polity. The tribal structure became less important. Worship was centralized in Jerusalem, the "City of David," implying that it belonged to the monarch as representative of the people as a whole rather than to any particular tribe. The older centers of power, particularly the military, the priesthood, and the tribal judges, clearly were discontented with the centralization provided by David. Economically, Solomon acted to unify the markets of Jerusalem with those of Syria in the north. Many among the northern tribes felt that the economic resources of the Galilee and northern Israel were being harnessed to subsidize the capital city of Jerusalem. In constructing the Temple in Jerusalem, Solomon also imposed a religious unity in his capital city. The Temple was famed for its splendor. In principle, three times yearly Jews everywhere were enjoined to make pilgrimages to Jerusalem and worship at the Temple. Lastly, Solomon expanded the diplomatic horizons of the Jewish State—including an alliance with the Phoenicians instrumental in the construction of the Temple, a diplomatic marriage to the daughter of Pharaoh, and extensive trade with Arabia and perhaps even India.

To be sure, these moves came at a price. The diplomatic alliance with Phoenicia came at the price of surrender of twenty Israelite cities in the Galilee—perhaps the earliest recorded instance of cession of territory in a diplomatic rather than a military process. To build the Temple, a *corvee* or forced labor was imposed upon the Israelite tribes. Lastly, the marriage with the daughter of Pharaoh aroused considerable antagonism by those who argued that it would bring idolatry and a dilution of monotheism into Jerusalem and the royal household. The Bible draws an apparent link between Solomon's intermarriage and the subsequent schism within his kingdom.

Divided Monarchy

The natural splits between the northern and southern tribes recurred after the death of Solomon. David's kingdom was divided, and the northern tribes established political independence together with rival centers of worship in Dan and Bethel. Not only were the Israelites weakened from within, but the resurgence of the superpowers—Assyria and Egypt—meant the eclipse of the Jewish kingdom into international insignificance. Although there were periods of Israelite prominence, the Jewish story of the next hundred years is one of intermittent civil war between northern and southern kingdoms, interrupted by occasional unity in the face of external threats.

An important archeological source, the Mesha Stone, records how the Moabites threw off Israelite rule and massacred Jews in the area of the Arnon River, a tributary of the Jordan. The Bible also records considerable resurgence of paganism within ancient Israel during this period. To some extent this represents the incomplete triumph of the monotheistic ideal among the people. In other respects it expresses a political conflict over the centralization of Jerusalem as the capital of Judaism. In still other respects, the resurgence of paganism reflects a desire for a physical symbol for the deity. To the ancient mind, there were few ideas within Judaism that were more difficult to absorb than the notion that God cannot be physically represented.

Lastly, while the biblical record blamed the breakup of the Davidic kingdom on the excesses of Solomon and his son Rehoboam, it is important to recognize that the unity provided by David and Solomon was itself unnatural. David brilliantly overcame tribal disunity. Over the course of time, the natural divisions of the people reasserted themselves.

To be sure, our history is written through the eyes of David's supporters. Theologically, those who upheld the centrality of Jerusalem would naturally denigrate the political and religious practices of their rivals in the north. The covenantal theology of Genesis was transmitted through the religious centralization in Jerusalem, in which the Temple represented the primary locale for Divine worship. Moreover, the presence of the Temple in Jerusalem stood as living embodiment of the enduring nature of the covenant between God and the Jews, now represented via the Davidic dynasty. The northern kingdom could hardly compete with the imagery and splendor, or the theology, of the Jerusalem Temple.

Reading: Judges I: 1–8, 19–21

The book of Judges *details the period between the death of Joshua and the rise of the Israelite monarchy. Its constant refrain is that absent a sovereign monarch in the land, anarchy prevailed. Judges arise intermittently to restore order, but only temporarily. The opening chapter in particular suggests a much more difficult conquest of Canaan by the Jewish people than the series of dramatic victories portrayed in the book of* Joshua. Judges *portrays a slow and painful process of conquest with many defeats along the way.*

[1]After the death of Joshua, the Israelites inquired of the Lord, "Which of us shall be the first to go up against the Canaanites and attack them?" [2]The Lord replied, "Let [the tribe of] Judah go up. I now deliver the land into their hands." [3]Judah then said to their brother-tribe Simeon, "Come up with us to our allotted territory and let us attack the Canaanites, and then we will go with you to your allotted territory." So Simeon joined them.

[4]When Judah advanced, the Lord delivered the Canaanites and the Perizzites into their hands, and they defeated ten thousand of them at Bezek. [5]At Bezek, they encountered Adoni-bezek, engaged him in battle, and defeated the Canaanites and the Perizzites. [6]Adoni-bezek fled, but they pursued him and captured him; and they cut off his thumbs and his big toes. [7]And Adoni-bezek said, "Seventy kings, with thumbs and big toes cut off, used to pick up scraps under my table; as I have done, so God has requited me." They brought him to Jerusalem and he died there.

[8]The Judahites attacked Jerusalem and captured it; they put it to the sword and set the city on fire.

[19]The Lord was with Judah, so that they took possession of the hill country; but they were not able to dispossess the inhabitants of the plains, for they had iron chariots. [20]They gave Hebron to Caleb, as Moses had promised; and he drove the three Anakites out of there. [21]The Benjaminites did not dispossess the Jebusite inhabitants of Jerusalem; so the Jebusites have dwelt with the Benjaminites in Jerusalem to this day.

Reading: II Samuel XII: 1–14

Samuel II *chronicles the story of the Davidic monarchy. Of particular interest to us is David's affair with Bathsheba, resulting in the killing of Bathsheba's husband, Uriah. Chapter XII, in particular, is remarkable, for the prophet Nathan serves as the conscience of the king, reprimanding him for his violations of morality. The message of the Davidic monarchy is, first, that no sovereign is above the law, and the greatness of David is not that he is without sin, but rather his willingness to own up to and take responsibility for his misdeeds.*

[1]But the Lord was displeased with what David had done, and the Lord sent Nathan to David. He came to him and said, "There were two men in the same city, one rich and one poor. [2]The rich man had very large flocks and herds, [3]but the poor man had only one little ewe lamb that he had bought. He tended it and it grew up together with him and his children: it used to share his morsel of bread, drink from his cup, and nestle in

his bosom; it was like a daughter to him. [4]One day, a traveler came to the rich man, but he was loath to take anything from his own flocks or herds to prepare a meal for the guest who had come to him; so he took the poor man's lamb and prepared it for the man who had come to him."

[5]David flew into a rage against the man, and said to Nathan, "As the Lord lives, the man who did this deserves to die! [6]He shall pay for the lamb four times over, because he did such a thing and showed no pity." [7]And Nathan said to David, "That man is you! Thus said the Lord, the God of Israel: 'It was I who anointed you king over Israel and it was I who rescued you from the hand of Saul. [8]I gave you your master's house and possession of your master's wives; and I gave you the House of Israel and Judah; and if that were not enough, I would give you twice as much more. [9]Why then have you flouted the command of the Lord and done what displeases Him? You have put Uriah the Hittite to the sword; you took his wife and made her your wife and had him killed by the sword of the Ammonites. [10]Therefore the sword shall never depart from your House—because you spurned Me by taking the wife of Uriah the Hittite and making her your wife.' [11]Thus said the Lord: 'I will make a calamity rise against you from within your own house; I will take your wives and give them to another man before your very eyes and he shall sleep with your wives under this very sun. [12]You acted in secret, but I will make this happen in the sight of all Israel and in broad daylight.'"

[13]David said to Nathan, "I stand guilty before the Lord!" And Nathan replied to David, "The Lord has remitted your sin; you shall not die. [14]However, since you have spurned the enemies of the Lord by this deed, even the child about to be born to you shall die."

Reading: James Pritchard, *The Ancient Near East*

Lastly, we print two documents containing references to Israel from the archaeological records of the ancient world. The earlier document, the Merneptah stele, *records the victory of the Egyptian pharaoh Merneptah over Israel in the late thirteenth century* B.C.E. *This is probably the oldest reference to Israel currently extant. The phrase "Israel is laid waste" has often been interpreted as referring to the Jews as a people rather than as a specific homeland, in contrast to the other references to peoples together with lands. If this interpretation is correct, it may refer to the wanderings of Israel in the desert, thereby identifying Merneptah as the pharaoh of the Exodus. The second document is the Mesha Stone, recording the victories of Moab over Israel and particularly the revenge exacted from the Israelite house of Omri, the most powerful monarch of the Northern Kingdom of Israel.*

The Ancient Near East

Hymn of Victory of Mer-ne-ptah ("Israel Stella")

The princes are prostrate, saying "Mercy!"
Not one raises his head among the Nine Bows.

Desolation is for Tehenu; Hatti is pacified;
Plundered is the Canaan with every evil;

Carried off is Ashkelon; seized upon is Gezer;
Yanoam is made as that which does not exist;

Israel is laid waste, his seed is not;
Hurru is become a widow for Egypt!

All lands together, they are pacified;
Everyone who was restless, he has been bound by the king of Upper and Lower Egypt: Ba-en-Re Meri-Amon; the Son of Re: Mer-ne-Ptah Hotep-hir-Maat, given life like Re every day.

The Moabite Stone

I (am) Mesha, son of Chemosh-[. . .], king of Moab, the Dibonite—my father (had) reigned over Moab thirty years, and I reigned after my father,—(who) made this high place for Chemosh in Qarhoh [. . .] because he saved me from all the kings and caused me to triumph over all my adversaries. As for Omri, king of Israel, he humbled Moab many years (lit., days), for Chemosh was angry at his land. And his son followed him and he also said, "I will humble Moab." In my time he spoke (thus), but I have triumphed over him and over his house, while Israel hath perished for ever! (Now) Omri had occupied the land Medeba, and (Israel) had dwelt there in his time and half the time of his son (Ahab), forty years; but Chemosh dwelt there in my time.

And I built Baal-meon, making a reservoir in it, and I built Qaryaten. Now the men of Gad had always dwelt in the land of Ataroth, and the king of Israel had built Ataroth for them; but I fought against the town and took it and slew all the people of the town as satiation (intoxication) for Chemosh and Moab. And I brought back from there Arel (or Oriel), its chieftain, dragging him before Chemosh in Kerioth, and I settled there men of Sharon and men of Maharith. And Chemosh said to me, "Go, take Nebo from Israel!" So I went by night and fought against it from the break of dawn until noon, taking it and slaying all, seven thousand men, boys, women, girls and maid-servants, for I devoted them to destruction for (the god) Ashtar-Chemosh. And I took from there the [. . .] of Yahweh, dragging them before Chemosh. And the king of Israel had built Jahaz, and he dwelt there while he was fighting against me, but Chemosh drove him out before me. And I took from Moah two hundred men, all first class (warriors), and set them against Jahaz and took it in order to attach it to (the district of) Dibon.

It was I (who) built Qarhoh, the wall of *the forests* and the wall of the citadel; I also built its gates and I built its towers and I built the king's house, and I made both of its reservoirs for water inside the town. And there was no cistern inside the town at Qarhoh, so I said to all the people, "Let each of you make a cistern for himself in his house!" And I cut *beams* for Qarhoh with Israelite captives. I built Aroer, and I made the highway in the Arnon (valley); I built Beth-bamoth, for it had been destroyed; I built Bezer—for it lay in ruins—with fifty men of Dibon, for all Dibon is (my) loyal dependency.

And I reigned [*in peace*] *over* the hundred towns which I had added to the land. And I built [. . .] Medeba and Beth-diblathen and Beth-baal-meon, and I set there the [. . .] of the land. And as for Hauronen, there dwelt in it [. . . . And] Chemosh said to me, "Go down, fight against Hauronen. And I went down [and I fought against the town and I took it], and Chemosh dwelt there in my time. . . .

Bibliography for Further Reading

Alter, Robert. *The Art of Biblical Narrative,* Basic Books, 1981
Auerbach, Elias. *Moses,* Wayne State University Press, 1975
Sarna, Nahum. *JPS Torah Commentary: Exodus,* 1991
Rosenberg, Joel. *King and Kin,* Indiana University Press, 1986
Silver, Daniel Jeremy. *Images of Moses,* Basic Books, 1982
Walzer, Michael. *Exodus and Revolution,* Harper and Row, 1985

Unit III

Prophecy and Biblical Religion

Literary Prophecy

Perhaps the most renowned feature of biblical religion relates to Israelite prophecy. Prophecy in the sense of predicting the future, or soothsaying, was by no means restricted to ancient Israel. On the contrary, the Bible itself records the story of Balaam, a prophet among the gentiles. Interestingly, Balaam is probably the only character featured in the Pentateuch for whom an independent archeological record exists. In the late 1960's, a stele was discovered in Jordan indicating a person named Balaam son of Be'or as a figure well-known for dispensing advice concerning fertility, a description not terribly distant from the Balaam of the Hebrew Bible.

The Jewish prophets may be categorized into four distinct typologies: Some inclined to an early form of mysticism, forming ecstatic bands which would go about prophesying as if in a trance. When King Saul engaged in such mystical activity, it was marveled that he, too, had joined the ecstatic bands of prophets.

Other prophets were the traditional soothsayers—those who could see things not readily apparent. Thus, Samuel is referred to as a "seer," who can inform Saul as to where his missing donkeys may be found.

Yet a third type were referred to collectively as the false prophets. These were Israelite prophets who believed in monotheism, but who counseled the people to believe in a false and shallow optimism concerning the inviolability of Jerusalem.

Lastly, there were the court prophets—those who functioned both as courtier and conscience of the Israelite monarch. Nathan was perhaps the best known of this type, rebuking David over the Bathsheba affair and subsequently becoming involved in court intrigue over the question of David's succession. Although the court prophets were most obviously political, all four types had a political base and were involved in political activities. Some were more representative of aristocratic backgrounds, as is mentioned specifically concerning Isaiah, Jeremiah, and Ezekiel. Precisely on account of their political interests, the sociologist Max Weber referred to biblical prophets as the earliest political pamphleteers. To be sure, these categories were by no means exclusive—save for the distinction between "false" and "true" prophets.

The most famous of the prophets left behind literary records, which comprise some of the most beautiful documents in the entire Bible. It is important to note that the literary prophets by no means focused upon predicting the future. Rather, they defined prophecy as moral exhortation, urging the people to change their ways, and utilized predictions of the future only as a vehicle to articulate their moral themes. The predictive side of prophecy may have become the more popular, but the essential theme of moral exhortation clearly was far more important in the eyes of the biblical authors.

The literary prophets stressed a number of very specific themes: First, they were generally disgusted with the temple cult of animal sacrifices. To be sure, the prophet Isaiah criticized prayer as well. The prophets were by no means opposed to sacrifices per se. Rather, they opposed sacrifices that were unaccompanied by ethical content or moral force. Instead the prophets emphasized ethical behavior as the primary vehicle of personal and national salvation.

Secondly, the literary prophets emphasized the conditional nature of the Jewish covenant. Jerusalem and the Temple were by no means inviolable. They were liable to destruction if the Jews failed to fulfill the responsibilities of the covenant.

Thirdly, the literary prophets rejected the popular eschatology of an end of days accompanied by a triumph of the Jews. They warned that the end of days would be days of darkness accompanied by enormous human suffering. In this sense, they represented perhaps the earliest warnings against those who anticipate a messianic or apocalyptic end, even while articulating a vision of ultimate redemption.

Fourthly, the prophets are best known for their universalism. In their view, nations of the world would retain a place in God's Divine scheme. Their activities serve Divine purposes within history. The prophetic vision embraced all of humanity in its vision of a peaceful future. This prophetic vision of universalism by no means replaced the more particularistic or ethnocentric visions found elsewhere in the Bible. Rather, the prophets suggested a constant dialectic between the particular and the universal. To be a Jew meant to struggle constantly between these two poles, at times working entirely on issues unique to the Jewish community, at other times serving as a "light unto the gentiles," i.e. fulfilling the universalistic mission of bearing the message of ethical monotheism to the gentile world.

Lastly, the literary prophets usually articulated a clear-cut foreign policy to Israelite monarchs. Oftentimes, the monarchs rejected it as dissonant with their immediate needs and objectives. Jeremiah, in particular, counseled a foreign policy of accommodation with Babylonia, rather than rebellion against Babylonian rule. Indeed, the political theory of Jeremiah served the Jews as a counterbalance to the political theory of rebellion. Ultimately, as we shall see, after the failure of successive rebellions against Rome, the political theory of accommodation prevailed in Jewish life until modern times.

The literary prophets are perhaps best remembered today for their sophisticated literary value and for their emphasis upon bridging the social chasms between rich and poor. In that sense, they are perceived today as transmitting a message of Jewish universalism and ethical responsibility at a time of growing social chasm. These messages, however, can by no means be taken out of the context of a battle to preserve monotheism and a political struggle over the appropriate policies for the Jewish State to pursue.

Political Developments

The northern kingdom of Israel, with its capital in Samaria, and consisting of the ten northern tribes, excluding Judah, Benjamin, and portions of the landless Levite tribe, began to collapse in the middle of the eighth century B.C.E. In 738 B.C.E, the Assyrian monarch Tiglath-Pileser III conquered a coalition of several nations in the vicinity of ancient Canaan. He deported Arameans from Damascus and replaced them with new inhabitants. Aram had previously served as a safety belt between Israel and Assyria. This population exchange was designed to prevent revolts by undermining the native ethnic population. Religion was a key tool in undermining the national character of the conquered area, for the Assyrians expected the new population to bring their religious traditions with them, resulting in new forms of religious syncretism. Thus, religious policy would serve national aims.

In 722 B.C.E., the Assyrian king Sargon II conquered Samaria and treated the Israelite state in ways similar to how his predecessor had treated Aram. Most likely, only the higher classes were deported and were resettled on the Chebar River near the Assyrian-Babylonian border.

Similarly, the Assyrians brought in new settlers from the far reaches of the Assyrian empire to settle in Samaria. These new settlers blended with the indigenous Israelite inhabitants and are recorded in the Bible as syncretizing Jewish and pagan practices. These mixed populations are the origins of the still-existing Jewish sect known as Samaritans. Over the years, the Samaritans clearly became more monotheistic, but were generally excluded from the Jewish body politic. Samaritan theology centralized Mount Gerizim in Samaria in contrast to Jerusalem. On Mount Gerizim the Samaritans built their own temple, which lasted until Maccabean times. To this day, the Samaritans sacrifice the Paschal lamb every Passover on Mount Gerizim. Lastly, the Samaritan Pentateuch—which is actually a Hexateuch, for it includes the Book of Joshua, whose hero was a member of the tribe of Ephraim and was therefore regarded as a Samaritan ancestor—contains a number of textual differences from the Jewish version of the Pentateuch.

Despite their small numbers, the Samaritans retained a distinctive existence into the twentieth century. They are recorded as rebelling on several occasions against Rome and are featured prominently in the New Testament, hence the origin of the phrase "Good Samaritan." At several points in Jewish history, the Samaritans were closely allied with the surrounding Jewish communities. At most points, however, the Samaritans were considered a sect set apart. Lacking a diaspora, with the exception of Samaritan communities in Egypt and Syria, the Samaritan center remained Palestine. In 1950, the benefits of the Law of Return were extended by the newly-formed State of Israel to the Samaritans. Their High Priest continues to reside in Nablus to this day.

The Ten Lost Tribes

The destruction of the northern kingdom and the emergence of the Samaritans as a Jewish sect are closely related to one of the most colorful myths of Jewish history, that of the Ten Lost Tribes. Throughout the Middle Ages, various travelers spun fantastic legends about what had become of these Ten Lost Tribes, the powerful kingdoms that they had created, and predictions of their eventual return to the Jewish body politic. Most of this material was legendary in nature and fed upon the desires of medieval Jews to hear of a place where Jews were powerful and sovereign, rather than subject and defeated.

The question does remain, however, what became of the Ten Lost Tribes. Clearly, Jews believed that these tribes had somehow disappeared but would rejoin the Jewish people at some far-off future date. In fact, however, it is not much of a mystery as to what became of them. First, not all Jews were deported from ancient Samaria. The Bible records Jewish tribes as continuing to live in the area of northern Israel after the Assyrian conquest and as linking up with the Jews of Jerusalem. Others were deported to the far reaches of the Assyrian Empire and most likely assimilated in the surrounding environment. Still others possibly joined the later exiles of Jerusalem to the River Chebar during the Babylonian conquest of the early sixth century B.C.E. Others, of course, evolved into latter day Samaritans.

To be sure, we do find Jewish tribes in southern Russia and Afghanistan who have traditions of being the descendants of the Ten Lost Tribes. These "mountain Jews" came into greater prominence in the twentieth century under the former Soviet Union. Some have since immigrated to the State of Israel. One cannot validate the authenticity of their traditions as being of the Ten Lost Tribes. All one can say is that they have such traditions.

In short, however, there is little mystery as to what became of the Ten Lost Tribes. Some, perhaps most, evolved into the Samaritans or linked up with the Jews remaining in Canaan. Others assimilated into the Assyrian Empire. Others linked up with the later Judean exiles to Babylonia. Some, possibly, may have retained their distinctiveness as Jewish tribes in southern Russia. Other tales of the Ten Lost Tribes, identifying them with American Indians or Chinese Jews or the Bene Israel of Bombay, are far more legend than history.

Religious Reform

Under the leadership of the literary prophets, Jerusalem witnessed significant reforms in Jewish religion and practice. These were the years known as the "Deuteronomic Reform" in which the principles of the Book of Deuteronomy became greatly emphasized within ancient Judaism. For example, the Book of Kings underscores the principle of personal responsibility, insisting that fathers will not die for the sins of their sons nor will sons die for the sins of fathers. As a result, although the assassins of a Jerusalem monarch were brought to justice, no punishment was inflicted upon the children of the assassins—a principle of personal responsibility sharply at odds with the ancient code of Hammurabi, which suggested, for example, that if an architect built a house and the house collapsed killing the son of the purchaser, the son of the architect must be killed. The Deuteronomic Reform sharply emphasized the theme of personal accountability and individual responsibility.

Moreover, worship was centralized in Jerusalem. The Jewish king Hezekiah removed the high places outside Jerusalem on which sacrifices were being placed, to bring the people closer to Jerusalem and its Temple. Hezekiah is lavishly praised for his actions in the biblical record, even though he astonished much of the ancient pagan world which could not believe that the Jewish God would be satisfied with fewer rather than more sacrifices. Although the Assyrians sought to conquer Jerusalem as well, in the year 700 B.C.E., they abandoned the siege of Jerusalem following a miraculous plague decimating the army of the Assyrian king, Sennacherib. Remarkably, this plague is also recorded by the Greek historian Herodotus, who notes that the plague occurred to Sennacherib's army while it was invading Egypt. Of course, the biblical story recording the lifting of the siege of Jerusalem by Sennacherib only corroborated the already prevailing myth that Jerusalem was inviolable and could never be destroyed.

The culmination of the Deuteronomic Reform occurred during

the reign of the boy king Josiah. The long reign of Josiah's predecessor, Menassah, served as the sole period in the history of the southern kingdom of Judah of official idolatry. Menassah was completely subservient to the Assyrians, and, perhaps related to that subservience was his willingness to transform Jerusalem into an idolatrous city and to murder those who opposed this transformation.

After his death, Josiah, an eight-year-old descendant, began the process of restoring the Temple in Jerusalem and purifying the cult. Under the tutelage of the High Priest Hilkiah, Josiah initiated efforts to rebuild the center of Israelite monotheism. During the course of these efforts, a book was found within the Temple precincts which mandated Judaic practices widely at variance with what was known at the time. Possibly this was the Book of Deuteronomy, although there is no explicit mention to that effect. However, the reforms that Josiah initiated following the discovery of this book appear to have corresponded closely with the dictates of the Book of Deuteronomy. Again, there was an insistence upon removal of places of sacrifice outside Jerusalem; the holiday of Passover was reinstituted as a central time of pilgrimage to Jerusalem for Jews everywhere; lastly, it became the special province of the king to recite this book at a national gathering. Although there is no conclusive proof for the identification of the book with Deuteronomy, the evidence of the reforms based upon it appear to correspond with the content of Deuteronomy.

One cannot, however, divorce the religious reforms of Josiah from his political agenda. Clearly, the reforms were tied to resurgent nationalism and rebellion against Assyrian rule. Josiah, in fact, reconquered the northern areas of Samaria and the Galilee. In annexing northern Israel, he wished to rid the Jews of Assyrian religious influence. In fact, Josiah died at Megiddo in the north while resisting an attack from Egypt.

The biblical praise of Josiah is lavish. He is recorded as exceeding in righteousness all of his predecessors in Jerusalem and all those who followed him. In retrospect, the Bible views his reign as the last period of glory in the history of the Judean monarchy. His successors essentially presided over a state in decline, culminating in the Babylonian exile and destruction of Jerusalem in 586 B.C.E.

Reading: Isaiah I:1–27

The Book of Isaiah is, perhaps, the finest statement of literary prophecy. Isaiah defines prophecy not as predicting the future, but as moral exhortation. The opening chapter of Isaiah serves as the prophet's indictment of Judean society for having abandoned the ethics of Judaic law. Note, in particular, his disdain for ritual sacrifice, preferring instead ethical action.

[1]The prophecies of Isaiah son of Amoz, who prophesied concerning Judah and Jerusalem in the reigns of Uzziah, Jotham, Ahaz, and Hezekiah, kings of Judah.

[2]Hear, O heavens, and give ear, O earth,
For the Lord has spoken:
I reared children and brought them up
And they have rebelled against Me!

[3]An ox knows its owner,
An ass its master's crib:
Israel does not know,
My people takes no thought.

[4]Ah, sinful nation!
People laden with iniquity!
Brood of evildoers!
Depraved children!
They have forsaken the Lord,
Spurned the Holy One of Israel,
Turned their backs [on Him].

[5]Why do you seek further beatings,
That you continue to offend?
Every head is ailing,
And every heart is sick.

[6]From head to foot
No spot is sound:
All bruises, and welts,

And festering sores
Not pressed out, not bound up,
Not softened with oil.

[7]Your land is a waste,
Your cities burnt down;
Before your eyes, the yield of your soil
Is consumed by strangers
A wasteland as overthrown by strangers!

[8]Fair Zion is left
Like a booth in a vineyard,
Like a hut in a cucumber field,
Like a city beleaguered.

[9]Had not the Lord of Hosts
Left us some survivors,
We should be like Sodom,
Another Gomorrah.

[10]Hear the word of the Lord,
You chieftains of Sodom;
Give ear to our God's instruction,
You folk of Gomorrah!

[11]What need have I of all your sacrifices?
Says the Lord.
I am sated with burnt offerings of rams,
And suet of fatlings,
And blood of bulls;
And I have no delight
In lambs and he-goats.

[12]That you come to appear before Me
Who asked that of you?
Trample My courts

[13]no more;
Bringing oblations is futile,
Incense is offensive to Me.
New moon and sabbath,
Proclaiming of solemnities,

Assemblies with iniquity,
I cannot abide.

[14]Your new moons and fixed seasons
Fill Me with loathing;
They are become a burden to Me,
I cannot endure them.

[15]And when you lift up your hands,
I will turn My eyes away from you;
Though you pray at length,
I will not listen.
Your hands are stained with crime

[16]Wash yourselves clean;
Put your evil doings
Away from My sight.
Cease to do evil;

[17]Learn to do good.
Devote yourselves to justice;
Aid the wronged.
Uphold the rights of the orphan;
Defend the cause of the widow.

[18]Come, let us reach an understanding,
says the Lord.

Be your sins like crimson,
They can turn snow-white;
Be they red as dyed wool,
They can become like fleece.

[19]If, then, you agree and give heed,
You will eat the good things of the earth;

[20]But if you refuse and disobey,
You will be devoured [by] the sword.
For it was the Lord who spoke.

[21]Alas, she has become a harlot,
The faithful city
That was filled with justice,
Where righteousness dwelt
But now murderers.

[22]Your silver has turned to dross;
Your wine is cut with water.

[23]Your rulers are rogues
And cronies of thieves,
Every one avid for presents
And greedy for gifts;
They do not judge the case of the orphan,
And the widow's cause never reaches them.

[24]Assuredly, this is the declaration
Of the Sovereign, the Lord of Hosts,
The Mighty One of Israel:
Ah, I will get satisfaction from My foes;
I will wreak vengeance on My enemies!

[25]I will turn My hand against you,
And smelt out your dross as with lye,
And remove all your slag:

[26]I will restore your magistrates as of old,
And your counselors as of yore.
After that you shall be called
City of Righteousness, Faithful City.

[27]Zion shall be saved in the judgment;
Her repentant ones, in the retribution.

Bibliography for Further Reading

Albright, William Foxwell. *From the Stone Age to Christianity,* Anchor Books, 1957

Bright, John. *A History of Israel,* Westminster Press, 1972

Grant, Michael. *The History of Ancient Israel,* Scribners, 1984

Heschel, Abraham J. *The Prophets,* Harper and Row, 1962

Kaufman, Yehezkhel. *The Religion of Israel,* Schocken, 1972

Redford, Donald. *Egypt, Canaan, and Israel in Ancient Times,* Princeton University Press, 1992

Unit IV

Destruction and Exile

Foundations of Diaspora Autonomy

Babylonian Exile

Josiah's reign ended at Megiddo in 609 B.C.E. The Babylonian king Nebuchadrezzar proceeded to defeat Egypt at the Battle of Carchemish (606 B.C.E.) and capture Jerusalem in 597 B.C.E. The Babylonian Chronicle, the annals of the Babylonian kingdom, records that, following Nebuchadrezzar's defeat of Egypt, he advanced to take "all of the land of Hatti including the city of Judah."

The capture of Jerusalem in 597 B.C.E. resulted, not in the destruction of the Temple, but rather in the exile of the upper classes of the population including the king, Jehoiachin. Nebuchadrezzer in turn replaced him with a presumably more subservient Zedekiah, an uncle of Jehoiachin and therefore also a member of the royal Davidic line.

However, the party of rebellion quickly urged Zedekiah to abandon the policies of accommodation advocated so eloquently by the prophet Jeremiah. Eleven years later, in 586 B.C.E., Judah was again in revolt and the Babylonian army had reentered Canaan. In addition to the biblical record of this rebellion, we have a fascinating glimpse of it through the Lachish Letters written from the front to headquarters in Jerusalem. The Jewish generals at Lachish complain against certain nobles who are weakening the hand of the people with their counsels of despair and surrender. Here appears to be an extra-biblical reference to Jeremiah, who was imprisoned by King Zedekiah precisely because he argued that surrender to the Babylonians would mean life, while continued rebellion would mean catastrophe.

As Jeremiah prophesied, this rebellion too ended in failure, marked by the destruction of Jerusalem and the burning of Solomon's Temple. Again an exile of the Jews occurred to Babylonia, but sizable numbers remained in the area surrounding Jerusalem. A new governor, Gedaliah, sympathetic to Jeremiah and to the Babylonians, was empowered by the Babylonian authorities. Scripture records that his policies of accommodation provided considerable economic relief to the remaining population. However, the forces of rebellion assassinated Gedaliah, resulting in a return of the conquering Babylonian army in 582 B.C.E. and yet a third exile of the remaining Jewish population. The Jewish diaspora in fact spread further, for Jeremiah himself joined the exiles to Egypt, which now received a Jewish community that would become quite sizable and significant in later diaspora history.

Factors that Account for Jewish Survival in Exile

The critical question for the historian is what accounted for Jewish survival in exile. Most nations which lost their homeland naturally assimilated into the surrounding environment. For Jews, the tragedy was compounded by the loss of the Temple, the central symbol of Judaism in the ancient world. Judaism was now associated with a religion of defeat, having forfeited both claims to national sovereignty and to religious centralization.

At least five factors help account for continued Jewish survival in the exile. First, one must note the geographical site of exile. Jews are recorded as living by the River of Chebar, perhaps not coincidentally the place of the Israelite exile by the Assyrians some 140 years previously. The ability to link up with an already existing community has been one of the most critical features in facilitating Jewish immigration throughout the millennia.

Secondly, one must note the role of Jewish leadership. The Davidic family, represented by Jehoiachin and his five sons, became royal pensioners of the Babylonian monarchs. Archeological evidence testifies to their continued prominence among the

Babylonian exiles. One Jewish tradition ascribes the beginning of the institution of self-government known later as the exilarchate to Jehoiachin in Babylonia. Whether this tradition is accurate or not, it reflects the continued presence of Jewish leadership in the exile, serving as symbolic anchor for Jews to tie themselves to as Jews.

Nor should one underestimate the importance of Jeremiah's own leadership, even though he himself went to Egypt rather than Babylonia. In an important letter from Jerusalem to the Babylonian exiles, he counseled what later became the dominant Jewish political theory of diaspora: "Build houses and plant gardens... and seek the welfare of the city in which you are living because in its welfare will be your peace" (Jeremiah 29:5–7). Jeremiah's advice, consistent with his advice in Jerusalem, was for the Jews to accommodate themselves to the prevailing diaspora rulers. Rebellion against them would be futile at best, destructive at worst. The most important thing for the exiles to do was to go about their day-to-day business, to build constructive lives, to marry and to raise families. It is this political theory of accommodation with the diaspora that ultimately became the prevailing model of Jewish perception of gentile rule down into modern times.

Thirdly, the archeological record, reflected in the economic records known as the Murashu documents, suggests a portrait of a diversified Jewish economy. We find Jews engaged in commerce, in agriculture, in banking, in contracting, and in rent collecting. This diversification of the Jewish economy, in turn, functioned to safeguard Jewish existence, for Jews were not overly concentrated in a single economic sector.

Fourthly, one must look at the Jewish relationship to Babylonian culture. Jews adopted Babylonian names. For example, in the Book of Esther we encounter, for the first time, names such as Mordecai and Esther, clearly approximations of the Babylonian Marduk and Astarte. In terms of the Jewish calendar, while the rules governing the calendar remained the same as those prevailing in Canaan, new names were given to the months, reflecting the Babylonian calendar—e.g. Kislev and Nisan. By adopting Babylonian proper names and the names of the months of the Babylonian calendar, Jews were communicating the need for some accommodation with the prevailing Babylonian culture. The values of Judaism remained distinctive, yet the forms in which those values were communicated were consonant with the institutions and expectations of Babylonian society.

Last and by no means least, the responses of Judaism as a religious system to the Babylonian exile were critical in ensuring Jewish continuity and survival. The prophet Ezekiel elaborated on the doctrine of individual retribution already articulated during the period of the Deuteronomic reform. In the aftermath of the catastrophe of 586 B.C.E., this doctrine took on greater importance. The message to the Jews of the exile was that they bore responsibility only for their own actions. Were they to change their ways, the covenant with the Jews and its promise of future restoration would continue to prevail. By preaching personal responsibility and national redemption, Ezekiel was helping overcome the natural despair of the people who had witnessed the catastrophe that seemed to augur national destruction.

Literature of the Exile

Theologically, two classics of Jewish literature written during this period helped articulate the doctrine of Jewish continuity. The Book of Lamentations, ostensibly an elegy over the destruction of Jerusalem, wrestled with the question of why and what Jews were to make of the destruction. The author of Lamentations, by tradition the prophet Jeremiah, yet in all likelihood a contemporary of somewhat different political views, set forth a dual theology in attempting to wrestle with the reasons behind the catastrophe. On the one hand, the author of Lamentations suggests that Jerusalem sinned and therefore was punished. The covenant had been violated by the Jews, and therefore the Jews lost their homeland. This "punishment for sin" theology appears to have been inadequate, however, to justify the suffering of the exiles. Doubtless many felt that no sin justified the destruction of innocent children. As a result, in chapter three, the author of Lamentations takes a different approach. There he expresses anger and resentment against God for having brought about the destruction.

This anger and resentment, as Elie Wiesel noted correctly over two thousand years later, really connotes an affirmation of God. Neutrality to God would be denial. Efforts to justify God are irrelevant at best, misplaced at worst. Rather expressions of anger and resentment permit the individual simultaneously to affirm belief in God's presence, yet at the same time to express disagreement and dissent from actions in history. This theme of anger at God originates in Abraham's defiant pleas to God to spare the city of Sodom. Later Hasidic writings would elevate human anger at God into a virtue, as a means of holding God accountable for what takes place in history.

Chapter four of Lamentations again invokes the conditional nature of the covenant. The author states that "the kings of the land and the inhabitants of the world did not believe that an enemy and oppressor would enter the gates of Jerusalem" (Lamentations 4:12), meaning that the myth of the invincibility of Jerusalem prevailed throughout the ancient world. That the Babylonians had entered Jerusalem corroborated the conditional nature of the covenant with the Jews. Jeremiah had been correct, and the false prophets were wrong, to argue that Jerusalem could never be destroyed. Yet, while acknowledging the conditional nature of the covenant, the author looks forward to a future restoration. The Davidic monarchy has been defeated, but Jerusalem will be restored. A new covenant that will not be broken will ultimately cement Jewish ties to homeland and Torah.

The Book of Job wrestles with these issues on a more personal level. Job is a righteous man who experiences personal tragedy. His faith is tested as he raises the problem of theodicy—why do righteous men suffer while evil prevails. Job's friends counsel him that most likely he has sinned and therefore is suffering. Job rejects the advice of his friends because he knows that no sin warranted the punishment he has received.

Significantly, Job does not receive any final answer to his problem of theodicy, perhaps because no satisfying answer indeed exists. One of his friends, Eliphaz, argues for the disciplinary value of suffering—a test of the intentions of the righteous. Zophar argues for God's omniscience—namely that what, from our perspective appears to be evil, from a Divine perspective may very well be good. Job rejects these answers, and the text justifies his rejection. For Job, the answer lies not in any specific message but rather in God's "voice out of the whirlwind"—a statement that God exists. Human understanding is limited and can never fathom these issues of ultimate justice. God confronts Job by challenging him as to who he thinks he is to question God's ways. Is Job a creator who builds and destroys worlds? Job in turn has no answer. His comment is simply that he is satisfied. Until now, he had only heard of God. Now he realizes God's presence and revelation out of the whirlwind. In seeing a vision of Divine creation, Job realizes precisely how unknowable are the ways of God. Previously, Job had not questioned God's power but rather His justice. Now he understands that Divine justice cannot be measured by human scales.

To be sure, this answer does not solve the philosophical problem. To say that Divine justice transcends human categories does not minimize the reality of Job's loss. What does comfort Job is God's presence. He still does not have an answer to why evil exists, but he now acknowledges that God is the only ultimate. God's presence alone reassures Job that the human endeavor is worth continuing.

The opening chapter of Job also raises the question of the relationship between Divine omnipotence and the reality of evil. Job is the first book to set forth a portrait of Satan. Satan as the evil angel has a limited but very real domain. Yet the opening chapter of Job states clearly and unequivocally that Satan can be no more and no less than an agent of God. Satan, like other angels, is purely a messenger. He has no independent moral force or freedom.

The author of the Book of Job may be arguing against the prevailing Zoroastrian theory of two powers in heaven, one for good and one for evil. As Jews encountered Persian culture, they encountered the Persian or Zoroastrian theology of dualism that explains evil and its existence as a result of perpetual conflict between a God of light and a God of darkness. This dualism suggested an independent realm of the demonic. Jewish monotheism by definition rejected dualism. As a result, it had to confront the reality of evil's existence and question how a Divine deity who was wholly good could create or permit evil to occur. The opening chapter of Job is a clear affirmation that whenever evil occurs, God must bear responsibility. Satan is not a free agent, but simply a messenger of the Divine. The rejection of dualism, in turn, underscores the issue of theodicy as critical for the monotheist. Job, like other theologians, cannot answer that issue completely. Rather, he affirms Divine presence even while questioning Divine justice.

These questions of Job became all the more significant in the aftermath of the Holocaust. The traditional punishment-for-sin theology sounded crude at best when so many innocent children had suffered. Irving Greenberg has argued eloquently that no theological statement may be made about Auschwitz unless one is prepared to make it in the presence of children in the ovens. Similarly, Job rejects efforts to justify God's actions. In the aftermath of Auschwitz, any justification of God rings hollow. Yet Job's affirmation that God exists remains every bit as relevant.

Restoration

In 539 B.C.E. Cyrus I, King of Persia and Media, conquered Babylon. Shortly thereafter he issued a declaration authorizing the Jews to return to their homeland and to rebuild the Temple in Jerusalem. Cyrus's declaration represented a policy of the Persian Empire of showing respect for the local deities of the peoples whom they had conquered.

To be sure, only a minority of Jews accepted the invitation to return to Palestine. From 586 B.C.E. until our own day in the 1990's a majority of Jews consistently has lived outside of the borders of Israel. Although that pattern may be changing today, in light of population growth in Israel and assimilation and demographic erosion in the diaspora, two fundamental observations about Jewish history continue to prevail: First, the primary reasons for Jewish immigration to Israel have had more to do with economic opportunities, secondarily perhaps with persecution, and only marginally with ideological convictions concerning a Jewish homeland. Secondly, the nature of Jewish history since 586 B.C.E. has been a story of interplay between diaspora and homeland. The minority of Jews—perhaps 40,000–50,000—who accepted Cyrus's invitation and immigrated to Palestine were early actors in the diaspora-Israel interchange.

Leadership among the Jews now shifted from king and prophet to priest. The royal line was initially represented by Zerubavel, a figure of Davidic lineage who appears to have disappeared mysteriously. The last of the prophets, Malachi, rails against the three primary abuses of the returning Jews—intermarriage, failure to redeem vows, and the degeneracy of the priesthood. However, with the rebuilding of the Temple as the central orientating event of the return from Babylonia, the priesthood assumed renewed significance. The Samaritans were rebuffed in their offer to assist in the rebuilding of the Temple, probably because of their incomplete monotheism and because collaboration with the remaining Samaritans may have gone beyond the authorization of Cyrus, or because the returnees did not wish to be dominated by them politically. If Cyrus's primary motivation in permitting a Jewish restoration was to establish a friendly population near his westernmost border with Egypt, a Jewish alliance with the Samaritans might have created too strong a buffer zone that would not have been to his liking. In any case, Samaritan intervention with Persia possibly halted the building for many years. Only under Darius I, in 516 B.C.E., was the work completed. The new Temple was far inferior to Solomon's structure, yet it symbolized the Jewish restoration, coincidentally exactly 70 years after the destruction of the first Temple.

The Persian period in Jewish history lasted for over 200 years, to the conquest of Alexander the Great in 330 B.C.E. However, the period remains an incredibly dark one in terms of our knowledge of the Jewish encounter with the Persian Empire. The Book of Esther fails to give us a concrete historical context for Jewish life in the Persian Empire, although it does articulate an outspoken cultural criticism of the hedonism of the Empire, with its constant partying and arbitrary justice. At the flick of a lottery, the Jews could be eliminated entirely. The author of the Book of Esther is suggesting the precariousness of Jewish life in the diaspora. Mordecai as a court Jew owes his success as much to good fortune as to his own survival skills.

More historically authenticated are the Persian foundations for diaspora Jewish autonomy. In the middle of the fifth century B.C.E., the Persian government granted Ezra authority to punish those who violated the Torah. This represented a novel precedent whereby Jews were not only permitted to live by Jewish law, but rather were compelled by the secular authority to enforce Jewish law. This pattern of the secular state facilitating diaspora Jewish autonomy reappears throughout diaspora Jewish history. Clearly the Persians desired a stable Jewish community and felt that empowering Jewish leaders to enforce Jewish law would provide precisely that stability.

As noted earlier, during this period for the first time Jews encountered the significant issue of intermarriage with surrounding gentile nations. Ezra sought to prevent intermarriage and encourage marriage between Jews—a pattern Jewish leaders would emulate for millennia afterwards. To be sure, one possible alternative for coping with intermarriage was conversion to Judaism. A book probably written at this time, the Book of Ruth, remains the classic statement of conversion, in which Ruth joins with the Jewish people, abandons her family and nation of origin, and accepts Judaism with the words "your people shall be my people" (Ruth I: 16). The Book of Ruth amounts to an eloquent statement on the importance of conversion as entering the Jewish covenant not only of faith but also of destiny and peoplehood.

Most significantly, Ezra, together with his colleague Nehemiah, reinstituted the covenant of faith establishing the Torah as the official constitution of the Jews. In so doing, they established the foundations of Jewish existence under gentile rule in accordance with principles of tradition and Jewish heritage. Finally, the doctrine of the Messiah, or a future redeemer, first appears during this period, suggesting a promise of a final redemption and future restoration of the entire Jewish people in its homeland.

In addition to the ongoing exilic community in Babylonia-Persia, a sizable military colony of Jews appears to have flourished at Elephantine, near the Egyptian-Ethiopian border at the First Cataract of the Nile. The inhabitants consisted primarily of Jewish soldiers acting on behalf of the Persian government. They built their own temple at Elephantine and continued to offer animal sacrifices. The last records of Elephantine Jewry date from approximately 400 B.C.E., at which time the temple was still standing, although it had ceased offering sacrifices.

The Elephantine colony is historically significant in several respects. First, its presence suggests the image of the Jew as warrior and soldier in ancient times. Secondly, the colony underlines the importance of Israel-diaspora relations, as the Jews of Elephantine corresponded with their coreligionists in Jerusalem regarding the observance of the Passover holiday. Lastly, the records of Elephantine Jewry reveal that both women and men were able to initiate divorce proceedings—a practice at variance with traditional Jewish law. Certainly Elephantine Jewry deviated from the Judaism of homeland. The very fact that they had a temple offering animal sacrifices—to say nothing of the pious affectations offered on behalf of pagan deities—suggests how far removed they were from the mainstream of ancient Judaism. Nevertheless, the very presence of the Elephantine colony points to the growing importance of diaspora Jewry as a force in the historical development of the Jewish people.

Reading: Jeremiah XXIX: 1–10

The Book of Jeremiah also serves as a paradigm of literary prophecy. Jeremiah has historically been seen as the prophet of doom—hence the term "jeremiad." Actually, Jeremiah's prophecies express far more than doom-saying. His "Letter to the Exiles," reprinted here, stands as a classic statement of Jewish political theory—namely, continued aspiration for redemption, yet focusing on the here and now while in exile and seeking the welfare of the land to which the Jews have been exiled. Jeremiah's advice guided not only the Judean exiles to Babylonia, but also much of rabbinic political wisdom even into modern times.

[1]This is the text of the letter which the prophet Jeremiah sent from Jerusalem to the priests, the prophets, the rest of the elders of the exile community, and to all the people whom Nebuchadnezzar had exiled from Jerusalem to Babylon—[2]after King Jeconiah, the queen mother, the eunuchs, the officials of Judah and Jerusalem, and the craftsmen and smiths had left Jerusalem. [3][The letter was sent] through Elasah son of Shaphan and Gemariah son of Hilkiah, whom King Zedekiah of Judah had dispatched to Babylon, to King Nebuchadnezzar of Babylon.

[4]Thus said the Lord of Hosts, the God of Israel, to the whole community which I exiled from Jerusalem to Babylon: [5]Build houses and live in them, plant gardens and eat their fruit. [6]Take wives and beget sons and daughters; and take wives for your sons, and give your daughters to husbands, that they may bear sons and daughters. Multiply there, do not decrease. [7]And seek the welfare of the city to which I have exiled you and pray to the Lord in its behalf; for in its prosperity you shall prosper.

[8]For thus said the Lord of Hosts, the God of Israel: Let not the prophets and diviners in your midst deceive you, and pay no heed to the dreams they dream. [9]For they prophesy to you in My name falsely; I did not send them—declares the Lord.

[10]For thus said the Lord: When Babylon's seventy years are over, I will take note of you, and I will fulfill to you My promise of favor—to bring you back to this place.

Reading: Esther I

The Book of Esther is a diaspora-centered work. It has but one reference to Zion, and there are no explicit references to the Deity. Rather, the book of Esther is an example of wisdom literature, trying to guide Jewish life in exile. Of particular interest in the first chapter is the critique of the hedonism of Persian society and its arbitrary sense of justice. The author mocks the extensive partying in which wine flows so freely, as if society has nothing more important to do than engage in constant partying. Similarly, the deposition of Queen Vashti at the whim of the Persian monarch and his advisors suggest the arbitrary nature of diaspora existence. The author implies that in such a society, the moral order favored by Judaism is absent. Mordechai and Esther restore that moral vision and thereby save the Jewish people. The precariousness of diaspora Jewish existence stands as the most powerful theme within the book.

[1]It happened in the days of Ahasuerus—that Ahasuerus who reigned over a hundred and twenty-seven provinces from India to Nubia. [2]In those days, when King Ahasuerus occupied the royal throne in the fortress Shushan, [3]in the third year of his reign, he gave a banquet for all the officials and courtiers—the administration of Persia and Media, the nobles and the governors of the provinces in his service. [4]For no fewer than a hundred and eighty days he displayed the vast riches of his kingdom and the splendid glory of his majesty. [5]At the end of this period, the king gave a banquet for seven days in the court of the king's palace garden for all the people who lived in the fortress Shushan, high and low alike. [6][There were hangings of] white cotton and blue wool, caught up by cords of fine linen and purple wool to silver rods and alabaster columns; and there were couches of gold and silver on a pavement of marble, alabaster, mother-of-pearl, and mosaics. [7]Royal wine was served in abundance, as befits a king, in golden beakers, beakers of varied design. [8]And the rule for the drinking was, "No restrictions!" For the king had given orders to every palace steward to comply with each man's wishes. [9]In addition, Queen Vashti gave a banquet for women, in the royal palace of King Ahasuerus.

[10]On the seventh day, when the king was merry with wine, he ordered Mehuman, Bizzetha, Harbona, Bigtha, Abagtha, Zethar, and Carcas, the seven eunuchs in attendance on King Ahasuerus, [11]to bring Queen Vashti before the king wearing a royal diadem, to display her beauty to the peoples and the officials; for she was a beautiful woman. [12]But Queen Vashti refused to come at the king's command conveyed by the eunuchs. The king was greatly incensed, and his fury burned within him.

[13]Then the king consulted the sages learned in procedure. (For it was the royal practice [to turn] to all who were versed in law and precedent. [14]His closest advisers were Carshena, Shethar, Admatha, Tarshish, Meres, Marsena, and Memucan, the seven ministers of Persia and Media who had access to the royal presence and occupied the first place in the kingdom.) [15]"What," [he asked,] "shall be done, according to law, to Queen Vashti for failing to obey the command of King Ahasuerus conveyed by the eunuchs?"

[16]Thereupon Memucan declared in the presence of the king and the ministers: "Queen Vashti has committed an offense not only against Your Majesty but also against all the officials and against all the peoples in all the provinces of King Ahasuerus. [17]For the queen's behavior will make all wives despise their husbands, as they reflect that King Ahasuerus himself ordered Queen Vashti to be brought before him, but she would not come. [18]This very day the ladies of Persia and Media, who have heard of the queen's behavior, will cite it to all Your Majesty's officials, and there will be no end of scorn and provocation!

[19]"If it please Your Majesty, let a royal edict be issued by you, and let it be written into the laws of Persia and Media, so that it cannot be abrogated, that Vashti shall never enter the presence of King Ahasuerus. And let Your Majesty bestow her royal state upon another who is more worthy than she. [20]Then will the judgment executed by Your Majesty resound throughout your realm, vast though it is; and all wives will treat their husbands with respect, high and low alike."

[21]The proposal was approved by the king and the ministers, and the king did as Memucan proposed. [22]Dispatches were sent to all the provinces of the king, to every province in its

own script and to every nation in its own language, that every man should wield authority in his home and speak the language of his own people.

Reading: Jeremiah LII

The concluding chapter of Jeremiah *consists of an historical account of the Babylonian conquest and destruction of Jerusalem. The author concludes, however, on a positive note with the liberation of the Judean king from the Babylonian prison, thereby affirming the temporary nature of the Babylonian exile and the continued vitality of Jewish life after the exile.*

[1]Zedekiah was twenty-one years old when he became king, and he reigned in Jerusalem for eleven years. His mother's name was Hamutal, daughter of Jeremiah of Libnah. [2]He did what was displeasing to the Lord, just as Jehoiakim had done. [3]Indeed, Jerusalem and Judah were a cause of anger for the Lord, so that He cast them out of His presence.

Zedekiah rebelled against the king of Babylon. [4]And in the ninth year of his reign, on the tenth day of the tenth month, King Nebuchadrezzar moved against Jerusalem with his whole army. They besieged it and built towers against it all around. [5]The city continued in a state of siege until the eleventh year of King Zedekiah. [6]By the ninth day of the fourth month, the famine had become acute in the city; there was no food left for the common people.

[7]Then [the wall of] the city was breached. All the soldiers fled; they left the city by night through the gate between the double walls, which is near the king's garden—the Chaldeans were all around the city—and they set out for the Arabah. [8]But the Chaldean troops pursued the king, and they overtook Zedekiah in the steppes of Jericho, as his entire force left him and scattered. [9]They captured the king and brought him before the king of Babylon at Riblah, in the region of Hamath; and he put him on trial. [10]The king of Babylon had Zedekiah's sons slaughtered before his eyes; he also had all the officials of Judah slaughtered at Riblah. [11]Then the eyes of Zedekiah were put out, and he was chained in bronze fetters. The king of

Babylon brought him to Babylon and put him in prison, [where he remained] to the day of his death.

[12]On the tenth day of the fifth month—that was the nineteenth year of King Nebuchadrezzar, the king of Babylon—Nebuzaradan, the chief of the guards, came to represent the king of Babylon in Jerusalem. [13]He burned the House of the Lord, the king's palace, and all the houses of Jerusalem; he burned down the house of every notable person. [14]The entire Chaldean force that was with the chief of the guards tore down all the walls of Jerusalem on every side. [15]The remnant of the people left in the city, the defectors who had gone over to the king of Babylon, and what remained of the craftsmen were taken into exile by Nebuzaradan, the chief of the guards. But some of the poorest elements of the population—[16]some of the poorest in the land—were left by Nebuzaradan, the chief of the guards, to be vine-dressers and field hands.

[17]The Chaldeans broke up the bronze columns of the House of the Lord, the stands, and the bronze tank that was in the House of the Lord; and they carried all the bronze away to Babylon. [18]They also took the pails, scrapers, snuffers, sprinkling bowls, ladles, and all the other bronze vessels used in the service. [19]The chief of the guards took whatever was of gold and whatever was of silver: basins, fire pans, sprinkling bowls, pails, lampstands, ladles, and jars. [20]The two columns, the one tank and the twelve bronze oxen which supported it, and the stands, which King Solomon had provided for the House of the Lord—all these objects contained bronze beyond weighing. [21]As for the columns, each was eighteen cubits high and twelve cubits in circumference; it was hollow, and [the metal] was four fingers thick. [22]It had a bronze capital above it; the height of each capital was five cubits, and there was a meshwork [decorated] with pomegranates about the capital, all made of bronze; and so for the second column, also with pomegranates. [23]There were ninety-six pomegranates facing outward; all the pomegranates around the meshwork amounted to one hundred.

[24]The chief of the guards also took Seraiah the chief priest and Zephaniah, the deputy priest, and the three guardians of the threshold. [25]And from the city he took a eunuch who was in command of the soldiers; seven royal privy councilors, who

were present in the city; the scribe of the army commander, who was in charge of mustering the people of the land; and sixty of the common people who were inside the city. [26]Nebuzaradan, the chief of the guards, took them and brought them to the king of Babylon at Riblah. [27]The king of Babylon had them struck down and put to death at Riblah, in the region of Hamath.

Thus Judah was exiled from its land. [28]This is the number of those whom Nebuchadrezzar exiled in the seventh year: 3,023 Judeans. [29]In the eighteenth year of Nebuchadrezzar, 832 persons [were exiled] from Jerusalem. [30]And in the twenty-third year of Nebuchadrezzar, Nebuzaradan, the chief of the guards, exiled 745 Judeans. The total amounted to 4,600 persons.

[31]In the thirty-seventh year of the exile of King Jehoiachin of Judah, on the twenty-fifth day of the twelfth month, King Evil-merodach of Babylon, in the year he became king, took note of King Jehoiachin of Judah and released him from prison. [32]He spoke kindly to him, and gave him a throne above those of other kings who were with him in Babylon. [33]He removed his prison garments and [Jehoiachin] ate regularly in his presence the rest of his life. [34]A regular allotment of food was given him by order of the king of Babylon, an allotment for each day, to the day of his death—all the days of his life.

Bibliography for Further Reading

Alter, Robert. *The Art of Biblical Poetry,* Basic Books, 1985, esp. ch. 4

Bickerman, Elias. *From Ezra to the Last of the Maccabees,* Schocken Books, 1962

———. *Four Strange Books of the Bible,* Schocken Books, 1967

Kates, Judith A. and Reimer, Gail Twersky, eds. *Reading Ruth,* Ballantine, 1994

Unit V

Athens and Jerusalem

Conflict and Synthesis

Alexander the Great

In 350 B.C.E., Philip of Macedonia united Greece under Macedonian rule. His son Alexander, surnamed the Great, in turn conquered the entire Persian empire uniting Greece with the ancient Near East. This gave birth to what came to be called Hellenistic civilization, meaning a synthesis of Greek culture with the civilization of the ancient Near East.

In Jewish history Alexander has generally received a favorable press. There are many legends of his encounters with subject peoples such as the Jews and the Samaritans. The Jewish legend records the High Priest of Jerusalem greeting Alexander. Although this legend is no doubt unhistorical, it does reflect a generally positive perception of Alexander, despite his conquest of Persia, which had permitted the Jews to return to Palestine and rebuild the Temple in Jerusalem. By contrast, the Samaritan account of their meeting with Alexander appears to have been far more historical. Alexander apparently authorized the building of the Samaritan temple on Mount Gerizim. Subsequently, however, the Samaritans rebelled against Alexander and burned his representative to death. The rebellion may have been an act of support for the last Persian emperor, Darius III, against whom Alexander was warring. Alexander's troops quelled the rebellion and installed a Macedonian garrison in Samaria.

After Alexander's death in 323 B.C.E., his generals proceeded to divide the empire. In 312 B.C.E., Ptolemy I captured Palestine, deporting thousands of Jews to Egypt. For the next century, Palestine and Egypt were joined under Ptolemaic rule. Continued trade between Egypt and Palestine stimulated further Jewish migrations to Egypt. More significantly, although the Ptolomies generally did not intervene in the internal practice of Judaism, the period of Ptolemaic rule witnessed incipient Hellenization among the Jewish population.

The symbol of this increased Hellenization was the translation of first the Torah and then the rest of the Bible into Greek. This was the classic Septuagint, according to legend requested by Ptolemy II Philadelphus, ostensibly for his personal library. More likely, Ptolemy was interested in checking out the requests of the Jews for exemption from certain statutes under Egyptian law, lest they conflict with the practices of Judaism. Alternatively, the translation may have been deemed necessary by the Jews themselves due to decreased Judaic literacy. Although other translations existed, only the Septuagint was celebrated as a momentous occasion. On the one hand, the translation was regarded as so accurate as to be near-miraculous. On the other hand, the day of the completion of the translation was equated to the day on which the Jews built the Golden Calf.

This dual view of the Septuagint reflected the overall Jewish ambivalence toward Greek culture. Exposure to Greek culture offered new opportunities for potential synthesis between Judaism and Hellenism. Conversely, for a minority to survive in a majority culture, that minority required greater distinctiveness of language, values, ritual, and family practices. Moreover, the Septuagint clearly was an apologetic document. Certain changes were introduced into the text to avoid offending Hellenistic sensitivities. Other changes were introduced to explain apparent anthropomorphisms—statements in the Bible that ascribed human features to the Almighty—in a non-literal way, or as figures of speech. This approach to rationalizing difficult or irrational passages in the text is also found in medieval philosophic literature. For example, Maimonides stated that the Torah spoke in language which human beings could hear. It was not necessarily meant to be taken literally. The Jewish philosopher Philo, living in Egypt in the first century C.E., went to great lengths in developing this allegorical interpretation of Scripture.

Politically, there was little change from the Persian period. The

Ptolemies maintained Jewish autonomy. The Tobiad family became powerful as tax collectors among the Jews. The High Priests in Jerusalem apparently had the right to print coins, a primary symbol of autonomy and also a carry-over from the Persian period.

Culturally, probably the most significant work emanating from this period is the Book of Ecclesiastes, perhaps the most characteristically Hellenistic work within the Bible. It is unclear precisely when the book was written. Tradition ascribes it to King Solomon, although the text does not say so explicitly. Rather the work seems to have emanated from aristocratic Jewish circles in Jerusalem. Its style of Hebrew is noticeably late for the biblical period, and its status as a canonized book was questioned even as late as rabbinic times.

Ecclesiastes is a classic of wisdom literature, which offers ethical advice on man's role within society. Its view of history is cyclical; whatever has happened is fated to recur. Consistently the author questions whether human endeavor actually matters, or whether all of our affairs are mundane and transitory. Yet the author's overall conclusion is decidedly optimistic. Although individuals can do little to affect the overall course of history, on an individual basis human beings can hope to obtain marginal improvements. Thus the author struggles with philosophical skepticism. Is there a purpose in human existence or does the inevitability of death mandate that we regard our lives as transitory and relatively meaningless? He seems to favor acceptance of this reality even as he questions its advantages.

In this respect, the author of Koheleth, or Ecclesiastes, articulates a view far less pessimist than the radical existentialism of certain twentieth century philosophers. Although Koheleth states repeatedly that all is vanity, he also concludes that meaning to human existence is real. Perhaps at times that meaning is veiled, the purpose to our existence may be unknowable, but there is a worthwhile struggle to be waged for internal mastery over our soul and emotions. Despite the author's toying with philosophical skepticism, he asserts a classically Jewish message that human life contains meaning, must be lived to its fullest, and ought to be celebrated. For these reasons, although controversy persisted over the canonization of the book, the rabbis of the Talmud concluded that Koheleth occupied a deserved place in the canon of holy books.

The Maccabean Revolt

Ptolemaic rule was succeeded by Seleucid rule in Palestine. In approximately 200 B.C.E., Antiochus III, a member of the Seleucid dynasty in Syria and heir to the Alexandrian empire in Asia, wrested Palestine from the hands of the Ptolemies. Antiochus III reaffirmed Jewish autonomy and urged the Jews to live in accordance with "*patrioi nomoi*" or the laws of their ancestors.

Yet the tendency toward increased Hellenization persisted. In 170 B.C.E. a dispute erupted over the priesthood in which Jason, a Hellenizer, purchased the priesthood and promised to hellenize Jerusalem. He, in turn, was ousted by Menelaus, an extreme Hellenizer who wished to transform Jerusalem into a Greek *polis.*

Symbolic of this transformation was the Greek institution known as the gymnasium. On the surface, the gymnasium appeared to be a harmless institution in which young men could exercise physically. In practice, it symbolized the conflict between Judaic and Hellenistic values. Young men parading naked in the gymnasium personified the cult of the body. Circumcision, a universal rite among Jewish males, was held as a mark of physical degradation. Some Jews even sought to reverse its physical effects. Last and by no means least, the reverence accorded homosexuality within Greek culture radically contradicted the Judaic emphasis upon heterosexual marriage.

These cultural trends, however, were strictly internal, reflecting a cultural war among Jews. What prompted the Maccabean rebellion were the policies of Antiochus IV outlawing the practice of Judaism and compelling Hellenization. These policies, initiated in 168 B.C.E., have long baffled historians. Some have attributed them to acts of personal lunacy, although Antiochus IV was well-known for conducting a rational foreign policy. Others suggested the policies of coercive Hellenization emanated from religious conviction and zealotry. However, Antiochus IV had otherwise been quite skeptical of the Greek gods. He personally inclined to Epicurean views that the gods cared little about human affairs. Nor could the policies be ascribed to a desire for political unification, for Antiochus IV supported the maintenance of Phoenician temples dedicated to non-Greek deities. Lastly, these policies of coercive Hellenization were restricted entirely to the Land of Israel. In Antioch and elsewhere in the Seleucid Empire, Jews probably continued to maintain their freedoms and privileges to practice Judaism.

The policies of coercive Hellenization ought be understood in the context of the internal conflict within Palestine between Hellenists and anti-Hellenists. Antiochus IV intervened on behalf of those parties closest to him. This struggle may also be related to a political conflict between Jews who supported restoration of Ptolemaic rule and Jews who favored the new Seleucid rule. Again, Antiochus IV seemed to have intervened on behalf of his allies in an attempt to eliminate his opponents.

The Maccabean rebellion itself consisted of two primary stages. In the initial years, 167–163 B.C.E., the rebellion was a quest for religious freedom. This stage enjoyed a broad consensus among the Jewish people to eliminate coercive Hellenization and to restore monotheistic faith centered in Jerusalem. After a series of Maccabean victories, the Seleucids abandoned the policies of Antiochus IV, restored religious freedom, and once again offered autonomy to the Jews of Palestine. This stage culminated in the purification of the Temple in Jerusalem and its rededication with a cruse of oil on the twenty-fifth day of Kislev, inaugurating the new holiday of Chanukah.

Judah the Maccabee and his brothers, known as the Hasmonean family, however, were not satisfied with the restoration of religious liberty. Their rebellion continued into a second stage for political independence and a restoration of Jewish sovereignty. Significantly, when the goals of the rebellion became secular and political, it lost its broad consensus within the Jewish people. Many deserted Judah's army, indicating their satisfaction with a restoration of religious liberty and autonomy under Greek rule. Judah himself was left with only 800 soldiers in his last battle in 161 B.C.E.

The second stage of the rebellion was nowhere nearly as successful as the first. Judah and two of his brothers were killed by Greek armies, and following his death, the Maccabees were reduced to a small guerilla group operating in the mountains of Palestine.

Yet Judah's youngest brother, Jonathan, was in many ways far more successful than his older and more renowned brother. For Jonathan turned to diplomacy as a vehicle to obtain by peaceful methods what he could not obtain on the battlefield. He followed Judah's lead in seeking Roman intervention, which made success possible through Rome's policies of "divide and conquer." Also, the internal problems of the Seleucid empire made Judean independence conceivable. Jonathan served as a master diplomat, playing off one side against another. Although he had been little more than a bandit after Judah's defeat, by 153 B.C.E. he had become a major player in the complicated world of Seleucid politics. The fact that Jonathan bore the good will of Rome, the rising power in the West, granted him considerable clout and legitimacy as a potential ally and king-maker within the struggles of the Seleucid empire. Although he also met a tragic end, by 142 B.C.E. an independent Jewish State was proclaimed with the last surviving Hasmonean brother, Simon, as ruler. Complete sovereignty was obtained under his son, John Hyrcanus (134–104 B.C.E.).

To be sure, this Hasmonean state (142–65 B.C.E.), the last period of independent Jewish sovereignty in Palestine until the twentieth century, was again a function of the relative eclipse of the superpowers from the immediate region of Palestine and her neighbors. The Seleucid empire was in decline, and therefore Jonathan and the Hasmoneans enjoyed a broad range of latitude. Although the power of Rome was rising, Rome was not yet in a position to intervene militarily in Palestinian affairs. The moral and diplomatic support offered the Hasmoneans by Rome of course increased their leverage within the declining Seleucid empire. Once Rome did determine to intervene in Palestine, Judean sovereignty and independence would quickly end.

The immediate problem confronting the Hasmoneans, however, was neither that of Rome nor of foreign policy generally, but of establishing their legitimacy within the Jewish body politic. The Hasmoneans suffered from two problems. They were members neither of the royal Davidic line nor of the High Priestly line. As a result, Maccabean propaganda struggled to establish an alternate legitimacy for the Hasmonean dynasty. The Books of the Maccabees, particularly Maccabees I and Maccabees II, found in the Apocrypha, or non-canonized books, articulate consistently that the family origin of the Maccabees was irrelevant, for they were chosen by God to lead Israel. The Dead Sea Scrolls may suggest an alternative version of Hasmonean propaganda by referring to a Levitic messiah prevailing over a Davidic messiah. Possibly this refers to the Levitic origin of the Hasmoneans in the absence of Davidic ancestry. Lastly, the Maccabees undertook a campaign to underscore the legitimacy of the Temple in Jerusalem, regardless of the identity of the particular High Priest.

Conversely, in approximately 145 B.C.E., the former high priest Onias IV obtained permission to build a new temple to rival that of Jerusalem at Leontopolis in Egypt. The Leontopolis temple functioned for over 200 years until closed by the Romans in 73 C.E. after their victory at Masada. Symbolically, the Leontopolis temple signified, like its predecessor at Elephantine, continued sacrificial rites in the Egyptian diaspora.

Yet what was most devastating about Hasmonean rule was its retreat from the principles of the Maccabean rebellion. It was the Hasmoneans who introduced into Jewish history the infamous policy of coercive conversion by compelling the pagan residents of Galilee and of Idumea either to accept conversion to Judaism or to be killed. This forcible conversion policy, so notorious in later Jewish history, unfortunately was introduced by the Jews themselves.

Culturally, the Hasmoneans reverted to many of the features of Hellenistic civilization. The names of Hasmonean monarchs were distinctively Hellenistic—Jannai, Aristobulus, etc. Their large building campaigns were also Greek-like, as was their practice of declaring days of victory as national holidays. Judah Aristobulus went so far as to call himself "Philhellene" on his coins. Moreover, the reticence regarding the use of the term king, out of respect for the Davidic legacy, now lapsed.

By the time of Alexander Jannai, the break between the Hasmoneans and the people at large became quite clear. Jannai is recorded as crucifying 800 members of the Pharisaic or rabbinic party, suggesting a fundamental break between the Hasmoneans and rabbinic leadership. Interestingly, the rule of the Hasmoneans was almost ended during Jannai's tenure. Cleopatra, Queen of Egypt, nearly annexed Palestine, but withdrew her armies because of pressure from two Jewish generals who argued that conquest of Palestine by Cleopatra would alienate Egyptian Jews in Alexandria—perhaps the first case in Jewish history of diaspora Jewry applying political pressure to safeguard the center of Jewish life in Palestine.

Externally, the Hasmoneans were regarded as barbarians by advocates of Greek culture. Their policy of forced conversion toward the peoples they conquered offended the pagan values of pluralism and religious tolerance. Hellenistic intellectuals now accused the Jews of robbing Palestine from the hands of the ancient Canaanites—a charge that would be repeated in later centuries.

The last Hasmonean monarch was the queen Salome Alexandra. In large measure she acted to restore the harmony between the Hasmoneans and rabbinic leadership. However, this harmony was short-lived. Very quickly the Jewish body-politic degenerated into civil war between supporters of each of her two sons, Hyrcanus and Aristobulus. Some seemed to have so despaired of Hasmonean rule that they sent a delegation to the Roman general Pompey, then perched in Syria, requesting his intervention to overthrow the Hasmoneans and to restore Jewish autonomy under Roman rule. Although Pompey would probably have acted in such a fashion in any case, this provided him a pretext to intervene in Palestinian politics. In the long run, to be sure, Hasmonean sovereignty was very much a function of Roman disinterest in the area. Once Rome became engaged in the ancient Near East, maintaining Jewish independence was in any case largely illusory.

The legacy of the Maccabees is complex. They did restore religious freedom and are permanently remembered through the holiday of Chanukah. Their rule was clouded, however, by images of religious intolerance towards outsiders and the reincorporation of Hellenistic culture within Judaism. Nevertheless, as the last sovereign Jewish entity for the next two thousand years, they retained a powerful image of effective Jewish leaders who presided over the last period of Jewish sovereignty. Throughout the many centuries of Rome rule, there were many who longed for a restoration of Hasmonean rule.

Reading: Ecclesiastes I

The book of Ecclesiastes reflects the encounter of Judaism with Hellenistic culture. The author constantly struggles to find meaning in a world in which so much appeared empty. Ultimately he opts for Wisdom, or Torah, meaning that despite the apparent vanity of so much of human endeavor, performing ethical actions and the pursuit of wisdom are preferable to folly despite the apparent worthlessness of so many human endeavors.

[1]The words of Koheleth son of David, king in Jerusalem.

[2]Utter futility!—said Koheleth—
Utter futility! All is futile!

[3]What real value is there for a man
In all the gains he makes beneath the sun?

[4]One generation goes, another comes,
But the earth remains the same forever.

[5]The sun rises, and the sun sets—
And glides back to where it rises.

[6]Southward blowing,
Turning northward,
Ever turning blows the wind;
On its rounds the wind returns.

[7]All streams flow into the sea,
Yet the sea is never full;
To the place [from] which they flow
The streams flow back again.

[8]All such things are wearisome:
No man can ever state them;
The eye never has enough of seeing,
Nor the ear enough of hearing.

[9]Only that shall happen
Which has happened,
Only that occur
Which has occurred;
There is nothing new
Beneath the sun!

[10]Sometimes there is a phenomenon of which they say, "Look, this one is new!"—it occurred long since, in ages that went by before us. [11]The earlier ones are not remembered; so too those that will occur later will no more be remembered than those that will occur at the very end.

[12]I, Koheleth, was king in Jerusalem over Israel. [13]I set my mind to study and to probe with wisdom all that happens under the sun.—An unhappy business, that, which God gave men to be concerned with! [14]I observed all the happenings beneath the sun, and I found that all is futile and pursuit of wind:

[15]A twisted thing that cannot be made straight,
A lack that cannot be made good.

[16]I said to myself: "Here I have grown richer and wiser than any that ruled before me over Jerusalem, and my mind has zealously absorbed wisdom and learning." [17]And so I set my mind to appraise wisdom and to appraise madness and folly. And I learned—that this too was pursuit of wind:

> [18]For as wisdom grows, vexation grows;
> To increase learning is to increase heartache.

Reading: I Maccabees I:1–57

Maccabees I *is the primary account of the Hasmonean rebellion against Greek rule. The author is avowedly pro-Hasmonean and underscores their legitimacy claiming that God at this time had chosen the Hasmonean family to save Israel. The opening chapter details the onset of Greek persecution. Note, in particular, the author's claim that "lawless men" of Israel had initiated approaches to Antiochus IV inviting introduction of Greek practices within Palestinian Judaism. Note also the author's emphasis on Jewish martyrdom in the face of persecution.*

Chapter One, Alexander's Conquests and Legacy

[1]It came to pass after Alexander, the son of Philip of Macedon, who marched from the land of Chittim, defeated Darius, king of the Persians and Medes, and seized his throne. [2]And he waged many wars, in which he captured fortified towns, and slew kings; [3]and moved steadily forward to the ends of the earth, plundering many nations. At last the world lay quiet under Alexander's rule, and he was full of pride. [4]He built up a very mighty army, and ruled over countries, peoples and principalities; all paid him tribute.

[5]Afterward he took ill, and knowing that he was dying, [6]he summoned his generals, men who had been brought up with him from his youth, and divided his empire among them while he was still alive. [7]Alexander had reigned twelve years when he died. [8]His generals took over the rulership, each in his own province. [9]At his death they were all crowned as kings, and their descendants after them for many years. They brought much misery upon the world.

[10]From among these there descended a wicked individual, Antiochus Epiphanes, the son of King Antiochus. He had been a hostage in Rome before he succeeded to the throne of Syria in the year 137 of the Greek era.

[11]In those days there arose out of Israel a group of lawless men, who misled many of their people. "Let us enter into a treaty with the pagans around us," they proposed, "for ever since we separated ourselves from them, many misfortunes have come upon us." [12]The people considered this a good plan, and some of them were eager to carry it out. [13]They went to the king, and he gave them the authority to introduce the customs of the pagans. [14]They built a stadium in Jerusalem, in the pagan style. [15]They removed the marks of their circumcision, and rejected the Holy Covenant. They intermarried with the pagans, and turned to evil ways.

[16]And when, in Antiochus' opinion, his kingdom was solidly established, he determined to become the ruler of Egypt, so that he might reign over two kingdoms. [17]He invaded Egypt with a powerful force of chariots, elephants, cavalry and a great fleet. [18]He waged war against Ptolemy, king of Egypt, but Ptolemy panicked, fled, and many fell wounded. [19]The fortified cities were captured and the land of Egypt was plundered.

[20]After conquering Egypt, in the year 143, Antiochus turned back and marched up against Israel and Jerusalem with a strong force. [21]In his arrogance he entered into the Temple, and carried off the golden altar, and the lamp for the light, and all its equipment, [22]the table of the showbread, the cups, the bowls, and the golden censers, the curtain, the crowns; and the golden adornment on the front of the Temple he stripped off completely. [23]He seized the silver, the gold, and precious vessels, and whatever hidden treasures he found. [24]And having taken everything, he carried them away to his own country. He had massacred many people and gloated over all he had done.

> [25]Great was the sadness throughout Israel. [26]Rulers and elders groaned; girls and young men were depressed, the beauty of women faded away. [27]Every bridegroom did lament, and every bride sat grieving in her chamber. [28]The

land trembled for its inhabitants, and the whole house of Jacob was clothed in shame.

[29]After two years, the king sent to the towns of Judea a chief tax official, who arrived at Jerusalem with a strong force. [30]His conversation was clever and they trusted him. But, having won their confidence, he suddenly attacked the city. He dealt it a powerful blow, and killed many people of Israel. [31]He plundered the city, setting it to blaze. He tore down the houses in it and the walls around it. [32]And they took the women and children captive, and seized the cattle. [33]Then they fortified the City of David with a great, strong wall, with strong towers, and it was made into a citadel. [34]And they garrisoned there pagan people and violators of the Law. [35]They accumulated weapons and provisions, collected together the spoils of Jerusalem, and stored them there. [36]There they lay in ambush, a serious threat to the Temple, and a steady menace to Israel.

[37]They shed innocent blood round the Temple, they defiled the Sanctuary. [38]The inhabitants of Jerusalem fled for fear of them. She became the dwelling place of strangers, she became a stranger to her offspring, her children deserted her. [39]Her Temple became desolate as a wilderness, her festivals turned to mourning, her Sabbaths to shame, her honor to contempt. [40]Her dishonor was as great as her glory had been, and her pride was bowed low in grief.

[41]Then the king issued a decree throughout his kingdom that they should all become one people and abandon their own laws and religions. [42]And all the pagan nations accepted the royal command. [43]And many in Israel agreed to this form of worship, sacrificing to idols and profaning the Sabbath. [44]The king also sent written word by messengers to Jerusalem and to the cities of Judah that they should follow customs foreign to the country, [45]and that they should stop the burnt-offerings, sacrifices, and drink-offerings in the Temple. [46]Sabbaths and festivals were to be profaned. The Temple and its priests were to be polluted. [47]Altars, sacred groves, and shrines for idols were to be established; swine and other unclean animals were to be offered in sacrifice. [48]They must leave their sons

uncircumcised, and defile themselves in every way unclean and abominable. [49]So that they might forget the Law and change all of their religious ordinances. [50]Whoever would not obey the order of the king was to die. [51]Such was the decree which the king issued for the whole of his kingdom. He appointed officials over all the people, and he commanded the towns of Judea, every one of them, to offer sacrifice. [52]Many of the people, who were willing to forsake the Law, joined them and did evil in the land. [53]Their wicked conduct caused Israel to hide in places of refuge. [54]On the twenty-fifth day of Kislev in the year 146, he erected a dreadful desecration upon the altar, and in the surrounding cities of Judah they erected altars. [55]They offered incense at the doors of the houses and in the streets. [56]The Scrolls of the Law which they found, they tore to shreds and they burnt. [57]Anyone discovered in possession of a Book of the Covenant, or fulfilling the Law, was put to death by the king's sentence.

Bibliography for Further Reading

Bickerman, Elias. *The Jews in the Greek Age,* Harvard University Press, 1988

DeLange, Nicholas. *Apocrypha,* Viking Press, 1978

Tcherikover, Avigdor. *Hellenistic Civilization and the Jews,* Athenaeum, 1970

Unit VI

Jewish Sectarianism

Josephus records four distinct sects as living in Second Commonwealth times. The sects do not appear to have been particularly large. Josephus tells us that there were 6,000 Pharisees and 4,000 Essenes. He notes that the Sadducees were not particularly numerous, although he declines to give us any specific estimate. In Josephus's opinion the majority of Jews did not belong to any particular sect. Rather, the sects were battling for the minds and hearts of the Jewish people at large.

Pharisees

Perhaps the best known, and certainly the core group within Judaism that eventually triumphed, were the Pharisees. The Pharisees have been given a negative reputation primarily on account of the description of them in the Gospels as rigid obscurantists who had lost touch with the real needs of the people. In contemporary parlance, the term Pharisee has become a term of opprobrium, indicating a rigid legalism oblivious to the human needs of society and individuals.

In practice, the Pharisees were far more progressive and forward-looking than any of the other sects. The term Pharisee is probably derived from the Hebrew word for "separate." The term suggests Pharisaic insistence on separating from the people at large in observance of the laws of purity and impurity. The Hebrew reference to "interpretation" refers to a central tenet of pharisaism—namely, the existence of an Oral Law interpreting Scripture without which the Written Law of the Torah would be simply inexplicable.

The Pharisees believed in a dual Torah: a written Torah consisting of the Five Books of Moses, coupled with an oral tradition explaining what that Written Law actually meant. Jews believe that this oral tradition dates far back in history. Although its origins are uncertain, we revere it as if it were commanded by God to Moses at Sinai. Pharisaic tradition consists of the development of this Oral Law to the point that it had to be written down, lest it be forgotten. Around 200 C.E., Rabbi Judah the Patriarch, the generation's outstanding exponent of the Pharisaic tradition, committed the Oral Law to writing in the form known as the *Mishna.* In subsequent generations interpretations of the *Mishna* multiplied both in Palestine and Babylonia. These interpretations, known as the *Gemara,* were also committed to writing. The Talmud consists of the *Mishna* plus the *Gemara.* The Babylonian Talmud is generally considered more complete and comprehensive; the Palestinian Talmud more concise and less complete. As a result, the Babylonian Talmud has been the primary object of Talmudic study to this day, although specialists continue to consult the Palestinian Talmud as well. These two Talmuds form the corpus of Rabbinic Judaism. Over time, the Pharisees evolved from a small sect into the mainstream Judaism that triumphed in the aftermath of the destruction of the Second Temple.

Contrary to the image of the Pharisees in the New Testament, the Pharisaic rabbis provided effective leadership both in terms of adapting to the day-to-day needs of the Jews as a people and to the historical challenges of reconstructing Judaism in the aftermath of the destruction. For example, the *Prozbul* of Hillel represents a fascinating case study of Pharisaic legislation at work. The written Torah ordains that every seventh year, society shall provide the debtor class with a fresh start. All debts are cancelled, and the individual is given an opportunity to start anew. However, as the economy became more complex, and people required larger sums of money to borrow, creditors would cease loaning money as the sixth year came to an end, on the grounds that their debts could not be collected in the seventh year. The situation did not meet the needs of the Jews of the time, and the burdens fell especially upon the poor, who would no longer be able to borrow funds. Therefore

Hillel instituted the *Prozbul*, a document indicating that the individual who possesses the document may not collect the debts owed to him, but the court is empowered to collect the debts on his behalf. Through the *Prozbul* a number of goals were accomplished. The principle was maintained that in the seventh year the individual refrain from collecting debts. However, to facilitate the needs of a more complex economy, the public square, i.e., the court, was empowered to collect debts on the creditor's behalf. The memory of the principle was retained, even as its implementation was nullified because of the needs of a changing economy.

The Pharisees justified their actions as part of a chain of rabbinic authority dating back to Moses. A remarkable *Midrash*, or biblical commentary, illustrates this process. The Pharisees told the legend that Rabbi Akiba, one of the greatest exponents of the Pharisaic tradition, was teaching Torah in heaven. Moses entered his class and discovered that he understood nothing. When Moses was ready to complain to God concerning his lack of understanding, he heard Rabbi Akiba pronounce "and all this we know by virtue of the Oral Law given to Moses at Sinai." When Moses heard this statement, he was immediately gratified and ceased to protest. The story is remarkable for several reasons. First, it acknowledges significant development within the Oral Law from Moses's written Torah. Were the Oral Law literally Mosaic in origin, Moses would have had little difficulty in comprehension. Secondly, however, it asserts an authority for the Oral Law as if it were Mosaic in origin. In effect, the statement is made that we do not know the precise origin of these laws. They are quite ancient in character. They are revered as if they were Mosaic. Finally, when Moses himself hears all this, he is gratified that so much has been accomplished in his name.

Perhaps the most famous, and most misunderstood, example of Pharisaic legislation relates to the *lex talionis*. The written Torah ordains explicitly, "an eye for an eye." This is the usual origin of the notion of "Old Testament justice" as signifying vengeful retribution. However, the Oral Torah recognized that Jewish society could not exist on the basis of literally exacting an "eye for an eye." As a result, the Oral Torah explicitly interpreted this verse as referring to monetary compensation and not to shedding of the perpetrator's eye. This was again justified as the Oral Torah taught to Moses at Sinai, meaning that the written Torah never was meant to be interpreted literally as "an eye for an eye". The principle of retribution in kind was maintained, but implemented in a way that society could function, not in a way that would lead to the dissolution of human bonds within a societal framework. Needless to add, the reference to "Old Testament justice" maliciously suggests that it has been superseded by the New Testament, which presumably is more humane and just.

Pharisaic Judaism was by no means the only option for Judaic self-definition in Second Commonwealth times. The Pharisees had numerous competitors. That Pharisaic Judaism ultimately captured the minds and hearts of the people and evolved into the prevailing rabbinic Judaism is an enormous credit to the historical sense of the Pharisees, their flexibility and capacity to respond to the religious and human needs of the Jews at large, and their remarkable creativity in being able to cope with national challenges.

Sadducees

The primary competitors to the Pharisees were the Sadducees. The term Sadducees probably derived from the name Zadok, a High Priest in the time of David, connoting that the Sadducee party represented the legitimate priestly family. They centered around the Temple in Jerusalem and generally captured a majority of the wealthier classes. Many were close to the Hasmonean dynasty.

The central doctrine of the Sadducees was denial of the Pharisaic Oral Law. That is not to say that they denied Oral Law per se, for they recognized that the Mosaic law required interpretation. What they did deny was Pharisaic authority in determining oral tradition. In other words, they had their own traditions and argued that only the priests could determine what those traditions were. The battle between Sadducees and Pharisees was in some measure a struggle over authority within the Jewish community. Should priests lead or should the rabbis?

Some Sadducee doctrines bespeak a certain rationalism. The Sadducees denied the concepts of immortality and afterlife—ostensibly on the grounds that these were not found within the written Torah. Josephus records that the Sadducees did not believe in angels, suggesting an incipient rationalism. That is not to say that the Sadducees were Hellenists. On the contrary, they seemed to have been deeply religious. After the destruction of the Second

Temple, they continued to bring sacrifices to the Temple Mount, despite the fact that doing so, in express violation of Roman orders, endangered their very lives. Most Sadducees disappeared after 70 C.E., precisely because their definition of Judaism was so Temple-centered, and they failed to develop alternatives by which Judaism could be reconstructed without a physical temple in Jerusalem.

Essenes

The third sect Josephus describes are the Essenes—a term referring either to spiritual healers or derivative from the Greek word for holy. Some suggest that the Essenes evolved from the Hasidim, a group of Jews from Maccabean times who had refused to join the rebellion of Judah the Maccabee.

Clearly the Essenes did separate from the mass body-politic of the Jews. Most Essenes lived near Ein Gedi, in the desert. Their rules were communitarian in nature. Josephus informs us that they did not marry, for they regarded women as bothersome and a diversion from spirituality. That meant the sect could survive only via conversion of Jews who had not been born as Essenes. The sect, in fact, imposed a year of probation upon new initiates.

The Essenes also seemed to have practiced an early form of communism, sharing property in common. Essenes could partake only of foods prepared by other members of the sect. Those who were expelled from the sect often faced starvation because of their vows that they would not eat the food of outsiders.

The Essenes rejected the Jerusalem Temple. Probably they opposed as well the validity of the Jerusalem priesthood. However, their political nationalism was by no means quieted because of their distance from the center of Jewish life. Most likely the majority of Essenes were killed by the Roman armies during the great rebellion against Rome of 66 C.E.

Zealots

Josephus tells us that the fourth philosophy was that of the Zealots. In all probability, Josephus describes them as a specific sect in order to articulate his apologia that the Jews were by no means a rebellious people. The Roman governors, in Josephus's view, were too harsh, and as a result, the people at large fell under the sway of Zealot hotheads. Whether Josephus's interpretation of the rebellion against Rome is accurate or forms a model of historical apologetics is a subject we shall return to subsequently. What is clear is that the Zealots refused to accept Roman rule. They crystallized as a rebellious group in the first century of the Common Era and ultimately captured a majority of Jewish public opinion by the time of the rebellion.

An example of the Zealot interpretation of Jewish law may be seen in their attitude toward taxes. Ultimately Pharisaic Judaism argued that in matters of taxation, "The law of the State is the law," meaning that Jewish law supported the obligation to pay one's fair share of taxes. However, a Zealot source informs us that when the Roman tax collector comes to town, one is permitted to cheat him. Underlining this dictum is the Zealot rejection of Roman rule, and therefore it was permissible to cheat the Romans of their taxes. The Pharisees, in turn, negated this position on the grounds that society cannot function unless individuals paid their fair share of taxes. As we shall see, part of the Pharisaic reconstruction of Judaism in the aftermath of the Destruction was an accommodation to both the reality and the validity of Roman authority.

An extreme sect within Zealotism was the group known as the Sicarii. For them, as a matter of religious principle, foreign rule was, by definition illegitimate. These radicals believed in political assassination of Jew and Roman alike with whom they disagreed. The term Sicarii refers to "wielders of the knife," i.e. cloak-and-dagger men who would stab opponents in the back. In the Talmud, they are referred to as *biryonim* or terrorists. Most likely, they ended their lives in Masada, an action of collective suicide that remains controversial to this day.

Minor Sects

The Samaritans continued their sectarian presence within Palestine often in tension with the Jews as a people. The Samaritans had their Temple on Mount Gerizim, but this was destroyed in 129 B.C.E. by the Hasmonean King John Hyrcanus I. Possibly this action constituted revenge for Samaritan acquiescence in the decrees of Antiochus IV. At that time the Samaritans had dedicated their temple to Zeus and shunned any role in the Maccabeen rebellion.

The most exotic of the Jewish sects, and the one most widely debated to this day, is the so-called Dead Sea sect who came to be known through the Dead Sea Scrolls. Although identified with virtually every group in Palestine at the time, including the early Christians, the Dead Sea sect in their doctrines appear closest to the Essenes. They believed that they were the "true Israel." The world was divided between "children of light" and "children of darkness," and the members of the sect were incorporated within the "children of light." They, too, practiced communal living and were concerned with the legitimacy of the priesthood of Jerusalem.

More specifically, the Dead Sea scrolls tell the story of a Teacher of Righteousness who was murdered by a Wicked Priest. The identity of these individuals has been a subject of controversy ever since the discovery of the Dead Sea Scrolls in the late 1940's. It would, of course, be by no means unusual for sectarian groups to splinter into even more sectarian groups, and, in that respect, the Dead Sea sect may well have been an Essene offshoot.

Conclusion

The more interesting question, and more basic one, concerns the reasons for the wide proliferation of sects at this time. Perhaps it reflected a growing social chasm among the classes. As we shall see, for example, the rebellion against Rome to some extent was an uprising of the lower classes. In other contexts, the sects are marked by their millenarianism—their expectation that the end of days was at hand, again a theme prevalent in various rebellions against Rome. Similarly, the sects seemed to have retained considerable belief in the power of magic. For example, sectarian writings such as the *Book of Enoch* record the story of the fallen angels subsequently immortalized in Milton's "Paradise Lost," a legend that explains the origins of evil yet at the same time arrogates to Satan independent powers bordering on dualism. To the extent that the rabbinic establishment rejected the independent power of magic, the millenarian sects may have clung to these popular beliefs.

Lastly, each of the sects reflects a counter-establishment thrust. To appreciate this, one must return to the portrait of the Pharisees within the Gospels. The negativity expressed toward the Pharisees reflects the resentment of the establishment by disenfranchised groups. Whether the establishment be the Hasmonean monarchy, the Temple in Jerusalem, or the leadership of the rabbis, sectarianism was a vehicle for expressing the natural resentment toward those in power by those who feel disenfranchised.

That sectarianism suggests several conclusions: First, there probably has never been a single form of Judaism. Rather, there have been a variety of forms, each struggling to capture the minds and hearts of the Jewish people.

Secondly, one cannot minimize the reasons for the Pharisaic triumph. Their program adapted to the needs of the Jews in the aftermath of the Roman destruction. The Pharisaic rabbis provided effective leadership at a time when the existence of Jews and Judaism was endangered. The Pharisees triumphed not by coercion, but rather by force of persuasion and teaching. In so doing, they revolutionized the nature of Jewish education and created the parameters for Jewish life to continue for the next two millennia. Thereby the Pharisees created and formed a Jewish unity in place of a proliferation of sects.

The legacy of Jewish sectarianism is two-fold: First, diversity has often been the norm in Jewish history. However, the ultimate triumph of the Pharisees represents unity amidst that diversity. So long as Jews could form a common whole in which what they shared in common as Jews far outweighed their differences, the Jewish community could function as a viable people. Significantly, marriageability served as the key to preserving that commonality. Once sects could no longer marry with one another, they fell outside the Jewish body-politic.

Reading: ***Ethics of the Fathers*** **1: 1**

The Ethics of the Fathers *is a work of rabbinic Judaism offering advice on the conduct of human affairs. Its opening statement articulates the Pharisaic doctrine that Jews have received the Oral Law in a chain of tradition going back to Moses.*

> Moses received Torah from Sinai and delivered it to Joshua, and Joshua to the Elders, and the Elders to the Prophets, and the Prophets delivered it to the men of the Great Synagogue. These said three things: Be deliberate in judging, and raise up many disciples, and make a hedge for the Torah.

Reading: Josephus, *Antiquities* 18:1

Josephus, an historian of Second Commonwealth Judaism, wrote the Antiquities *to demonstrate to the Roman world that the Jews had been in existence even before the founding of Rome. Possession of antiquity, in the classical world, was a sign of legitimacy. Therefore, Josephus surveys the broad sweep of Jewish history and brings it up to his own time. In the following selection, he takes the opportunity to describe the range of Jewish sects in first-century Judaism.*

The Jews had had for a great while three sects of philosophy peculiar to themselves, the sect of the Essenes, the sect of the Sadducees, and the third sort of opinions was that of those called Pharisees. And although I have already spoken of these sects in the second book of the Jewish War, yet will I touch a little upon them also now.

As for the Pharisees, they live simply, and despise delicacies, and follow the guidance of reason, as to what it prescribes to them as good, and think they ought earnestly to strive to observe its dictates. They also pay respect to such as are in years; nor are they so bold as to contradict them in anything which they have introduced. And when they say that all things happen by fate, they do not take away from men the freedom of acting as they think fit; since their notion is, that it has pleased God to mix up the decrees of fate and man's will, so that man can act virtuously or viciously. They also believe that souls have an immortal power in them, and that there will be under the earth rewards or punishments, according as men have lived virtuously or viciously in this life; and the latter souls are to be detained in an everlasting prison but the former will have power to live again. On account of these doctrines they have very great influence with the people, and whatever they do about divine worship, a soul, prayers, or sacrifices, they perform according to their direction. Such great testimony do the cities bear them on account of their constant practice of virtue, both in the actions of their lives, and in their conversation.

But the doctrine of the Sadducees is that souls die with the bodies; nor do they pretend to regard anything but what the law enjoins on them; for they think it virtue to dispute with the teachers of the philosophy which they follow, and their views are received by only a few, but those are of the highest rank. But they are able to do hardly anything so to speak, for when they become magistrates, as they are unwillingly and by force sometimes obliged to do, they addict themselves to notions of the Pharisees, because the people would not otherwise put up with them.

The doctrine of the Essenes is that all things are left in the hand of God. They teach the immortality of souls, and think that the rewards of righteousness are to be earnestly striven for. And when they send what they have dedicated to God to the temple, they do not offer sacrfices, because they have more pure lustrations of their own; on which account they are excluded from the common court of the temple, and offer their sacrifices by themselves. But their course of life is better than that of other men, and they entirely addict themselves to husbandry. It also deserves our admiration, how much they exceed in justice all other men that addict themselves to virtue, to such a degree as has never appeared among any other men, either Greeks or barbarians, and that not for a short time, but it has endured for a long while among them. This is shown by that institution of theirs, which will not suffer anything to hinder them from having all things in common, so that a rich man enjoys no more of his wealth than he who has nothing at all. There are more than four thousand men who live in this way, and they neither marry wives, nor are desirous to keep slaves, thinking that the latter tempts men to be unjust, and that the former gives a kindle to domestic quarrels; but as they live by themselves, they minister to one another. They also appoint good priests to receive their revenues, and the fruits of the ground, so as to get their corn and food. They live all alike, and mostly resemble those Dacae who are called Polistae.

But Judas the Galilaean was the author of a fourth sect of Jewish philosophy. Its pupils agree in all other things with the Pharisaic notions, but they have an inviolable attachment to liberty, and say that God is the only ruler and lord. They also do not mind dying any kinds of death, nor indeed do they heed the tortures of their relations and friends, nor any such fear make them call any man lord. Since this immovable resolution of theirs is well known to a great many, I shall speak no further about that matter; for I am not afraid that anything I have said of them should be disbelieved but rather fear that what I have said comes short of the resolution they show when they undergo pain. And it was in Gessius Florus' time, who was our procurator, that the nation began to suffer from this madness, for by the abuse of his auhority he made the Jews go wild and revolt from the Romans. And these are the sects of Jewish philosophy.

Bibliography for Further Reading

Neusner, Jacob. *From Politics to Piety: The Emergence of Pharisaic Judaism,* KTAV, 1979

Schiffman, Larry. *Reclaiming the Dead Sea Scrolls,* Jewish Publication Society, 1995

Simon, Marcel. *Jewish Sects in the Time of Jesus,* Fortress Press, 1967

Stone, Michael. *Scriptures, Sects, and Visions,* Fortress Press, 1980

Unit VII

Rome and Jerusalem

Herod the Great

Rome installed Antipater as puppet ruler in 47 B.C.E. He descended from a family of Idumean origin which had converted to Judaism during the forcible conversions initiated by the Hasmonean monarchs. To some this represented poetic justice, in the sense that the policy of forcible conversions initiated by the Hasmoneans in turn proved the undoing of their dynasty.

Antipater captured the support of Julius Caesar, who exempted Jews from appearing in court on the Sabbath and from serving in the Roman Army. Herod succeeded his father, Antipater, as Roman vassal. He was crowned by the Romans after deposing a Hasmonean descendant, Antigonus, who had been installed temporarily in Jerusalem by the Parthians. The arrival of Parthia, or Persia, in Palestine shortly after the assassination of Julius Caesar in 44 B.C.E. created an expectation of Parthia as a redeemer of the Jewish people. Parthia was Rome's primary rival in international politics. Parthian troops evicted the Roman garrison in Jerusalem and restored the traditional Hasmonean line. For the next 600 years of Roman domination, Jews looked to Parthia as would-be redeemer. During rebellions against Rome, Jews hoped for Parthian intervention. Moreover, the Jewish community of Babylonia, the leading Jewish community in the world outside of Palestine, were loyal Parthian citizens and looked to Parthia for protection. The Talmud goes so far as to state that one will know that the Messiah has arrived when one sees a Parthian horse in the Land of Israel suggesting that the Parthian cavalry formed a concrete vehicle to which were attached hopes for Jewish messianic redemption.

Parthian intervention in Palestinian politics, however, did not last. Herod succeeded in deposing Antigonus and restoring Roman troops to Jerusalem. Although he chose poorly in the internecine Roman wars between Augustus Caesar and Mark Antony, Herod succeeded in demonstrating his value to the Romans as their loyal representative at the crossroads to Asia.

His relationship to the Hasmonean family was complicated. He married Mariamne, a Hasmonean princess, and appointed her brother as high priest. Later, Herod murdered them when hearing of a Hasmonean conspiracy against him. Other random murders of family members who seemingly threatened him prompted his patron Augustus Caesar to remark, "It is better to be a pig in Herod's house than a member of his family," meaning that, as a Jew, Herod would not consume or kill pigs, but would be likely to murder family members.

The Talmud, however, sees Herod in somewhat more ambivalent terms. For the rabbis, Herod was a "middle-of-the-road" king—neither good nor bad. The Talmud praises some of his accomplishments, such as building great cities, assisting the Jews during times of famine through remission of taxes, and protection of diaspora Jewry. Perhaps best known was Herod's reconstruction of the Temple in Jerusalem, a structure that was now over five centuries old and badly in need of repair. Herod's reconstruction, of which the Western Wall of the courtyard remains to this day the holiest place within Judaism, aroused the admiration of Jews everywhere. The Talmud praises it lavishly, saying that one who has not witnessed Herod's reconstruction has never witnessed a building in his life.

Yet Herod was vicious in dealing with his opponents. The Hasmonean family was virtually decimated. He abolished the consulting power of the Sanhedrin or high court of the Jews. Josephus records that he had 200,000 of his opponents killed. Although this is doubtless an exaggeration, it does testify to Herod's merciless massacre of his opponents. One historian has suggested that Herod had a "messiah complex," believing that Israel was to be saved through Rome and via himself, Herod. Rome represented the salvation of the world, and Herod served as its representative.

Leading the Pharisees at this time was Hillel, perhaps the greatest of the early Pharisaic teachers. Although Hillel was best known for his formulation of the golden rule ("Do unto others as you would have others do unto you"), his primary significance probably lies in his formulation of the major principles of biblical exegesis—comparison and analogy, generalization of specific cases, etc. These formed the basic "thirteen principles" by which the Oral Law interpreted the Written Torah.

Hillel built an entire school within Pharisaic thought. Generally, his views were considered more liberal and inclusive than those of his rival, Shammai. Perhaps the best example of this liberality and openness was the story of his reaction to a would-be proselyte. The proselyte initially came to Shammai and demanded that the Torah be taught to him while standing on one foot. Shammai quickly grew disgusted with the individual and chased him away. Hillel, in turn, responded that the entire Torah is contained in the phrase "'What is hateful to you, do not do to your neighbor'—the rest is commentary. Go and learn."

Herod died in 4 B.C.E. At his death, two Pharisees encouraged the people to tear down the Roman eagle from the gate to the Jerusalem Temple. Such an act of rebellion, of course, meant instant and terrible reprisals, which formed the epitaph to Herod's bloody reign.

He was succeeded initially by his son Archelaus. However, Archelaus was unable to maintain the control over the people his father had exerted. Civil war ensued, and after ten years Archelaus was banished to Gaul. Herod's other sons proved similarly incompetent, and Rome substituted imperially appointed procurators for Herodian rule. Generally, these were the political friends of the emperor, who regarded Palestine as a reward for past favors or as a potential steppingstone to imperial greatness. The best of the procurators did not understand Jewish sensibilities. The worst tyrannized and exploited the people. Perhaps the best known and most typical of the procurators was Pontius Pilate, whose name has been immortalized as presiding over Palestine during the ministry and crucifixion of Jesus. As an example of his lack of sensitivity to his subjects, the custom had been that Roman troops on entering Jerusalem would point their shields inward, so as not to offend the people with a public demonstration of the Roman deities inscribed on the shields. Pilate reversed this order, provoking a revolt, which was put down only with considerable bloodshed. Ultimately, the Roman Emperor Tiberius overruled Pilate's decree.

Similarly, when Pilate tried to improve living conditions in Jerusalem, he did so in ways that were insensitive and offensive to the feelings of the Jews. During a water shortage he used a fund for Temple sacrifices to transport water to the city. Similarly, he would utilize his power of appointment arbitrarily to remove and replace a series of high priests.

Nor was Pilate by any means the worst of the governors. Others exploited the people and tyrannized them. Tiberius Alexander, perhaps the best and certainly the most understanding of the Roman procurators, symbolized Jewish frustrations on account of his apostacy from Judaism.

Therefore, it should be no surprise that the Zealot party grew considerably during the reign of the procurators. In all likelihood the Zealots originated in Herodian times, and their numbers increased, especially in the Galilee, which became a hotbed of Jewish nationalism. To be sure, not all extremists were Zealots. The Sicarii represented an extreme group who believed in utilization of political assassination against their enemies—both Romans and moderate Jews. For example, the High Priest Jonathan fell victim to Sicarii assassins. Frequently they would kidnap Jews in order to ransom their own political prisoners. The Roman procurators, in turn, agreed to such ransom demands provided the Jews paid for them. The Talmud refers to these extremists as *"biryonim,"* an unclear term probably meaning Jewish terrorists.

Other extreme groups opposed the use of terror. The Apocalyptists believed that Divine intervention would destroy Rome. Human action was unnecessary. Still other groups were messianic in nature. An Egyptian prophet gathered thousands to the Mount of Olives by promising to deliver the Roman garrison into their hands, an action that, of course, ensured quick Roman response and violence.

The proliferation of these groups suggests how widespread the dissatisfaction with Roman rule had become. From the perspective of Jewish leadership, the tendency toward violence and political extremism meant the collapse of normal day-to-day activities within Palestine. From the perspective of the Romans, the growth of such movements symbolized the breakdown of order and stability represented by Herod. Jews and Romans were on a collision course. In this context, the relatively charitable rabbinical evaluation of Herod becomes more understandable. In retrospect, Herod appeared to have been an evil king, yet one who had maintained the peace by preserving Jewish interests in Rome and sustaining Roman interests in Palestine. Although Herod's murders were unforgivable, in comparison with the Roman procurators, his reign had marked a lengthy period of stability and accommodation with Rome, in contrast to the violence and degenerate anarchy that marked the period of the procurators.

To be sure, the alternatives were not limited to direct Roman rule via the procurators or substitute Roman rule via Herod. Over time, rabbinic leadership succeeded in formulating a new concordat with the Romans by which the rabbis would preserve Jewish autonomy in Palestine while inculcating loyalty and obedience to Roman rule. That rabbinic political theory of accommodation, however, could take hold only after the political theory of rebellion against Rome had proven bankrupt.

The Great Revolt, 66–73 C.E.

Under the last of the procurators, Gessius Florus, conditions deteriorated to the point of open rebellion against Rome. Josephus blames the rebellion on the greed and insensitivity of Florus, who antagonized virtually all classes of Jews. While this was doubtless a factor in crystallizing the revolt, several longer-term currents were at work to ensure an uprising in any case. These included the growth of Zealotism, rejecting Roman rule, along with the growth of messianism, which believed that Rome represented the fourth kingdom of Daniel, whose destruction would usher in the messianic era. This view was mirrored by the Roman historian Suetonius, who wrote of the widespread conviction that the result of the Jewish war against Rome would determine the ultimate fate of the Roman Empire.

On a more practical level, Jews hoped again that Parthia would intervene. However, the Parthians congratulated the Roman general Vespasian on his successful conduct of the war against the Jews. Finally, one cannot overlook the economic motives behind the rebellion. One of the leaders, Simon Ben Giora, posed as a champion of the slaves. He and his colleague Jochanan of Gush Halav opposed the pro-Roman Jewish aristocracy and burned the archives of the Jewish moneylenders.

But the revolt was by no means limited to extremist elements among the Jews. Josephus's protest to the contrary, most of the Pharisees, Sadducees, and Essenes seem to have supported the rebellion. That is not to say that all Jews favored the uprising. Some, like Josephus himself, initially supported the rebellion, yet came to believe that rebellion itself was futile. Josephus later exhorted the people to surrender.

The last of the Herodians was represented by Agrippa II and his sister and paramour, Berenice, an incestuous relationship that scandalized Jewish religious leadership. His father, Agrippa I, a grandson of Herod and his Hasmonean princess Mariamne, had been beloved by Jews, and his short reign, 39–44 C.E., had been universally praised. However, he died prematurely, possibly at Roman instigation, and his plans for broader Jewish independence, in turn, were nullified. His son Agrippa II and daughter Berenice were Roman collaborators. Both were close to the Roman general Titus and counseled the Roman authorities on how best to quell the rebellion.

The Pharisaic leadership was divided. Most Pharisees, especially the House of Shammai, apparently supported the rebellion. Jochanan Ben Zakkai represented a minority opinion, urging that the rebellion be abandoned in favor of seeking an accommodation with Rome. His opinion ultimately prevailed and enabled the reconstruction of Judaism and Jewish life after the destruction. Needless to say, that was a politically unpopular opinion while the reality of the revolt was in full swing.

The rebellion ended with the devastation of Judea, the razing of Jerusalem, and the destruction of the Temple. Josephus actually exonerates Titus from the destruction, claiming it was an independent action by a Roman soldier. To be sure, Josephus's account is here suspect, given that he wrote under the patronage of his friend and emperor, Titus. The rabbis blamed Titus for the destruction, and the Roman historian Tacitus claims that the destruction was justified. The Arch of Titus in Rome symbolizes to this day his victory over the Jews as did the coins he printed on which were inscribed the phrase, "Judea Capta."

The last act of the rebellion was the collective suicide at Masada, a massive fortress overlooking the Dead Sea. For three years the remnants of the Zealots held out at Masada, harassing the Roman troops. After the Romans had succeeded in building a ramp enabling them to storm the fortress, the men at Masada determined upon the collective suicide of all the inhabitants—men, women, and children. Two women and their children are said to have hidden in the caves and told the story of the suicide to the Romans upon their entry into the fortress.

The story remains problematic and controversial as an act and historical symbol to this day. The suicides deprived the Romans of complete victory. Yet the men of Masada do not seem to have considered the alternatives. One alternative, perhaps the most constructive one, was to join the Pharisees in seeking an accommodation with Rome. A second alternative was surrender—an act that doubtless would have meant the death of many and the slavery of others. However, the Jewish community of Rome successfully redeemed large numbers of Jewish captives, and presumably the men, women, and children of Masada who were brought to Rome might ultimately have been ransomed by the Jewish community there. Lastly, Masada was not strictly speaking a suicide on the part of all. The women and children involved found that the decision was made on their behalf. For them, the action at Masada may have been closer to murder than to suicide.

Interestingly, Masada was rarely mentioned in medieval Jewish sources. One source actually changes the narrative from a collective suicide to a defeat at the hands of the Romans. Suicide is generally frowned upon in Jewish tradition, and the men of Masada, being the remnants of the Zealots and Sicarii, could by no means have been viewed favorably by rabbinic tradition. Most importantly, Masada symbolized exactly what the rabbis were seeking to prevent—namely, continued rebellion against Rome rather than an accommodation to Roman sovereignty that would enable Judaism and Jewish life to continue.

Josephus wrote The Jewish War *to demonstrate to the Romans that the Jews were by no means a rebellious people, but rather, that if governed fairly, they would function as loyal citizens of Rome. Conversely, to the Jews, Josephus's message was the futility and folly of rebellion against Rome. The concluding section of* The Jewish War *is our primary con-*

temporary source for the collective mass suicide at Masada which, for Josephus, underscored the destructiveness of Jewish extremism.

Reading: Josephus, *The Jewish War* VII:8–9

However, neither did Eleazar once think of flying away, nor would he permit any one else to do so; but when he saw their wall burnt down by the fire, he could devise no other way to escape or offer hope for further courage, and setting before their eyes what the Romans would do to them, their children, and their wives if they got them into their power, he consulted about having them all slain. Now, as he judged this to be the best thing they could do in their present circumstances, he gathered the most courageous of his companions together, and encouraged them to take that course in a speech made to them in the following manner. "Since we, long ago, my generous friends, resolved never to be servants to the Romans, nor to any other than to God Himself, who alone is the true and just Lord of mankind, the time is now come that obliges us to make that resolution true in practice. And let us not at this time reproach ourselves for self-contradiction, while we formerly would not undergo slavery, though it were then without danger; but we must now, together with slavery, choose such punishments as are also intolerable; I mean this, upon the supposition that the Romans once reduce us under their power while we are alive. We were the very first that revolted from them, and we are the last that fight against them; and I cannot but esteem it as a favor that God has granted us that it is still in our power to die bravely, and in a state of freedom, which has not been the case of others who were conquered unexpectedly.

"It is very plain that we shall be captured within a day's time; but it is still possible to die in a glorious manner, together with our dearest friends. This is what our enemies themselves cannot by any means prevent, even though they are very eager to take us alive. Nor can we propose any more to ourselves to fight them and beat them. It might have been proper indeed for us to have wondered at God's purpose much sooner, and at the very first, when we were so desirous of defending our liberty, and when we received such sore treatment from one another and worse treatment from our enemies, and to have been aware that the same God, who had of old taken the Jewish nation into His favor, had now condemned them to destruction; for had He either continued favorable, or been in a lesser degree displeased with us, He would not have overlooked the destruction of so many men, or delivered His most holy city to be burnt and demolished by our enemies. To be sure, we faintly hoped to have preserved ourselves, and ourselves alone, still in a state of freedom, as if we had been guilty of no sins ourselves against God, nor been partners with those of others; we who taught other men to sin.

"Wherefore, consider how God has convinced us that our hopes were in vain, by bringing such distress upon us in our present desperate state, which is beyond all our expectations; for the nature of this fortress, which was in itself unconquerable, has not proved a means of our deliverance; and even while we still have great abundance of food and a great quantity of arms, and other necessities more than we need, we are openly deprived by God Himself of all hope of deliverance; for that fire which was driven upon our enemies did not, of its own accord, turn back upon the wall which we had built: this was the effect of God's anger against us for our manifold sins, which we have been guilty of in a most insolent and extravagant manner with regard to our own countrymen; the punishments for which let us receive not from the Romans but from God Himself, as executed by our own hands, for these will be more moderate than the other. Let our wives die before they are abused, and our children before they have tasted of slavery; and after we have slain them, let us bestow that glorious benefit upon one another mutually, and preserve ourselves in freedom, as an excellent funeral monument for us. But first let us destroy our money and the fortress by fire; for I am well assured that this will be a great grief to the Romans that they shall not be able to capture our bodies, and shall fail of our wealth also: and let us spare nothing but our provisions; for they will be a testimonial when we are dead that we were not subdued for want of necessities; but that, according to our original resolution, we have preferred death to slavery."

This was Eleazar's speech to them. Yet the opinions of all the auditors did not acquiesce to his plan; but although some of them were very zealous to put his advice in practice and were in a manner filled with pleasure at it and thought death to be a good thing, yet those that were most emotional felt pity for their wives and families; and while these men were especially moved by the prospect of their own certain death, they looked wistfully at one another, and by the tears in their eyes, declared their dissent from his opinion. When Eleazar saw these people in such fear, their souls dejected at so prodigious a proposal, he was afraid lest perhaps these emotional persons should, by their lamentations and tears, enfeeble those that heard what he had said courageously; so he did not leave off exhorting them, but stirred himself up, recollecting appropriate arguments for raising their courage; he undertook to speak more briskly and fully to them concerning the immortality of the soul. So he uttered a groan of lamentation, and fixing his eyes intently on those that wept, he spoke thus: "Truly, I was greatly mistaken when I thought I was listening to brave men who have struggled hard for their liberty, and to those resolved either to live with honor or else to die; but I find that you are such people as are no better than others, either in virtue or in courage, and are afraid of dying though you be delivered thereby from the greatest miseries, while you ought to make no delay in this matter, nor to expect anyone to give you good advice; for the laws of our country, and of God Himself, have, from ancient times, and as soon as ever we could use our reason, continually taught us, and our forefathers have corroborated the same doctrine by their actions and their bravery of mind, that it is life that is calamity to men, and not death; for this last offers our souls their liberty and sends them into their own place of purity, where they are to be liberated from all sorts of misery; for while souls are tied down to a mortal body, they are partakers of its miseries; and really, to speak the truth, they are themselves dead; for the union of what is divine to what is mortal is disagreeable. It is true, the power of the soul is great even when it is imprisoned in a mortal body; for by moving it in a way that is invisible, it makes the body a sensible instrument, and causes it to advance further in its actions than mortal nature could otherwise do. However, once it is freed from that weight which draws it down to the earth and is connected with it, it obtains its own proper place, and does then become a partaker of that blessed power and those abilities which are then every way incapable of being hindered in their operations. It continues invisible, indeed, to the eyes of men, as does God Himself; for certainly it is not itself seen, while it is in the body; for it is there in an invisible manner, and when it is freed from it it is still not seen. It is this soul which has one nature, and an incorruptible one at that; but yet it is the cause of the change made in the body; for whatsoever it be which the soul touches, that lives and flourishes; and from whatsoever it is removed, that withers away and dies; such a degree is there in it of immortality. Let me produce the state of sleep as a most evident demonstration of the truth of what I say; wherein souls, when the body does not distract them, have the sweetest rest depending on themselves and conversing with God, by their alliance to Him; they then go everywhere, and foretell many future events beforehand; and why are we afraid of death, while we are pleased with the rest we have in sleep? And how absurd a thing is it to pursue liberty while we are alive, and yet to deny it to ourselves where it will be eternal!

"But put the case that we had been brought up under another persuasion, and taught that life is the greatest good which men are capable of, and that death is a calamity; however, our present circumstances ought to be an inducement to us to bear such calamity courageously, since it is by the will of God, and by necessity, that we are to die; for it now appears that God has made a decree against the whole Jewish nation that we are to be deprived of this life which we would not make a due use of; for do not ascribe your present condition to yourselves, nor think the Romans the true reason that this war we have had with them has become so destructive to us all: these things have not come to pass by their power, but a more powerful cause has intervened and made us offer them an occasion for their appearing to be conquerors over us. What Roman weapons, I pray you, were those by which the Jews of Caesarea were slain? On the contrary, when they were no way disposed to rebel but were all the while keeping their seventh day festival and did not so much as lift up their hands against the citizens of Caesarea, yet did those citizens run upon them in great mobs, and cut their throats and the throats of their wives and children, and this without any regard to the Romans themselves, who never took us for their enemies till we revolted from them. But some may be ready to say that truly the people of Caesarea always had a quarrel against those that lived among them, and that when an opportunity offered itself, they only satisfied their old rancor. What then shall we say to those of Scythopolis, who ventured to wage war with us on account of the Greeks? They were slain, they and their whole families, in the most inhumane manner, which was all the requital made them for the assistance they had offered the others; for that very same destruction which they had prevented from falling upon the others, they suffered themselves from them, as if they had been ready to be the actors against them.

"It would be too long for me to speak at this time of every destruction brought upon us: you must know that there was not a single Syrian city which did not slay its Jewish inhabitants and were not more bitter enemies to us than the Romans themselves: nay, even those of Damascus, once they were able to allege no tolerable crime against us, filled their city with the most barbarous slaughter of our people and cut the throats of eighteen thousand Jews, along with their wives and children. And as to the multitude of those slain in Egypt, and that by torture also, we have been informed they were more than sixty thousand; indeed, being in a foreign country and so naturally having nothing with which to oppose their enemies, they were killed in the aforementioned manner.

"As for all those of us who have waged war against the Romans in our own country, had we not sufficient reason to have sure hopes of victory? For we had arms, and walls, and fortresses so prepared as not to be easily captured, and courage not to be moved by any dangers in the cause of liberty, which encouraged us all to revolt from the Romans. But then, these advantages sufficed us but for a short time and only raised our hopes, while they really appeared to be the origin of our miseries; for all we had has been taken from us, and all has fallen under our enemies, as if these advantages were only to render their victory over us the more glorious and not disposed to preserve those by whom these preparations had been made.

"And as for those already dead in the war, it is reasonable we should esteem them blessed, for they are dead in defending and not in betraying their liberty; but as to the multitude of those now under the Romans, who would not pity their condition? And who would not make haste to die before suffering the same miseries with them? Some were put upon the rack and tortured with fire and whippings, and so died. Some were half devoured by wild beasts, and yet were preserved alive to be devoured by them a second time, in order to afford laughter and sport to our enemies; and such of those as are still alive are to be looked on as the most miserable, who, being so desirous of death, could not achieve it.

"And where is now that great city, the metropolis of the Jewish nation, which was fortified by so many walls, which had so many fortresses and large towers to defend it, which could hardly contain the instruments prepared for war, and which had so many ten thousands of men to fight for it? Where is this city that was believed to have God Himself inhabiting therein? It is now demolished to its very foundations, and has nothing but that monument of it preserved, I mean the camp of those that destroyed it which still dwells upon its ruins; some unfortunate old men also lie upon the ashes of the Temple, and a few women are there preserved alive by the enemy, to our bitter shame and reproach. Now, who is there that revolves these things in his mind and yet is able to bear the sight of the sun, though he might live out of danger? Who is there so much his country's enemy or so unmanly and so desirous of living as not to repent that he is still alive? And I cannot but wish that we had all died before we had seen that holy city demolished by the hands of our enemies, or the foundations of our holy Temple dug up in so profane a manner.

"But since we had a generous hope that deluded us, that we might perhaps have been able to avenge ourselves on our enemies, though it has now become vanity and has left us alone in this distress, let us make haste to die bravely. Let us take pity on ourselves, our children, and our wives, while it is in our power to show pity to them; for we are born to die, as well as those whom we have begotten; nor is it in the power even of the most happy to avoid it. But for abuses and slavery, and the sight of our wives led away in an ignominious manner, with their children, these are not such evils as are natural and necessary among men; although such as do not prefer death to those miseries when it is in their power so to do, must undergo even them, on account of their own cowardice. We revolted from the Romans with great pretensions to courage; and when, at the very last, they invited us to preserve ourselves, we would not comply with them. Who will not, therefore, believe that they will certainly be in a rage against us, in case they take us alive? Miserable will then be the young men strong enough in their bodies to sustain many tortures! Miserable also will be those of elder years who will not be able to bear those calamities which young men might sustain! A man will be obliged to hear the voice of his son imploring the help of his father, when his hands are bound! But certainly our hands are still at liberty, and have a sword in them! Let them be subservient to us in our glorious design; let us die before we become slaves under our enemies, and let us go out of the world, together with our children and our wives, in a state of freedom.

"This it is that our laws command us to do; this it is that our wives and children desire at our hands; nay, God Himself has brought this necessity upon us; while the Romans desire the contrary, and are afraid lest any of us die before we are captured. Let us therefore make haste, and instead of affording them so much pleasure as they hope for in getting us under their power, let us leave them an example which shall at once cause their astonishment at our death, and their admiration of our hardiness therein."

So these people died with this intention that they would leave not so much as one soul among them all alive to be subject to the Romans. Yet there was an old woman, and another who was kin to Eleazar and superior to most women in prudence and learning, with five children, who had concealed themselves in caverns under ground, and had carried water thither for their drink, and had hidden there when the rest were intent upon the slaughter of one another. Those others were nine hundred and sixty in number, the women and children being withal included in that computation.

Now the Romans expected that they should be fought in the morning, when accordingly they put on their armor, and laid bridges of planks upon their ladders from their banks, in order to make an assault upon the fortress, which they did; but they saw nobody as an enemy, only a terrible solitude on every side, with a fire within the place as well as a complete silence. So they were at a loss to guess what had happened. At length they made a shout, as if at a blow given by the battering-ram, to test whether they could bring anyone out that was within; the women heard this noise and came out of their underground cavern, and informed the Romans what had been done; and the second of them clearly described both what was said and what was done, and the manner of it; yet the Romans did not easily heed such a desperate undertaking, and did not believe it could be as the women said; they also attempted to put the fire out, and quickly cutting themselves a way through it came within the palace, and so met up with the multitude of the slain, but could take no pleasure in the fact even though it were done to their enemies. Nor could they do other than wonder at the courage of the Jews' resolution and the immovable contempt of death which so great a number of them had shown when they went through with such an action as that was.

And here we shall put an end to our history, wherein we earlier promised to deliver the same with all accuracy to those desirous of understanding in what manner this war of the Romans with the Jews was managed. Of which history, how good its style must be left to the determination of the readers; but for the agreement with the facts, I shall not scruple to say, and boldly, that truth has been my sole aim through its entire composition.

Bibliography for Further Reading

Alon, Gedaliah. *The Jews in Their Land in the Talmudic Age,* Harvard University Press, 1989

Cohen, Shaye J.D. *From the Maccabees to the Mishnah,* Westminster Press, 1987

Grant, Michael. *Herod the Great,* American Heritage Press, 1974

———. *The Jews in the Roman World,* Weidenfeld and Nicolson, 1973.

Unit VIII

Destruction and Renewal

Aftermath to Destruction

After the destruction of the Second Temple, Jewish leaders had to cope with the very viability of a Judaism that had lost its center and anchor and was now associated with a defeated religion. To be sure, there was little religious oppression that ensued. Titus, Vespasian's son, who completed the conquest of Jerusalem, refused to abolish the privileges of the Jews of Antioch, despite repeated requests to do so. Some have attributed this to his sexual liaison with Berenice, sister of Agrippa II. More likely, the Jews of the Roman Empire as a whole retained their privileges despite the destruction of Judea. Rome maintained respect for the power of the Jewish diaspora, and Judaism continued to be a *religio licita,* or legal religion of the Empire.

Two stories in the Talmud (*Gittin* 55b-56a) reflect the efforts at reconstructing Judaism internally. First, the Talmud tells its own story of the destruction. There were two enemies with similar names, Kamza and Bar Kamza. A man made a party but invited Bar Kamza, the wrong individual, to attend. When he showed up, he was asked to leave. The rabbis of Israel were said to have been present, but refused to save Bar Kamza from his embarrassment. Such was his anger that he convinced the Roman authorities that the Jews were a rebellious people, and proved it by placing a blemish on a sacrifice to be made in the name of the Emperor. When the rabbis saw the blemish, they were inclined to be permissive regarding the sacrifice out of respect for the Emperor. However, when one of their number pointed out that sacrificing the animal would be absolutely forbidden, they acknowledged his point and refused to offer the sacrifice. The story concludes that on account of the excessive scrupulousness of the rabbis was the Temple destroyed.

The story is instructive on many levels. First, it attributes the destruction to internal conflicts among the Jews themselves. Rome is by no means the natural enemy of the Jews. Rather Jewish disunity brought about the destruction.

Secondly, the story is remarkable in that the rabbis engage in self-criticism. They should have intervened at the party to ensure that an individual was not embarrassed publicly. Then they should have intervened on behalf of the Jewish people so as to prevent giving offense unnecessarily to the Roman Emperor. Their willingness to blame themselves suggests that they understood the demands of leadership as needing to meet the real needs both of individual Jews and of the Jewish people at large.

The second Talmudic story similarly provides insight into how the rabbis perceived themselves and how they defined effective Jewish leadership. In the final days of the siege of Jerusalem, one of the leading rabbis, Jochanan Ben Zakkai, called his nephew who was the leader of the Jewish terrorists and asked him how he could continue to destroy the people. The terrorist replied that he would like to desist, but the others would never permit it. In that case, Jochanan asked for his cooperation in leaving the city and making overtures to the Roman general. Ben Zakkai left via a ruse, pretending to be dead, for corpses were not buried within Jerusalem's precincts, and entered the Roman camp, where he greeted Vespasian with the title Emperor. Vespasian engaged him in dialogue as to how he knew this, and soon a herald arrived proclaiming him to be Emperor. In gratitude, Vespasian offered him three requests. Jochanan asked for the town of Javneh and its sages, protection for the family chain of Rabban Gamaliel, descendants of Hillel and of the Davidic dynasty, and physicians to heal Rabbi Zadok. Some of the rabbis criticized Rabbi Jochanan for asking for so little. He felt, however, that had he asked for more, i.e. to spare the Jews entirely, he would have ended up with nothing.

This Talmudic tale is also instructive for its insight into how the rabbis coped with the destruction through the emergence of a new rabbinic leadership acceptable to Rome. Javneh may have been a Roman prison camp. Jochanan realized that he would be sent there. What he wished was permission to reinstitute the Jewish Academy, the Sanhedrin, among the sages there.

Secondly, he asked that the family chain of Hillel be spared. Most likely, Gamaliel represented those Pharisaic leaders who had joined the Zealot party. Jochanan wished to establish continuity with pre-rebellion Pharisaic leadership. Therefore, he asked that Gamaliel and his family be spared so as to be able to reinstitute Hillelite leadership among the Jews. The restitution of the Hillel chain, which traced its lineage to David, would constitute a powerful symbol of ongoing Jewish leadership and sovereignty, despite the loss of Jerusalem and the Temple.

Lastly, Jochanan requested physicians to heal Rabbi Zadok. Most likely, many of the rabbis had been wounded or injured during the rebellion. He was asking for appropriate medical relief to be provided by the Roman authorities.

Underlying these requests, however, lies an alternative political theory from that of the Zealots and a new relationship with Rome. Jochanan Ben Zakkai acknowledges the futility of the rebellion. His nephew, the leader of the Jewish terrorists, agrees with him, yet is unable to do anything about it because of the extremism of those in revolt. Even some of the rabbis regarded Jochanan as foolish in requesting too little in exchange for his support for Rome. Yet Jochanan strikes a deal with the Romans that enables them to feel that they have loyal allies among the rabbinic leadership, while at the same time granting the rabbis the authority to reconstitute Jewish life anew.

In turn, Jochanan utilizes Javneh as the vehicle both to absorb the tragedy of the destruction of the Temple and simultaneously to recover from its loss. Consider, for example, his legislation in Javneh. Jochanan decreed that if the Jewish New Year fell on Shabbat, the shofar could be sounded in Javneh. Previously, this was done only within the Temple precincts. The message now was to remember the destruction but not be overwhelmed by it. Life continues, and although Javneh can never be a surrogate for the Temple itself, it can reconstitute itself as the center of Judaism and Jewish peoplehood.

In this context, Pharisaic leadership, personified by Jochanan and the Hillelite chain which he restored, captured the imagination and support of the Jewish body politic. The Sadducees appeared to have completely disappeared. For one thing, their power base, the Temple, was gone. Moreover, they had no religious program comparable to the Pharisees. The Pharisaic theology of crisis emphasizing resurrection and immortality of the soul provided considerable comfort and meaning to a people bereft of its political and national treasures. Last, and by no means least, where the Pharisees struck an accommodation with Rome, making them acceptable in the eyes of Roman leadership, the Sadducees continued to defy Rome by bringing sacrifices to the Temple Mount, even though the Temple had been destroyed.

The Pharisees provided an alternative leadership model, distinct both from Herod and from the Roman procurators. In external affairs, the Pharisees counseled acceptance of Roman rule and refraining from rebellion. Internally, the Pharisees reconstituted Jewish life upon the principles of Torah—both Written and Oral. Their leadership succeeded in meeting the needs of contemporary Jews. Politically, they wisely abstained from further rebellion. Religiously, they pointed to the continuing salience and wisdom of Judaism as a religious tradition that could effectively guide the day-to-day lives of contemporary Jews.

To be sure, there were difficulties in effecting this transition. Rabbinic leadership had enormous difficulty in handling dissent or minority opinion. Thus, the rabbis told the story of a rabbi who invoked heaven and earth to demonstrate the correctness of his opinion (*Bava Metzia* 59b). Although various supernatural signs attested that he was right, the rabbinic response was that "it is not in heaven," meaning that authority within the Jewish community must be lodged in contemporary rabbinic leadership. The rabbis may make mistakes, yet the community has to continue running its affairs with the knowledge that mistakes may be made. Rabbinic leadership recognized the limitations of human frailties and foibles. Nevertheless, Jewish survival required empowering the rabbis to go on, even at the risk of making mistakes. The dissenting rabbi, unfortunately, was placed under the ban of excommunication for his refusal to accept that the power to interpret Torah was now given over to human beings and was "not in heaven."

Similarly, the rabbis expressed the idea of the human role in creating Torah through a beautiful legend of the angels in heaven opposing giving the Torah to the Jews. The angels argued to God that if the Torah were given over to human hands, a perfect document would be relativized and rendered imperfect. God's response was that the Torah takes on meaning only when given over to human hands. In effect, the interpretation of Torah, with all the risks of relativization and imperfection, must be put in the hands of contemporary Jewish leadership.

Others, including leading figures from within rabbinic leadership, rejected the political philosophy of accommodation with Rome. In 115 C.E., a rebellion broke out against Roman rule in a number of cities within the Jewish diaspora. In Egypt, Cyprus, Cyrenaica, and perhaps Mesopotamia, Jews rose up in revolt against Roman authorities. At this time the Roman Emperor Trajan was engaged in battle with Parthia, and perhaps the hope for a Parthian victory again became expressed in messianic agitation among the Jews.

The Roman sources report considerable Jewish atrocities against their victims. These stories probably reflect widespread civilian murders that were replicated by native inhabitants upon the Jews. For example, in Alexandria, the great synagogue of the Jews was destroyed, and the community, reputed to be one of the largest in the Jewish world, was never able to recover completely. The Cyprus Jewish community appears to have been completely destroyed, and Jews were prohibited from settling there afterwards.

It is unclear whether the Jewish community in Palestine participated in this rebellion. One Talmudic source reports a "day of Trajan," possibly referring to a promise granting the Jews permission to rebuild the Temple and therefore explaining why Palestine remained quiet during these disturbances. Other historians see this rebellion as a dress rehearsal for the far more costly rebellion of Bar Kokhba, fifteen years later in Palestine. Finally, Salo Baron regards the rebellion of 115 C.E. as more reflective of tensions between Jews and their Greek neighbors in the diaspora than of an anti-Roman political rebellion as occurred subsequently in Palestine.

The Bar-Kokhba Revolt

The causes of this final revolt remain unclear: The Roman historian Dio-Cassius attributes it to the desire to transform Jerusalem into a pagan city. The church historian Eusebius counters that the transformation of Jerusalem to Aelia Capitolina constituted punishment for the rebellion. The rebellion itself occurred because of the continuing spirit of contentiousness among the Jews. The Roman Emperor Hadrian's biographer, Spartianus, attributes it to Hadrian's revoking the permission of the Jews to practice circumcision—an exemption which the Jews had heretofore enjoyed. A legendary Jewish source attributes it to Hadrian's revoking the promise given by his predecessor to rebuild the Temple in Jerusalem. Nor should one discount the fact that the rebellion occurred just over 60 years after the destruction of the Second Temple. Doubtless there were those who recalled that the Second Temple had been rebuilt exactly 70 years after the destruction of the First. Was it not, therefore, appropriate to initiate steps leading to the construction of the Third Temple 70 years after the destruction of the Second?

Several tentative conclusions emanate from this diversity of opinion. First, the Bar Kokhba revolt, 132–135 C.E., aroused considerable attention within contemporary Roman and Christian circles. Secondly, the rebellion may not have been due to any single cause, but rather through a combination of several causes. Lastly, certain of the prohibitions against the practice of Judaism which were in effect after the rebellion may well have preceded the rebellion and, in fact, led to it.

The rebellion appears to have been initially quite successful and widespread. Rabbi Akiba is said to have pronounced Bar Kokhba the Jewish messiah, changing his name from Bar Kosiba to Bar Kokhba or "son of the star." Certainly Bar Kokhba reestablished some form of Jewish autonomy, minted coins bearing his name, and rededicated Jerusalem as a Jewish center. However, by the latter years of the rebellion, considerable dissent had emerged in opposition to Bar Kokhba's leadership. Letters from Bar Kokhba to his troops indicate that his own generals were not following his orders. Rabbinic legends describe Bar Kokhba as a cruel individual who trained his troops by mutilating their limbs. The rabbis referred to Bar Kokhba not as "son of the star," which Akiba had called him, but rather as Bar Kosiba or "son of a lie." The rabbis assign Bar Kokhba an ignominious end, strangled by a snake in his last stand at the village of Betar, rather than a glorious end fighting the Romans. Bar Kokhba, in the rabbinic reading of history, became little more than one in a long line of false messiahs, rather than a glorious military hero.

In the aftermath of the rebellion, the Romans declared martial law and prohibited the public teaching of Judaism in Palestine. Rabbinic ordination was banned, Rabbi Akiba had to leave Palestine for Parthia to engage in regulation of the calendar, a public symbol of rabbinic authority over Jews everywhere. Hadrian attempted to uproot dimensions of Judaism that might lead to further rebellion. For example, Jews were barred now from entering Jerusalem. The very name of the land of Israel was changed to "Palestine," or land of the Philistines, in an attempt to rob it of its Jewish roots. Rabbi Akiba and some of his colleagues were imprisoned for their continued willingness to teach Torah in public and suffered martyrdom for their efforts.

These persecutions did not last long. Hadrian's successor, Antoninus Pius, did not enforce these decrees and relaxed the persecutions. They were, in any case, difficult to enforce, and Antoninus Pius had no desire to offend the Jews of the diaspora or their sympathizers in Rome, the "Fearers of the Lord," who adopted a number of Jewish practices without openly converting to Judaism.

As a result, Pharisaic leadership was able to emerge from underground and reassert itself. Its most powerful figure was Rabbi Judah the Patriarch, who was said to have formed a close working alliance with the Roman emperor of the time. It was Judah who was the primary architect of Roman-Jewish accommodation. He enlarged the authority and autonomy of the patriarchate as ethnarch and tax collector among the Jews and as primary Jewish representative to the Roman empire. He transformed Pharisaic leadership from essentially academic and religious in nature to political and even military. The center of Jewish life during his tenure shifted from Javneh to the Galilee—to Tiberias and Sepphoris. Although Judea had been destroyed, Jewish life was able to revive and continue as previously in the northern agricultural areas of the Galilee. Judaism continued as a *religio licita* of the Roman empire. The sole limitation was the ban on Jewish proselytizing activity—a ban that was observed probably more in the breach than in reality. Jewish judicial and political autonomy prevailed, and persecutions by the Romans ceased for the next 200 years, until Rome became a Christian empire.

As a result, Judaism as a system was able to flourish. Judah the Patriarch insisted that the Oral Law be committed to writing, lest it be forgotten by the Jews. He composed the *Mishna,* a codification of the Oral Law regulating all aspects of Jewish life both in Palestine and in the diaspora. Study of the *Mishna,* namely the *Gemara,* continued as the Oral Law became the primary constitution and basis on which to reconstruct Jewish life.

The rabbis formed a tightly-knit class. Conservative estimates place their numbers at no more than 400 in Palestine, with perhaps an additional 400 in Babylonia. Unofficially, they functioned as a "ruling class" for the Jewish communities of Palestine and Babylonia. By regulating the calendar, the liturgy, civil law, marriage and divorce, and, of course, tax collecting, the rabbinic sages influenced day-to-day life within the Jewish community. The power of the Patriarch gave this influence official sanction and authority.

All this could occur only once the Jews recognized the bankruptcy of the political theory of rebellion and Masada in favor of accommodation and reconciliation with Rome. The Talmud reflects this new political theory in several ways. The Maccabean rebellion is remembered in the Talmud not as a military victory, but that a cruse of oil was able to last for eight days in the Temple, suggesting spiritual purification rather than military victory. Rabbinic literature contains admonitions against those who would try to calculate the end of days, let alone hasten its presence. Similarly, the rabbis suppressed apocalyptic literature revealing the nature of the end of days. Lastly, the rabbis emphasized the principle that "the law of the state is the law," meaning that the authority of Roman law was recognized by rabbinic leadership.

As to Bar Kokhba, the rabbis blurred the memory of him as military hero in favor of the memory of him as failed messiah. The rabbis redefined the very concept of heroism not as military victory, but as the capacity to control one's passions. The site of Bar Kokhba's last stand, the village of Betar, was portrayed by the rabbis less as a military fortress and more as a center for Torah study.

To be sure, some opposition continued. When Rabbi Judah the Patriarch tried to abolish the fast of the ninth of Av if it fell on Shabbat, probably to effect greater Roman-Jewish reconciliation, he was opposed by the rabbis, who argued that fasting on the ninth of Av was too sacred a tradition for Jews to forget. Others were opposed to his tendency toward one-man rule, especially as reflected in his personal wealth, personal standing army, and power of appointment to office.

Yet Judah's theory of accommodation prevailed and created the groundwork for Jewish political life and autonomy throughout medieval Jewish history. For the next two centuries Roman rule (140–313 C.E.) was noticeably free of persecution. Nor were there Jewish rebellions against the Romans, demonstrating the validity of the Pharisaic perspective that the Jews were by no means a rebellious people. Jews lived in peace with a Roman government that granted them autonomy and freedom of religious practice. As representative of the Hillelite and Davidic line, Judah and his successors symbolized continuing Jewish sovereignty despite the loss of State and Temple. The memories of the Temple, of course, persisted. Once a year, on the ninth of Av, Jews bribed the Roman authorities to be able to enter Jerusalem to mourn the destruction of the Temple. The basic message, however, was one of reconstruction and renewal. Rabbinic leadership emphasized not memory of the failed rebellion, but rather the need to reconstruct Jewish life upon the principles of the Oral Torah and to relegate to a far-off future the hope for a Jewish restoration.

Reading: *Tractate Gittin* 55b–56a

Tractate Gittin *of the Talmud addresses primarily questions of divorce. However, like many other Talmudic tractates, it intersperses a wide array of topics and information.* Tractate Gittin, *at length, recounts the destruction of Jerusalem at the hands of the Romans. Its material, while legendary, served didactic purposes in specifying what lessons Jews ought learn from the destruction. Most importantly, rabbinic Judaism ascribed the destruction to the loss of Jewish unity and urged Jews to rebuild their common sense of peoplehood.*

> The destruction of Jerusalem came through a Kamza and a Bar Kamza; the destruction of Tur Malka came through a cock and a hen; the destruction of Bethar came through the shaft of a leather. The destruction of Jerusalem came through a Kamza and a Bar Kamza in this way. A certain man had a friend Kamza and an enemy Bar Kamza. He once made a party and said to his servant, Go and bring Kamza. The man went and brought Bar Kamza. When the man [who gave the party] found him there he said, See, you tell tales about me; what are

you doing here? Get out. Said the other: Since I am here, let me stay, and I will pay you for whatever I eat and drink. He said, I won't. Then let me give you half the cost of the party. No, said the other. Then let me pay for the whole party. He still said, No, and he took him by the hand and put him out. Said the other: Since the Rabbis were sitting there and did not stop him, this shows that they agreed with him. I will go and inform against them to the Government. He went and said to the Emperor, The Jews are rebelling against you. He said, How can I tell? He said to him: Send them an offering and see whether they will offer it [on the altar]. So he sent with him a fine calf. While on the way he made a blemish on its upper lip, or as some say on the white of its eye, in a place where we [Jews] count it a blemish but they do not. The Rabbis were inclined to offer it in order not to offend the Government. Said R. Zachariah b. Abkulas to them: People will say that blemished animals are offered on the altar. They then proposed to kill Bar Kamza so that he should not go and inform against them, but R. Zachariah b. Abkulas said to them, Is one who makes a blemish on consecrated animals to be put to death? R. Johanan thereupon remarked: Through the scrupulousness of R. Zechariah b. Abkulas our House has been destroyed, our Temple burnt and we ourselves exiled from our land.

He [the Emperor] sent against them Nero the Caesar. As he was coming he shot an arrow towards the east, and it fell in Jerusalem. He then shot one towards the west, and it again fell in Jerusalem. He shot towards all four points of the compass, and each time it fell in Jerusalem. He said to a certain boy: Repeat to me [the last] verse of Scripture you have learnt. He said: *And I will lay my vengeance upon Edom by the hand of my people Israel.* He said: The Holy One, blessed be He, desires to lay waste his House and to lay the blame on me. So he ran away and became a proselyte, and R. Meir was descended from him.

He then sent against them Vespasian the Caesar who came and besieged Jerusalem for three years. There were in it three men of great wealth, Nakdimon b. Gorion, Ben Kalba Shabua' and Ben Zizith Hakeseth. Nakdimon b. Gorion was so called because the sun continued shining for his sake. Ben Kalba Shabua' was so called because one would go into his house hungry as a dog [*keleb*] and come out full [*sabea'*] Ben Zizith

Hakeseth was so called because his fringes [*zizith*] used to trail on cushions [*keseth*]. Others say he derived the name from the fact that his seat [*kise*] was among those of the nobility of Rome. One of these said to the people of Jerusalem, I will keep them in wheat and barley. A second said, I will keep them in wine, oil and salt. The third said, I will keep them in wood. The Rabbis considered the offer of wood the most generous, since R. Hisda used to hand all his keys to his servant save that of the wood, for R. Hisda used to say, A storehouse of wheat requires sixty stores of wood [for fuel]. These men were in a position to keep the city for twenty-one years.

The *biryoni* were then in the city. The Rabbis said to them: Let us go out and make peace with them [the Romans]. They would not let them, but on the contrary said, Let us go out and fight them. The Rabbis said: You will not succeed. They then rose up and burnt the stores of wheat and barley so that a famine ensued. Martha the daughter of Boethius was one of the richest women in Jerusalem. She sent her manservant out saying. Go and bring me some fine flour. By the time he went it was sold out. He came and told her, There is no fine flour, but there is white [flour]. She then said to him, Go and bring me some. By the time he went he found the white flour sold out. He came and told her, There is no white flour but there is dark flour. She said to him, Go and bring me some. By the time he went it was sold out. He returned and said to her. There is no dark flour, but there is barley flour. She said, Go and bring me some. By the time he went this was also sold out. She had taken off her shoes, but she said, I will go out and see if I can find anything to eat. Some dung stuck to her foot and she died. Rabban Johanan b. Zakkai applied to her the verse, *The tender and delicate woman among you which would not adventure to see the sole of her foot upon the ground.* Some report that she ate a fig left by R. Zadok, and became sick and died. For R. Zadok observed fasts for forty years in order that Jerusalem might not be destroyed, [and he became so thin that] when he ate anything the food could be seen [as it passed through his throat.] When he wanted to restore himself, they used to bring him a fig, and he used to suck the juice and throw the rest away. When Martha was about to die, she brought out all her gold and silver and threw it in the street, saying, What is the good of this to me, thus giving effect to the verse, *They shall cast their silver in the streets.*

Abba Sikra the head of the *biryoni* in Jerusalem was the son of the sister of Rabban Johanan b. Zakkai. [The latter] sent to him saying, Come to visit me privately. When he came he said to him, How long are you going to carry on in this way and kill all the people with starvation? He replied: What can I do? If I say a word to them, they will kill me. He said: Devise some plan for me to escape. Perhaps I shall be able to save a little. He said to him: Pretend to be ill, and let everyone come to inquire about you. Bring something evil smelling and put it by you so that they will say you are dead. Let then your disciples get under your bed, but no others, so that they shall not notice that you are still light, since they know that a living being is lighter than a corpse. He did so, and R. Eliezer went under the bier from one side and R. Joshua from the other. When they reached the door, some men wanted to put a lance through the bier. He said to them: Shall [the Romans] say, They have pierced their Master? They wanted to give it a push. He said to them: Shall they say that they pushed their Master? They opened a town gate for him and he got out.

When he reached the Romans he said, Peace to you, O king, peace to you, O king. He [Vespasian] said: Your life is forfeit on two counts, one because I am not a king and you call me king, and again, if I am king, why did you not come to me before now? He replied: As for your saying that you are not king, in truth you are a king, since if you were not a king Jerusalem would not be delivered into your hand, as it is written, *And Lebanon shall fall by a mighty one. 'Mighty one'* [is an epithet] applied only to a king, as it is written, *And their mighty one shall be of themselves* etc.; and Lebanon refers to the Sanctuary, as it says, *This goodly mountain and Lebanon.* As for your question, why if you were a king, I did not come to you till now, the answer is that the *biryoni* among us did not let me. He said to him: If there is a jar of honey round which a serpent is wound, would they not break the jar to get rid of the serpent? He could give no answer. R. Joseph, or as some say R. Akiba, applied to him the verse, [*God*] *turneth wise men backward and maketh their knowledge foolish.* He ought to have said to him: We take a pair of tongs and grip the snake and kill it, and leave the jar intact.

At this point a messenger came from Rome saying, Up, for the Emperor is dead, and the notables of Rome have decided to make you head [of the State]. He had just finished putting on one boot. When he tried to put on the other he could not. He tried to take off the first but it would not come off. He said: What is the meaning of this? R. Johanan said to him: Do not worry: the good news has done it, as it says, *Good tidings make the bone fat*. What is the remedy? Let someone whom you dislike come and pass before you, as it is written, *A broken spirit drieth up the bones*. He did so, and the boot went on. He said to him: Seeing that you are so wise, why did you not come to me till now? He said: Have I not told you?—He retorted: I too have told you.

He said: I am now going, and will send someone to take my place. You can, however, make a request of me and I will grant it. He said to him: Give me Jabneh and its Wise Men, and the family chain of Rabban Gamliel, and the physicians to heal R. Zadok. R. Joseph, or some say R. Akiba, applied to him the verse, *'[God] turneth wise men backward and maketh their knowledge foolish'*. He ought to have said to him: Let them [the Jews] off this time. He, however, thought that so much he would not grant, and so even a little would not be saved.

Reading: Eusebius, *The History of the Church*

Eusebius (263–339 C.E.) was one of the Church Fathers. His general history of the Church serves as a primary source both for the early history of the Church and the later history of the Roman Empire. This selection provides a Christian record of the Bar Kokhba revolt. Note, in particular, his reference to Jerusalem being forbidden to Jews and the transformation of the city into a pagan town named in honor of the Emperor Hadrian.

The final siege of the Jews

When the Jewish revolt again grew to formidable dimensions, Rufus governor of Judaea, on receiving military reinforcements from the emperor, took merciless advantage of their crazy folly and marched against them, destroying at one stroke unlimited numbers of men, women, and children alike, and—as the laws of war permitted—confiscating all of their lands. The Jews at that time were under the command of a man called Bar Cochba, which means a star—a bloodthirsty bandit who on the strength of his name, as if he had slaves to deal with, paraded himself as a luminary come down from heaven to shine upon their misery.

The climax of the war came in Hadrian's eighteenth year, in Betthera, an almost impregnable little town not very far from Jerusalem. The blockade from without lasted so long that hunger and thirst brought the revolutionaries to complete destruction, and the instigator of their crazy folly paid the penalty he deserved. From that time on, the entire race has been forbidden to set foot anywhere in the neighbourhood of Jerusalem, under the terms and ordinances of a law of Hadrian which ensured that not even from a distance might Jews have a view of their ancestral soil. Aristo of Pella tells the whole story. When in this way the city was closed to the Jewish race and suffered the total destruction of its former inhabitants, it was colonized by an alien race, and the Roman city which subsequently arose changed its name, so that now, in honour of the emperor then reigning, Aelius Hadrianus, it is known as Aelia. Furthermore, as the church in the city was now composed of Gentiles, the first after the bishops of the Circumcision to be put in charge of the Christians there was Mark.

Bibliography for Further Reading

Avi-Yonah, Michael. *The Jews of Palestine*, Schocken Books, 1975

Finkelstein, Louis. *Akiba: Scholar, Saint and Martyr*, Jason Aronson, 1990

Harkabi, Yehoshafat. *The Bar Kokhba Syndrome*, Rossel Books, 1983

Levine, Lee I. *The Rabbinic Class of Roman Palestine in Late Antiquity*, Jewish Theological Seminary, 1989

Mintz, Alan. *Hurban*, Columbia University Press, 1984

Neusner, Jacob. *First Century Judaism in Crisis*, Abingdon Press, 1975

Schorsch, Ismar. "On the History of the Political Judgment of the Jew," *From Text to Context*, Brandeis University Press, 1995

Steinberg, Milton. *As a Driven Leaf*, Behrman House, 1996

Unit IX

Origins of Christianity

Life of Jesus

Jesus appears to have begun his career as a teacher seeking to strengthen Jewish doctrines rather than to overthrow them. The Sermon on the Mount is a classic statement of compassion for the poor and underprivileged. Repeatedly, Jesus states that he came to fulfill the law rather than overthrow it, promising that he would change "neither a jot nor a tittle."

To be sure, the Synoptic Gospels (Matthew, Mark, Luke) record in their accounts of the life of Jesus considerable tension between him and the Pharisees. The Pharisees accused Jesus of violating the law. He responded that the Pharisees were obsessed with the literal meaning of the law rather than the spirit underlying it. This critique of Pharisaism as rigid legalism would be repeated by Christian theologians down to the twentieth century. In Paul, the critique would give rise to the doctrine of supersessionism—the belief that the covenant with Jesus at Golgotha, or the Crucifixion, had superseded the covenant with the Jews, and that the New Testament had made the Old Testament virtually obsolete.

That is not to say that there were not significant differences between the teachings of Jesus himself, as expressed at the Sermon on the Mount, and the teachings of traditional Judaism. Jesus condemns divorce, for example, for any reason other than "unchastity." Rabbinic Judaism, by contrast, permitted divorce in marriages that were beyond repair.

Philosophically, Jesus preached, "Love your enemies and pray for your persecutors"—the origin of the doctrine of Christian love embracing all. Twentieth-century Christian thinkers, particularly Leo Tolstoy, elevated this into a form of Christian pacifism, a doctrine of non-resistance, even toward radical evil. Rabbinic Judaism rejected this pacifism. The doctrine of loving one's enemy was rejected as an unrealistic assessment or expectation of human nature. Moreover, in the case of radical evil, such as the doctrine of Amalek in the Bible, traditional Judaism argued specifically for resistance and combat rather than turning the other cheek.

Most specifically, Jesus clashed with the Pharisees over the application of points of Jewish law and teaching to contemporary life. The Gospel of Matthew, for example, records that Jesus permitted his disciples to pluck corn from the field on the Sabbath. When the Pharisees reproached Jesus for permitting his disciples to violate the Sabbath, he responded, "The son of man is sovereign over the Sabbath."

Similarly, Jesus entered into the Temple in Jerusalem and criticized the practices there as emphasizing payments of tithes but overlooking the "end of the Law, justice, mercy, and good faith." Jesus promised to tear down every stone in the Temple and to rebuild it as a new and purified Temple.

These clashes between Jesus and the Pharisees, whom he condemned repeatedly as hypocrites, led ultimately to the trial and the crucifixion of Jesus. The Gospels record that one of Jesus's disciples, Judas Iscariot, betrayed him to the High Priest and the Pharisees. The Pharisaic Council, or Sanhedrin, deliberated Jesus's fate and found him guilty of stating "I can pull down the Temple of God and rebuild it in three days." They queried him as to whether he regarded himself as the Messiah, which he did not deny. The Roman governor, Pontius Pilate, tried to spare Jesus. However, the people insisted that he be crucified.

The Gospels lay the blame for deicide collectively on the Jews. In Matthew, Pilate states explicitly, "My hands are clean of this man's blood," but the people respond, "His blood be on us, and on our children." This is the origin of the Christian teaching of contempt—that Jews are to be held in contempt for rejecting the Lord and demanding his crucifixion. Only Vatican II, in 1965, removed the teaching of contempt from Catholic education. For centuries Jews were regarded as an accursed people because, in rejecting Jesus, they were guilty of deicide.

To be sure, the account in the Gospels must be evaluated historically. Clearly, the Jewish Sanhedrin did not enjoy the power of capital punishment independently. The Jews could recommend capital punishment, but it was the Roman authorities that implemented it. Moreover, crucifixion is not a Jewish form of punishment but rather a Roman one. That the Gospels exempt the Roman authorities probably has more to do with the recognition that Christianity developed within the Roman Empire than it does with historical conditions of first-century Palestine.

Moreover, the Romans shared with the Pharisees a common motive in wishing to eliminate Jesus. By claiming that he was the Jewish Messiah, the King of the Jews, Jesus represented as much a threat to Roman authority as to that of the Pharisees. Although the Gospels exempt the Roman authorities from responsibility for the Crucifixion, the latter most likely agreed with the Pharisees that Jesus was a seditious personality.

Lastly, one must look at the rabbinic accounts of the Crucifixion. The Talmud records in Sanhedrin 43a: "On the eve of Passover Jesus was hanged. For forty days before the execution took place, a herald went forth and cried, He is going forth to be stoned because he has practiced sorcery and enticed Israel to apostasy. Any one who can say anything in his favor let him come forward and plead on his behalf. But since nothing was brought forward in his favor, he was hanged on the eve of Passover. Ulla retorted: Do you suppose he was one for whom a defense could be made? Was he not a *mesith* (enticer), concerning whom Scripture says, 'Neither shall thou spare nor shall thou conceal him?' With Jesus, however, it was different, for he was connected with the government."

This Talmudic passage suggests that the rabbis were prepared to take responsibility for the killing of Jesus. The rabbinic accounts of Jesus's life portray him as a magician and sorcerer—probably a reference to Jesus's many miracles—and as one who enticed Israel to apostasy. Clearly the rabbis regarded him as guilty. The source obviously makes no mention of the Crucifixion, for that was a distinctively Roman punishment. Rather, Jesus is said to have been stoned.

Interestingly, the miracles attributed to Jesus invite comparison with the miracles recorded in the Talmud as having been performed in the Talmud by Honi Ha-Me'agal ("Circle-Drawer"). Honi seems to have brought rain to end a drought. He did so by drawing a circle, hence his name. Yet the leader of the Pharisees of the time, Rabbi Shimon Ben Shetach, who was best known for his closeness to the Hasmonean monarchs Alexander Jannai and Queen Salome, did not take kindly to Honi's actions. He wished to place him under ban and refrained from doing so only because he recognized Honi's effectiveness (and popularity).

The incident does reflect Pharisaic distaste with miracles and wonder-workers. The Pharisees identified magic with idolatry and naturally suspected a popular religion that placed its trust in miracles and works of wonder.

What, then, can we conclude? Clearly Jesus saw his original message as "directed to the lost sheep of the House of Israel alone." The Jews at the time failed to resonate either to his miracles or to his message. The Pharisees, in particular, seem to have regarded him as a false prophet, one who was seeking to lead astray the House of Israel. Together with the Romans, they agreed that Jesus was a dangerous character, specifically in his claims to messiahship and his promise to destroy the Temple. Pharisaic rabbis living outside the Roman Empire several centuries later had no trouble in taking responsibility for his death. To exempt the Roman authorities completely, however, is certainly an unrealistic assessment of first-century Palestinian politics and the nature of Roman rule in Palestine.

Paul and Jewish Christianity

After Jesus's death his followers continued to observe Jewish law while believing in his messiahship and imminent second coming. They noted that Jesus himself had a favorable attitude toward the law. The changes he introduced were quite limited in scope and were mostly related to his claims to being the Apocalyptic Messiah.

Moreover, the association with Judaism was beneficial to the early Christians. Judaism possessed a past, which was a symbol of legitimacy in the ancient world. Moreover, Judaism possessed Scriptures, which could now be combed and reinterpreted for apparent prophecies predicting the coming of Jesus. Lastly, within the Roman Empire Judaism possessed the status of *religio licita.* Forming a distinctly new religion, as Christianity would later become, would entail considerable persecution by the Roman authorities.

Paul represented a parting of the ways between Judaism and

Christianity. In Paul's *Epistle to the Romans,* he rejects Jewish law as having been once valuable but now outmoded. Paul was overwhelmed with the theme of original sin—that all humanity is born in sin and that sin is transmitted sexually from generation to generation. The nature of the sin is human pride. Jewish law was granted to the Jews as a vehicle of salvation, but it was inadequate to raise humanity from the status of sin into grace. If anything, the law may very well have been counterproductive, for it falsely encouraged mankind to believe that human beings could work out their own salvation. The law is intellectual, and the study of it only increases human pride, which is, at heart, the nature of original sin.

Original sin is so overwhelming that only a free act of grace by God can raise humanity out of sin into grace. Therefore, God became man in the persona of Jesus and died for our sins vicariously to provide us with atonement. Salvation can be had through faith in Jesus—a free gift which was given to humanity via Jesus's life and death. Salvation cannot be had by the intellectual study and observance of the Jewish law.

In other words, the law for Paul was fundamentally flawed. It falsely offered the hope of salvation, but the reality of sin was so powerful that the law was inadequate to the task. Jewish history had actually proved this. The Jews had been given the law, yet had failed to observe it, and in turn were punished. Because the Jews were the possessors of the law, Jesus had come to them first. Given that they had rejected his message, Jesus's teachings were now the common possession of humanity. That Jews continued to observe the law in this new age reflected only Jewish obstinacy. That the Temple was destroyed within one generation after the Crucifixion was proof positive, in the eyes of many Christians, that the Jews were being punished for their rejection of Jesus. This Christian reading of Jewish history mirrored the Jewish reading—namely, that the Jews had lost their Temple and were in exile because they had sinned. The difference between these two readings of history lay in what constituted the sin.

As a result, the gap between Jews and Christians progressively widened. The Gospels themselves reveal an unmistakable increase in hostility as time advances. To some extent this reflects an attempt within the Gospels to appease Roman authorities. In another sense, the anti-Judaism expressed so vividly in the Gospels, which would plague later Jewish history, symbolizes a daughter faith seeking to break fundamentally and irretrievably from the mother religion.

Conversely, the Talmud makes no effort to embrace Jewish Christianity. Talmudic references to Christianity are generally contemptuous. These references were often censored by Christian authorities in the medieval period. Clearly the Pharisees saw little that was attractive in the teachings of Jesus that was not already found in rabbinic Judaism. The miracles Jesus was said to have performed were regarded as inferior to the miracles of the Bible. Lastly, the rabbis did regard Jesus as seditious, both in terms of his relationship to Jewish law and in the implications of his claims to being the Jewish Messiah. Paul begins as a Pharisee, but breaks sharply with Pharisaism upon realizing the nature of the revelation to Jesus. He therefore urges Jewish Christians to separate themselves fundamentally from Jewish law and custom. Although one can find Jewish Christians observing Jewish law yet believing in the imminence of the coming of Jesus for many years after Paul, the break between Judaism and Christianity is clearly evident by the second century C.E.

Bar Kokhba is said to have persecuted the Christians during his rebellion. Bar Kokhba's defeat was regarded by Christians as additional proof of Divine punishment for the Crucifixion. By Bar Kokhba's time there were more Christians than Jews in the Roman Empire. Christians generally feared that their followers might relapse into Judaism. Early Christian Councils, e.g. the Elvira Council (300–303 C.E.), sought to limit contact between Jews and Christians. Christians were prohibited from socializing with Jews and, of course, from marrying with them.

One other contemporary source preserves references to the life of Jesus. The Jewish historian Josephus refers to Jesus on two occasions. In one account, he refers to Jesus's family and depicts him as having lived and taught in the first century. In a second reference, Josephus refers to Jesus as "a wise man, if it be lawful to call him a man; for he was a doer of wonderful works, a teacher of such men as had a veneration for truth. He drew over to him many of the Jews and many of the Gentiles: He was the Christ." These last four words, "He was the Christ," are strange coming from the pen of Josephus. The term Christ refers to messiah, suggesting that Josephus himself believed in Jesus as the messiah. Given that this contradicts all of Josephus's political theory, which sought to discourage messianic frenzy and encouraged Jews to live in accordance with the Pharisaic doctrine relegating messianic hopes to the far-off future, Jewish historians generally believe these words were an interpolation into the text of Josephus. Nevertheless, because they were early testimony to the life of Jesus, these words were preserved over the centuries by Christian authorities.

Several conclusions emanate from this reading of the origins of Christianity and its relationship to rabbinic Judaism: First, the primary messages of Jesus were that of a Jewish teacher articulating a doctrine of love and compassion for the underprivileged. The doctrines themselves were by no means incompatible with traditional Judaism, although there were significant differences. Rather, Jesus's conflict with the Pharisees and his probable claims to being the Messiah insured the enmity of contemporary Jewish leadership. Nevertheless, the teachings of Jesus alone would not have necessitated a fundamental break between Judaism and early Christianity.

However, Paul's teachings distinguishing between an Israel after the flesh, a physical Jewish people, who had sinned, and an Israel after the spirit, which had been saved, marked the fundamental break between Judaism and Christianity. The symbol of the Jewish law was physical—i.e. circumcision. Paul desired a spiritual circumcision. The physical attributes of the Jews as a people reminded one only of the past heritage of Judaism and its current rejection of Jesus. An Israel after the spirit would be truly saved through faith in Jesus. This duality of flesh and spirit symbolized the fundamental break between Judaism and Christianity. Judaism remained a this-worldly religion, focusing upon a particular people, homeland, and set of laws. Christianity was universal, focusing upon a spiritual Jerusalem rather than an earthly one. The believing Christian connoted one who had been given the free gift of grace or faith in Jesus as savior. To be a Jew meant that one was a member of God's original Chosen People, which had erred fundamentally in rejecting Jesus as Messiah.

Lastly, this break between Judaism and Christianity set down the parameters for later Jewish-Christian relationships. Although there were many ups and downs in that relationship over the millennia, the basic Christian doctrine remained that the covenant with the Jews had been superseded by the covenant with humanity at Golgotha. The Jews were to be revered as the original possessors of God's teaching, and therefore Jesus had come to them initially. However, the covenant with the Jews was now outdated. Jewish reverence for a physical law would not lead one to salvation. On the contrary, it might be counterproductive, for it would only encourage humanity in the false belief that human beings can work out their own salvation. For these reasons, Christian Scriptures were divided between "Old Testament" and "New Testament." The very terms "old" and "new" implied the doctrine of supersessionism. Jews have preferred to use the term Hebrew Bible, thereby suggesting that the texts of the Jews were by no means outdated or anachronistic.

Reading: The Gospel of Mark XIV:60–72, XV:1–39

The Gospel of Mark *is one of the four gospels within the New Testament. Mark, Matthew, and Luke are known as the Synoptic Gospels, in that they all tell the story of the life of Jesus.* Mark *is considered to be the oldest and therefore the most historical of the Gospels. Chapters 15 and 16 are accounts of the crucifixion and the resurrection. Note, in particular, the ascription of responsibility to the Jews alone.*

[60]Then the High Priest stood up in his place and questioned Jesus: 'Have you no answer to the charges that these witnesses bring against you?' [61]But he kept silence; he made no reply.

Again the High Priest questioned him: "Are you the Messiah, the Son of the Blessed One?' [62]Jesus said, 'I am; and you will see the Son of Man seated on the right hand of God and coming with the clouds of heaven.' [63]Then the High Priest tore his robes and said, 'Need we call further witnesses? [64]You have heard the blasphemy. What is your opinion?' Their judgement was unanimous: that he was guilty and should be put to death.

[65]Some began to spit on him, blindfolded him, and struck him with their fists, crying out, 'Prophesy!' And the High Priest's men set upon him with blows.

[66]Meanwhile Peter was still in the courtyard downstairs. One of the High Priest's serving-maids came by [67]and saw him there warming himself. She looked into his face and said, "You

were there too, with this man from Nazareth, this Jesus.' [68]But he denied it: 'I know nothing.' he said; 'I do not understand what you mean.' Then he went outside into the porch; the cock crew, [69]and the maid saw him there again and began to say to the bystanders, 'He is one of them'; [70]and again he denied it.

Again, a little later, the bystanders said to Peter, 'Surely you are one of them. You must be; you are a Galilean.' [71]At this he broke out into curses, and with an oath he said, 'I do not know this man you speak of.' [72]Then the cock crew a second time; and Peter remembered how Jesus had said to him, 'Before cock crows twice you will disown me three times.' And he burst into tears.

Chapter 15

[1]When morning came the chief priests, having made their plan with the elders and lawyers and all the Council, put Jesus in chains; then they led him away and handed him over to Pilate. [2]Pilate asked him, 'Are you the king of the Jews?' He replied, 'The words are yours.' [3]And the chief priests brought many charges against him, but he answered nothing. [4]Pilate questioned him again: 'Have you nothing to say in your defence? You see how many charges they are bringing against you.' [5]But, to Pilate's astonishment, Jesus made no reply.

[6]At the festival season the Governor used to release one prisoner at the people's request. [7]As it happened, the man known as Barabbas was then in custody with the rebels who had committed murder in the rising. [8]When the crowd appeared asking for the usual favour, [9]Pilate replied: 'Do you wish me to release for you the king of the Jews?' [10]For he knew it was out of spite that they had brought Jesus before him. [11]But the chief priests incited the crowd to ask him to release Barabbas rather than Jesus. [12]Pilate spoke to them again: 'Then what shall I do with the man you call king of the Jews?' [13]They shouted back, 'Crucify him!' [14]'Why, what harm has he done?' Pilate asked. They shouted all the louder, 'Crucify him!' [15]So Pilate, in his desire to satisfy the mob, released Barabbas to them; and he had Jesus flogged and handed him over to be crucified.

[16]Then the soldiers took him inside the courtyard (the Governor's headquarters) and called together the whole company.

[17]They dressed him in purple, and having plaited a crown of thorns, placed it on his head. [18]They began to salute him with, 'Hail, the King of the Jews!" [19]They beat him about the head with a cane and spat upon him, and then knelt and paid mock homage to him. [20]When they had finished their mockery, they stripped him of the purple and dressed him in his own clothes.

They then took him out to crucify him. [21]A man called Simon, from Cyrene, the father of Alexander and Rufus, was passing by on his way in from the country, and they pressed him into service to carry his cross.

[22]They brought him to the place called Golgotha, which means 'Place of a skull'. [23]He was offered drugged wine, but would not take it. [24]Then they fastened him to the cross. They divided his clothes among them, casting lots to decide what each should have. [25]The hour of crucifixion was nine in the morning, [26]and the inscription giving the charge against him read, 'The king of the Jews.' [27]Two bandits were crucified with him, one on his right and the other on his left.

[28]The passers-by hurled abuse at him: [29]'Aha!' they cried, wagging their heads, 'you would pull the temple down, would you, and build it in three days? [30]Come down from the cross and save yourself!' [31]So too the chief priests and the doctors of the law jested with one another: 'He saved others,' they said, 'but he cannot save himself. [32]Let the Messiah, king of Israel, come down now from the cross. If we see that, we shall believe.' Even those who were crucified with him taunted him.

[33]At midday darkness fell over the whole land, which lasted till three in the afternoon; [34]and at three Jesus cried aloud, '*Eli, Eli, lema sabachthani?*' which means, 'My God, my God, why hast thou forsaken me?' [35]Some of the passers-by, on hearing this, said, 'Hark, he is calling Elijah.' [36]A man came running with a sponge, soaked in sour wine, on the end of a cane, and held it to his lips. 'Let us see,' he said, 'if Elijah is coming to take him down. [37]Then Jesus gave a loud cry and died. [38]And the curtain of the temple was torn in two from top to bottom. [39]And when the centurion who was standing opposite him saw how he died, he said, 'Truly this man was a son of God.'

Reading: Epistle to the Romans XI: 1–12

Paul's Epistle to the Romans *served as a defining statement of early Christianity. Paul distinguished between Israel after the flesh, whom God had rejected, and Israel after the spirit, in whom salvation through Jesus lies. As a result, Paul's* Epistle to the Romans *served as the cornerstone of the doctrine of Christian supersessionism, that the New Testament had eclipsed the Old Testament and that Jewish law was now obsolete. Salvation came, not via the Law, but rather through faith in Jesus alone. All individuals are born in sin, but the power of faith in Jesus is so great that it may save humanity.*

[1]I ask then, has God rejected his people? I cannot believe it! I am an Israelite myself, of the stock of Abraham, of the tribe of Benjamin. [2]No! God has not rejected the people which He acknowledged of old as His own. You know (do you not?) what Scripture says in the story of Elijah—how Elijah pleads with God against Israel: [3]'Lord, they have killed thy prophets, they have overthrown thine altars, and I alone am left, and they are seeking my life.' [4]But what does the oracle say to him? 'I have left myself seven thousand men who have not done homage to Baal.' [5]In just the same way at the present time a 'remnant' has come into being, selected by the grace of God. [6]But if it is by grace, then it does not rest on deeds done, or grace would cease to be grace.

[7]What follows? What Israel sought, Israel has not achieved, but the selected few have achieved it. The rest were made blind to the truth, [8]exactly as it stands written: 'God brought upon them a numbness of spirit; he gave them blind eyes and deaf ears, and so it is still.' [9]Similarly David says:

'May their table be a snare and a trap,
Both stumbling-block and retribution!
[10]May their eyes be darkened so that they do not see!
Bow down their back for ever!'

[11]I now ask, did their failure mean complete downfall? Far from it! Because they offended, salvation has come to the

Gentiles, to stir Israel to emulation. [12]But if their offence means the enrichment of the world, and if their falling-off means the enrichment of the Gentiles, how much more their coming to full strength!

Bibliography for Further Reading

Klausner, Joseph. *Jesus of Nazareth,* Beacon Books, 1964

Sanders, E.P. *Paul, the Law and the Jewish People,* Fortress Press, 1983

Sandmel, Samuel. *A Jewish Understanding of the New Testament,* KTAV, 1974

Travers-Herford, R. *Christianity in Talmud and Midrash,* KTAV, 1975

Unit X

The Church and the Jews

Judaism and Christianity as Competitive Religions

Rome accepted Christianity in the early part of the fourth century C.E. The status of Judaism officially was unchanged, inasmuch as it remained a *religio licita* of the Roman Empire. However, as Christianity became more important within the Roman Empire, the relationship with Jews and Judaism underwent serious revision. The turning point came in the fourth century, under Constantine the Great, who recognized Christianity's official status, converted to Christianity himself, and reconstituted his capital in the East at Constantinople. Under Constantine, the nature of Christian legislation toward Jews was defensive in nature. Rather than engage in offensive anti-Semitism, Christian concern was with protecting confessing Christians from contact with Jews lest they relapse into Judaism.

Both Judaism and Christianity were proselytizing faiths in the declining centuries of the Roman Empire. Christianity, to be sure, possessed many of the advantages of Judaism—monotheism, scriptures—but without the defect of being associated with a defeated faith. However, Christian leaders feared that converts to Christianity might well become targets for conversion to Judaism as well. Therefore they sought to limit Jewish proselytizing activity and minimize Jewish-Christian contacts.

Constantine himself restored two privileges to the Jews, which were critical in Palestine. First, he allowed Jews to reside in places from which Jerusalem could be sighted, e.g. Bethlehem. Secondly, he allowed Jews to enter Jerusalem one day a year, on the ninth of Av. Previously this had been done only illegally, usually through bribery of Roman soldiers. These grants given to Jews were very important in terms of Christian doctrine. By focusing attention upon the Roman destruction of Jerusalem, which had occurred so shortly after the Crucifixion, Constantine was demonstrating that the Jews were being punished for their rejection of Jesus. No sooner had they engaged in the crime of deicide than, within a generation, they had lost their homeland and the central symbol of their faith, the Jerusalem Temple.

Moreover, the concern with Palestine reflected a broader desire to infuse Christian symbols and institutions in the Holy Land. Theologically, Christianity had substituted a spiritual Jerusalem for an earthly Jerusalem. Yet practically, Palestine had been the land in which Jesus had preached and lived, and refocusing attention upon it, via Christian pilgrimages, would provide a physical symbol for Christianity's past heritage. Constantine built churches in Palestine, especially in areas in which Jesus was said to have lived. Moreover, he created holy places, or objects of pilgrimage, for devout Christians seeking to pay tribute to the life of their savior.

The years following Constantine marked the major translation of Scriptures into Latin, the Vulgate translation of Saint Jerome. The Vulgate enabled Christians to study Scripture on their own and, in turn, to make them less dependent upon Jewish interpreters.

Some of the new legislation was social in nature. At the Council of Antioch in 341 C.E., it was decreed that Christians may not visit Jews on the Passover holiday, nor may they eat matzot together with them. At the Council of Laodicea in 360 C.E., Christians were enjoined from accepting gifts from Jews on the holiday of Purim. Secondly, it was noted that Christians must work on Saturday and observe Sunday as the Christian Sabbath—again an attempt to prevent Christians from lapsing into Judaizing practices. In 357 C.E., the ban on Jewish proselytization was extended even to conversion to Judaism absent missionary activity. Conversely, Jews were enjoined from assaulting or harassing any Jewish converts to Christianity. Similarly, Jews were banned from possessing any gentile slaves, for it was generally expected that the slave of a Jew in effect become a semi-proselyte. Holding slaves meant that one had a captive audience for conversionist activity, especially if conversion to Judaism meant freedom and emancipation. Christians now interpreted the biblical dictum of "the elder serving the younger brother" as referring to Jewish subservience to Christianity. For Jews to possess Christian slaves would violate that principle.

To be sure, the ban on conversion to Judaism was observed more in the breach than in reality. We find conversions to Judaism continuing well into the Middle Ages. Increasingly, Jews suffered for accepting converts both in Christian and in Moslem lands. The fact that they continued to do so reflects the continuing esteem for conversion within Jewish history. By the end of the Middle Ages, conversion to Judaism had ceased, and at the beginning of modern times, Jewish abstention from conversionary activity became articulated as a Jewish value—namely, that others seek converts but Jews do not. Only very recently, under the leadership of Reform Judaism in America, has conversion to Judaism reentered the basic ethos of Jewish teachings and values. In articulating a program to stimulate conversion to Judaism, the Reform movement reinvoked a major theme of classical Jewish history.

One fourth century Roman Emperor rejected Christianity. Julian I, "the Apostate" (361–363 C.E.), sought to weaken Christianity and restore the philosophical paganism articulated by neo-Platonists. To accomplish these aims, Julian sought to strengthen Judaism in Palestine at the expense of Christianity. Therefore, he ordered a rebuilding of the Jerusalem Temple. This may also have been motivated by political concerns—his ongoing war with Parthia and his desire to gain the support of Parthian Jewry—again an illustration of how diaspora Jewry's influence affected conditions in the Jewish homeland. Theologically, by rebuilding the Temple, Julian would destroy the fundamental Christian proof that the destruction of the Jerusalem Temple had signified the validity of Christianity.

Work on the Temple commenced but was destroyed by fire. Christians saw this as an act of God; Jews charged Christian sabotage. Both views may be substantiated. An earthquake in Palestine in that year may well have set off underground fires, suggesting natural causes for the conflagration. However, a similar undertaking to restore a pagan temple with animal sacrifices in Antioch was also destroyed by fire. That Christian preachers had predicted that rebuilding the Temple would meet with Divine retribution may have, of course, stimulated some to instigate a fire deliberately.

In any event, the damage of the fire was by no means extensive. Rather, it provided an excuse to delay work on the Jerusalem Temple until Julian had returned from his war with Parthia. During that war, Julian was killed by a Christian soldier, and the project was abandoned permanently. Significantly, there is no evidence that the Palestinian Jewish Patriarchate cooperated in the venture. Julian may, in fact, have damaged the Patriarchate by abolishing the tax on diaspora Jewry raised to support it.

Christian Ascendancy

By the fifth century, Roman legislation concerning Judaism went much more on the offensive, inasmuch as Christianity had now become *the*—rather than *an*—official religion of Rome. Thus Theodosius I in 390 C.E. prohibited construction of new synagogues. To be sure, he equally prohibited the destruction of existing synagogues, although, unfortunately, this at times did occur. As a result, when Jews wished to repair a synagogue, they now claimed that the synagogue had been constructed prior to Theodosius I.

In 415 C.E. Gamaliel VI, the last of the Palestinian Jewish Patriarchs, was accused of building a synagogue as well as of circumcising slaves and adjudicating disputes among Christians. The Patriarch was punished and humiliated, setting the stage for the abolition of the institution upon his death in 429 C.E. Taxes previously directed for the Patriarchate were now directed to the imperial treasury, and the continuing symbol of Jewish autonomy and sovereignty, which traced its lineage to Davidic times, was now abolished. To be sure, outside the boundaries of the Roman Empire, in Babylonia, the exilarch of the Jews continued to claim Davidic ancestry and served as the symbol of ongoing Jewish autonomy and even sovereignty. Yet within the Roman Empire, the church had now gone on the offensive. Palestine became essentially a Christian land. Although Judaism remained a *religio licita* of the Roman Empire, it could be nowhere near as prominent and assertive as it had been in the last centuries of a pagan rather than Christian Rome.

The Church itself had to reconsider the place of Jews and Judaism in its theology. The Church father Augustine is perhaps best known for reformulating Christian theology at the time both of

Rome's decline and of her becoming Christian. Augustine's *City of God* is a classic statement of Christian dualism. The book was inspired by the sack of Rome by Alaric the Visigoth in 410 C.E. Augustine posed the appropriate question of how Rome could have been sacked almost immediately after she had become Christian. The answer lay in Christian dualism. Rome represented only the city of man. The ultimate city of God was a spiritual entity that was not at all subject to devastation by barbarian hordes.

This dualism also explained the vision of Jews and Judaism in Christianity. The Jews represented Israel after the flesh. Their doctrine of an earthly restoration to Jerusalem was fundamentally misguided. Like their ancestors who had rejected Jesus, the Jews of today committed a similar mistake in thinking in earthly rather than in spiritual terms. The Jews prayed every day for a physical rebuilding of their Temple. What they did not realize was that true salvation lay through faith in Jesus and not through physical expression of peoplehood and flesh.

This dualism led Augustine to articulate a fundamental theological conflict between Jewish and Christian teachings. For Augustine, salvation was a matter of predestination. As Paul had stated, "The just shall live by faith," meaning that those who have been given the free gift of grace through faith in Jesus would be awarded salvation. This is not subject to free will. Man had lost his free will at the time of original sin and the fall of man from Eden. Individual human beings were chosen by an act of God. Human activity was relatively insignificant in determining whether one would be saved or not. Jewish tradition, by contrast, emphasized the centrality of free will and human action. Rabbinic Judaism had decreed that all is in the hands of heaven, except the fear of heaven—meaning that Divine rule was providential in history, but every human being is free to work out his or her own destiny. Salvation in Judaism is awarded not on the basis of a Divine gift, but to those who merit entry into Paradise. Meriting entry is very much a function of human action and inaction.

Augustine illustrated this point by drawing a distinction between himself and his mother. He, the intellectual, had been tortured for many years by doubt, leading him to try every form of Christian heresy. In the *Confessions* he documents his intellectual journey until he finally arrived at a position of faith in Jesus. His mother, by contrast, a woman of pure faith, was able to accept

Jesus freely and lovingly. Augustine indicates, as Dante did subsequently in the *Divine Comedy,* that he preferred his mother's pristine faith to his own journey of doubt and intellectual struggle. Rabbinic Judaism, by contrast, placed much greater emphasis on the role of intellectual struggle. The rabbis emphasized, "Go out and study"—meaning that questions were by no means to be avoided, but rather must be intellectually engaged.

Yet this contrast of Judaism and Christianity is part and parcel of the larger struggle between their views of human nature. Because Christianity saw humanity as beset by original sin, men and women were simply incapable of working out their own salvation. Jewish law was criticized because, as an intellectual doctrine, it was accessible to the human mind, and mastery over it would only increase human pride and thereby sin. Judaism saw the law as a vehicle of salvation. By studying it one came to practice it, and through practice one entered into the heavenly paradise of the soul. Thus Judaism and Christianity differed fundamentally over the question of human capacity to work out personal salvation. Judaism was far more this-worldly and optimistic about human nature and emphasized the continuing relevance of Jewish law as a vehicle of salvation. Christianity was far more pessimistic, seeing man as irretrievably mired in original sin and therefore incapable of working out personal salvation. To such a mind-set, the continued presence of Judaism signaled an obsolete faith which had lost its purpose in contemporary society.

Doctrine of the Witness

Yet in practice, the Jews continued to exist centuries after the Crucifixion and the destruction of the Temple. Augustine and the other Church Fathers wrestled with this question of why Judaism continued if it had apparently lost its purpose? Augustine's answer lay in the "Doctrine of the Witness." This doctrine suggested that the continuing physical presence of the Jews was desirable because the Jews themselves provided testimony to the truth of Christianity in two ways: First, the Jews possessed Scriptures, thereby proving that Scriptures were by no means invented retrospectively by Christians to predict the coming of Jesus. Many years before Jesus had been born, the Jewish Scriptures were in existence. Christian interpreters now combed Hebrew Scriptures for alleged proofs that the authors knew of Jesus and predicted his coming.

Secondly, the physical status of the Jews provided testimony to the truth of Christianity. The Jews existed in a subjugated, second-class status as a defeated people. The origins of that subjugation lay in the destruction of the Temple in Jerusalem in 70 C.E., only 40 years after the Crucifixion. The perpetual servitude of the Jews reminded the world that the Jews are being punished for their rejection of Jesus. Therefore it was desirable that the Jew remain in Christian society. As long as Jews retained their second-class status, they would remind the world of their crime in rejecting Jesus and the validity of Jesus's teachings.

Augustine confessed that he had no clear picture as to what would take place in the Second Coming, but he was convinced that one step in the messianic age would be the final conversion of the Jews to faith in Jesus. As a result, Christian rulers were enjoined from eliminating the Jews. Although the Jews' status would always be second-class, the Church Fathers decreed that the Jews must be protected and not eliminated. In this context medieval Christian anti-Semitism provided a protective mechanism against the elimination of the Jews. Or, as Duns Scotus, a thirteenth century Christian theologian, put it, the Jews could be persecuted and virtually eliminated, but some of them would have to be kept alive on a deserted island until the Second Coming.

Thus a certain ambivalence appears in Christian teachings concerning Judaism. The Church Fathers developed the teaching of contempt—that Jews represented Israel after the flesh and were guilty of the crime of deicide. The typology of the Jew was that of the murderous elder brother—the Cain who murdered Abel, the younger brother symbolizing Christianity. The destruction of the Temple, as prophesied by Jesus, constituted fitting retribution for the crimes of the Jews.

Yet the Jews remained a valued people in terms of God's having chosen them initially, for Jesus's having been sent to them at first, and currently as witnesses to the truth of Christianity. In other words, the Jews retained their status as the people of Scripture, who had been chosen by God to receive His holy Word and Law. Therefore they had been privileged to hear first the message of Jesus. In our own day, the Jewish presence must be preserved, for the Jews are witnesses to the truth of Christianity.

Despite this ambivalence—reverence for the Jews as God's chosen people, yet contempt for Jews for the crime of deicide—Christian doctrine remained supersessionist. The Jews, at best, connote a fossil faith, one whose greatness lay behind it rather than in its future. Jewish aspirations for the future—visions of a restoration to Palestine and Jerusalem—reflected the Jewish obsession with the earthly and their incapacity to grasp the truly spiritual. The Jewish Christians, in this view, were equally mistaken, for they did not recognize that the law of the Jews had been made obsolete by the ministry of Jesus.

Gnosticism

Christian heresy also inclined toward anti-Judaism. The Gnostics argued that the God of the Hebrew Bible was really the Demiurge, a demonic deity who had hidden the ultimate God and had thereby created this world and revealed himself to the Jews. The true God had remained hidden for many years, but had become flesh via the person of Jesus in order to penetrate the Demiurge and allow humanity to believe in Him.

Yet the world as we know it continued to be ruled by the Demiurge. Therefore evil holds sway in this world. Against Augustine and Orthodox Christians who believed that the presence of evil was at most an illusion or the absence from good, the Gnostics, like mystics subsequently, argued for the reality of evil. Satan was alive and well and ruled on earth. The Jews, in this view, were the best representations of the power of Evil. The God of Israel, or the Demiurge, prevented the world from obtaining salvation through the person of Christ. The True God remained hidden in a world governed by the Demiurge, who had created this world, given the Torah to the Jews, and had prevented the full flowering of Jesus's ministry.

Gershom Scholem once described Gnosticism as "the greatest case of metaphysical anti-Semitism." Yet the primary concerns of the Gnostics were probably more with anti-Judaism than anti-Semitism. Marcion, the leading Gnostic theologian, demonstrated little concern with actual Jews, but was far more concerned with demonizing Judaism and with uprooting Christianity from its Judaic roots.

Gnosticism remained a Christian heresy. Orthodox Christians cannot believe in a dichotomy between the God of Israel and Jesus. The message of Christianity remained that of the Trinity constituting a unity of Father, Son, and Holy Ghost. However, the Gnostic heresy, to the extent that it became a popular doctrine owing to the power of mystical thought and its interpretation of the reality of evil, represented an extreme form of anti-Judaism. The Gnostics, in effect, laid the groundwork for subsequent identification of Jews with the devil and the Jewish messiah with the anti-Christ.

Palestine and Palestinian Jewry remained until the mid-seventh century under the sway of the Eastern Roman Empire or Byzantium. The dominant form of Christianity in Byzantium was Greek Orthodoxy, and it featured strong imperial intervention in theological matters. For example, the Byzantine Emperor Justinian in the sixth century prohibited the Jews from studying the Oral Law and encouraged the utilization of the Greek translation of the Torah (thereby detracting from the Oral Law) during the prayer service.

In 614 C.E. the Persians again invaded Palestine and, with Jewish assistance, expelled the Roman authorities for three years. Jews were given partial control over Jerusalem. This represented the last period of Jewish political control in Palestine until the twentieth century. The Byzantines reconquered Palestine in 629 C.E., but were in turn reconquered themselves by the Moslems in 638 C.E.

Augustine, in The City of God, *asks how, so shortly after adopting Christianity, did Rome decline so badly. Theologically, his question is, if Christianity offered salvation, why did its acceptance means Rome's destruction? Augustine's answers lie in Christian dualism. The earthly city of man may be destroyed, but it ultimately pales into insignificance when compared with the city of God. True reality is spiritual rather than earthly. Significantly, rabbinic Judaism responded that God would not enter the heavenly Jerusalem until He had first entered the earthly Jerusalem, suggesting that rebuilding the physical city of man took precedence over entering the heavenly city of God.*

Augustine's City of God, *then, serves as a Christian statement of a philosophy of history. Human history is divided into several epochs. The current epoch of life after the birth, crucifixion, and resurrection of Jesus is fundamentally different from the preceding epoch in which the Jews had lived under the Law. Yet the world stands unredeemed until the second coming of Jesus, which all are awaiting. Augustine here offers his forecast of the "end of history," acknowledging that he is by no means certain of the precise order of events. This vision of history moving toward a definite end colored much of the Christian reading of history for the next two millennia.*

Reading: Augustine, *City of God,* Book XXI, ch. 30

Heaven, too, will be the fulfillment of that Sabbath rest foretold in the command: 'Be still and see that I am God.' This, indeed, will be the ultimate Sabbath that has no evening and which the Lord foreshadowed in the account of his Creation: 'And God rested on the seventh day from all his work which he had done. And he blessed the seventh day and sanctified it: because in it he had rested from all his work which God created and made.' And we ourselves will be a 'seventh day' when we shall be filled with His blessing and remade by His sanctification. In the stillness of that rest we shall see that He is the God whose divinity we ambitioned for ourselves when we listened to the seducer's words, 'You shall be as Gods,' and so fell away from Him, the true God who would have given us a divinity by participation that could never be gained by desertion. For, where did the doing without God end but in the undoing of man through the anger of God?

Only when we are remade by God and perfected by a greater grace shall we have the eternal stillness of that rest in which we shall see that He is God. Then only shall we be filled with Him when He will be all in all. For, although our good works are, in reality, His, they will be put to our account as payment for this Sabbath peace, so long as we do not claim them as our own; but, if we do, they will be reckoned as servile and out of place on the Sabbath, as the text reminds us: "The seventh day . . . is the rest of the Lord. . . . Thou shalt not do any work therein.' In this connection, too, God has reminded us, through the Prophet Ezechiel: 'I gave them my sabbaths, to be a sign between me and them, that they might know that I am the Lord that sanctifies them.' It is this truth that we shall realize perfectly when we shall be perfectly at rest and shall perfectly see that it is He who is God.

There is a clear indication of this final Sabbath if we take the seven ages of world history as being 'days' and calculate in accordance with the data furnished by the Scriptures. The first age or day is that from Adam to the flood; the second, from the flood to Abraham. (These two 'days' were not identical in length of time, but in each there were ten generations.) Then follow the three ages, each consisting of fourteen generations, as recorded in the Gospel of St. Matthew; the first, from Abraham to David; the second, from David to the transmigration to Babylon; the third, from then to Christ's nativity in the flesh. Thus, we have five ages. The sixth is the one in which we now are. It is an age not to be measured by any precise number of generations, since we are told: 'It is not for you to know the times or dates which the Father has fixed by his own authority.' After this 'day,' God will rest on the 'seventh day,' in the sense that God will make us, who are to be this seventh day, rest in Him.

There is no need here to speak in detail of each of these seven 'days.' Suffice it to say that this 'seventh day' will be our Sabbath and that it will end in no evening, but only in the Lord's day—that eighth and eternal day which dawned when Christ's resurrection heralded an eternal rest both for the spirit and for the body. On that day we shall rest and see, see and love, love and praise—for this is to be the end without the end of all our living, that Kingdom without end, the real goal of our present life.

I am done. With God's help, I have kept my promise. This, I think, is all that I promised to do when I began this huge work. From all who think that I have said either too little or too much, I beg pardon; and those who are satisfied I ask, not to thank me, but to join me in rejoicing and in thanking God. Amen.

Bibliography for Further Reading

Parkes, James. *The Conflict of the Church and Synagogue,* Athenaeum, 1969, 1977

Reuther, Rosemary. *Faith and Fratricide,* Beacon Books, 1974

Schiffman, Lawrence. *Who Was A Jew,* KTAV, 1985

Unit XI

Jewry and Islam

Mohammed and the Jews

Mohammed lived in seventh-century Arabia and appears to have been influenced by both Christians and Jews. He demonstrated considerable knowledge of both the Jewish Bible and legendary midrashic materials. Muslim tradition, however, claimed that the Jews distorted Scriptures. In the original version of the text of Genesis, Ishmael was the favorite son of Abraham and was to have received the promise of the Abrahamic Covenant. The Jews distorted this record making Isaac Abraham's heir.

Nevertheless, Mohammed reflected the influence of Judaism in numerous places in the Koran. He insisted upon the unity of God, denying the Christian doctrine of Trinity. Similarly, he constantly emphasized the importance of law, a Judaic doctrine in pronounced contrast to the Christian emphasis upon faith. Moreover, he stressed the role of the prophet, the Day of Judgment, resurrection, and angelogy—all of which, in varying degrees, reflect the influence of Jews and Judaism.

Furthermore, Moslems believed in the importance of *hadith,* oral traditions which are said to go back to Mohammed and which are necessary to interpret Islamic Scriptures. This notion of oral tradition seems far more indebted to Jews and Judaism than to Christianity or other faiths.

Mohammed referred to the bearers of other monotheistic faiths as "Peoples of the Book"—a term suggesting considerable reverence and respect for fellow monotheists in contrast to pagan infidels, against whom Mohammed preached recourse to *jihad,* "holy war."

In particular, a number of rituals introduced by Mohammed seemed oriented toward the Jews of Arabia. For example, prayer was directed toward Jerusalem. Mohammed emphasized ritual ablutions and abstention from pork.

There were, of course, Jewish communities in Arabia. These dated from Second Commonwealth times. Most likely Jews had emigrated to Arabia for trade opportunities that existed in the Roman Empire. Several Jewish kingdoms had arisen. The last of these was destroyed by the Byzantine Emperor Justinian in the generation prior to Mohammed's birth.

By the time of Mohammed, several Jewish tribes populated various areas of the Arabian peninsula. Most likely these possessed only fragmentary knowledge of Judaism, having been so removed from the centers of Jewish life for centuries. Mohammed seems to have come in contact with them and absorbed much of their Jewish teachings. However, his fragmentary knowledge of Judaism may well explain the considerable degree of confusion regarding Jewish thought in his teaching. In particular, the constant confusion between Jewish texts and legends is characteristic of Mohammed's writings about the Bible.

Mohammed originally lived and preached in Mecca. His flight, or Hegira, to Medina is the central orientating event in Islamic heritage and constitutes year one of the Islamic calendar. This flight to Medina appears to have been motivated by a search for new allies. The Jews of Medina, in Mohammed's view, constituted fertile targets to receive his message.

However, the Jews of Arabia felt little attraction to Islam. Those doctrines of Islam that appeared close to Judaism were already available to Jews. By contrast, Mohammed's insistence that he represented the "seal of prophecy"—the last and greatest of the prophets—pointedly contradicted the Judaic notion that no prophet after Moses was as great as he. Similarly, Mohammed regarded Jesus as a prophet, a doctrine which Jews could not accept, having taught that Jesus was a false messiah. Lastly, Jews most likely regarded Mohammed's depictions of Judaism as a caricature rather than an accurate representation, owing to the constant confusion between legend and history.

As a result, Mohammed attacked the Jewish tribes in the Arabian Peninsula with his army. He offered them the alternatives of conversion to Islam or expulsion. Although there were few converts to Islam, some resisted Mohammed militarily and were exterminated. Others were reduced to very heavy tribute. Mohammed preached that ideally the Arabian peninsula should be free of all non-Islamic elements. As a result, Islamic doctrine declared Arabia off-limits to Jews and Christians. In practice, however, echoes of Arabian Jewry have persisted into modern times. The image of Arabia as "*judenrein*" was more theoretical than real. However, even during the 1991 Gulf War, Jewish soldiers stationed in Arabia were instructed not to display Jewish symbols openly, so as to avoid offending Moslem sensitivities.

Theologically, the Jewish roots of Islam were significant. As a monotheistic faith, Islam more closely approximated Judaism than Christianity. Where Judaism profoundly contradicted the Christian doctrine of Trinity and the resurrection of Jesus, the conflict with Islam appears to be more limited in scale, focused on whether Mohammed represented the actual "seal of prophecy". Later Jewish thinkers, particularly Maimonides, studied Islamic philosophy and appeared heavily indebted to Moslem theologians. Certainly conversion to Islam was regarded by some Jewish thinkers as considerably less reprehensible than conversion to Christianity. All agreed on the fundamentally monotheistic ideals of Islam. By contrast, Jewish thinkers were divided as to how they should view Christianity. Most acknowledged that Christianity was preferable to paganism, but controversy ensued as to how Jews ought interpret the doctrine of the Trinity.

To be sure, Islam suggested a new theological conflict with Judaism virtually absent from Jewish-Christian relations—namely a conflict over territory and territorial imperatives. Moslem theologians divided the world into *dar al-Islam,* or "territory of Islam" and *dar al-harb* or "territory of the nations." Theologically, territory that had passed over into Islamic hands could never revert to territory of the nations. The land of Israel, having once been Islamic land, could never revert to Jewish hands. By that reasoning, of course, the State of Israel today becomes a theological travesty, reflected in the uncompromising rejection of Israel's existence as a state by fanatical Islamic groups such as Hamas or Islamic Jihad. The acceptance of Israel as a Jewish State requires greater secularization, or at least a reform of traditional Islamic theology.

Jewry and the Islamic Empire

Shortly after Mohammed's death in 632 C.E., the Arabian tribes began their conquest of the Mediterranean world under the banner of Islam. Palestine itself became a Moslem territory in 638 C.E. The Arabian tribes extended their domain to Persia in the East and as far as Spain in the West. The Zoroastrian faith virtually disappeared, although some Parsees persist to this day, and Zoroastrian influence concerning dualism and the reality of evil can be traced in Christian sectarian thought, emphasizing the devil and the anti-Christ, throughout medieval and modern times.

This conquest had pronounced implications for Jews internationally. Politically, the Arabic conquest virtually unified world Jewry for the first time in over a millennium. The overwhelming majority of Jews now lived under Islamic rule. One principle of Jewish survival throughout the Greek and Roman periods had been that the presence of two Jewish communities acted as a safety valve ensuring Jewish survival. If Jewish life were endangered under one form of gentile rule, Jews could emigrate to another political authority. Persecutions in Byzantium, for example, might be countered by Jewish migrations to Babylonia. Political unity, therefore, posed a theoretical threat to Jewry.

In practice, Jewish unity under Islam was far more beneficial than harmful. It permitted Talmudic authority, expressed via the Pharisaic rabbis, to spread throughout the international Jewish community. The growth of the Arabic language provided a common medium for the transmission of culture and heritage. Lastly, the unity afforded by Islam was never absolute. Some Jews lived outside the boundaries of Islam, particularly in Christian Europe. Thus originated the ethnic, cultural, and religious distinctions between Ashkenazi and Sephardi Jews. Although the division between Ashkenazim and Sephardim is by no means an absolute distinction between Jews living in Christian Europe and Jews living under Islamic rule, the chasm between these two groups of Jews owes its origin partially to the Islamic conquest, which did not extend to areas such as Germany and France, which, in turn, became the strongholds of Ashkenazi Jewry.

Generally, Islamic rule tolerated Jews but denied them equal status. The term *dhimmi* denoted a protected people, but one with second-class status. Many Jews converted to Islam, given that Islam represented the ascendant force, while Judaism was associated with a defeated faith. Historian Salo Baron claims that Jews had once represented close to one-third of the population of Egypt, Palestine, and Syria, and 10 percent of the Roman Empire. Yet Jewish numbers declined radically during the years of the Moslem conquest, as social status rose with conversion to Islam. Conversely, Moslems were prohibited from converting to Judaism.

The Jews fulfilled critical functions for the Islamic Empire. They acted as international traders providing a link between the Islamic and Christian worlds. There was even some involvement of Jews in the slave trade, although Jews owned very few slaves themselves, and the leading perpetrators of the slave trade were Moslem and Syrian Christian rather than Jewish. Lastly, Jews fulfilled certain bureaucratic needs of the Islamic Empire, freeing Moslems to serve in the military.

Jewish status under Islam was confirmed by four basic freedoms: Jews were promised protection from injury to life, limb, and property. To be sure, some religious persecution did exist. For example, during the reign of the fanatical Caliph, Al-Hakim, 1012–1020 C.E., synagogues were burned, and pogroms against Jews ensued owing to a *hadith,* or oral tradition, that Mohammed had prophesied that within 500 years of his death all Jews were to be converted. Similarly, in the 1140's, the Almohades, a Moslem tribe, compelled Jews in Spain to convert to Islam. However, these persecutions and pogroms were sporadic during the years of Islamic rule. On a day-to-day basis, Jews living under Islam reasonably could expect protection of their personal lives and property.

Secondly, Jews were guaranteed freedom of worship. This provided full freedom for the development of the trappings of a religious community—education, welfare, religious services, etc. The sole exception was the ban on Jewish proselytization. However, into modern times Jews enjoyed religious freedom in Islamic lands. Although political freedoms would lapse, especially in the context of the conflict with Zionism, religious freedoms were maintained, at least in theory and usually in practice.

Thirdly, Jews were granted the freedom of settlement and movement within the borders of the Islamic Empire. This freedom of settlement did not extend to the two holy cities of Islam, Mecca and Medina, for Mohammed had decreed there was no room for nonbelievers within the Hejaz itself. However, the freedom to settle and move elsewhere in the Islamic Empire greatly assisted the Jews to function as international traders. There was no Jewish "ghetto" or area of the city in which Jews had to reside. To be sure, there was usually a Jewish quarter in which Jews voluntarily resided, but they were not compelled to limit their residence to a particular section of town.

Lastly, Jews enjoyed freedom of occupation and economic pursuit. This freedom greatly improved Jewish economic status and clearly made Jewish life under Islam preferable to living under Christianity. Jews were not compelled to adopt any particular form of economic activity. They availed themselves of the diversity of occupations Islam proffered. To be sure, Jews were encouraged to fulfill certain economic functions so as to leave Arabs free for military conquest. However, in theory, Jewish economic life was free and diverse, in pronounced contrast to Jewish life under medieval Christendom.

Yet the term *dhimmi* clearly denoted second-class status. Jews were subject to heavy taxes simply on the grounds of being Jewish. In addition to imposing economic disabilities and providing an inducement to convert to Islam, these taxes were humiliating. Only *dhimmis* had to pay them, and they symbolized the inferior status of those who were fellow monotheists but not full Moslems.

Other restrictions denoted the special and inferior status of *dhimmis.* Jews were prohibited from building new synagogues that were taller or higher than neighboring mosques. When passing a Moslem in the street, the Jew had to stand aside, denoting the inferior status of the *dhimmi.* Special garments, forerunners of the infamous yellow badge, were meant to designate clearly who was a Moslem and who was a *dhimmi.* Although many of these restrictions were more theoretical than real, they symbolized the protected yet second-class status of *dhimmis.* Islam waged holy war against the infidels but permitted the "peoples of the book" to remain in peace, so long as they accepted second-class status. Many Jews, to be sure, preferred conversion to Islam. Jewish historian Salo Baron estimated that by the year 1200 there were only 2 million Jews left in the world, given the losses resulting from conversion coupled with the destruction of Jewish lives in the various rebellions against Rome.

These restrictions also signalled some of the differences in treatment of Jews in Islamic as distinct from Christian lands. In Islamic lands, restrictions on garb were meant to communicate who were the rulers and who were the ruled. In Christian lands, by contrast, restrictions on dress were meant initially to segregate Jews and ultimately to exclude them from Christian society. As Mark R. Cohen has argued, only from the fifteenth century onward did the treatment of Jews in Islamic countries approximate the day-to-day treatment of Jews under medieval Christendom.

This picture of protected but second-class status for Jews in the Islamic Empire has several implications for contemporary Moslem-Jewish relations. First, the status of Jews under Islam was far more protected and offered greater economic opportunities than under Christendom. Moreover, Judaism shared more in common with Islam as a religious system than it did with Christianity.

However, it is a myth to speak in terms of an utopian era of Jews and Moslems living in equality and harmony. Arab historians in recent years have capitalized on this myth, suggesting that anti-Semitism was unknown in the Moslem world and that its modern manifestations were strictly a function of the Arab-Zionist conflict. On the contrary, *dhimmi* status did mean humiliating and second-class status for Jews and Judaism. Periods of persecution were by no means unknown, although they were more sporadic than under Christendom. The Arab-Zionist conflict did not invent tensions between Jews and Arabs. On the contrary, their contacts over the centuries often were filled with tension and animosity. Lastly, when Islamic lands experienced social and economic decline, as they did in the latter part of the Middle Ages and modern periods, the pressure against Jews and Judaism became more intense. Deteriorating social and economic conditions often increased religious fanaticism, resulting in increased persecution, pogroms, and even compulsory conversion. This deterioration occurred long before there was a modern Zionist movement. To say that Arabs and Moslems cannot be anti-Semitic for they are Semites themselves amounts to little more than semantic delusion. Rather, Moslem anti-Semitism, while very different from Christian anti-Semitism, possesses its own checkered history independent of the Christian record.

Jewish Communal Organization

Islam did encourage strong Jewish self-government. The Moslem caliphs wished to rule over all of Islam, so they encouraged the Jewish authorities to develop centralized Jewish leadership closely connected to the Moslem caliphs. In particular, the Islamic conquest encouraged the growth of the two primary Jewish institutions—the *gaonate* and *exilarchate,* located in Baghdad, the capital of the Islamic Empire.

These two institutions had existed in the pre-Islamic period. However, they gained in power and stature under Islamic rule. The *geonim,* or heads of the Jewish academies, had four major tasks: As academic deans, they presided over Talmudic research. Legislatively, they issued regulations affecting the day-to-day lives of Jews in the Islamic Empire. As public educators, they sponsored two months per year of general adult Jewish education. For the months before the High Holy Days and Passover, the *geonim* closed the regular Talmudic academies and transformed them into open universities for Jewish learning. The nature of study became more popular, and Jews throughout the Islamic world were encouraged to come for a month to Baghdad to study with great Jewish scholars. This model of universal adult education communicated a most powerful message that being a Jew meant the ongoing study of Jewish texts and tradition. Lastly, through the literature of responsa, by which *geonim* answered questions concerning Jewish law put to them by Jews living far from Baghdad, the *geonim* were able to assert their authority over their co-religionists everywhere in the Islamic Empire. This genre of responsa literature—questions and answers concerning points of Jewish law—remains a treasure of Jewish legal literature to this day.

The exilarchs or "heads of the exile" date to pre-Islamic, rabbinic times and traced their ancestry to the House of David. The exilarch symbolized the ongoing sovereignty of Jewish political power and the Davidic dynasty. Jews everywhere revered the exilarch as a symbol of continued Jewish glory.

Islamic authorities elevated the status of the exilarch to virtually a political officer within the Islamic empire. The caliph appears to have taken an active interest in searching for qualified candidates.

Although the power of the exilarchs eroded after the split within the Islamic caliphate in the tenth century, they continued to hold office until the Mongolian invasions of 1401.

Clearly both exilarchs and *geonim* lost much of their power and influence as the Islamic Empire declined. The fortunes of these institutions in many ways paralleled the fortunes of Islamic rule. In their heyday, they symbolized a powerful and autonomous Jewish community which, under Islamic rule, nurtured both the welfare of Jews as individuals and as family members and the welfare of Judaism as a religious system.

Reading: *The Koran*

The Koran *is the Moslem Scripture, allegedly revealed to Mohammed by the Angel Gabriel. It is divided into* suras, *many of which refer to material in biblical Scriptures as well as in midrashic commentary. Through such material, Mohammed laid claim to the heritage of both Judaism and Christianity.*

We showed Moses and Aaron the distinction between right and wrong, and gave them a light and an admonition for righteous men: those who truly fear their Lord and dread the terrors of Judgment-day.

And in this We have revealed a blessed counsel. Will you then reject it?

We bestowed guidance on Abraham, for We knew him well. He said to his father and to his people: 'What are these images to which you are so devoted?'

They replied: 'Our fathers worshipped them.'

He said: 'Then you and your fathers erred grossly.'

'Is it the truth that you are preaching,' they asked, 'or is this but a jest?'

'Know, then,' he answered, 'that your Lord is the Lord of the heavens and the earth. It was He that made them: to this I bear witness. By the Lord, I will overthrow your idols as soon as you have turned your backs.'

He broke them all in pieces, except their supreme god, so that they might return to Him.

'Who has done this to our deities?' asked some. 'He must surely be a wicked man.'

Others replied: 'We have heard a youth called Abraham speak of them.'

They said: 'Then bring him here in sight of all the people, that they may act as witnesses.'

'Abraham,' they said, 'was it you who did this to our deities?'

'No,' he replied. 'It was their chief who smote them. Ask *them*, if they can speak.'

Thereupon they turned their thoughts to their own folly and said to each other: 'Surely you are sinful men.'

But they soon returned to unbelief and said to Abraham: 'You know that they cannot speak.'

He answered: 'Would you then worship that, instead of Allah, which can neither help nor harm you? Shame on you and your idols! Have you no sense?'

They cried: 'Burn him and avenge your gods, if you must punish him!'

'Fire,' We said, 'be cool to Abraham and keep him safe.'

They sought to lay a snare for him, but they themselves were ruined. We delivered him and Lot, and brought them to the land which We had blessed for all mankind.

We gave him Isaac, and then Jacob for a grandson; and We made each a righteous man. We ordained them leaders to guide mankind at Our behest, and enjoined on them charity, prayer and almsgiving. They served none but Ourself.

To Lot We gave wisdom and knowledge and delivered him from the Wicked City; for its inhabitants were men of iniquity and evil. We admitted him to Our mercy; he was a righteous man.

Before him Noah invoked Us and We heard his prayer. We saved him and all his kinsfolk from the great calamity, and delivered him from the people who had denied Our revelations. Evil men they were; We drowned them all.

And tell of David and Solomon: how they passed judgment regarding the cornfield in which strayed lambs had grazed by night. We gave Solomon insight into the case and bore witness to both their judgments.

We bestowed on them wisdom and knowledge, and caused

the birds and mountains to join with David in Our praise. All this We have done.

We taught him the armourer's craft, so that you might have protection in your wars. Will you then give thanks?

To Solomon We subdued the raging wind: it sped at his bidding to the land which We had blessed. We have knowledge of all things.

We assigned him devils who dived into the sea for him and performed other tasks besides. We kept a watchful eye over them.

And tell of Job: how he called on his Lord, saying: 'I am sorely afflicted: but of all those that show mercy You are the most merciful.'

We heard his prayer and relieved his affliction. We restored him to his family and as many more with them: a blessing from Ourself and an admonition to worshippers.

And you shall also tell of Ishmael, Idris, and Dhulkifl, who all endured with fortitude. To Our mercy We admitted them, for they were upright men.

And of Dhul-Nun: how he went away in anger, thinking We had no power over him. But in the darkness he cried: 'There is no god but you. Glory be to You! I have done wrong.'

We heard his prayer and delivered him from affliction. Thus We shall save the true believers.

And of Zacharias, who invoked his Lord, saying: 'Lord, let me not remain childless, though of all heirs You are the best.'

We heard his prayer and gave him John, curing his wife of sterility. They vied with each other in good works and called on Us with piety, fear, and submission.

And of the woman who kept her chastity: We breathed into her of Our spirit, and made her and her son a sign to all men.

Your religion is but one religion, and I am Your only Lord. Therefore serve Me. Men have divided themselves into schisms, but to Us they shall all return. He that does good works in the fullness of his faith, his endeavors shall not be lost: We record them all.

Reading: Bernard Lewis, ed., *Islam*

The pact of Omar is a document concerning the treatment of non-Moslems by Islamic rulers. Jews, Christians, and Zoroastrians were considered dhimmis, *or protected peoples, albeit with second-class status. As a result, Jews in the Islamic empire enjoyed a number of freedoms although their status was clearly designed to be inferior to that of Moslems. Although the document as here reproduced is directed at Christians, it applied equally to Jews.*

The Pact of 'Umar (c. Seventh Century)

We heard from 'Abd al-Rahman ibn Chanam [died 78/697j as follows: When 'Umar ibn al-Khattab, may God be pleased with him, accorded a peace to the Christians of Syria, we wrote to him as follows:

In the name of God, the Merciful and Compassionate.

This is a letter to the servant of God 'Umar [ibn al-Khattab], Commander of the Faithful, from the Christians of such-and-such a city. When you came against us, we asked you for safe-conduct *(am'in)* for ourselves, our descendants, our property, and the people of our community, and we undertook the following obligations toward you:

We shall not build, in our cities or in their neighborhood, new monasteries, churches, convents, or monks' cells, nor shall we repair, by day or by night, such of them as fall in ruins or are situated in the quarters of the Muslims.

We shall keep our gates wide open for passersby and travelers. We shall give board and lodging to all Muslims who pass our way for three days.

We shall not give shelter in our churches or in our dwellings to any spy, nor hide him from the Muslims.

We shall not teach the Qur'an to our children.

We shall not manifest our religion publicly nor convert anyone to it. We shall not prevent any of our kin from entering Islam if they wish it.

> We shall show respect toward the Muslims, and we shall rise from our seats when they wish to sit.
>
> We shall not seek to resemble the Muslims by imitating any of their garments, the *qalansuwa,* the turban, footwear, or the parting of the hair. We shall not speak as they do, nor shall we adopt their *kunyas.*
>
> We shall not mount on saddles, nor shall we gird swords nor bear any kind of arms nor carry them on our persons.
>
> We shall not engrave Arabic inscriptions on our seals.
>
> We shall not sell fermented drinks.
>
> We shall clip the fronts of our heads.
>
> We shall always dress in the same way wherever we may be, and we shall bind the *zunnar* round our waists.
>
> We shall not display our crosses or our hooks in the roads or markets of the Muslims. We shall only use clappers in our churches very softly. We shall not raise our voices in our church services or in the presence of Muslims, nor shall we raise our voices when following our dead. We shall not show lights on any of the roads of the Muslims or in their markets. We shall not bury our dead near the Muslims.
>
> We shall not take slaves who have been allotted to the Muslims. We shall not build houses overtopping the houses of the Muslims.
>
> (When I brought the letter to 'Umar, may God be pleased with him, he added, "We shall not strike any Muslim.")
>
> We accept these conditions for ourselves and for the people of our community, and in return we receive safe-conduct.
>
> If we in any way violate these undertakings for which we ourselves stand surety, we forfeit our covenant [*dhimma*], and we become liable to the penalties for contumacy and sedition.

'Umar ibn al-Khattab replied: Sign what they ask, but add two clauses and impose them in addition to those which they have undertaken. They are: "They shall not buy anyone made prisoner by the Muslims," and "Whoever strikes a Muslim with deliberate intent shall forfeit the protection of this pact."

Bibliography for Further Reading

Cohen, Mark R. *Under Crescent and Cross: The Jews in the Middle Ages,* Princeton University Press, 1994

Goitein, S.D. *Jews and Arabs: Their Contacts Throughout the Ages,* Schocken, 1970

Lewis, Bernard. *The Jews of Islam,* Princeton University Press, 1984

Stillman, Norman. *The Jews of Arab Lands,* Jewish Publication Society, 1979

Unit XII

Jewish Messianism and Sectarianism

Messianism

In studying Jewish messianism, we must distinguish between the messianic idea, messianic calculations, and messianic movements. The messianic idea promised a future restoration of the Jews to Palestine, coupled with a universalist vision of a world at peace. Jewish thinkers often divided between those who saw a future messianic era as gradually evolving out of present-day conditions, a medieval form of the modern idea of progress, and those who argued that the messianic era would be totally unlike anything that existed today. This latter, more apocalyptic view saw messianism as the direct obverse of the idea of progress. In this view, the world would deteriorate to the point that only a radical cataclysm could alter the course of history and usher in the Redemption.

Of particular interest in this messianic idea was the theme of the warrior-messiah, the Messiah son of Joseph. This messiah would precede the Davidic messiah, do battle with the enemies of Israel, and in fact, die in battle.

The precise origins of this doctrine of the Messiah son of Joseph are unclear. Some suggest they lie in attempting to account for a failed messiah, e.g. Bar-Kokhba. More likely, the doctrine relates to the age-old hope of the Jews for restoration of the unity of Israel and the return of the Ten Lost Tribes. A Messiah son of Joseph who dies in battle on behalf of the people of Israel would signify both the return of the Ephraimite tribes to the Jewish people and the final ascendancy of the House of David over the House of Joseph. Lastly, Prof. David Berger. following the late Louis Ginzberg, has argued for a typological explanation, relating the Messiah Son of Joseph to the Rabbinic legend of a failed exodus of the tribe of Ephraim from Egypt 30 years prior to the exodus of the Jews generally. In other words, an early precursor, albeit unsuccessful, of redemption is paralleled by a later precursor of a final redemption.

Messianic calculation usually involved attempts, based upon biblical data, to fix the date for the arrival of the messiah. The dates fixed often were sufficiently far off in the future as to be relatively meaningless to contemporary Jews. Some calculators of the end of days, however, were themselves guilty of arousing messianic frenzy by fixing a date in the relatively near future.

Messianic movements dot the entire course of medieval Jewish history. These generally reflected counter-establishment movements, led by charismatic false messianic personages, who themselves inspired followers to take up the cudgels of a messianic movement. If the establishment focused upon preservation of Jewish life in the diaspora based upon the foundations of Jewish law, these counter-establishment messianic movements advocated return to Palestine sometimes coupled with abrogations of the Jewish legal system.

The rabbis encouraged the messianic idea, which set a future vision of where Jewish history should lead. They were highly ambivalent about messianic calculation, for it could be quite destructive. They were most opposed to messianic movements, for these at best would result in widespread disappointment and at worst would shatter the *modus vivendi* Jewish leaders had worked out for living in the diaspora.

The rabbis had codified this view of messianic activity by claiming that the Jews had vowed not to return to Palestine *en masse* or to rebel against the nations in exchange for a promise that the gentile nations would not overly oppress the Jews. These vows, which ultra-Orthodox opponents of Zionism regard as binding to this day, reflected the view of the rabbinic establishment throughout the medieval period. The most important things for Jews to do consisted of building their own lives as constructively as possible and recognizing gentile power and authority. Jews prayed daily for a future restoration, but no messianic activity ought be undertaken directly. Observance of Jewish law bound one to the Jewish community and acceptance of rabbinic authority. Messianic activity, by contrast, would not only constitute a violation of rabbinic authority, but would also be perceived as revolutionary and destructive by the gentile authorities and a rebellion against their sovereignty. Lastly, even if such messianic activity would be viewed benignly by the gentile authorities, the failure of any particular messianic movement would engender only widespread disappointment and sadness within the Jewish community at large.

The messianic idea, in other words, was a particularly this-worldly idea. The rabbis downplayed messianic hysteria or fantastic dreams of other-worldly redemption. Jews were taught to think in terms of a redemption in this world involving a return to the Jewish homeland of Palestine. However, the way to reach that end was to go about one's day-to-day work in accordance with Jewish law, rather than to engage in concrete political activities or rebellion against gentile authority.

To be sure, conflicts between world powers generally fed messianic speculations. The rise of Islam, the conquest of the Byzantine empire by the Persian Empire, or the conflict between Christendom and Islam all nurtured Jewish speculations about an end of days in which the fourth kingdom envisioned by Daniel would be destroyed and in its destruction the fifth kingdom or Kingdom of God would commence. Daniel had calculated that the messianic era would commence after "time, times and half-a-time," an indeterminate period 3 1/2 times of which would theoretically provide the date of the messiah's arrival. Historians have generally interpreted this as 3 1/2 years, meaning the time of the Syrian Greek persecution which the Hasmoneans overthrew, and on which Daniel was commenting. However, throughout the medieval period and even into modern times, Jews witnessing cataclysmic world events invoked the "time, times and half-a-time" calculation as a vehicle for determining messianic dates.

Ironically, the dates chosen often turned out to be years of destruction rather than redemption. World-wide cataclysmic events often had catastrophic rather than redemptive effects upon world Jewry. 1096, 1492, and 1648—dates predicted to be "messianic"—all represented years of pogroms or expulsions. The Talmud itself offered several dates suggesting the Messiah would arrive several hundred years following the destruction of the Temple. More generally, the rabbis believed that the era of redemption was far off in the future and that Jews should concern themselves with the here and now rather than be concerned overly with the far-off future. In addressing messianism, the Talmud cited the view that the messianic era will not differ greatly from the current era. The world will continue as usual, with the difference that the Jews would be restored to their rightful place among the nations and will dwell in security. One Talmudic rabbi went so far as to say that none of the prophecies of messianic personage recorded in the Bible will come to pass. They were all meant to refer to the biblical King Hezekiah, and since the Jews were not worthy in his time, none of these prophecies have future validity. To be sure, the rabbis rejected this view, but they did not condemn it as heresy.

To Moses Maimonides, Jewish messianism was also a modified form of the idea of progress. Change will come in a slow and evolutionary way, and the arrival of the messiah will only culminate a long period of human activity. Jewish mysticism articulated a similar view that the messiah will essentially be expected to usher in a period of universal peace, restoring the harmony of the cosmos, rather than an age of worldwide cataclysms. For Maimonides, skepticism concerning particular messiahs does not imply disbelief in the messianic idea. Rather skepticism toward messiahs reflects leadership responsibility and reasonable caution.

These views of the rabbinic establishment did not resonate with those severely discontented with the status quo. First, the voices of moderation essentially asked the Jews to be content with gentile rule, exile from homeland, and the status of a defeated nation. Messianic voices, by contrast, appealed to memories of past Jewish glories and dreams of future Jewish sovereignty. Generally these movements set themselves in opposition to the prevailing rabbinic order. The rabbis, by contrast, cooperated with the Islamic and Christian governments to quell such movements. Gerson Cohen has noted that the Sephardic ambience was more messianically oriented than the Ashkenazi one. The political successes of Jews living in Islamic lands whetted their appetites for messianism. Secondly, the greater skepticism of Sephardim encouraged greater challenge to rabbinic authority, as compared with the absolute faith and piety more characteristic of Ashkenazim, reflected in the greater tendency to Jewish martyrdom in Ashkenazic lands. Lastly, a rational society posited a Deity who was predictable—hence the value in efforts to predict an end to history.

Some of the messianic movements themselves serve as good examples of these tensions. In 450 C.E. Moses of Crete led Jews into the Mediterranean, promising to part the waters to enable them to walk to Palestine. The Christian text records that as Moses and his followers drowned, so great was the disappointment among the remaining Jews of Crete that widespread conversions to Christianity ensued.

In the eighth century a Jew named Abu-Issa claimed to be a prophet and precursor of the messiah. He abolished divorce, prohibited meat, and instituted prayer on a seven-times-per-day basis. Arab armies regarded him as a potential threat to Islamic rule and killed him, although his followers could be found as late as the tenth century C.E.

Perhaps the most romantic figure was David Al-Roy, a twelfth century Baghdad Jew who claimed magical powers. Two impostors acting in his name urged Baghdad Jews to assemble on the rooftops to fly to Jerusalem. Jewish authorities cooperated with the Moslem authorities in having Al-Roy arrested and subsequently killed. British Prime Minister Benjamin Disraeli would later immortalize him in an historical novel.

Messianic movements continued well into the nineteenth and twentieth centuries. In 1840, with the failure of the messianic movement slated for the year 5600, conversions to Christianity ensued, including rabbinical authorities. Yemen, in particular, was a hotbed of messianic activity in the late nineteenth century. In the twentieth century messianism has been the province of two contrasting movements: Religious Zionism and Lubavitch Hasidism. For the religious Zionists, the creation of the State of Israel was the first step in the messianic redemption. Chief Rabbi Abraham I. Kook had hailed World War I as the final apocalyptic battle of Gog and Magog. His son, Rabbi Zvi Yehuda Kook, greeted the Six-Day War with its conquest of Judea and Samaria and the unification of Jerusalem as ultimate acts of redemption. In this view, potential surrender of territory of the historical land of Israel would negate the imminent coming of the messiah. The most extreme forms of this messianism expressed itself in a Jewish underground in the early 1980's, involving terrorist activity against Arab civilians.

Lubavitch messianism, by contrast, was rooted more in the personality of Rabbi Menachem Mendel Schneersohn, the seventh Lubavitcher Rebbe. Schneersohn died without heirs. In his final years speculation increased, especially among the Lubavitcher youth movement, that he was destined to be the messiah. Although Schneersohn himself never gave official sanction to such statements, and in fact his leading advisors repudiated them, widespread belief that the Rebbe was himself the messiah increased during Schneersohn's last years. His passing in 1994 raised all of the questions associated with failed messianic movements and disappointed many within the Lubavitch camp. Surprisingly, the messianic fervor continues, often expressed in advertisements placed in the *New York Times* and other media concerning the imminent coming of the messiah. Needless to add, this excitement stands in pronounced contrast to the realistic caution of Moses Maimonides in his *Epistle on Martyrdom*: " (If the messiah comes,)—life will be more pleasant. If he does not come, we have not lost anything; on the contrary we have gained by doing what we have to do."

Sectarianism

Similar observations should be made concerning Jewish sectarianism. Jewish sects represented a rebellion against the ruling rabbinic establishment, often accompanied by Palestine-centered activity.

The most important of the sects were the Karaites, a word referring to either their emphasis upon Scripture or their "calling" to serve the Lord. The founder of Karaism was Anan Ben David, an eighth-century member of the exilarchic family who had been passed over by the ruling rabbinic establishment in his candidacy for the exilarchate. The rabbis did acknowledge his scholarship but, in all likelihood, felt that his character was insufficiently stable for a position of communal leadership. Anan proceeded to establish a rival Jewish sect, allegedly based upon the principle of reverence for Scripture, or the Written Law, while denying the oral tradition of the rabbis. His followers were known originally as Ananites. In subsequent generations they became known as Karaites.

Anan did invoke his own interpretation of Scripture. He greatly extended the number of forbidden marriages between relatives. He banned intercourse and circumcision on the Shabbat and Jewish holidays. Most significantly, he interpreted literally the biblical statement "Do not light fire on the Sabbath day" to mean that no lights whatsoever were permissible on the Shabbat, effectively transforming the day into one of sadness and gloom rather than joy and light.

Although leading a dissenting Jewish movement, Anan himself appears to have been highly intolerant of those who questioned his leadership and authority. He counseled that anyone guilty of misinterpreting the Bible should be subject to the death penalty.

Karaism spread remarkably in the medieval period and continues to enjoy followers to this day. The Karaites may have built upon the survival of an older tradition of Jewish sectarianism already present in Second Commonwealth times, which rejected rabbinic authority particularly as it concerned the Oral Law. Moreover, Karaism incorporated a number of Moslem features, particularly contact with Moslem intellectuals, Scriptural prayer, inheritance laws that were similar to Islam, and comparable laws of exogamy or refraining from marrying blood relatives. Thirdly, Karaism represented a counter-establishment force emphasizing return to Palestine and rejection of the Jewish establishment. It can be seen as a struggle against rabbinic efforts to fix *the* normative interpretation of Judaism. Lastly, Karaism's ability to survive may be attributed partially to its willingness to reinterpret Jewish law in light of new conditions. Karaite thinkers argued, in direct contrast to rabbinic thinkers, that later generations of Jews in fact possessed greater authority than earlier generations because resting on the shoulders of those who preceded them, they could see further. This Jewish version of a battle between "ancients and moderns" as to who has greater authenticity, those who precede us or those in our own day, enabled Karaite jurists to reinterpret Karaite doctrine in light of new and changing historical conditions. More generally, the Karaites possessed the classic symbols of legitimacy in medieval Jewish history—an aristocracy of Jewish learning coupled with an aristocracy of Davidic descent.

Of particular importance was Karaite emphasis upon Palestine and the return to Zion. Some Karaites prohibited partaking of meat and wine as a gesture of permanent mourning for the destruction of Zion. Their position approximated the view of a sectarian group known as "Mourners of Zion," who argued that since the destruction of the Temple, it was appropriate that Jews spend their time only on mourning the destruction. Rabbinic wisdom, by contrast, marginalized this view. The rabbis sought to contain mourning rather than expand it. They argued that both wine and meat were permissible and outlawed the excessive mourning practices of the "Mourners of Zion." Rabbinic tradition came to understand the breaking of the glass at the wedding feast as meaning that Jewish life must continue; the destruction must be remembered, but it cannot be allowed to prevent further Jewish celebrations and rejoicing.

Polemics between Karaites and Rabbanites were particularly vigorous. The Karaites accused the Rabbanites of being anthropomorphic, focusing upon rabbinic legends such as God wearing the *tallith* and phylacteries. Conversely, the Rabbanites, in particular Saadiah, the greatest of the *geonim*, carefully refuted Karaite doctrines and thereby reduced their impact and significance.

Yet surprisingly, relations between Karaites and Rabbanites remained close in the early Middle Ages. Marriageability was the key. As long as Jews could marry one another, they maintained a single Jewish people. In marriages between Karaites and Rabbanites it was generally noted that each partner would refrain from violating the traditions of the other partner. Often Karaite leaders functioned within Jewish communal institutions as leaders of a united Jewish community consisting of Rabbanites, Karaites and Samaritans.

By the sixteenth century, however, Karaites and Rabbanites had diverged significantly. At that point rabbinic authority placed a total ban on marital unions between the two groups. Once they could no longer marry one another, a joint concept of peoplehood was obsolete—a theme of considerable significance for the definition of Jewish peoplehood today.

In the nineteenth century Karaite communities in southern Russia sought exemption from Czarist anti-Jewish legislation by claiming that Karaites were not united biologically with the Jewish people, but rather were descendants of the Jewish kingdom of the Khazars, which had governed southern Russia in the eighth to tenth centuries. This claim, although patently false, was politically motivated to convince the Russian authorities that Jews were foreigners, while Karaites were native Russians. In practice, the fabled Khazar kingdom converted to Judaism in the eighth century, probably under the influence of both Karaite and Rabbanite teachers. The Khazars' knowledge of Judaism was quite meager. Probably only the royal family converted. The sources speak of Khazar rule being extremely tolerant, for Jews, Moslems, Christians, and pagans lived together harmoniously. By the tenth century the Khazar kingdom was no longer Jewish. It was overthrown completely by the Mongolian invasions of the thirteenth century. Nevertheless, memories of the Khazar kingdom continued to inspire Jews throughout the Middle Ages with the message that elsewhere Jews continue to enjoy statehood and sovereignty. By identifying Karaites and Khazars, nineteenth-century Karaites essentially were driving a wedge between themselves and the Jewish people in order to claim exemption from anti-Semitic legislation.

Surprisingly, Karaite communities were also able to evade the Nazi destruction by claiming to be outside the Jewish people. The Nazi authorities accepted the Karaites' claim that their origins lay not in Jewish blood but among the Khazar rulers of southern Russia. Jewish historians at the time echoed this mistaken idea, precisely to encourage more lenient treatment of Karaites by the Nazis. Ultimately, the Karaites represented too small a group in Nazi-occupied Europe to merit the attention of the Final Solution.

Most Karaites continued to live outside the Nazi orbit in any case, in Palestine and in Egypt. Today there are approximately 4,000 Karaites in the State of Israel. Under the Law of Return, Karaites were not defined as Jews but were given the benefits of the Law of Return as a group which consistently looked to Palestine throughout the centuries of its existence.

The implications of Karaite sectarianism are significant for Jewish history. First, the growth of sectarianism reflects discontent with the prevailing rabbinic establishment. The stronger the establishment became, the greater and more natural the tendency to dissent. Secondly, the Karaites built upon the undercurrent of traditional attachment to Palestine. The rabbis counselled that Jewish life ought focus upon the diaspora, for dreams of a return to Palestine were unrealistic and, in many respects, counterproductive. Karaite popularity reflected the Jewish underpinnings of memories of a lost homeland and desire to return to it. Lastly, the Karaite experience demonstrates the limits of peoplehood. When Jews can no longer marry one another, their sense of remaining part of a united Jewish people withers away. Once Karaite practice made marriages to Jews impossible, Karaites and Rabbanites could no longer consider themselves as members of the same people. Although it is clearly a mistake to identify contemporary Jewish divisions and schisms with the Karaite-Rabbanite split of the medieval period, the principle of marriageability remains. As long as Jews can marry one another, they will retain their concept of peoplehood. Once, however, questions of personal status prevent marriages among Jews, the very definition of united peoplehood is called into question.

Reading: Moses Maimonides, "Epistle to Yemen"

The "Epistle to Yemen" by Moses Maimonides was a letter addressed to the Jews of Yemen, among whom a messianic pretender had arisen. Maimonides takes the opportunity to set forth his view of messianism, discouraging messianic activity as counterproductive. In general, he argues that we should not anticipate the messianic days as a period of massive upheaval, but rather as a restoration of order. In the meantime, rather than engage in unfruitful messianic speculation, we ought best go about our daily business.

You have adverted to the computations of the date of the redemption, and Rabbi Saadiah's opinion on the subject. First of all, it devolves upon you to know that no human being will ever be able to determine it precisely, as Daniel has intimated: *For these words are secret and sealed* [Dan. 12:9]. Indeed many hypotheses were advanced by scholars who fancied they had discovered the date. This was anticipated in his declaration: *Many will run to and fro, and opinions will be multiple* [Dan. 12:4], that is, there will be numerous views concerning it. Furthermore, God has communicated through His prophets that many people will calculate the time of the advent of the Messiah, but they will be disappointed and fail. He also cautioned us against giving way to doubt and distrust because of these miscalculations. The longer the delay the more fervently we hope, as He states: *For there is a prophecy for a set term, a truthful witness for a time, that will come. Even if it tarries, wait for it still; for it will surely come, without delay* [Hab. 2:3].

Reading: Leon Nemoy, ed., *Karaite Anthology*

Anan Ben-David is considered the founder of Karaism. The document presented here is his statement on the Sabbath and raises all of the issues of the Karaite-Rabbanite polemic. Who possessed accurate claim to interpretation of the written law? Had rabbinic Judaism not clearly departed from the spirit of Scripture in permitting the use of fire on Shabbat, so long as it had been pre-lit or kindled by a gentile? At stake here was not an arcane dispute over hermeneutics, but a conflict over authority to interpret scripture and over the rabbinic interpretation of the Sabbath as a day of delight and pleasure, in contrast to the day of gloom suggested by Karaite exegesis.

Sabbath

1. Carrying a burden, which is forbidden on the Sabbath, signifies only the act of carrying upon one's shoulder, since it is written: *they carried upon their shoulders* (Num. 7: 9).

2. [It is forbidden to light fire in Jewish homes on the Sabbath or to permit fire kindled before the arrival of the Sabbath to continue burning into the Sabbath, as it is written: *Ye shall not kindle fire in all your dwellings upon the sabbath day* (Exod. 35:3).]

3. One might perhaps say that it is only the kindling of fire on the Sabbath which is forbidden, and that if the fire had been kindled on the preceding weekday it is to be considered lawful to let it remain over the Sabbath. Now the Merciful One has written here: Ye *shall not kindle fire,* and elsewhere: *thou shalt not perform any work* (Exod. 20:10), and both prohibitions begin with the letter *taw.* In the case of labor, of which it is written: *thou shalt not perform any work,* it is evident that even if the work was begun on a weekday, before the arrival of the Sabbath, it is necessary to desist from it with the arrival of the Sabbath. The same rule must therefore apply also to the kindling of fire, of which it is written: *Ye shall not kindle,* meaning that even if the fire has been kindled on a weekday, prior to the arrival of the Sabbath, it must be extinguished.

4. In the case of work, just as one is forbidden to perform it himself, so also is he forbidden to have others perform it for him. [So, too, in the case of fire, one is forbidden to make others

kindle it for him on the Sabbath, just as one is forbidden to kindle it himself.] Thus it is clear that we are forbidden to leave either a lamp or any other light burning on the Sabbath in any Jewish home.

Bibliography for Further Reading

Cohen, Gershon D. "Messianic Postures of Ashkenazim and Sephardim," *Studies in the Variety of Rabbinic Cultures,* Jewish Publication Society, 1991

Kochan, Lionel. *Jews, Idols, and Messiahs,* Blackwell, 1990

Saperstein, Marc, ed. *Essential Papers on Messianic Movements and Personalities in Jewish History,* New York University Press, 1992

Scholem, Gershom. *The Messianic Idea in Judaism,* Schocken, 1972

Abba Hillel Silver, *A History of Messianic Speculation in Israel,* Beacon Books, 1959

Unit XIII

Medieval Jewish Philosophy and Mysticism

Jewish Philosophy

Harry Wolfson, a preeminent historian of Jewish philosophy, has argued that medieval Jewish philosophy began with Philo and modern Jewish philosophy with Spinoza. Although Philo actually lived in the Greco-Roman period (first century B.C.E.), he anticipated many of the major themes of medieval Jewish philosophy. First was the apologetic motif. Philo argued that the Jews taught philosophy to the Greeks. The basic principles of Judaism were completely harmonious with the principles of Hellenism. In attempting to argue that Judaism would pass the test of Greek culture, Philo correctly anticipated the purpose of much of medieval Jewish philosophy—to translate Judaism for intellectual circles and to prove that Jewish thought occasioned no conflict with general culture. Obviously Philo's comment that Jews taught philosophy to the Greeks is unhistorical, but it does provide an insight to the apologetic mind-set of medieval Jewish philosophers. They consistently portrayed Jews as serving as mentors for general culture and philosophy.

Secondly, the idea that Greek and Jewish philosophy could be harmonized led directly to the "double-truth" theory so popular in the Middle Ages. Faith and reason were by no means incompatible. Rather they served as two alternate sources of truth headed in parallel directions. To believe in the truths of Scripture did not require suspending one's reason. Both Jewish Scriptures and Greek philosophy aimed to inculcate the same set of truths. They simply did it via different methods.

To be sure, this "double-truth" theory posed major dilemmas, especially in cases where the record of Scripture seemingly contradicted one's perception of rational truth. This was particularly the case with reference to apparent anthropomorphisms in the Bible, wherein Scripture depicted God in human form. Statements such as "and God went down" therefore were described as strictly allegorical in meaning. For educational purposes Scriptures spoke in "a language of humanity," meaning that to enable all to understand, Scripture ascribed to God human characteristics. These could, however, in no sense be taken literally. The Talmud itself had wrestled with these apparent anthropomorphisms and had dismissed them simply as conventions of language to make the Torah accessible to humanity.

Somewhat more problematical were Scriptural stories that seemed to contradict reason. Did miracles actually occur? Was the world truly created in six days? Here too Philo argued on behalf of allegorical interpretation of Torah. The stories that clearly contradicted reason ought to be rejected so as not to demean the Almighty. By Philo's reasoning, miracles, if taken literally, suggested that nature was by no means perfect and Divine, but rather required supernatural intervention. In that sense, it was best that miracles be interpreted via natural causes. That is not to say that they did not occur, but that they can be explained naturalistically as phenomena occurring within the regular course of events. What made them miraculous was their occurring precisely at this time.

For example, the six days of creation need not be taken as six 24-hour periods but as six aeons. Joshua did not necessarily make the sun stand still; rather a solar eclipse took place at that time.

Yet Philo and his successors imposed strict limits upon allegorical interpretation. Throughout medieval Jewish philosophy virtually all Jewish thinkers insisted on the primacy of the miracle of the revelation at Sinai. This miracle was regarded as so preeminent as to defy allegorical interpretation.

In other cases Philo argued that allegorical interpretation should not mean rejection of the biblical story per se. Total rejection of the story would ultimately mean rejection of Jewish law itself. Rather, allegorical interpretation meant only attaching a level of significance to the event that transcends physical reality. Allegorical interpretation permits the rational reader to accept the truth of Scripture without accepting its literal truth. The story of the Tower of Babel, for example, may not mean literally a tower built to the heavens. Abraham, for example, need not actually have been visited by three angels, but may have imagined such an encounter. What Philo and his successors rejected wholeheartedly were attempts to have the allegorical interpretation replace completely the literal interpretation. Extreme allegorizers argued that Jewish law did not remain salient—only the ideas that the law represented remained so. Of course, this distinction in interpreting Scripture and law literally or allegorically later became a fundamental distinction between Judaism and Christianity.

Finally, Philo sought to harmonize Jewish Scriptures with Greek Platonism. The platonic theory of ideas suggested that this world was only an imperfect representation of the world of ideas. Every physical object in this world represented a perfect and unchanging idea of that object in the world of ideas or forms. This platonic dualism between physical reality and the world of forms harmonized the ancient Greek dispute over whether the world is unchanging or is constantly in flux. The world of forms was permanent and unchanging. Physical reality, by definition, was imperfect and constantly in flux.

Philo transformed this platonic dualism through his concept of *Logos,* or an intermediary which transformed the world of forms to the world of physical reality. The *Logos* roughly translates as the Word, meaning that God, acting through His spoken Word, utilized the world of forms as a blueprint for this world, transforming it into physical reality. Philo was arguing that the platonic world of forms is by no means alien to Judaism. The Torah was preexistent in the world of forms. However, to make the Torah meaningful to humanity, it required physical embodiment, expressed via creation and ultimately revelation.

The Talmud says specifically that the world was created through ten "sayings" of the Almighty bringing into existence physical reality. More pointedly, the rabbis told the legend of the angels arguing with God against granting the Torah to the Jews. The angels noted that the Torah was perfect and unchanging. Handing it over to humanity would, by definition, mean relativization and dilution. Nevertheless, God rebuked the angels, saying the Torah is meaningless unless it is given over to humanity. This beautiful Midrash in effect empowers humanity to go forward with the Torah, even if it means committing errors in its interpretation and implementation. Similarly, for Philo the world of forms is perfect. Creating a physical universe by definition means imperfection and change. Nevertheless, Philo agrees that absent the principle of creation, the world of forms remains meaningless and irrelevant to history.

This idea of the *Logos* became quite influential in later philosophy and theology. The neo-Platonists developed an entire theory of creation via emanation from God into this world—a theory adopted, in turn, by some Jewish philosophers and mystics. The kabbalists transformed the entire theory of emanations to one of "*sefirot*" or aspects of the Divinity that had been emitted by the Infinite One into this world. Lastly, of course, for Christianity the *Logos* became flesh—meaning that the word of God assumed human form so as to make God accessible to all of humanity.

Thus one can understand why Wolfson ascribes the beginning of medieval Jewish philosophy to Philo. Philo originated the apologetic motif of harmonizing Judaism with Greek culture, initiated the allegorical interpretation of Scripture as the vehicle of doing so, and created a precedent for later Jewish thinkers to harness philosophy as the handmaiden of theology. Thus Philo accomplished the primary purposes of medieval Jewish philosophy—the defense of Judaism, rationalization of Scripture, and invocation of philosophical reason to prove the truths of Jewish theology.

Medieval Jewish philosophy engaged the questions of philosophy generally. How do we know that God exists? What do we mean by the recorded attributes of God as portrayed in Scripture? How should we understand anthropomorphisms in the Bible? Most problematically, are the twin ideas of Divine providence and human freedom compatible?

Behind these questions lies again the principle of philosophy serving as the handmaiden of theology. Believers were indeed perplexed by questions of do we really know that God exists, what can we say of Him, and is freedom real or illusory: By attempting to answer these questions, philosophy assumed the goal and objective of defending theological truths to individuals impressed with the power of reason. Thus, Maimonides entitled his magnum opus *The Guide for the Perplexed*—meaning that those who doubted the truths of religion because of the persuasiveness of reason would find their appropriate guide in Maimonides's philosophical work. Again, philosophy would serve as the handmaiden of theology.

Several proofs for God's existence permeated medieval Jewish philosophy. These were often indebted to Aristotle—particularly the cosmological and the teleological proofs. The cosmological proof suggested that all that exists must have a creator. All physical objects had an efficient cause—one that brought it into existence. God served as the first cause, the initial mover who got the ball rolling by initiating the process of creation.

This proof assumed that creation occurred *ex nihilo,* that God invoked matter where nothing had previously existed. Creation occurred in time; before creation absolute nothingness existed. It was unclear, following Aristotle, what God had been doing since the moment of creation. If God served strictly as first cause, in effect there was nothing for Him to do since that time. Aristotle had conceded as much, arguing that since God was perfect, it was only appropriate that He contemplate perfection, and since God was the only perfection, Aristotle argued that God was contemplating Himself since the moment of creation. God became "Thought-thinking-Thought."

Although the cosmological proof resonated with many medieval Jewish thinkers, Aristotle's teleological proof went further in corroborating Scripture. For Aristotle, all that existed had a final cause—a purpose that explained its existence. The teleological proof served as an argument from design. If creation was so purposeful, then a Divine mind must have brought it into existence, for only such a Divine mind could have created a nature in which all that existed possessed a specific purpose or Final Cause.

Similarly, medieval Jewish philosophers were perplexed by the apparent anthropomorphisms or attributes ascribed to the Almighty. For most, these attributes were purely figures of speech—the limitations of human language in discussing phenomena that were beyond the capacity of human articulation. To say that God was "great" meant nothing save that there was no aspect of weakness within Him. The term "great" was purely a human construction that could by no means be ascribed to the Almighty. The theology of negative attributes argued that we cannot ascribe positive characteristics to God. We can only describe the absence of negative attributes. The conventions of human language dictate that we speak in a language that might appear to be anthropomorphic. The true essence of God lies beyond the capacity of language to describe effectively.

Most problematic was the apparent contradiction between Divine providence and human freedom. If God supervised individual behavior, how could that behavior truly be free? More tellingly, if God knew the future, as Divine omniscience necessitated, how could human beings truly be free to follow their own conscience?

Scripture had pointed in this direction when suggesting that God had hardened the heart of Pharaoh, preventing him from allowing the Israelites to leave. If the record of Scripture were taken literally, then there would really be no room to hold Pharaoh accountable, for he had no real choice as to whether to permit the Israelites to leave. Moreover, Scripture states explicitly that God knew that Pharaoh would not permit the Israelites to leave. If God knew the future concerning Pharaoh's decision, Pharaoh did not really have much choice in whether to listen to Moses's plea, "Let my people go."

For medieval Jewish philosophy, this question was pivotal, for it focused sharply upon the moral issues of human freedom and accountability. There could be neither merit nor demerit in human action if those actions were foreordained by God. If God knew the future, how could we really speak in terms of moral freedom rather than the determinism of human behavior?

Medieval Jewish philosophers answered this question in a variety of ways. In tenth-century Baghdad Saadiah argued again that this was a limitation of language. We speak in terms of God knowing the future, but Divine knowledge does not mean causation. Maimonides argued that what we mean by Divine knowledge is not human knowledge and therefore we can not ascribe human categories of knowledge to God. God's knowledge cannot be measured in human terms. We are therefore unable to comprehend how this problem may be solved.

Other Jewish philosophers felt that the problem of foreknowledge and free will cut more deeply than the limitations of language. In fourteenth-century France Gersonides went so far as to argue that there was indeed a contradiction between foreknowledge and free will, and therefore foreknowledge had to be limited so as to leave room for freedom of action. Gersonides argued that God knows the future in terms of the general course of history, but does not know the particulars so as to leave human behavior free on a daily basis. Hasdai Crescas, in fourteenth-century Spain, by contrast, argued that Divine providence was so central to Judaism that freedom was really only an illusion. We operate as if we are free, but Divine providence necessitates that our actions are known to God and therefore our freedom is illusory or symbolic rather than real.

Christianity, by contrast, was less perplexed by the issue of freedom. Augustine had noted that original sin required predestination of human behavior. For purposes of social construction, we operate as if we are free. Real freedom, however, was not terribly important theologically, for, in any case, all of humanity was born collectively into original sin and required a Divine act of grace to release us from sin. Judaism, by contrast, by emphasizing the law and human activity as pathways to salvation, was troubled by the prospective absence of freedom, for there could be no way of either praising or criticizing human action if people were not truly free to forge their own destinies.

Jewish Mysticism

Mysticism dealt with similar problems as did philosophy, but came to different conclusions. All religions were troubled by the apparent distance between man and God. Philosophy posited bridging that distance via the "*Logos*" or the word of God serving as a bridge between God and man. Observing God's word would, in philosophic terms, bring man closer to God.

The mystic, by contrast, posited a direct bridge within one's soul between God and humanity. The mystic aimed for more intimate union between the soul and God. Knowledge of God, for the mystic, was not simply knowledge of God's word or *Logos*, but a direct, intimate, almost carnal union between the human being and the Divine essence.

The mystics claimed that the Torah was truly a mystical document. The biblical patriarchs had obtained mystical knowledge of God. The true meaning of Torah lay not in this world of physical reality but rather in the world of the cosmos. This world and Jewish law served only to provide entry into the ultimate world of the cosmos. The mystics were arguing for alternative levels of meaning and interpretation within Torah. The literal meaning was the public and exoteric meaning. Only a small coterie of initiates knew the ultimate meaning or the mystical interpretation of Torah. This interpretation was available through the mystical text known as the *Zohar,* ascribed to a second-century Talmudic rabbi, but most likely composed in thirteenth-century Spain.

The essence of Jewish mysticism is knowledge of the *sefirot,* or Divine emanations, through which God relates to this world. Kabbalistic theosophy is knowledge of the *sefirot*—a doctrine heavily indebted to earlier forms of emanationist theory, which held that God had emanated aspects of the Divine essence to bring this world into existence. One can never truly know God—one can know only His emanations or *sefirot.* However, God does become accessible to us through these external emanations. We perceive them as if they were independent from God. Yet they constitute emanations emitted from His divine essence.

The ten *sefirot* are portrayed along the lines of the human body. The right side of the body, representing the masculine emanations of God, are symbolized by mercy or compassion. The feminine side of God, the left side of the body, symbolizes restraint or *gevurah,* implying strictness, judgment, and mastery over the passions. The distinction between masculinity and femininity suggests that neither gender can be ascribed to God. Divine emanations contain both masculine and feminine elements. Moreover, a third dimension of the *sefirot,* representing the central arteries of the body, served to unite the masculine and feminine dimensions. The last of the *sefirot,* symbolizing the human reproductive organs, not only synthesizes the *sefirot* but translates them into this world of physical reality. The symbolism of reproduction is especially poignant, in that human beings again assume roles as co-creators with God—meaning that the human capacity for reproduction enables us to translate Divine attributes and emanations into this world.

As noted earlier, this knowledge remained quite esoteric for many years. Only in Spain in the thirteenth century did Kabbala attain a more popular following. At times it was revered as much as was *halakha* itself. All kabbalists insisted upon the centrality of *halakha.* Without *halakha* there could be no mysticism. Yet mystics were suggesting that the *halakha* provided only one level of reality.

Mystics aimed at a higher level, in which unification of the human soul with the Divine emanations was possible. As this Kabbala became public, it would attain increased significance in Jewish history, particularly after the expulsion of the Jews from Spain in 1492.

Reading: ***Three Jewish Philosophers***

Next to Maimonides, Saadiah Gaon stood as the greatest of Jewish philosophers. His Book of Doctrines and Beliefs *served as a cardinal statement of medieval Jewish philosophy and a rationalist interpretation of Scripture. In the section reprinted here, Saadiah details his views concerning the messianic age. Note, in particular, that his views are inherently rational, preferring a vision of world peace to a fantastic vision of great miracles.*

> (I) In the messianic age it is expected that all creatures will believe in God and proclaim His unity, as is said, 'And the Lord shall be King over all the earth; in that day shall the Lord be one and His name One' (Zech. 14.9), but do we not see them still clinging to their errors and denial of God ? (2) In the messianic age the faithful are supposed to be free and not forced to pay tribute in money and food to other nations, as it says, 'The Lord hath sworn by His right hand . . . Surely I will no more give thy corn to be food for thine enemies; and strangers shall not drink thy wine for which thou hast laboured' (Isa. 62.8). But do we not see that every nation is compelled to pay tribute and obedience to the nation to which it is subject? (3) In the messianic age we expect the abolition of all wars between men and complete disarmament, as it says, 'And they shall beat their swords into ploughshares, and their spears into pruning-hooks; nation shall not lift up sword against nation, neither shall they learn war any more' (Isa. 2.4). But do we not see the nations fighting and contending with each other more violently than ever before? Should one try to explain that Scripture only means to say that there will be no more wars under the banner of religion, is it not the fact that religious wars and

quarrels are today more intense than ever? (4) In the messianic age the animals are expected to live peacefully one beside the other, the wolf feeding with the lamb, the lion eating straw, and the young child playing with a snake and the basilisk, as is said, 'And the wolf shall dwell with the lamb . . . and the cow and the bear shall feed . . . They shall not hurt nor destroy. . . .' (Isa. 11.6–9), whereas we see that the evil nature of the wild animals is still the same and they have not changed in any way. Should, again, someone explain that Scripture only means to say that the wicked people will live peacefully alongside with the virtuous, the facts are precisely to the contrary. For nowadays the tyranny and violence of the strong against the weak are more ruthless than ever before.

All these facts prove conclusively that the prophetic messages of comfort have not yet been fulfilled. Our refutation of the opinion held by the people we have referred to applies also to the Christians.

Gershom Scholem, ed., *The Zohar*

The Zohar, *or The Book of Splendor, is the basic text of Jewish mysticism. Much of it reads as an interpretation of* Genesis, *with the assumption that the Torah has many meanings; however, in the minds of the kabbalists, the real meaning was the hidden or secret one. In particular, the mysteries of creation were known only to the initiate. Kabbalistic knowledge, therefore, connotes the true knowledge of the wisdom of the Torah. The selection from the* Zohar *printed here refers to the kabbalistic* sefirot*—emanations from the Deity, which caused this world to come into being. Kabbalistic theosophy, or knowledge of God, is therefore knowledge of the* sefirot. *Note, in particular, how the Deity is referred to as the* Eyn Sof, *or the Infinite. This world, of course, is finite. Therefore, the* sefirot *were the mechanism by which the Infinite Deity emanated aspects of the Divine so as to bring this world into reality. Note, finally, that the author portrays this view of creation as stemming from the Talmudic reference to the world coming into existence through ten "words" uttered by God. In effect,* The Zohar *equates "words" with* sefirot*—namely, emanations from the Deity into this world.*

In this same wise has the Cause of causes derived the ten aspects of his Being which are known as *sefirot,* and named the crown the Source, which is a never-to-be-exhausted fountain of light, wherefrom he designates himself *eyn sof,* the Infinite. Neither shape nor form has he, and no vessel exists to contain him, nor any means to apprehend him. This is referred to in the words: "Refrain from search after the things that are too hard for thee, and refrain from seeking the thing which is hidden from thee."

Then He shaped a vessel diminutive as the letter *yod,* and filled it from him, and called it a Wisdom-gushing Fountain, and called himself wise on its account. And after, he fashioned a large vessel named sea, and designated it Understanding [*binah*] and himself understanding, on its account. Both wise and understanding is he, in his own essence; whereas Wisdom in itself cannot claim that title, but only through him who is wise and has made it full from his fountain; and so Understanding in itself cannot claim that title, but only through him who filled it from his own essence, and it would be rendered into an aridity if he were to go from it. In this regard, it is written, "As the waters fall from the sea, and the river is drained dry" [Job 14:11].

Finally, "He smites [the sea] into seven streams" [Isa. 11:15], that is, he directs it into seven precious vessels, the which he calls Greatness, Strength, Glory, Victory, Majesty, Foundation, Sovereignty; in each he designates himself thus: great in Greatness, strong in Strength, glorious in Glory, victorious in Victory, "The beauty of our Maker" in Majesty, righteous in Foundation [cf. Prov. 10:25]. All things, all vessels, and all the worlds does he uphold in Foundation.

In the last, in Sovereignty, he calls himself King, and he is "the greatness, and the strength, and the glory, and the victory, and the majesty; for all that is in heaven and in the earth is Thine. Thine is the kingdom, O Lord, and Thou are exalted as head above all" [I Chron. 29:11]/ In his power lie all things, be it that he chooses to reduce the number of vessels, or to increase the light issuing therefrom, or be it the contrary. But over him, there exists no deity with power to increase or reduce.

Also, he made beings to serve these vessels: each a throne

supported by four columns, with six steps to the throne, in all, ten. Altogether, the throne is like the cup of benediction about which ten statements were made [in the Talmud], harmonious with the Torah, which was given in Ten Words [The Decalogue], and with the Ten Words by which the world was created.

Bibliography for Further Reading

Funkenstein, Amos. *Perceptions of Jewish History,* University of California Press, 1993

Guttmann, Julius. *Philosophies of Judaism,* Schocken, 1973

Husik, Isaac. *A History of Medieval Jewish Philosophy,* Athenaeum, 1969

Scholem, Gershom. *Major Trends in Jewish Mysticism,* Schocken, 1955

———. *Kabbalah,* Quadrangle Books, 1974

Wolfson, Harry. *Philo,* Vols. 1–2, Harvard University Press, 1947

Unit XIV

The Crusades and the Jews

Doctrine of the Witness

According to the Church Fathers, Jews bore witness to the truth of Christianity. "Israel after the flesh," i.e. the Jews, continued to have a place in God's Divine scheme because their sheer being testified to the pre-Christian existence of Scriptures. Antiquity was a sign of legitimacy in the medieval world. Jewish presence provided Christianity with antiquity and thereby testified to the truth of Christianity.

Secondly, Jewish existence testified to Christian truth in a more political and physical sense. The low status of Jews in medieval Europe signified their punishment for their rejection of Jesus. The Crucifixion had occurred in approximately the year 30 C.E. Only one generation later, in 70 C.E., had the Jerusalem Temple been destroyed, signifying the onset of the exile. Christians connected these events. No sooner had the Jews rejected Jesus than God had rejected the Jews as a people. Continued Jewish existence in medieval Christendom, coupled with their low status as a people, served as a constant historical reminder of the punishment of the Jews and the triumph of Christianity. Augustine, summarizing much of the sentiment of the Church Fathers, advised that the Jews should be maintained in a lowly status, but should not be destroyed. On the contrary, they must be kept alive for, at the end of days, they will be converted to the true faith as part of the Second Coming.

The Doctrine of the Witness signified yet another aspect of the complicated relationship between Jewry and medieval Christendom. On the one hand, Jews were cursed for having rejected Jesus. On the other hand, they were revered as God's Chosen People and the people of the Old Testament. Thus, for example, Pope Gregory the Great in the seventh century issued a papal bull, "*Sicut Judaeis*," condemning the compulsory baptism of Jews. Persuading Jews to convert was Gregory's preferred model. However, if forcibly converted, Jews may not return to Judaism. Gregory offered tax benefits for Jews to convert and permitted Jews to live in accordance with traditional Roman law. Jewish property must be protected. Simultaneously, Gregory condemned Judaism as a "superstitio" and a "perditio."

Inside the Jewish community, the most critical innovations of the time were spearheaded by the leading interpreter of rabbinic law, Rabbenu Gershom of Mainz, commonly referred to as "the light of the exile." Gershom's most significant innovations lay in the area of Jewish family law. For the first time he outlawed bigamy. Similarly, he decreed that no one may divorce a wife against her will. Clearly these *takkanot*, or rabbinic legislations, were motivated by a desire to improve the condition of women. Although one could by no means impose twentieth-century egalitarian categories upon tenth-century rabbinic legislation, one can detect a growing evolution in rabbinic legislation demonstrating greater concern and sensitivity to the position and rights of women within Jewish family law.

The Crusades

Ambivalence concerning Jews reflected itself most vividly during the period of the Crusades, which were ostensibly efforts to liberate Palestine from the hands of the Moslems, yet, in practice, were often preceded by general pogroms against Jews. Calls for Crusades emanated from the senior leadership within the Church. Yet Crusader violence often stemmed from below. The clergy generally offered whatever protection there was to be had for Jews. Simultaneously, the violent sermons of clergy against Jews provided the ideological rationale and justification for Crusader anti-Jewish violence. The Popes ordered the Crusaders to desist from attacking Jews and to restore their lost property. However, the very same authorities that called for the Crusades often issued the most incendiary anti-Jewish sermons and statements.

The tangible impact of Crusader violence against Jews was in fact quite limited. Approximately 5,000 Jews died during the First Crusade of 1096. These killings formed part of a general pattern of anarchy and lawlessness. The major Jewish communities of Worms, Mainz, and Cologne were destroyed. However, Jewish life subsequently was reconstructed. In other areas, the Jews were barely touched by the Crusades. The Crusades did not mark a fundamental turning point in medieval Jewish existence. They did mark a shift in Jewish values and self-perception under the impact of the Crusades. That impact was considerably more cultural and psychological than physical or political. After the First Crusade, those Jews who had converted to Christianity under duress were permitted to return to Judaism, despite the theological opposition of the Church to their doing so.

More significantly, Jews expressed a range of reactions to Crusader violence. The instinctive reaction was to appeal to the authorities for protection. This often came from the secular emperor or nobles, as well as church figures themselves. Secondly, wherever possible, Jews engaged in self-defense. The myth of Jewish powerlessness is clearly overstated. Thirdly, the Jews dealt directly with the Crusaders, frequently resorting to bribery. Fourthly, Jews turned to their neighbors for assistance as well as rescue. Jews invoked the model of Queen Esther and her response to Haman—fasting, bribery, appealing to the king for protection, and finally self-defense. As a result, the Purim holiday symbolized throughout the medieval period the one day during the year when Jews felt free to vent their frustrations at Christian authorities and "turn the tables" by satirizing Christian oppressors.

The willingness to undergo martyrdom served only as the last, albeit best-known, of these responses. What Jews feared most was their children falling into Christian hands. Hence, they were willing to undergo martyrdom rather than see their children become Christians. Martyrdom was generally approved by rabbinic authorities. Jews turned to the Talmud for precedents, noting that 400 young Jewish men and women had drowned in the Mediterranean rather than be brought to Rome by Titus where they presumably would be violated and reared under pagan auspices.

Theologically, this became the ideology of *kiddush Hashem,* or "sanctification of God's name"—a willingness to undergo martyrdom for the sake of the Almighty. The rabbis in the Talmud had discussed this notion in terms of three sins to be avoided under all circumstances, even at the price of martyrdom—namely, committing murder, adultery, and worshiping pagan deities. However, the ideology of *"kiddush Hashem,"* had different levels. First was the willingness to allow oneself to be killed. This constituted the preferred model of martyrdom—permitting oneself to be martyred rather than commit a crime. Suicide constituted only the second level. Some precedents existed (e.g. the Talmudic tale of the young men and women whom Titus had captured), but clearly suicide was by no means the preferred model. Far more preferable was waiting until the oppressor actually committed the murder. The final level, and the most problematical, was taking the lives of others, particularly women and children. This was totally unjustified in Jewish tradition and blurred the lines between suicide and murder. Although it reflected the heightened religiosity of the times and milieu, perhaps invoking Jewish memories of bringing sacrifices to the Temple or Abraham's intention to sacrifice Isaac, this killing of children could not be justified by recourse to Jewish tradition.

Significantly, this ideology of martyrdom, or sanctification of God's name, constituted an Ashkenazic response to persecution rather than a Sephardic one. Sephardim prided themselves on being able to accept externally a new faith yet secretly preserve Judaism. The Ashkenazic sources pointed to the Maccabean model of Hannah and her seven children, who were willing to die rather than submit to Greek paganism. Theologically, Ashkenazic authorities had interpreted the exile and its travails as a punishment for sin. Now they viewed the travails of exile as a test of the righteous. Just as Abraham had been tested in being asked to sacrifice Isaac, so the Jews of today were being tested by God via the Crusaders. Perceiving these travails as a test, rather than punishment, in turn made Divine reward inevitable. Again the dream of restoration constituted the message of consolation during a time of troubles.

Moreover, the ideology of martyrdom served as the mirror image of the Crusaders themselves. The Crusaders believed that they were doing God's work in removing the infidels. They were prepared to engage in sacrifice of self and were certain of receiving eternal reward and final vindication. The martyrs thus perceived themselves much as the Crusaders perceived themselves.

To be sure, the killing of children constituted a radically new element. The only comparable incident had been that of Masada, yet Masada had been long forgotten and certainly did not serve as a model for medieval Jewish existence. Leading rabbinic authorities generally were not prepared to endorse the actions of those who killed their children, although at least one attempted such a defense. They treated suicide with ambivalence, saying that under the circumstances suicide could not be considered a sin. However, they usually remained silent concerning the action of the martyrs in killing their children. Such an extreme action could not be justified no matter how noble the motives.

In later Jewish history the imagery of martyrdom became the dominant imagery of the Crusades. However, it is most important to remember that martyrdom was only the most extreme of a wide series of reactions ranging from self-defense to bribery to the search for allies. The ideology of martyrdom, of course, was developed further as an expression of Jewish religious superiority. Ashkenazic Jews modelled their behavior on Temple sacrifices. Sacrifices reflected a vicarious atonement for the Jews of the future, and were a paradigm for martyrdom—giving oneself totally to service to God.

Rabbinic leadership faced the challenge of reconstructing Jewish life in the aftermath of the Crusades. In particular, the rabbis were concerned to merge the commemoration of sadness with joy. For example, the *yizkor* memorial prayer was recited on holidays and days of Jewish celebration. The rabbis rejected the "mourners of Zion" who would eat no meat and perpetually mourned Jerusalem. Instead, rabbis developed *memorbuchs* and recorded the names of those who had been martyred. They also developed "second Purim" days, commemorating redemption of Jews from medieval oppressors. Their message was to remember the past but to continue into the future.

Medieval Charters

The Crusades exposed the vulnerability of the Jews and their need for protection if they were to persevere in Europe. As a result, medieval rulers began issuing special charters of protection to Jews, under which Jews fell directly under the sovereignty of the Crown. On the one hand, this reflected a further reduction in the status of the Jews, for they became, by the 1230s, "serfs of the royal chamber," meaning the direct property of the king. On the other hand, as they were the direct property of the king, damage to Jews necessitated payment to the royal crown.

Where pre-Crusade Jewry had been involved in building cities in Europe, post-Crusade Jewry was now increasingly pushed into usury as its primary economic function. The Church regarded interest and wealth as sinful, and prevented Christians from engaging in credit loans. Jews fulfilled this function for Christians by issuing loans, often at extremely steep interest rates, because the risk was so great and the danger of never receiving repayment quite high. The rise of capitalism, to be sure, removed this last economic function from Jews, as a credit economy became universal in the European world.

Indeed, Jews began leaving Western Europe in the centuries following the Crusades. They were expelled from England in 1290, from France in 1306 and again in 1394, and from Spain in 1492. Throughout the sixteenth century a variety of German states and principalities took their turns at expelling the Jews, so that by 1600 there were few Jews left in Western Europe.

However, in Eastern Europe during these years Jews were being invited to settle. The Polish monarchy was interested in settling Jews along its frontier areas and issued charters inviting Jews to settle there. Polish Jewry experienced a significant demographic growth spurt, so that by 1600 Poland represented the largest demographic reservoir of world Jewry. Poland, in effect, became the center of world Jewry until the partitions of Poland in the eighteenth century marked her collapse as a nation-state. Communal autonomy, meaning the right of the Jews to regulate their own affairs—as to education, law, tax collecting, and religious and welfare services, continued to be the hallmark and mainstay of diaspora Jewry and now found its most vivid expression in Polish Jewry.

In the aftermath of the Crusades, the papacy attained its greatest influence and stature in Europe. Every pope would renew Jewish rights by issuing a special "*constitutio pro judaeis.*" Jews greeted each new pope and requested the renewal of their rights. Popes consistently condemned the blood libel and promised continued Jewish security. Simultaneously, of course, the popes proclaimed the Jews to be in perpetual servitude, owing to the guilt of the Crucifixion. Thomas Aquinas, perhaps the leading Christian theologian of the Middle Ages, summarized the position of the Church succinctly. For Aquinas, the key was not to eliminate the Jews, but rather to prevent their fostering heresies among the Christian population. The Church began intervening in the internal literature of the Jews, particularly the Talmud. Churchmen argued that Jews in fact knew the truth of Christianity, but nevertheless they rejected Jesus. In contrast to Augustine, who argued that Jews did not know the truth of Jesus, the new charge against the Jews lay in their steadfastness—their unwillingness to confront reality.

A number of debates were held concerning the Talmud itself. Churchmen argued that the Talmud was a pernicious document and had to be destroyed. Popes such as Innocent IV defended Jewish possession of the Talmud, yet the Talmud was now censored so as not to offend Christianity. References to Jesus were excised. Thus, Church censorship of the Talmud placed the Church authorities in the curious position of determining Jewish text.

Jewish attitudes to Christianity also ranged. Although they generally exempted Islam from the charge of paganism, owing to its insistence upon the unity of God, Jewish thinkers remained divided as to whether this applied to medieval Christianity as well. Perhaps the majority sentiment was that the Christian doctrines of Trinity and Incarnation qualified it as idolatrous. The most liberal position was suggested by Rabbi Menahem Meiri, in the eleventh century, who exempted Christianity from the charge of idolatry. Generally, Jewish thinkers agreed that both Christianity and Islam constituted significant progress in history over classical paganism. They disagreed over whether the classical strictures against paganism applied to contemporary Christianity. Moses Maimonides assigned Christianity a status higher than paganism and called both Christianity and Islam effective preparers, "those who straighten the road," for the messianic era.

The overall picture remained one of oppression. Attitudes toward Jews deteriorated during the years of the Black Death, when there were charges that Jews had polluted the wells of Europe. The conception of the Jew in the latter part of the Middle Ages portrayed Jewry as allied with the devil, as possessing a tail and emitting a foul stench. Most strikingly, the infamous blood libels now recurred repeatedly, despite being condemned by virtually every authority. Following a charge that the Jew desecrated the Christian host, namely the wafer used in the sacrament of transubstantiation, a pogrom ensued in 1298 known as the Rindfleisch Massacres, which claimed at least 3,400 martyrs.

Clearly, the physical security of the Jews had deteriorated. In England, despite the absence of Jews after 1290, the sermons of the English friars became vitriolic in their anti-Jewishness. Medieval anti-Semitism, precisely because of its theological roots, provided protection against the complete elimination of the Jews. The Doctrine of the Witness rationalized continued Jewish existence and insisted that Jews must be preserved until the end of days. While medieval society excluded Jews and even condemned them, it still protected them and prevented the wholesale elimination that became the horror of twentieth-century Nazism.

Lastly, Jews preserved their communal autonomy throughout the medieval period. Jews were able to regulate their own affairs, adjudicating disputes in Jewish courts, collecting their own taxes, appointing their own religious officials, and educating their young. The powers of medieval Jewish *kehillot,* or communities, were quite considerable. The *kehilla* enforced its will through the *herem,* or ban of excommunication. In extreme cases, its power even extended to capital punishment, most notably in cases of informers against the community.

The most renowned Jewish communal leader in the aftermath of the Crusades was Rabbi Solomon Itzhaki, better known as Rashi. Justly renowned for his biblical and Talmudic commentary which effectively provided a guide to virtually all of the books of the Bible and most of the Talmudic tractates, Rashi assumed also a role of communal leadership given the crises of the late eleventh and early twelfth centuries. Most importantly, when Jews who had accepted baptism were allowed to return to Judaism, Rashi counseled tolerance and acceptance. Although others criticized these Jews for failure to live up to the ideals of martyrdom, Rashi recognized both the human limitations and communal needs mandating welcome and acceptance of those who had suffered so severely during the Crusader trauma.

Reading: Robert Chazan, *European Jewry and the First Crusade*

The Crusade Chronicle *of Solomon Bar-Simson recorded the travails of the Jews during the First Crusade. Of particular importance was its ideology of martyrdom, extolling those Jews who were prepared to accept death rather than submit to conversion to Christianity. Note in particular the analogy to the sacrifice of Isaac. The martyrs of the Crusades perceived themselves as eternal sacrifices—"like sheep to the slaughter" for the sake of the Almighty.*

The enemy, immediately upon entering the courtyard, found there some of the perfectly pious with Rabbi Isaac ben R. Moses the dialectician. He stretched out his neck and they cut off his head immediately. They had clothed themselves in their fringed garments and had seated themselves in the midst of the courtyard in order to do speedily the will of their Creator. They did not wish to flee to the chambers in order to go on living briefly. Rather, with love they accepted upon themselves the judgment of heaven. The enemy rained stones and arrows upon them, but they did not deign to flee. They struck down all those whom they found there, with "blows of sword, death, and destruction."

Those in the chambers, when they saw this behavior on the part of those saintly ones and that the enemy had come upon them, all cried out: "There is nothing better than to offer ourselves as a sacrifice." There women girded themselves with strength and slaughtered their sons and daughters, along with themselves. Many men likewise gathered strength and slaughtered their wives and their children and their little ones. "The tenderest and daintiest" slaughtered "their beloved children. " They all stood—men and women—and slaughtered one another. The young women and the brides and the bridegrooms gazed through the windows and cried out loudly: "Behold and see, our God, what we do for the sanctification of your holy Name, rather than deny you for a crucified one, a trampled and wretched and abominable offshoot, a bastard and a child of menstruation and lust. " "The precious children of Zion," the children of Mainz, were tested ten times, like our ancestor Abraham and like Hananiah, Mishael, and Azariah. They offered up their children as did Abraham with his son Isaac. They accepted upon themselves the yoke of the fear of heaven, of the King of kings, the Holy One, blessed be he, willingly. They did not wish to deny the awe of our King or to exchange it for [that of] "a loathsome offshoot, " a bastard born of menstruation and lust. They stretched forth their necks for the slaughter and commended their pure souls to their Father in heaven. The saintly and pious women stretched forth their necks one to another, to be sacrificed for the unity of the [Divine] Name. Likewise men to their children and brothers, brothers to sisters, women to their sons and daughters, and neighbor to neighbor and friend, bridegroom to bride, and betrothed to his betrothed. They sacrificed each other until the blood flowed together. The blood of husbands mingled with that of their wives, the blood of parents with that of their children, the blood of brothers with that of their sisters, the blood of teachers with that of their students, the blood of bridegrooms with that of their brides, the blood of cantors with that of their scribes, the blood of infants and sucklings with that of their mothers. They were killed and slaughtered for the unity of the revered and awesome Name. At such reports "the ears of those who hear must surely tingle." "For who has heard the like? Who has ever witnessed such events?" "Ask and see." Were there ever so many sacrifices like these from the days of Adam? Were there ever a thousand one hundred sacrifices on one day, all of them like the sacrifice of Isaac the son of Abraham? For one the world shook, when he was offered up on Mount Moriah, as is said: "Hark! The angels cried aloud!" The heavens darkened. What has been done [this time]? "Why did the heavens not darken? Why did the stars not withdraw their brightness?" . . . and light—"why did they not darken in their cloud cover," when one thousand one hundred holy souls were killed and slaughtered on one day, on the third day of Sivan, a Tuesday—infants and sucklings who never transgressed and never sinned and poor and innocent souls? "At such things will you restrain yourself, O Lord?" "For your sake they were killed"—innumerable souls. "Avenge the blood of your servants that has been spilled" in our days and before our eyes speedily. Amen.

Reading: Solomon Grayzel, ed., *The Church and the Jews in the Thirteenth Century*

The edict of Innocent III is an example of papal edicts offering protection to Jews. It forbids compulsory conversion or baptism as well as violence against Jews. Note the critique of Judaism as misunderstanding its doctrine of law and the continued humiliation of Jewry, even if Jews are not to be completely destroyed. Papal pronouncements such as these emanated directly from the Doctrine of the Witness, which simultaneously insisted that the Jews be kept low yet forbade violence against them.

September 15, 1199—An Edict in Favor of the Jews

Although the Jewish perfidy is in every way worthy of condemnation, nevertheless, because through them the truth of our own Faith is proved, they are not to be severely oppressed by the faithful. Thus the Prophet says, "Thou shalt not kill them, lest at any time they forget thy law," or more clearly stated, thou shalt not destroy the Jews completely, so that the Christians should never by any chance be able to forget Thy Law, which, though they themselves fail to understand it, they display in their book to those who do understand.

Therefore, just as license ought not to be granted the Jews to presume to do in their synagogues more than the law permits them, just so ought they not to suffer curtailment in those (privileges) which have been conceded them. That is why, although they prefer to remain hardened in their obstinacy rather than acknowledge the prophetic words and the eternal secrets of their own scriptures, that they might thus arrive at the understanding of Christianity and Salvation, nevertheless, in view of the fact that they begged for our protection and our aid, and in accordance with the clemency that Christian piety imposes, we, following in the footsteps of our predecessors of happy memory, the popes Calixtus, Eugene, Alexander, Clement, and Coelestine, grant their petition and offer them the shield of our protection.

We decree that no Christian shall use violence to force them to be baptized as long as they are unwilling and refuse, but that if anyone of them seeks refuge among the Christians of his own free will and by reason of his faith, (only then,) after his willingness has become quite clear, shall he be made a Christian without subjecting himself to any calumny. For surely none can be believed to possess the true faith of a Christian who is known to have come to Christian baptism not willingly, and even against his wishes.

Moreover, without the judgment of the authority of the land, no Christian shall presume to wound their persons, or kill (them) or rob them of their money, or change the good customs which they have thus far enjoyed in the place where they live. Furthermore, while they celebrate their festivals, no one shall disturb them in any way by means of sticks or stones, nor exact from any of them forced service, except that which they have been accustomed to perform from ancient times. In opposition to the wickedness and avarice of evil men in these matters, we decree that no one shall presume to desecrate or reduce the cemetery of the Jews, or, with the object of extorting money to exhume bodies there buried. If any one, however, after being acquainted with the contents of this decree, should presume to act in defiance of it (which God forbid), he shall suffer loss of honor and office, or he shall be restrained by the penalty of excommunication, unless he shall have made proper amends for his presumption.

We wish, however, to place under the protection of this decree only those (Jews) who have not presumed to plot against the Christian Faith.

Bibliography for Further Reading

Chazan, Robert. *European Jewry and the First Crusade,* University of California Press, 1987

Cohen, Jeremy. *The Friars and the Jews,* Cornell University Press, 1982

Stow, Kenneth R. *Alienated Minority: Jews of Medieval Latin Europe,* Harvard University Press, 1992

Unit XV

Islamic Jewish Culture

The Spanish Golden Age and Moses Maimonides

The Golden Age of Spain

Jewish life in medieval Moslem Spain remains the critical era of Islamic-Jewish symbiosis. To be sure, the concept of the Golden Age was perhaps more mythical than real. Politically, for example, the Golden Age was by no means free of persecution. In other respects, the Golden Age meant more to Jews and Jewish scholars than it meant to Spanish society, for the concept of the Golden Age of Spain became part of the intellectual baggage by which nineteenth-century Jewish intellectuals argued for Jewish emancipation and equality. Integrate the Jews into civil society, they insisted, and indeed the Jews will create a veritable Golden Age.

What the Spanish Golden Age did mean was that beginning with the Moslem conquest of Spain in 711 C.E. to the Almohade conquest in 1148, Jewish life in Spain was relatively secure (although the Moslem restrictions on *dhimmis* and insistence upon second-class status remained in force). The stability that Moslem rule provided and the relative absence of persecution generally nurtured a structure wherein Jewish culture could flourish. Jews contributed to virtually all areas of literature, from poetry to *halakhic* literature. Perhaps nineteenth-century Jewish scholars retrospectively overrated the quality of Spanish Jewish poetry and its centrality to Spanish culture. Yet one cannot overlook the diversity and richness of the poetry, covering virtually all subjects, both religious and secular, from liturgical elegies to military and even love poetry.

Sustaining this poetry was the adaptation of the Hebrew language to poetic meter. Jews argued that culturally whatever Moslems could accomplish, Jews could do better. Therefore they turned to Hebrew poetry to reply to the Moslem argument that Arabic was the most beautiful language and the Koran the most beautiful book. Jewish poets responded that the Hebrew language was truly the most aesthetic language. Apparent deficiencies in the Hebrew vocabulary existed only because many words had been forgotten and therefore had to be revised. Spanish Jewish grammarians advanced significantly the study of Hebrew grammar so as to facilitate the development of a Hebrew-language poetry.

Spanish Jewish culture also turned to history and historical scholarship. Rabbinic culture had by and large abandoned historical reasoning and historiography. As Jewish historian Yosef Yerushalmi has argued, in the medieval period Jewish memory replaced historical recording. However, in eleventh-century Spain Abraham Ibn Daud composed the *Sefer HaQabbalah,* a book that composed a chain of tradition from ancient to medieval times, legitimating rabbinic authority in Spain on the grounds that the rabbis of Spain were the heirs of the rabbinic academies of Babylonia, which in turn were the heirs of the rabbinic academies of Palestine. By writing the history of rabbinism, Ibn Daud thereby polemicized against Karaism, which claimed that rabbinic tradition was fraudulent and the Karaite tradition authentic. Moreover, Ibn Daud harnessed historiography to buttress rabbinic political theory. Rebellion against the gentiles had proven to be a failure. The rebellion of Bar Kokhba had resulted in a catastrophe to the Jewish people. By invoking historical precedent, Ibn Daud again articulated the rabbinic political theory of accommodation to gentile rule, working within the diaspora, and relegating messianic aspirations to the far-off future. Lastly, Ibn Daud told the tale of the story of four captives—four rabbinic scholars taken prisoner on a boat and ransomed by their respective Jewish communities. Although historians have cast doubt about the authenticity of the tale, it reflected the Jewish value of responsibility for the rescue of captives and, more importantly, served as a paradigm for the transmission of Jewish teaching from the Babylonian academies to

Spain. In effect, the Spanish Jewish academies claimed that they were the authentic bearers of Jewish tradition, because the teachings of Babylonia had been transmitted to Spanish rabbinical authorities.

Spain also became renowned for the quality of its biblical exegesis. Spanish exegesis specialized in explaining the text grammatically and rationalistically. Abraham Ibn Ezra stands as the finest example of the rationalist mode of exegesis. Ibn Ezra rarely departs from the plain sense of Scripture. Nor does he hesitate to take issue with other exegetes, e.g. Rashi, who at times substituted a homiletical meaning for a literal or historical one.

Spanish Jewish intellectuals also focused upon the writing of philosophy, following the criteria of medieval Jewish philosophy generally, which harnessed philosophy as the handmaiden for theology. Thus Solomon Ibn Gabirol, best known for his religious poetry, composed the *Fons Vitae* under the pen name of Avicebrol, a neo-Platonic tract on creation. Ibn Daud followed in the footsteps of Aristotle in his Hebrew book *Emunah Ramah.* Judah Halevi, perhaps the best known Spanish Jewish philosopher and poet, in his book *The Kuzari,* reacted against the Spanish admiration of Greek philosophy. Although Halevi, too, followed in Aristotle's footsteps in articulating a theology of negative attributes, he essentially relegated philosophy to second-class status. Jews, according to Halevi, had no need for philosophy, for theirs is the gift of prophecy. Salo Baron notes that Halevi was protesting the intellectualized Judaism of the upper classes. By insisting upon the chosenness of the Jews, Halevi was arguing that Jews did not require the culture of the gentiles and instead should be proud of their own heritage.

Halevi's vision of Judaism is often criticized as too exclusionary. For example, he goes so far as to argue that converts to Judaism can never attain prophecy, because that is exclusively a gift for the biological children of Abraham. Yet his emphasis upon Jewish national pride and love of homeland—as in his famous poem, "I am in the West and my heart is in the East"—served as an appropriate historical corrective to the heavy emphasis on diaspora and diaspora culture among Spanish Jewish leadership. Halevi reminded Spanish Jewry that exile remains exile and that the Jews as a people possess a historical homeland in the land of Israel.

This ambivalence about Spain and the Spanish exile can be found even among the Jewish courtier class, diplomats who rose to the highest positions in Spanish government. The court Jews frequently utilized their influential positions to patronize the flourishing of Jewish arts. Yet even as senior a diplomat as Hasdai Ibn Shaprut, *nasi* or prince of the Jewish community and physician and diplomatic representative of the caliph of Cordoba, wrote to the king of the Khazars in Southern Russia that he would gladly surrender all he had in Spain to live under a Jewish government and in a Jewish sovereign state.

Nevertheless, Spanish Jewry prided itself on its cultural eminence. Spanish Jews regarded themselves as the elite of European Jewry and as the most politically secure. Therefore, when persecution did come to Spain, it was all the more shocking. The Almohade invasion of 1148 signalled the end of the Golden Age. The Almohades derided Judaism as anthropomorphic in nature and offered Jews the alternatives of expulsion from Spain or conversion to Islam. Although Spanish Jewry was able to recover and persisted under Christian rule until 1492, never again did it attain the cultural preeminence that it had enjoyed during the Golden Age.

Moses Maimonides

Maimonides and his family fled Spain during the Almohade persecutions. Some have suggested that Maimonides's leniency toward forced converts to Islam reflected his own biographical experience. In his "Letter on Martyrdom," Maimonides advised converts to observe Islam externally, practice Judaism as much as possible in secret, and then leave at the earliest possible opportunity. This appears to have been the pattern of Maimonides's own family, which was caught in the Almohade persecutions and left shortly afterwards for North Africa, before finally settling in Egypt. Whether Maimonides himself ever actually became a Marrano cannot be proven. However, his experience mirrors the advice he gave to those undergoing persecutions.

In Egypt Maimonides rose quickly to the heights of communal leadership. He earned his living as physician and vizier to the Moslem caliphs and thereby became a spokesman for the Jews. He and his family for centuries afterwards occupied the Egyptian Jewish office of Nagid, or prince of the Jews, signifying ongoing Jewish communal self-government. The community was indeed a united community, combining Rabbanite, Samaritan, and Karaite elements. Its leaders possessed judicial authority, the power to supervise communal officials, and control over marriages and divorces. Those who defied its will were subject to the power of excommunication, forbidding Jews any social or economic contact with the individual. Thus Egyptian Jewry preserved all of the hallmarks of medieval Jewish autonomy.

What were the works of Maimonides? *The Mishneh Torah* served as a comprehensive code, summarizing and synthesizing all of Jewish law. *The Guide for the Perplexed,* his most famous work, began as an attempt to explain biblical anthropomorphisms and the theology of negative attributes. It moved from there to a host of other philosophical subjects, all of which concerned the "perplexed" of the day. The *Epistle to Yemen* was a letter downplaying messianic ferment. He cautioned the Jews of Yemen not to believe in any messianic pretender until such time as the individual had proven himself. On the contrary, at the end of days there would doubtless be a flurry of messianic pretenders. Messianism itself raised unrealistic expectations. Maimonides sought to repudiate these by arguing that at the end of days the world will continue as normal. No major upheavals will take place. Rather peace will prevail, and the Jews will live in security.

Moreover, Maimonides cautioned that Jewish experience with messianic movements had been counterproductive. Many had tried to predict the end of days, and all had failed. Astrological predictions, in particular, he derided as utter nonsense. But focusing on messianism itself was unhealthy, for it would insure the wrath of gentile nations, divert the Jews from their real needs and day-to-day living, and discourage the masses when the predictions proved to be false.

Maimonides, like his rabbinic forebears, encouraged instead a constructive messianism focusing on the messianic idea and dream of restoration, rather than on concrete political efforts to change the political status quo. To Maimonides, the messianic idea approached the nineteenth-century idea of progress. The world will gradually improve via a long period of human endeavor. This vision of messianism offered political security, enabling the Jews to devote themselves to God. The messiah himself would remain a human being, a mortal who would ultimately succumb to death as well. This naturalized messianism was meant to dampen unrealistic expectations that were at best wasteful of Jewish energies, at worst likely to ensure psychological disappointment.

The *Epistle on Martyrdom* was one of Maimonides's earliest works. In it he advised on conduct during persecution. Islam should not be equated with idolatry, given the Islamic insistence upon monotheism. Therefore Maimonides justified temporary apostasy, out of compulsion but not out of belief, observing Judaism in secret, and ultimately emigration at the earliest possibility. Perhaps, as mentioned earlier, this was autobiographical. More likely it was meant to counteract charges concerning Jews who would not accept martyrdom. Maimonides argued that martyrdom was by no means the sole response to persecution. Jews ought not despair over their failure to embrace martyrdom.

Maimonides was functioning here as a communal leader taking responsibility for the fate of the Jews. Theologically, he maintained that Islam was monotheist. Conversion to Islam entailed a statement that "there was no God but Allah and Mohammed is his prophet." Although this statement would be regarded as false by any believing Jew, it did not constitute a profession of belief that contradicted the foundations of Jewish faith. Jews agreed on the unity of the deity, but rejected Mohammed as God's prophet. Conversion to Islam by no means entailed affirming a belief as alien as the Trinity of Christianity.

Maimonides's last work was his *Essay on Resurrection.* This was a response to his detractors, who argued that most likely Maimonides denied resurrection of the dead. He had not mentioned it in his philosophic works. To some extent, it contradicted his philosophic ethos that saw the greatest good in an afterlife in which the human soul will contemplate the Almighty. By this reasoning, what good was resurrection, if all it did was restore us to our earthly existence and thereby divert us from pursuing the highest good of intellectual contemplation of the Divine beauty?

In this essay, Maimonides responded that he did believe in resurrection. He regarded it as a dogma about which one cannot philosophize. Therefore he did not elaborate upon it, for he had nothing to add to it. However, he noted that resurrection will definitely take place at the end of days, although those resurrected will ultimately die again. Whether this was, as Leo Strauss has argued, "persecution and the art of writing"—namely a concession to the popular feelings of the day—or whether Maimonides truly believed in resurrection cannot be fully determined. Clearly, it did not fit into his philosophical system. Conversely, he did include resurrection within his catechism of thirteen principles, arguing that one who denied it had lost one's share in the world to come.

Throughout his writings Maimonides incorporated Aristotle's dictum of the Golden Mean—pursue moderation and avoid extremes. Perhaps he downplayed resurrection precisely because his focus was on the here and now. He did not wish to encourage belief in miracles that violated the natural order, nor did he wish people to do the good in expectation of receiving a reward.

Perhaps Maimonides was at his most daring in his method of study of Torah. He placed the Torah in the historical context of the times as a battle with paganism and an attempt to wean the Jews away from idolatry. Prohibitions in the Torah, in Maimonides's view, reflected prohibitions of pagan practices. Where paganism invoked magic and supernatural behavior, Judaism invoked ethics.

The most controversial of these analyses concerned the ritual of sacrifices. Maimonides believed that prayer clearly was superior to sacrifices, for prayer was universal and was not restricted to Jerusalem. The prophets, in fact, had criticized sacrifices. Maimonides argued that historical process was at work here. Judaism could not prohibit sacrifices overnight, but rather would have to permit animal sacrifices so as to prevent the Jews from sacrificing to false gods. To be sure, Maimonides argued that sacrifices will return at the end of days, for reasons that remain unclear. In practice, he implied that historical progress would make sacrifices unnecessary and undesirable.

That same historical process applies to monotheism itself. For Maimonides, the world had begun with monotheism, had lapsed into paganism, and Christianity and Islam had paved the way for a monotheistic restoration. Christians and Moslems who followed "the covenant of Noah,"natural law, as legislated by God, merited salvation.

The Maimonidean Controversy

Why, then, did the writings of Maimonides polarize the Jewish world? Some, as noted, have argued that he did not believe in resurrection. Others maintained that Maimonides suggested that his *Mishneh Torah* would supersede the study of Talmud. Still others focused upon his unequivocal rejection of astrology, which other Jewish thinkers regarded as legitimate and as a possible vehicle to resolving the problem of Divine omniscience and human freedom—i.e. that God knew the future by knowing the path of the stars but not by knowing human action.

Over the course of the next century, the controversy split the Jewish community. A ban was placed on some Maimonidean writings. Christian authorities burned the *Guide to the Perplexed* as a threat to orthodox Christianity as well as to orthodox Judaism. Needless to add, Maimonides's opponents failed to realize that this act would serve as a precedent for further Inquisitorial intervention in Jewish affairs.

At issue was Maimonides's rationalism and its place within Judaism. He had elevated the study of philosophy to a religious obligation. He had rejected literalism in explaining Scriptures. For example, he explained that the story of the talking ass of Balaam in the Book of Numbers was an imaginary vision rather than a physical reality. Similarly, he had tried to rationalize the biblical record by saying that individuals who were said to have lived lengthy time spans (e.g. 969 years) were by no means representative of most individuals at the time, who lived simply normal life spans. By downplaying resurrection and miracles, Maimonides had shaken some of the foundations of medieval Jewish faith.

Maimonides had written an esoteric work. Stories of angels were vehicles of popular education to inspire people. Those who are truly "perplexed" would not be satisfied by fantastic or unbelievable stories. On the contrary, one's faith should not rest upon doubtful points, for these could easily be shattered. Rather, Maimonides maintained he was establishing an elite Judaism which was all the stronger for having been influenced by general philosophy.

The controversy lasted for 100 years, culminating with a ban on the study of philosophy prior to age 25. Maimonides's supporters translated his works into Hebrew and other languages, making him accessible to Jews everywhere. Those who sought to limit the influence of Maimonides ended up scoring at most a Pyrrhic victory. The legacy of the Maimonidean controversy suggests that ideas cannot be censored. On the contrary, they gain only greater legitimacy via attempts to suppress them. Thus, for example, the aforementioned Rabbi Menahem Meiri, perhaps the most liberal Jewish thinker in Christian Europe, opposed the ban on secular learning, which he found useful for the study of Torah. Meiri noted that many Jews were, in fact, more suited to study philosophy than they were to study Talmud. Although Maimonides's detractors feared that the study of philosophy would undermine Torah and thereby imposed a ban on his writings, they served only to invite further inquisitorial intervention, polarize the Jewish community, and ultimately demonstrate that censorship was counterproductive.

Reading: Abraham Halkin and David Hartman, eds., *Crisis and Leadership: Epistles of Maimonides,* "The Epistle on Martyrdom"

The "Letter on Martyrdom" is one of the earliest works of Moses Maimonides. Note, in particular, how, rather than support the ideology of martyrdom, Maimonides advises people to accept conversion temporarily, observe Judaism in secret, and leave the area at the earliest possible opportunity. Historians suggest that this may have been autobiographical on his part. Theologians note that Maimonides could suggest such a course of action because of the theological proximity between Judaism and Islam as monotheistic faiths—a status he may well not have extended to Christianity with its doctrine of the Trinity.

Theme four deals with the difference between this persecution and others, and what a person should do. Remember that in all the difficulties that occurred in the time of the sages, they were compelled to violate commandments and to perform sinful acts. The Talmud lists the prohibitions, that they may not study Torah, that they may not circumcise their sons, and that they have intercourse with their wives when they are ritually unclean. But in this persecution they are not required to do anything but say something, so that if a man wishes to fulfill the 613 commandments secretly he can do so. He incurs no blame for it, unless he set himself without compulsion to desecrate the Sabbath, although no one forced him. This compulsion imposes no action, only speech. They know very well that we do not mean what we say, and that what we say is only to escape the ruler's punishment and to satisfy him with this simple confession. Anyone who suffered martyrdom in order not to acknowledge the apostleship of "that man," the only thing that can be said of him is that he has done what is good and proper, and that God holds great reward in store for him. His position is very high, for he has given his life for the sanctity of God, be He exalted and blessed. But if anyone comes to ask me whether to surrender his life or acknowledge, I tell him to confess and not choose death. However, he should not continue to live in the domain of that ruler. He should stay home and not go out, and if he is dependent on his work let him be the Jew in private. There has never yet been a persecution as remarkable as this one, where the only coercion is to say something. When our rabbis ruled that a person is to surrender himself to death and not transgress, it does not seem likely that they had in mind speech that did not involve action. He is to suffer martyrdom only when it is demanded of him to perform a deed, or something that he is forbidden to do.

A victim of this persecution should follow this counsel: Let him set it as his objective to observe as much of the Law as he can. If it happens that he has sinned much, or that he has desecrated the Sabbath, he should still not carry what it is not allowed to carry. He must not think that what he has already violated is far more grievous than what he observes; let him be as careful about observance as possible. Remember, a person must learn this fundamental principle. Jeroboam ben Nebat is chastised for making the calves, and for disregarding the regulations regarding the Sabbath that come immediately after a holiday, or the like. None can claim that he was guilty of a more serious sin. This principle is applicable only in man-made laws in this world. God inflicts punishment for grievous sins and for minor ones, and He rewards people for everything they do. Hence it is important to bear in mind that one is punished for every sin committed and is rewarded for every precept fulfilled. Any other view of this is wrong.

What I counsel myself, and what I should like to suggest to all my friends and everyone that consults me, is to leave these places and go to where he can practice religion and fulfill the Law without compulsion or fear. Let him leave his family and his home and all he has, because the divine Law that He bequeathed to us is more valuable than the ephemeral, worthless incidentals that the intellectuals scorn; they are transient, whereas the fear of God is eternal.

Reading: Jacob Marcus, ed., *The Jew in the Medieval World*

The letter of Hisdai Ibn Shaprut is a document from the Golden Age of Spain. Hisdai notes his influence and prestige within the Spanish court. Yet he also expresses some envy and disappointment at not being able to live in a sovereign Jewish land. The letters suggest the importance of the kingdom of the Khazars as a symbol for medieval Jewish history. As stable as Jewish lives were in Spain, Jews still recalled their status in exile and their history of defeat. Rumors of a Jewish kingdom, no matter how far distant, excited the medieval Jewish imagination.

The Letter of Rabbi Hasdai, Son of Isaac Ibn Shaprut, to the King of the Khazars, about 960

> I, Hasdai, son of Isaac, son of Ezra, belonging to the exiled Jews of Jerusalem in Spain, a servant of my lord the King, bow to the earth before him and prostrate myself towards the abode of your Majesty from a distant land. I rejoice in your tranquility and magnificence and stretch forth my hands to God in heaven that He may prolong your reign in Israel. . . .
>
> Praise be to the beneficent God for His mercy towards me! Kings of the earth, to whom his [Abd-al-Rahman's] magnificence and power are known, bring gifts to him, conciliating his favor by costly presents, such as the King of the Franks, the King of the Gebalim, who are Germans, the King of Constantinople, and others. All their gifts pass through my hands, and I am charged with making gifts in return. [Ibn Shaprut, who knew several languages, received these embassies.] Let my lips express praise to the God of heaven, who so far extends His lovingkindness towards me, without any merit of my own, but in the fullness of His mercies!
>
> I always ask the ambassadors of these monarchs who bring gifts, about our brethren the Israelites, the remnant of the captivity, whether they have heard anything concerning the deliverance of those who have languished in bondage and have found no rest. [He was anxious to know if the "lost ten tribes" existed as an independent Jewish state anywhere.]

At length mercantile emissaries of Khorasan [a land southeast of the Caspian Sea] told me that there is a kingdom of Jews which is called Al-Khazar. But I did not believe these words for I thought that they told me such things to procure my goodwill and favor. I was therefore wondering, till the ambassadors of Constantinople came [between 944 and 949] with presents and a letter from their king to our king, and I interrogated them concerning this matter.

They answered me: "It is quite true, and the name of that kingdom is Al-Khazar. It is a fifteen days' journey by sea from Constantinople, but by land many nations intervene between us; the name of the king now reigning is Joseph; ships sometimes come from their country to ours bringing fish, skins, and wares of every kind. [The Khazars, great traders, got their wares from the Russians to the north.] The men are our confederates and are honored by us; there is communication between us by embassies and mutual gifts; they are very powerful; they maintain numerous armies with which they occasionally engage in expeditions." When I heard this report I was encouraged, my hands were strengthened, and my hope was confirmed. Thereupon I bowed down and adored the God of heaven. [Hasdai was happy: Christians could no longer say the Jews were without a country as a punishment for their rejection of Jesus.]. . . .

I pray for the health of my lord the King, of his family, and of his house, and that his throne may be established for ever. Let his days and his sons' days be prolonged in the midst of Israel!

Bibliography for Further Reading

Ashtour, Eliyahu. *The Jews of Moslem Spain,* Vols. I-III, Jewish Publication Society, 1974–1984

Gerber, Jane. *The Jews of Spain,* The Free Press, 1992

Heschel, Abraham J. *Maimonides,* Farrar Straus Giroux, 1982

Yerushalmi, Yosef. *Zakhor: Jewish History and Jewish Memory,* University of Washington Press, 1982

Unit XVI

Jews and Christian Spain

Jewish Origins in Spain

Spanish Jewry dated its history from biblical times. The reference to "Sepharad" in the prophet Obadiah, historically probably a reference to Asia Minor, was read as meaning the Spanish diaspora. Spanish Jewry claimed that Solomon's ships had sailed as far westward as the Iberian Peninsula. Clearly, Jews had been in Spain since the heyday of the Roman Empire. The fact that they could trace their origins to biblical times, even mythologically, symbolized the pride and self-esteem of Spanish Jewry. It also served the interests of Jewish-Christian polemic. Spanish Jews argued that since they had arrived in Spain in biblical times, long before Jesus, they should be considered exempt from the collective charge of deicide or the teaching of contempt, leveled against the Jewish people as a whole.

Although this reasoning is both far-fetched and divisive in terms of the unity of the Jewish people, one can understand why Spanish Jews made recourse to such a polemical argument. The initial encounter with Christian rulers in Visigothic Spain of the sixth century was unquestionably negative. The Visigothic state persecuted Jews mercilessly. In 613 C.E., Jews were offered the alternative of baptism or expulsion. Although the Council of Toledo, under the leadership of Isadore of Seville, mandated that Jews be protected from compulsory baptism, these persecutions were renewed periodically during the Visigothic tenure. Jews frequently had to evade these decrees via bribery. As a result, it should occasion no surprise that Jews were accused of collaborating with the Moslems in planning the conquest of Spain at the beginning of the eighth century.

The Reconquista

During the Reconquista, the period of Christian reconquest of Spain, 1150–1391 C.E., Jews were frequently employed by Christian governments as potentially useful both in city- building and in reconciling Moslems to Christian rule. Although the Reconquista provided unstable political conditions, Jews were valued and enjoyed economic prosperity. By the thirteenth century, there were probably 100,000 Jews living in Spain.

Not surprisingly, these Jews continued to venerate secular learning. Most Spanish Jews supported Maimonides during the infamous Maimonidean controversy. Moreover, the Spanish Jewish *Aljama,* or *Kehilla,* was in fact strengthened, even to the point of exercising the power of capital punishment against Jewish informers. Some Jewish legal authorities, in fact, were astonished that the Jewish community enjoyed such powers and doubted the actual permissibility of capital punishment absent a Jewish supreme court or Sanhedrin.

Jewish-Christian polemics lay at the heart of Spanish-Jewish relations in the thirteenth century. The polemics focused primarily upon the Talmud. Although Jews remained tolerated, they were generally forced to listen to conversionist sermons. Nachmanides, or Rabbi Moses Ben Nachman, became the chief apologist of Jewish heritage during this period. His debate with Pablo Christiani remains one of the classic texts of Jewish-Christian polemic.

Thirteenth-century missionary activity sought to undermine Judaism rationally. Aquinas himself had argued that Judaism as a system was morally inferior because it countenanced moneylending. Nachmanides's antagonist, Friar Pablo Christiani, argued that the rabbis had referred to a messiah being born in the first century, therefore indicating that he had already come, and only Jesus matched that description. Nachmanides responded that even if he took that legend at face value, which he did not, it could not refer to Jesus, because the Temple was destroyed one generation following the death of Jesus and the Talmud refers only to a messiah born at that time. More generally, the Jews argued that the miracles of Jesus were unimpressive, the doctrines of Incarnation and Trinity were irrational, and Christian society reflected greater moral deficiency because so many wars occurred within it.

However, as Spain became increasingly unified under Christian rule, the degree of Jewish persecution intensified. The pogroms of 1391, in particular, shattered the pride and self-esteem of Spanish Jewry. The message of the 1391 pogroms was that distinctions between Spain and the rest of Europe were more illusory than real in terms of Jewish security. The pogroms reduced the Jewish population. Subsequently, Jews were eliminated from state service and subjected to heavy taxation.

It is no surprise that Jewish conversion to Christianity increased significantly. To some extent, of course, conversion was abetted by persecution, although rarely was conversion compulsory. However, there were several motivations that led to Jewish apostasy. Persecution was the most obvious stimulant to conversion. Intellectually, however, the critique of Judaism by the Jewish philosophic elite suggested that it did not really matter whether one worshiped God as a Jew or as a Christian. At a time when Jewish life became difficult, those who accepted this form of religious relativism could easily take the next step of converting to Christianity. Thirdly, the prospect of reduced taxation and economic opportunities available to new Christians created yet another inducement to conversion. Lastly, there were those who acknowledged the force of history as lying with Christianity ascendant while Judaism increasingly seemed to be a defeated faith.

Conversion to Christianity, therefore, was by no means a simple response to persecution. Jews had different stimuli influencing their decisions to accept the Cross. Given that religious conviction of the truth of Christianity was only one of these causes, it appeared to many that converted Jews made bad Christians.

In this context, one can understand why the Inquisition was brought into Spain to see to the spiritual welfare of new Christians. The Inquisition was not directed at Jews and Judaism. It was directed exclusively against those new Christians, or *conversos*, suspected of relapsing into Judaism. From the perspective of the Jewish community, the number of Crypto-Jews or Marranos (a term of opprobrium denoting pig) may have been quite small. Yet from the perspective of the Inquisition virtually every *converso* was potentially a Marrano.

The methods of the Inquisition unquestionably were extreme. In many ways they represent the darkest chapters of Catholicism. The ideology of the Inquisition was to torture the body in order to save the soul. Confession held the key to salvation, even if articulated under enormous duress. Often people died under the tortures of the Inquisition. Even their deaths, however, were acceptable so long as they had confessed, thereby obtaining salvation.

Aside from the physical effects of the Inquisition upon its victims, it also divided the Jewish community and *conversos* from one another. A *converso* who was observed changing bed sheets on Friday afternoons or leaving a light burning on Friday night automatically came under suspicion of the Inquisition. The Jewish community was requested to hand over any "Marrano" or Crypto-Jew. To be sure, not all *conversos* were Marranos because remaining a Jew was possible until 1492, and many Jews did indeed convert to Christianity without practicing Judaism secretly. However, since so many of the *conversos* made poor Christians, given their philosophic leanings or because economic inducements had been the primary reason for conversion, a great many fell under the suspicion of the Inquisition.

During this difficult period the Jewish community was led by the philosopher Hasdai Crescas. His critique of Aristotle's philosophy provided him with stature in both the Jewish and gentile communities. In 1393, for example, he received authorization to resettle Jews in Barcelona and Valencia after the terrible pogroms there. He was succeeded by Rabbi Joseph Albo who, in 1415, participated in the infamous disputation of Tortosa. Albo downplayed faith in messianism as a religious principle. Christians argued that the Talmud indicated that the messiah had already come, suggesting that the rabbis of the Talmud knew the truth of Christianity yet openly denied it. Albo responded by noting that the belief in the messiah was a tenet of Judaism, but was by no means central to Jewish dogma. The only dogmas were that of God's existence, Divine providence, and future reward and punishment. These principles suggested Albo's attack upon philosophic skepticism, which argued that God held little interest in the day-to-day affairs of this world.

The Spanish Expulsion

The expulsion of the Jews from Spain marked the final unification of Spain under Christian rule. The fall of Moslem Granada in 1492 created the prospect of a unitary Spanish faith, ridding Spain of her foreign elements, and strengthening Spanish absolutism. The official reason for expelling the Jews was to undermine their influence upon *conversos*. The biblical commentator Don Isaac Abarbanel led Spanish Jewry during this period. Both King Ferdinand and Queen Isabella hoped he would convert and stay. Nevertheless he left for Italy with his co-religionists. The primary motive for the expulsion seems to have been to secure greater numbers of Jewish converts to Christianity. Indeed, some historians have argued that Ferdinand and Isabella, who previously had protected Spanish Jewry, would have permitted them to stay if not for the influence of Torquemada, a zealous proponent of Christianity generally and the Inquisition in particular.

Estimates vary as to precisely how many Jews were affected by the expulsion decree. Some suggest the number may have been as high as 200,000; others set it as low as 40,000. Recent estimates vary widely. Most left for Portugal, which was the most convenient land route. Others departed to Italy and the Ottoman Empire. The last Jew left on July 31, 1492, the seventh day of Av, a day long associated with Jewish tragedy. Christopher Columbus set sail for the shores of America almost immediately thereafter, symbolizing the dawn of a new chapter in Jewish history.

The Jews who went to Portugal soon discovered that the arm of the Inquisition had followed them. In 1497 the Portuguese king told the Jews that they, too, would have to convert to Christianity or abandon Portugal. Realizing that the bulk of the population would leave, for, after all, most had left Spain already, the Portuguese monarch was determined not to lose their valuable economic assets. He declared the Jews converted and forbade their leaving Portugal. Portugal, therefore, had a greater Marrano problem than did Spain. In 1506, for example, a major pogrom occurred in Lisbon, after a group of *conversos* had allegedly been celebrating the Passover Seder. The Inquisition survived for several hundred years, claiming as many as 30,000 victims of autos-da-fe or self-confessions. Remarkably, Marranos retained a subterranean Jewish existence for over 250 years and vestiges of Jewish practice have been found among Portuguese-Christians who do not consider themselves Jewish.

The expulsion itself was a traumatic experience for Spanish Jewry. Many turned to messianism in the belief that the expulsion represented the end of Jewish travails. One Jewish visionary, David Reubeni, appeared in Italy to tell the Pope that his brother headed a Jewish kingdom, which would join hands with the mythical kingdom of Prester John to liberate Palestine. A Marrano Jew, Solomon Molcho, noted for his psychic predictions concerning the overflow of the Tiber river and the Lisbon earthquake, predicted the coming of the Messiah for 1540. Although both Reubeni and Molcho benefitted from the Renaissance fascination with the exotic and the visionary, they both found a ready audience among Marrano Jews and the Spanish exiles. Their talk of a coming messiah fed the imagination of Jews who felt the exile from Spain had been the final blow in the record of Jewish suffering.

Jewish leaders resorted to the classical model of discouraging messianic movements yet preserving the messianic ideal. The Spanish expulsion did signal the relative nearness of redemption, for the quota of Jewish punishment was nearly exhausted. Jewish leaders reminded the Jewish community that those who had oppressed the Jews in the past (e.g. the Visigoths, the Romans) had disappeared, yet a remnant of Jewry remained. The sin of Spanish Jewry lay in its degree of assimilation. Return to Judaism would signal the coming of the redemption. Moreover, the dispersal of the Jews was by no means completely disastrous. Spreading the Jews throughout the world would safeguard Judaism, for if trouble came to Jews in one corner of the world, other Jewish communities could serve as a refuge and safety valve. Although the exile of today was significant and marked the fulfillment of biblical prophecy, it also signaled that other biblical prophecies, i.e., those of redemption, would also be fulfilled. The end of Jewish sufferings, in short, was near, and the very scattering of the Jews over the earth heralded the final redemption.

Some Jewish leaders went further. Don Isaac Abarbanel claimed that Christianity represented the fourth kingdom prophesied by Daniel and calculated that the wars between Christians and Moslems would usher in the redemption in 1503, while the voyages to the New World would result in the return of the Ten Lost Tribes. To be sure, these messianic calculations, as did all others, resulted only in further disappointment and frustrated hopes.

Other Jewish intellectuals asked what lessons could be absorbed from the catastrophic event of the expulsion. Some turned to history to explain the tragedy. Most notable was Solomon Ibn Verga, who, in his important chronicle *The Rod of Judah,* departed from the traditional theology of punishment for sin. Ibn Verga argued that the Jews should learn from past experiences to avoid future tragedies.

Therefore, Ibn Verga argued, the lessons of the expulsion lie in the difference between the local clergy who fomented anti-Semitism and the responsible clergy who opposed it. The masses were the enemies of the Jews, while protection could be sought from above. Jewish enemies envied Jewish wealth, for Jews were guilty of excessive ostentation.

All this amounted to a program to insure future Jewish survival. Ibn Verga urged that the Jews ally with legitimate authorities, on the grounds that protection would be had from above while hostility would be encountered from below. Secondly, he urged Jewish communities to exercise voluntary restraint, especially in dealings with Christians socially. Jewish communities adopted sumptuary legislation limiting the amount of money that could be used, for example, for weddings or for external dress. Lastly, Ibn Verga urged discouraging messianism, as it would irritate gentile authorities and lead to little positive outcome.

This interpretation of history represents both continuity with and departure from classical rabbinic tradition. Ibn Verga's political theory remained within the rabbinic paradigm: work on day-to-day existence, cultivate gentile authority, and discourage messianism. Yet reading these events historically suggested a more secular mind-set. Ibn Verga was unwilling to view Jewish history in strictly theological terms. By invoking a sociological perspective on Jewish-gentile relations, he placed Jewish history on a human plane, enabling Jews to take greater control over their own destiny. By saying that the course of Jewish history is natural rather than theological, Ibn Verga also implied that the future fate of the Jews depended in great measure upon how Jews interacted with gentiles.

To be sure, this was far from being accurate history. As noted, the Spanish expulsion had more to do with the needs of the Spanish monarchy and its desire for religious unity than with Jewish misdeeds. What mattered, however, was encouraging the Jewish community to continue despite the reality of gentile oppression. Ibn Verga was greatly pessimistic about the reality of anti-Semitism, which would probably continue irrespective of what Jews do.

Moreover, he seemed to have had little faith in the reality of redemption. His faith did lie in the capacity of the Jews to remain Jewish, despite tragedy and oppression.

Ibn Verga may have hit upon the secret of Jewish survival—the Jews' willingness to defy reality and articulate a distinctive Jewish message and faith despite physical evidence to the contrary. Jews had the genius to articulate monotheism in an age of paganism. Jews had reconstructed Judaism after both the first and second destructions of the Jerusalem Temple. The Spanish exile symbolized the travails of the Jewish diaspora. The message of Ibn Verga, like that of his rabbinic forbearers, was to continue to build Jewish life and to articulate the Jewish message despite the tragedy. Providence, or the enduring Covenant with the Jews, continued to operate, albeit through natural causes rather than through miraculous intervention. For all that the Spanish exile was traumatic in terms of Jewish self-consciousness and self-perception, it also symbolized the dawn of a new era in which Jewish history would be very different and, at times, very positive.

Reading: Frank Talmage, ed., ***Disputation and Dialogue***

The disputation of Nachmanides with Pablo Christiani was one of the classic confrontations of medieval Jewish-Christian polemic. Although there were severe restraints on what Nachmanides could say, the core of his argument centered on the failure of Christian messianism. If the messiah truly had come, he argued, history since the time of Jesus had seen so much war as to make a mockery of his messiahship.

> On the day appointed, the king came to a convent that was within the city bounds, where was assembled all the male population, both Gentiles and Jews. There were present the bishop, all the priests, the scholars and the Minorites [i.e. the Franciscans] and the Preaching Friars [i.e. the Dominicans]. Fra Paulo, my opponent, stood up to speak, when I, intervening, requested our lord the king that I should now be heard. The king replied that Fra Paulo should speak first because he was the petitioner. But I urged that I should now be allowed to express my opinion on the subject of the Messiah and then afterwards he, Fra Paulo, could reply on the question of accuracy.

I then rose and calling upon all the people to attend said: 'Fra Paulo has asked me if the Messiah of whom the prophets have spoken has already come and I have asserted that he has not come. Also a Haggadic work, in which someone states that on the very day on which the temple was destroyed the Messiah was born, was brought by Fra Paulo as evidence on his behalf. I then stated that I gave no credence to this pronouncement of the Haggadah but that it lent support to my contention. And now I am going to explain to you why I said that I did not believe it. I would have you know that we Jews have three kinds of writings—first, the Bible in which we all believe with perfect faith. The second kind is that which is called *Talmud* which provides a commentary to the commandments of the Law, for in the Law there are six hundred and thirteen commandments and there is not a single one of them which is not expounded in the Talmud and we believe in it in regard to the exposition of the commandments. Further, there is a third kind of writing, which we have, called *Midrash*—that is to say sermonic literature [*sermones*] of the sort that would be produced if the bishop here should stand up and deliver a sermon which someone in the audience who liked it should write down. To a document of this sort, should any of us extend belief, then well and good; but if he refuses to do so no one will do him any harm. For we have scholars who in their writings say that the Messiah will not be born until the approach of the End-time when he will come to deliver us from exile. For this reason I do not believe in this book (which Fra Paulo cites) when it makes the assertion that the Messiah was born on the day of the destruction of the temple.

Furthermore, this (third kind of) literature is given by us the title *Haggadah* which is the equivalent of *razionamiento* in the current speech, that is to say that it is purely conversational in character. Nevertheless, as you wish, I shall accept in its literal sense that Haggadic narrative which Fra Paulo has quoted, because, as I have already remarked to you, it supplies manifest proof that your Jesus is not Messiah, inasmuch as he was not born on the day mentioned, the day of the destruction of the temple. In fact his whole career was already over long before. But you, our lord the king, more fittingly than the others put a question to me raising the objection that it was not customary for a man to live a thousand years. And now I shall give you a plain answer to your question. You will observe that the first man lived for a thousand years all but seventy and it is made clear in the Scripture that it was through his transgression that he died and, had he not sinned, he would have lived much longer or even forever. Also, Gentiles and Jews alike confess that the sin and the punishment of the first man will be rendered ineffective in the days of the Messiah. If this be so, then, after the Messiah shall come, transgression and its penalty will cease in all of us, but (especially) in the Messiah himself will they be entirely absent. Consequently it is appropriate that he who is the Messiah should live for thousands of years or for ever, as is said in Psalm 21:4: "He asked life of you, you gave it to him; even length of days for ever and ever." That point then has been explained. But our lord the king further has raised the question: "When then does the Messiah (meanwhile) reside? It is manifest from Scripture that the abode of the first man was in the garden of Eden which is upon the earth; and after he had sinned, as it is said in Genesis 3:23, "the Lord God sent him forth from the garden of Eden." That being the case, the Messiah, he who is exempt from the penalty incurred by Adam, had his abode in the garden of Eden, and so affirmed the scholars in the Haggadic writings to which I have referred.

Bibliography for Further Reading

Baer, Yitzhak. *History of the Jews in Christian Spain,* Vols. I-II, Jewish Publication Society, 1965

Chazan, Robert. *Barcelona and Beyond,* University of California Press, 1992

———. *Daggers of Faith,* University of California Press, 1989

Gerber, Jane. *Jews of Spain,* The Free Press, 1992

Kedourie, Elie, ed., *Spain and the Jews,* Thames and Hudson, 1992

Roth, Cecil. *The Spanish Inquisition,* Norton, 1964

Unit XVII

Renaissance and Reformation

Renaissance Humanism

As European intellectuals rediscovered the classics of Greek and Roman literature, they also turned to the study of the classical Jewish heritage as an extension of their veneration of the ancient world. For some, this meant an interest in the Kabbalah, in which they found similarities to Plato and neo-Platonism. Others wished to study the Hebrew language so as to be able to read classical texts in their original language. Thus, for example, the thirteenth-century humanist Raymond Lull advocated the study of Hebrew in the university curriculum.

To be sure, this renewed interested in Judaic heritage was not coupled with any particular love for Jews. On the contrary, Christian Kabbalists and Hebraists hoped that Christian scholarship about Judaism would strengthen conversionists' efforts to bring Jews closer to Christianity. In other words, Renaissance humanism would bring Jewish and Christian scholars into closer contact, enabling Christian missionaries to articulate a common language with Jews and ultimately bring them closer to Christianity. In effect, this meant a different approach to Jews—out of love rather than out of hatred—but with a similar intent of converting Jews to Christianity.

In that context humanists debated the appropriateness of Christian behavior toward Jews. Pico della Mirandola praised the expulsion of the Jews from Spain as a just event. Machiavelli, the foremost political theorist of the Renaissance, echoed this view, arguing that the expulsion represented the appropriate uses of religion to advance the purposes of the nation-state, thereby illustrating his call for a divorce between politics and morality.

Erasmus, perhaps the foremost humanist of the day, repudiated the use of the Talmud and Kabbalah by Christian scholars, even if done for conversionist motives. Thus Erasmus criticized the Christian veneration of the Kabbalah and Pico's argument that the study of Kabbalah approximated the truths of Trinitarian Christianity via its emphasis upon Godhead, *sefirot,* and the *Shekhinah,* or Holy Spirit. Pico had adhered to the theory of an "ancient theology"—the belief that a single thrust pervaded all cultures. In this view, Jewish, Christian, and pagan values were essentially harmonious. Pico believed that the Jewish Kabbalah provided the key to unlocking that harmony. Kabbalah, for Pico, represented a universalistic Judaism. He perceived it as a higher form of magic, enhancing man's capacity to control destiny and to assist humanity through constructive uses of Divine powers. Kabbalistic uses of letter permutations and recitation of the Divine Names represented appropriate harnessing of magic for constructive ends. Significantly, as Gershom Scholem has noted, this Christian Kabbalah failed to leave much of an impression upon Jewish contemporaries.

Erasmus, by contrast, seems to have been motivated by deeply-rooted Jew-hatred. He blamed the Jews for masterminding the Peasants' Revolt in sixteenth-century Germany. He bitterly attacked the Hebrew Scriptures as deficient morally. He even warned that the Church must be far more careful about accepting Jewish converts. Although Erasmus is best known as an advocate of tolerance with regard to the freedom to publish ideas, he reiterated many of the worst anti-Jewish canards, particularly defaming Pharisaic Judaism for excessive legalism, a hallmark of the later Protestant Reformation.

The foremost defender of Jews and Judaism during the Renaissance period was the German scholar Johannes Reuchlin. Reuchlin studied with the Italian Jewish scholar and biblical commentator Sforno, subsequently claiming that he had been overcharged. Nevertheless, he defended the study of Talmud and Kabbalah and opposed the persecution of the Jews. Like other humanists, however, he sought the peaceful conversion of the Jews to Christianity. In contrast to the Dominican Church, which argued for the suppression of Talmud and Kabbalah, Reuchlin maintained that Jewry will never accept Christianity if the primary image of the Christian was that of oppressor. He venerated the Kabbalah as a vehicle to recover the occult sciences to enable man to master nature. In this respect, the Renaissance marked a subtle and significant change in the approach to Jews and Judaism. Although this new attitude by no means connoted unequivocal love for Jews, it did open the door to breaking with traditional models, especially as related to how to approach Jews and Judaism.

For Jews the Renaissance meant a unique opportunity for involvement in European cultural life. Jewish historian Cecil Roth has argued that the Renaissance represented the high tide of Italian Jewry as a synthesis of Judaism with general culture and marked the involvement of Jews in all forms of intellectual endeavor including art, music, and astronomy. Thus, Immanuel of Rome, a Jewish poet, imitated Dante's vision of heaven and hell in a long poem entitled "The Composition of Tophet and Eden," although, significantly, Immanuel omitted any attempt to describe purgatory, a concept alien to Judaism.

The Renaissance Jewish scholar who may be credited with reviving the importance of historical study was the Italian Jew Azariah dei Rossi. In sixteenth-century Italy dei Rossi came into contact with Christian scholars interested in Judaism. He rekindled the study of Philo among Jews and questioned the realm of rabbinic authority outside the boundaries of Jewish law. For dei Rossi, as for Maimonides before him, the rabbis had no special expertise in areas that transcended the boundaries of the Oral Law. In those areas, modern knowledge and science might well be superior to rabbinic teaching. For example, dei Rossi challenged the traditional chronology, arguing that the rabbis had erred in assigning only 34 years to the Persian period in Jewish history. Rather than constituting an abstruse debate about dates, this question symbolized the authority of rabbinic statements concerning history. For dei Rossi and for historians after him, the historical statements in the Talmud could by no means be taken unquestioningly. Although dei Rossi insisted on the primacy of rabbinic authority in the realm of Jewish law, he essentially was searching for neutral, non-halachic grounds on which contemporary Jewish scholars could discourse with Renaissance culture. His willingness to challenge the authority of the rabbis reflected the broader Renaissance spirit of challenging inherited truths, individual research, and constant experimentation. Although dei Rossi revered rabbinic teaching, contemporary rabbis were not prepared to accept his challenge to inherited wisdom. They placed dei Rossi's work under a ban of excommunication although, over time, he paved the way for the revival of Jewish historical knowledge and scholarship. Significantly, the leading rabbinic authorities within Italy refused to support this ban, thereby upholding dei Rossi's work.

The Protestant Reformation

Renaissance humanists paved the way for the challenge to papal authority articulated by Martin Luther and the reformers. Luther initially echoed the Renaissance view that the Jews had resisted conversion because Christian treatment of them had been so illiberal. He urged that the mission to the Jews abandon hatred. However, given the refusal of the Jews to convert, Luther became vitriolically anti-Semitic. He abetted the expulsions of the Jews from the German principalities throughout the sixteenth century, arguing that the Jewish character was that of the *Book of Esther*—bloodthirsty and vengeful. Luther's critique of the Jews in some respects echoed the older critique of Paul. The Jews continued to be bound, in Luther's view, to the ceremonial and the ritual rather than the spirit and heart. He proposed a seven-point program for dealing with Jews that, in effect, meant the outlawing of Judaism and their expulsion from the German states. By 1600 Jews had effectively been forced out of Western and Central Europe and were increasingly settling in Eastern Europe, where they were welcomed.

Luther laid the groundwork for two contrasting directions in Protestant perspectives on Jews and Judaism. On the one hand, he argued for a different mission to the Jews. This mission clearly assumed that the purpose in continued Jewish existence was obsolete, that Jews adhered to an outmoded physical expression of religious practice while they had lost the spiritual values that those physical expressions represented. Luther's "liberal" perception of the Jews as a ceremonial rather than a spiritual people would be echoed in later liberal Protestant scholarship, particularly Immanuel Kant, Georg Wilhelm Friedrich Hegel, and Arnold Toynbee. Israeli philosopher Natan Rotenstreich has termed this "the recurring pattern" of liberal Protestantism—regarding Judaism as a "fossil" while counseling preservation and even emancipation of Jews. Conversely, by ultimately engaging in the outright persecution and expulsion of Jews, Luther provided a framework for even more vitriolic and vicious forms of anti-Semitic behavior.

John Calvin, founder of an alternative wing of Protestantism known today as Calvinism or Puritanism, refrained from vitriolic anti-Semitism but engaged in a critique of Jewish usury and of Jewish messianism as excessively materialistic. Calvin venerated the Hebrew Scriptures. Thus the early Puritans coming to America constantly invoked biblical names and places. However, he was clearly ambivalent concerning contemporary Jews. He lacked Luther's extreme anti-Semitism, but saw little value in the continuing presence of Jews and Judaism, whom he derided as materialists.

Increasingly, Jews found themselves on the defensive. In Germany they had to confront the persecution of Luther and his followers and therefore naturally sided with Luther's enemies, the Holy Roman Empire of Charles V. Influenced by his "court Jew" Yossel of Rosheim, Charles V tendered a grant of privileges to Jews in the Holy Roman Empire. This charter extended the medieval model of protecting the Jews as "serfs of the royal chamber." Like subsequent court Jews, Yossel succeeded in raising large sums on behalf of Charles V. The evaluation of whether such "court Jews" accomplished more for their people by embracing the government, or whether they did more harm, remains controversial to this day.

Moreover, the Catholic Counter-Reformation also charged Jews and Judaism as being the spirit behind Luther and Protestantism. The Council of Trent renewed prohibitions against Jews, while placing the Talmud on the Index of prohibited books. The first official Jewish "ghetto" originated in Venice in 1516. Previously, there had usually been a Jewish Quarter in which Jews had voluntarily resided. Now, under the impact of the Counter-Reformation, for the first time Jews were legally restricted to a particular impoverished area of the town. Pope Paul IV, in 1555, similarly enclosed Jews in a Roman ghetto while subjecting them to conversionist sermons.

Clearly the Reformation did not mark an end to Jew-hatred, but rather the beginning of new directions in modern anti-Semitism. It signified the increased importance of the nation-state and its capacities. In modernizing the nation-states, European governments would be compelled to raise the Jewish question—i.e., what do we do with a body of people who are residing in our state but do not share the nation's faith? Although the expulsions recurred in many sixteenth century German towns and principalities, the long-range response was that the nation-state cannot expel a sizable group of productive citizens, nor can it permit them to remain a nation apart. This view of the nation-state modernizing itself and integrating its citizens ultimately paved the road for Jewish emancipation.

Jews in Far-Off Lands

The Renaissance sparked interest in far-away places and featured many rumors of Jews living in exotic lands. Interest in far-off lands, as noted earlier, gave some credibility to the diplomatic mission of David Reubeni, claiming to represent a Jewish king beyond Europe. More substantively, Jews were now discovered in China, where they had apparently resided since the eighth century. Jewish traders, known as the Radhanites, had clearly reached China by the eighth century, utilizing, in part, the friendliness of the Khazar Jewish kingdom in Southern Russia as a vehicle to facilitate trade with the Orient. In the thirteenth century, Marco Polo met Jews in Peking and noted their political and economic influence. The Mongolian Khan who ruled China at the time of Marco Polo's visit had issued three decrees affecting Jews—that Christians, Jews, and Moslems were to be taxed equally, that Jews and Moslems were enjoined to join the army, and that Jews and Moslems were prevented from levirate marriage, or marriage to the wife of a deceased brother who had died childless. The existence of these decrees suggest a Jewish community of some size and significance.

In general, anti-Semitism was absent from China. Jews stressed the compatibility of Judaism and Confucianism. Surprisingly, the sole source of anti-Semitism in China was the presence of a Moslem population, which was often pitted against the Jews. The most important Jewish colony in China existed in Kaifeng, the capital of the Hunan province in south-central China. Kaifeng Jewry numbered in the thousands, and the community survived there for over 800 years. In Beijing (formerly Peking) the community disappeared by the eighteenth century. Most Jews either converted to Islam or moved to Kaifeng. Similarly, by the fourteenth century we have reports of intermarriage among Kaifeng Jewry and their dropping the religious prohibitions against pork. These early signs of assimilation pointed to the ultimate disappearance of Chinese Jewry.

The news of Jews living in China excited European Jewry. Some felt that these were remnants of the Ten Lost Tribes of ancient Israel. Jews in India regarded Chinese Jews as neighbors who had emigrated from Persia. Jewish leaders did attempt some correspondence with Chinese Jews. However, sadly, Christian missionaries expressed greater interest in meeting Chinese Jews than did their European Jewish brethren. By the nineteenth century Chinese Jewry remained at most an orphan colony of several hundred. No observance of Judaism persisted, and intermarriage with the Chinese population was the rule. Indeed, many Jews became Confucian by faith and entered into the Chinese civil service. Only in the twentieth century, with an influx of Russian Jews in the 1930's and subsequently a larger number of Jews escaping Hitler, did China again harbor a sizable Jewish population. Most of these, however, left China after 1948 to build new lives in the State of Israel.

The story of Chinese Jewry, although exotic, contains a larger lesson and implications for Jewish history. Jews survived as a numerically small body determined to maintain an ethnic heritage. Chinese toleration of Jews was remarkable in facilitating Jewish integration in China and encouraging an absence of persecution. Ultimately, however, Chinese Jewry was too far removed from the centers of Jewish life, too small, and too weak religiously to preserve itself as a corporate entity. By the time Chinese Jews became known to the rest of the Jewish world, there simply were not enough of them nor was there sufficient religious commitment to ensure their continuity. The fact that Jews disappeared in a country that tolerated them superbly raises disturbing implications for contemporary Jewish life.

The Jewish community that received the most attention and was perhaps the most exotic was the Ethiopian Jewish community, often known derisively as the Falashas, or "strangers." Many legends persist about the origins of Ethiopian Jewry. Moses is said to have spent some time in Ethiopia. Ethiopian Jews attribute their roots to the marriage of Solomon and Sheba, which produced the legendary king of Ethiopia, Menelik I. Clearly, in biblical times, there was an association with Ethiopia, and, quite possibly, Jews fled there after the destruction of the Temple in 586 B.C.E. More likely, however, given the presence of Jewish soldiers on the Ethiopian-Egyptian border in 600 B.C.E., a small Jewish community began to form there and emigrated southward into Ethiopia. Arabian Jews crossed over into Ethiopia after the destruction of the Arabian Jewish kingdom in the sixth century C.E. The origins of Ethiopian Jewry probably lie in Jewish migration to Ethiopia from Palestine and Arabia, coupled with conversion to Judaism by native Ethiopians.

Moreover, the legends of the Ethiopian Jews stated that they were once a mighty Ethiopian tribe. A Jewish kingdom was said to have been created in the tenth century, ruled by a powerful queen, Yehudit, who persecuted Christianity and engaged in intermittent warfare with other African tribes. Yet by the time European Jewry encountered Ethiopian Jewry, these were past memories and legends of a foregone time. By the seventeenth century Ethiopian Jewry had been overwhelmed, its lands confiscated, and many sold into slavery or forcibly converted to Christianity. The remnants who were allowed to return to Judaism were now known as the Falashas or outcasts. They were forbidden from owning land, and their numbers had been greatly reduced, so that by 1860 one could speak of 150,000 Falashas and only 50,000 by 1909.

The earliest reports of Ethiopian Jewry associated them with the lost biblical tribe of Dan. Indeed, rabbinic authorities in the sixteenth century proclaimed Ethiopian Jews to be the Biblical Danites. Unquestionably these associations date from the incredible ninth- century reports of Eldad Hadani, who most likely had little first-hand knowledge of Ethiopian Jewry but transmitted much legendary material about a powerful Jewish kingdom in Ethiopia lying beyond the mighty Sambation River, which rested every seventh day. Eldad also spoke of the other lost Jewish tribes and the fabled Khazar kingdom. Although his reports contained little historical value, they did boost the spirits of medieval Jews.

Jewish leaders and rabbinic authorities, upon receiving credible reports of Ethiopian Jewry, proclaimed Ethiopian Jews to be authentic Jews who required external support and assistance, particularly in the practice and understanding of Judaism. Ethiopian Jews had never been exposed to the Talmud. Their practices were heavily indebted to the Bible and Apocryphal literature and reflected heavy influence of Ethiopian Christianity. Nevertheless, one should not underestimate their degree of Jewish commitment.

Their famous trek to Palestine in the 1860's reflected a messianic hope to return to the Jewish homeland and reunite with the Jewish people. Chief Rabbi Abraham Isaac Kook reaffirmed the Jewishness of Ethiopian Jewry in 1921, as did Chief Rabbi Isaac Halevi Herzog in 1948. The benefits of the Law of Return, however, were extended to Ethiopian Jews only in 1975, for until then both Chief Rabbis did not agree on their Jewishness. Perhaps the most stirring aspects of Zionist history concerned the rescue of Ethiopian Jewry in Operation Moses in 1984 and, subsequently, Operation Solomon in 1992. The Zionist dream of ingathering the exiles and providing a homeland for all Jews is perhaps best reflected in the experience of Ethiopian Jewry. No finer statement could be made to the effect that Zionism clearly is not racism.

Readmission to England

This period also marked the return of the Jews to England, from which they had been expelled in 1290. Manasseh ben Israel, a rabbi in Amsterdam, composed in 1650 a series of *Humble Addresses,* in which he pleaded for England under Oliver Cromwell to grant Jews the right of return. He emphasized the economic importance of Jews to England and appealed to English traditions of justice and humanity, noting that other nations, particularly Holland, had profited by treating the Jews fairly.

Opposition to the potential return of the Jews arose quickly from clerical circles concerned with preserving England as a Christian state and from commercial circles worried about potential Jewish economic rivalry. Cromwell himself appeared to have been sympathetic to Manasseh's request, but remained relatively silent while claiming to be tolerant of non-Catholics.

At this juncture the Marrano community in London publicly proclaimed its Jewishness. During the Anglo-Spanish War these Marranos, living until now a subterranean existence, wished to be exempt from enemy status. They identified themselves as Marrano Jews and requested permission to build a synagogue. In effect, there were two parallel efforts occurring simultaneously to secure the right of the Jews to reenter England. Some Marranos may have worked within Cromwell's intelligence service, especially with respect to relations with Holland.

In 1655 at the Whitehall Conference, the widespread opposition to the Jewish presence became public. To some extent it emanated from Christian prejudices. In a more general sense, the Whitehall Conference proceedings indicated that Jews in England fared best when they stayed outside the public eye. So long as the "Jewish question" was not a matter of public discussion, there was little opposition to Jews. Placing it on the public agenda of English society triggered much of the latent hostility to Jews. Anglo-Jewish historians are fond of noting that British society has both disliked Jews personally yet at the same time accepted their presence within Britain.

Following the restoration of the English monarchy, it was ruled that Jews were permitted to remain in London, for no law existed to the contrary. The edict of expulsion of 1290 effectively was historicized to apply strictly to that time period. The English Restoration of the 1660's felt no need to revoke the changes in Jewish status that had occurred on the ground. Although the Whitehall Conference had rejected Manasseh ben Israel's formal request, Jews were now living in London, and there was nothing to prevent their further development as a community.

To be sure, the English Jewish community absorbed the lesson of adopting a low profile. They forbade the acceptance of converts to Judaism. They prohibited Jews from discussing religion with Christians. They were especially hard on Jewish criminals, for fear that these would upset the position of Jews in British society. Lastly, they even barred synagogues from welcoming non-Jewish guests, lest the absence of decorum in the synagogue create a negative impression concerning Jews and Judaism.

The new Jewish community organized quickly under Sephardic leadership. The major synagogue became the Bevis Marks Synagogue in East London. Ashkenazic immigration grew quickly and achieved parity with the Sephardic leadership, and soon thereafter Ashkenazim eclipsed Sephardim in importance.

Jews were permitted to return to England for a variety of reasons, ranging from the personal interest of Cromwell, who valued Jews as assets to the State, to the theological expectations of millenarian groups who thought the messiah would arrive quickly, to the mercantile interests of British commerce who hoped that Jews would increase the wealth of the state. In fact, Jews quickly became a valued asset in British society, although their self-imagery and self-consciousness dictated maintaining a low profile until the twentieth century.

Reading: Elkan Adler, *Jewish Travelers in the Middle Ages*

This reading is taken from the diary of David Reubeni, one of the strangest men of medieval Jewish history. His account is particularly consonant with the culture of the Renaissance with its interest in the exotic and in faraway places. His fantastic tale of a brother who was a Jewish king attracted more credibility in the culture of the Renaissance than it might otherwise have merited.

Jewish Travellers

This Judge came to my house because the King of Fez had heard about me and ordered him to go first to the King of Portugal, and then to come and see me, and he gave me letters from the Jews of Fez and from R. Abraham ben Zimori of Asfi-Safi and a third letter from the Captain of Tangier. Then the Judge asked me about my country, whether many Jews were there. And I answered that it is the wilderness of Habor, and that there are thirty myriad Jews in my country, and King Joseph, my brother, rules over them and has seventy counsellors and many lords, and I am a military lord over ways and war. And the Judge said to me, "What seekest thou from this kingdom that thou hast come from the east to the west?" I answered that from our youth we are trained in war, and our war is with the sword and lance and bow, and we wished to go, with God's help, to Jerusalem to capture the land of Israel from the Moslems, for the end and salvation has arrived, and I have come to seek wise handicraftsmen who know how to make weapons and firearms that they should come to my land and make them and teach our soldiers.

The Judge was much amazed at this, and said to me, "We believe that the kingdom will return to you this time, and if you return will you do kindness to us?" I said to him, "Yes, we will do kindness to you and to all who do kindness to Israel, which is in captivity under Ishmael and Edom," and I said to the Judge, "Do you also believe that the kingdom of the land of Ishmael will return to us?" And he replied to me, "In all the world they believe this." I said to him, "We are kings, and our fathers were kings from the time of the destruction of the temple till this day, in the wilderness of Habor. We rule over the tribes of Reuben and Gad, and half-tribe of Manasseh in the wilderness of Habor, and there are nine and a half tribes in the land of Ethiopia and other kings. The nearest to us are the tribe of Simeon and the tribe of Benjamin, and they are on the River Nile, above the kingdom of Sheba, and they reside between the two rivers, the blue river and the black river, which is the Nile. Their country is good and extensive, and they have a king and his name is Baruch, the son of King Japhet, and he has four sons, the eldest Saadiah, and the second Abraham, the third Hoter, and the fourth Moses, and their numbers are as ours in the wilderness of Habor, thirty myriads, and we and they take counsel together."

The Judge said to me, "Dost thou wish to write for me a letter to the King of Fez?" I answered, "I need not write, but you can say all this to him by the word of mouth and give him from me a thousand greetings and say to him that the Jews under his rule should be protected by him, and that he should honour them and this will be the beginning of peace between us and him, between our seed and his seed." The Judge also asked me, "What will you do with the Jews in all the lands of the west, will you come to the west for them and how will you deal with them?" I replied that we shall first take the Holy Land and its surroundings and that then our captains of the host will go forth to the west and east to gather the dispersed of Israel, and whoever is wise among the Moslem Kings will take the Jews under his rule and bring them to Jerusalem, and he will have much honour, greater than that of all the Moslem Kings, and God will deliver up all the kingdoms to the King of Jerusalem. Further, the Judge asked me, "Is it true that the Jews in Fez and its neighbourhood say, and the Moslems also, that you are a prophet and the Messiah?" and I answered, "God forbid, I am a sinner before the Lord greater than any one of you, and I have slain many men, and on one day I killed forty enemies. I am neither a prophet nor the son of a prophet, is neither a wise man nor a Kabbalist, but I am a captain of the host, the son of Solomon the King, the son of David, the son of Jesse, and my brother, the King, rules over thirty myriads in the wilderness of Habor. Moreover, the Marranos in the Kingdom of Portugal, and all the Jews in Italy and all the places that I passed also thought me to be a prophet, wise man, or Kabbalist, and I said to them, 'God forbid, I am a sinner and a man of war from my youth till now.'" Afterwards the Judge began to write to the Jews of Fez, and to R. Abraham ben Zimori of Asfi-Safi, and I wrote to them and handed the letters to him and he went on his way in peace.

After that there came before the King a great Moslem lord of the royal seed of Formosa, of the country of India, near to the wilderness of Habor. The cause of his coming was that a captain over the King's ship had slain his brother and taken all his money, and this captain was imprisoned because of the accounting for the ship's moneys which he had not brought to the King's treasury. The king honoured the Moslem lord and asked him also about me, and if he had any knowledge of the wilderness of Habor, and he replied to the King, "Yes, and in the wilderness of Habor there are many Jews and rich men who have herds, and they have a king at this time whose name is Joseph, and he has seventy counsellors, and the Jews do great things in the wilderness of Habor." And he told the King in private matters which could not be related in the presence of all his lords. There were then Marranos in the King's presence, and they came and told me all these things. Also Joseph Cordelia came to me and gave me a letter in the Arabic language from the King who rules in the west, beyond the kingdom of Fez. It is the world's end. There is no kingdom behind it, but only deserts, and they have neighbours, Arabs and Moslems, who have camps in this desert, and the King is a Moslem of the sons of the prophet Mahomet, and his name is Sherif. He is a strong and wise man and has in his kingdom Jews who reside on the mountain and the name of the mountain is Asum. It is at the world's end and those Jews sow and get in harvest and they are most of them poor but strong, and one of them came to me who was a Cohen, and his heart was as a lion's heart. They are not like the Jews who live under the rule of the Moslems, and in that letter it was written, "Behold, I have heard of thee, that thou art come to the King of Portugal from the tribes. Hast thou heard of this people who come out of the wilderness separating me from the blacks, for they have taken from us all the Arabs who dwell in the wilderness, them and their wives and their flocks and their young and all that is theirs. Not one of them returned of those they captured. We do not know if they have been slain or what has been done to them, but a fugitive who escaped came and told me this matter, and I sent the Jews that they should go and see them, but they did not return and we wondered about this people and I have written thee about them that thou, in thy kindness, mayest tell me and write from thy land all that thou knowed in fact, and do not hide anything from me, as to thy place and all the tribes; tell me everything."

Bibliography for Further Reading

Baron, Salo. *Ancient and Medieval Jewish History,* Rutgers University Press, 1972

Ross, Dan. *Acts of Faith,* St. Martin's Press, 1982

Roth, Cecil. *History of the Jews in England,* Oxford University Press, 1964

———. *The Jews in the Renaissance,* originally Jewish Publication Society, 1959; Harper Torch, 1965

Unit XVIII

The Marrano Phenomenon

Origins of Modernity

Jewish modernity may be said to have begun in 1492 with the expulsion of the Jews from Spain. Three changes in the social and intellectual lives of Jewry reflected the encounter with the modern ethos.

First, Jewish temperament and its assessment of modern culture fundamentally shifted. In medieval times Yehuda Halevi had argued that Jews ought reject Aristotle in favor of Jewish culture. At most, medieval Jewish thinkers legitimated gentile culture as potentially beneficial for the understanding of Judaism. By contrast, however, the modern Jewish temper desired acceptance by the standards of the external culture. Contra Halevi, modern Jewish thinkers acknowledged the greatness of gentile society. Gentile society was by no means something to be merely tolerated—rather it was to be emulated and internalized.

This change in temperament led to a philosophical change in terms of the breakdown of the medieval synthesis of faith and reason. Maimonides had placed faith over reason, arguing that while the two form alternative sources of truth, should they be in conflict with one another, the truths of faith or Scripture must take precedence over the truths of reason. By contrast, the Jewish encounter with modernity meant that the categories of reason would sit in judgment over the categories of faith. Jewish philosopher Benedict Spinoza, in that respect, personified the origins of modern Jewish thought. Spinoza rejected revelation and revealed religion as sources of truth. Reason stood as the sole criterion for truth. By that standard, Spinoza weighed Judaism and found it wanting. Judaism as a system made sense only when Jews had enjoyed a political state and sovereignty. The fact that the Jews had not disappeared given the destruction of their state was testimony only to their stiff-neckedness and stubbornness. Jewish identity in the modern world made no sense, for Judaism contradicted fundamentally the categories of reason and was therefore deficient as a religious system. As for why the Jews had survived, Spinoza's theory, popular among liberal and enlightened circles in later centuries, attributed Jewish survival strictly to gentile oppression. Remove persecution and anti-Semitism, and the Jew will gradually disappear. Spinoza's challenge to contemporary Jewish identity crystallizes the problem of the modern Jew: Why remain Jewish in a modern world prepared to accept the Jews as universal men and women?

Lastly, modernity symbolized the breakdown of Jewish communal structure and autonomy. That process culminated in the emancipation of the Jew as European citizen. Yet long before the grant of emancipation itself, a struggle ensued within the Jewish community as to the force of rabbinic authority and the extent of communal autonomy. The power of excommunication and Jewish legal control over education, taxation, and marriages had been the hallmarks of medieval Jewish life, but modernity represented the collapse of compulsory communal authority in favor of the voluntary force of moral persuasion.

Who Were the Marranos?

As noted earlier, in the eyes of rabbinic literature, the Marranos were often fallen Jews. In their own eyes, they constituted the heroes of Jewish history. From the perspective of the Inquisition, every *converso* was potentially a Marrano.

Clearly not all former Jews in Spain were Marranos. In all likelihood the upper classes were most ripe for conversion. At most a minority became Marranos, while others remained Jews.

The term Marrano refers to a pig and is a term of derision aimed at the Marranos by the Inquisition. Jews and Marranos referred to them as "*anusim*," meaning the compelled ones, i.e. they had no choice but to observe Christianity publicly while trying to preserve

Judaism in private. The inner life of the Marrano stressed biblical or Hebraic culture, for the Talmud was a closed book, whereas the Bible was accessible to Jew and Christian alike. In reading the Bible, the Marranos turned to the stories of Moses, who lived his life as an Egyptian, and Esther, who served as a Persian Queen, not telling her religion. Precisely through their "Marrano" identity these biblical personalities had saved the Jewish people. Therefore the Marranos regarded themselves as heroic in their capacity to preserve Judaism under the most extreme of circumstances. In practice, to be sure, Marrano Judaism often reflected a mixture of Jewish and Christian practices, e.g. kneeling. Many Marranos, in fact, entered the Christian clergy so as to escape the pressure of the Inquisition. Marranos tried to preserve a semblance of the fast of Yom Kippur as well as the minor fast of Esther, which now assumed symbolic importance owing to Esther's having lived as a Marrano.

In what sense, then, were the Marranos bearers of modernization? First, the Marranos represented a new economic and geographic phenomenon in Jewish life. The Marrano diaspora spread to the New World, as well as to Amsterdam, Salonika, London, Venice, and Constantinople—all major port cities interested in attracting trade. Marrano international connections thereby served as new sources for trade and capital. In Portugal the Marranos had become an entrepreneurial element. Now they were taking their capital out to the major centers of finance. German sociologist Werner Sombart ascribed to the Marranos the power of initiating modern capitalism. This thesis is incorrect with respect to industrial capitalism, in which few Marranos participated. It has some truth with respect to finance capitalism. For example, the Mendez family served as a classic example of an international Marrano economic network. Persecuted by the Inquisition, the members of the Mendez family fled to Holland and the Ottoman Empire. Because of their family and personal connections, they were able to advance the condition of Jews within the Ottoman Empire. One of the family members, Don Joseph Nasi, became an Ottoman foreign minister and initiated plans to resettle Jews in Tiberias in sixteenth-century Palestine. The naval battle of Lepanto, in 1572, ended his influence, for the victory of Venice over Turkey made Turkey turn away from the mercantilist policies which had enabled Nasi to rise in the imperial bureaucracy. His aunt, Dona Gracia Nasi, formed a virtual "underground passage" assisting Marranos to escape from Portugal and coordinated an international boycott of Ancona, Italy, in an unsuccessful effort to aid the Marranos there.

The story of the Mendez house is significant in yet another respect: Members of the family, upon leaving the lands of the Inquisition, did not immediately revert to Judaism. They felt that they could accomplish more for their people by remaining Marranos. Although the family members did ultimately return to Judaism, their example signaled that Marrano families would continue a subterranean Jewish existence over several generations. Marranos did not regard themselves as failed Jews for not reverting to Judaism immediately upon leaving the lands of the Inquisition. On the contrary, they prided themselves on their capacity to retain Jewish identity under extreme circumstances and to utilize their influence in Christian society to enhance the Jewish people. Moreover, rabbinic authorities criticized Marranos for preferring comfortable lives as Christians socially and economically to second-class status as Jews. Hence, as we shall see, Marranos were considerably more skeptical than most other Jews of the force of rabbinic authority.

Furthermore, the Marrano dispersion represents a new and distinctly modern form of a Jewish diaspora. The Jewish communities of London, Amsterdam, the Ottoman Empire, and Italy in large measure owe their origins to the geographic dispersion of the Marranos. Salonika, in the Ottoman Empire, was the only European city to harbor a Jewish majority until the twentieth century. The spread of the Marranos geographically placed a new focus upon a dispersed Jewish life in creating new centers of Jewish settlement.

Most importantly, however, the Marrano Jewish culture became quintessentially modern—personal and existential in terms of Jewish identity, and skeptical of rabbinic authority in the communal sphere. Upon reentering the Jewish community, Marranos encountered a Judaism of the Oral Law interpreted by the rabbinical establishment and widely at variance with their emphasis upon biblical Judaism. But overriding this clash of perspectives and interpretations of what was Jewish law, Marranos and the rabbinic establishment clashed fundamentally over the definition of what constituted ideal Jewish behavior. For the rabbis, the Marranos ought be tolerated and even respected for maintaining Judaism under difficult conditions, but at the same time criticized for having failed to live up to Jewish standards of martyrdom. The rabbis usually preferred martyrdom to publicly accepting Christianity and privately observing Judaism. From the perspective of the Marranos, however, they themselves were the true heroes of Jewish history, for they had preserved Judaism under the most extreme of conditions. It was this clash of perspectives that, in turn, reflected the modern ethos—to be distrustful of rabbinic authority and skeptical of rabbinic rulings.

Moreover, the religion of the Marranos had become deeply personal and existential. Every Marrano faced the choice of what to observe and what not to observe. Marranism indeed symbolized the fundamental condition and ethos of a modern Jew, weighing carefully what aspects of Jewish tradition continued to be salient and what aspects ought best be regarded as relics of a bygone era. In this sense, Marranism carried the banner of modern Judaism—the collapse of rabbinic authority replaced by personal, existential, and voluntary choice of what to observe and what not to observe.

The modern Jew clearly does not live under the specter of the Inquisition. However, in one sense most of us are like the Marranos, facing, on virtually a day-to-day basis, the existential choice of what aspects of tradition we incorporate and what aspects we do not. Spinoza captured the dilemma of the modern Jew perfectly in arguing that Judaism and modernity fundamentally conflict. His solution of abandoning Judaism clearly has been rejected by Jews who find value in retaining their Jewish identity. Their problem, a specifically modern and Marrano problem, is to find the points of intersection between the claims of Jewish tradition and those of modern culture. Given that modernity contains the hallmarks of personal choice and rebellion against communal authority and the power of tradition, the Marrano experience captures that ethos perfectly.

The Marranos represented the modern Jewish experience in yet another way—their reception within gentile society. The fact that Marranos who had converted to Christianity continued to suffer the opprobrium of Christian society reflected a new form of anti-Semitism—hatred of the Jew not on account of his professed religion, but rather on account of his racial origins. Spanish laws concerning *conversos* were called *statutes de limpieza* or cleansing statutes purging Christians of Jewish (or Moorish) origin from key positions in Spanish society. Clearly this was not the racism of the

Nazi experience. However, it did open the door to a new form of anti-Semitism in which racial origins counted more than professions of religion. Until now, conversion had always been a way to escape anti-Semitism. The Marrano experience demonstrated that anti-Jewishness lingers even when Judaism has been abandoned.

In short, the Marrano experience captured the modern ethos and dilemma of the Jews in four distinct ways: Economically, the Marranos represented new opportunities for entrepreneurial activity and investment capital. Geographically, the Marrano diaspora created a nexus of new Jewish communities which adopted leadership positions in the modern Jewish world. Marranos could be found in Mexico, and traces of Marrano descendants may be found in twentieth-century Portugal and even the postwar New World. Culturally and religiously, the Marranos represented a new form of Jewish identity—personal, existential, voluntary, and quite skeptical of rabbinic authority. Lastly, the Marrano experience demonstrated that the forms of modern anti-Semitism would be considerably different and in some ways more aggravated than the expressions of medieval Jew-hatred.

Furthermore, the Marrano Jewish experience demonstrated one aspect of the modern Jewish ethos which has been generally overlooked and only recently has become a focus of contemporary Jewish concerns. The overwhelming majority of Marranos lost their Jewishness within a span of several generations. Jewishness became at most an ancestral memory rather than a day-to-day human expression. In that sense, the heroism of the Marranos lay in their ability to preserve Judaism under such extreme conditions, but ultimately the experience was by no means a prescription for Jewish continuity. In some respects, it was incredible that Marrano Jewish identity should have survived for as long as 250 years. Conversely, the implications of the Marrano experience suggest that Jewish identity could not be preserved under such circumstances. The final aspect of the modernity of the Marranos, therefore, was their degree of assimilation.

American Jews today do not confront an Inquisition. There is no compelling force that asks the Jew to abandon his or her faith and accept the Christian church. However, as noted earlier, many are Marranos in the sense that contemporary Jewish identity is deeply personal, existential, and entirely voluntary. The experience of the Marrano suggests great opportunities for harnessing and developing one's Judaism coupled with enormous risks of assimilation and ultimately Jewish disappearance.

Interestingly, the nineteenth-century ultra-Orthodox rabbi Moses Sofer recognized the dangers of modernity in terms remarkably similar to Spinoza. Sofer echoed Spinoza in arguing that Judaism and modernity were incompatible. His advice, contrary to Spinoza, was to abandon modernity in favor of Judaism. The slogan of the ultra-Orthodox, following Sofer, became "whatever is new is forbidden from the Torah"—meaning an unabashed war against modern culture which persists in the ultra-Orthodox community to this day. Most modern Jews, however, are not prepared to accept either Spinoza or Sofer. While many have adopted outright assimilationist positions, and a tiny minority have clung to ultra-Orthodoxy, the broad mainstream of Jews as a people are groping to find points of interconnection between Judaic heritage and modern culture. Modern Jewish thought is an effort to respond to Spinoza, to identify the reasons why being Jewish makes sense in a modern framework and a modern context. Those efforts continue, and twentieth-century Zionism is but one in a long series of efforts by Jews to enter and embrace the modern world yet remain Jewish.

Spinoza carried his critique to yet another realm—the power of the Jewish community to compel obedience to its will. Spinoza argued in his *Theological-Political Treatise* that the state cannot compel religious observance. He argued for an early form of separation of church and state. The state may compel action, but it cannot compel belief. By that criterion, the Jewish community could no longer ensure adherence to its dictates. The power of excommunication had been the vehicle by which the Jewish community had insured compliance. What modernity now represented was the dilemma of keeping people Jewish without any compulsory force or penalties for doing so. The power of Judaism could now be only the power of moral persuasion. The dilemma of modern Jewry lies in finding ways of expressing morally persuasive positions in a culture in which Jewish practice and observance are at most optional.

Lastly, it is Spinoza who initiated a new language and formula for anti-Semitism. By arguing that Judaism was both an anachronism in the modern world and contrary to reason, Spinoza laid the groundwork for a new definition of anti-Semitism. Unlike the medieval world, where the expression of anti-Semitism was distinctly theological and religious, the modern expression was different in choice of idiom and language. No longer was the Jew condemned as Christ-killer, but as deficient in one or another modern category. For Spinoza to identify Judaism as an anachronism created the framework for a contemporary critique of Jews and Judaism as dissonant with or dangerous to modern European existence. Spinoza posed valid questions concerning the authenticity, historical accuracy, and Mosaic authorship of the Pentateuch. His answers to these questions, however, connoted the extinction of Judaism as a viable system. Judaism for him, too, became a fossil religion, failing to carry meaning in the contemporary world. That language of liberal anti-Semitism, opposing persecution of the Jews yet failing to find any internal merit in the preservation of Judaism, was echoed throughout the modern period.

For these reasons, one can both understand and criticize Spinoza's theory of Jewish survival—that the Jews survived solely on account of gentile persecution. One problem with the theory is that it is not true. Continued Jewish identity was more often a function of religious commitment and social cohesion than of gentile oppression. For that reason, Salo Baron, the greatest of Jewish historians, titled his work *Social and Religious History of the Jews* (18 volumes, Columbia University Press, 1952–1983) implying that it was Jewish society and religion that preserved Jews throughout the ages. Conversely, Baron negated the "lachrymose conception of Jewish history" which saw anti-Semitism as the central dominating feature of the Jewish historical experience. Secondly, and more importantly, Spinoza's theory of Jewish survival presupposed that Judaism lacked sufficient internal merit to be worth preserving on its own. That liberal thinking, echoed subsequently in the Enlightenment and in the twentieth century by no less a thinker than Jean-Paul Sartre, was pernicious in failing to respect the beliefs, values, and teachings of the Jews. It also suggested that the experience of the Jews with modern anti-Semitism would never be restricted to the political right. The political left, while most often disavowing attempts to persecute the Jews, saw little reason or merit in the Jews' preservation as a people. The Jewish romance with the left assumed that the left was free of anti-Semitism. Historical experience dictated that anti-Semitism would be found on both left and right.

Reading: Benedict Spinoza, *Theological-Political Treatise*

Spinoza's Theological-Political Treatise *is one of the earliest statements of modern biblical criticism. He argues that Moses could not have written the Pentateuch as indicated by historical anachronisms that simply would have been meaningless in Moses's time. To Spinoza, however, these are not simply points of intellectual dispute. The implication is rejection of the salience of Judaism in the modern world. Moses had designed a system that met the needs of a theocratic state. The answer for the Jews of today was to abandon Judaism in favor of joining the modern world. For that reason, some historians, particularly Arthur Hertzberg, have credited Spinoza with being the founder of modern anti-Semitism.*

Lastly, that in Deut. chapter iii., in the passage relating to Og, king of Bashan, these words are inserted: "For only Og king of Bashan remained of the remnant of giants: behold, his bedstead was a bedstead of iron; is it not in Rabbath of the children of Ammon? nine cubits was the length thereof, and four cubits the breadth of it, after the cubit of a man." This parenthesis most plainly shows that its writer lived long after Moses; for this mode of speaking is employed by one treating of things long past, and pointing to relics for the sake of gaining credence; moreover, this bed was almost certainly first discovered by David, who conquered the city of Rabbath (2 Sam. xii. 30) Again, the historian a little further on inserts after the words of Moses, "Jair, the son of Manasseh, took all of the country of Argob unto the coasts of Geshuri and Maachathi; and called them after his own name, Bashan-havot-jair, unto this day." This passage, I say, is inserted to explain the words of Moses which precede it. "And the rest of Gilead, and all Bashan, being the kingdom of Og, gave I unto the half tribe of Manasseh; all the region of Argob, with all Bashan, which is called the land of the giants." The Hebrews in the time of the writer indisputably knew what territories belonged to the tribe of Judah, but did not know them under the name of the jurisdiction of Argob, or the land of the giants. Therefore the writer is compelled to explain what these places were anciently so styled, and at the same time to point out why they were at the time of his writing known by the name of Jair, who was of the the tribe of Manasseh, not of Judah. We have thus made clear the meaning of Aben Ezra and also the passages of the Pentateuch which he cites in proof of his contention. However, Aben Ezra does not call attention to every instance, or even the chief ones; there remain many of greater importance, which may be cited. Namely (I.), that the writer of the books in question not only speaks of Moses in the third person, but also bears witness to many details concerning him; for instance, "Moses talked with God;" "The Lord spoke to Moses face to face;" "Moses was the meekest of men" (Numb. xii. 3); "Moses was wrathful with the captains of the host;" Moses, the man of God;" "Moses, the servant of the Lord, died;" "There was never a prophet in Israel like unto Moses," etc. On the other hand, in Deuteronomy, where the law which Moses had expounded to the people and written is set forth, Moses speaks and declares what he has done in the first person: "God spake with me" (Deut. ii. 1, 17, etc.), "I prayed to the Lord," etc. Except at the end of the book, when the historian, after relating the words of Moses, begins to speak in the third person, and to tell how Moses handed over the law which he had expounded to the people in writing, again admonishing them, and further, how Moses ended his life. All these details, the manner of narration, the testimony, and the context of the whole story lead to the plain conclusion that these books were written by another, and not by Moses in person.

We must also remark that the history relates not only the manner of Moses' death and burial, and the thirty days' mourning of the Hebrews, but further compares him with all the prophets who came after him, and states that he surpassed them all. "There was never a prophet in Israel like unto Moses, whom the Lord knew face to face." Such testimony cannot have been given of Moses by himself, nor by any who immediately succeeded him, but it must come from someone who lived centuries afterwards, especially as the historian speaks of past times. "There was never a prophet," etc. And of the place of burial, "No one knows it to this day."

We must note that some places are not styled by the names they bore during Moses' lifetime, but by others which they obtained subsequently. For instance, Abraham is said to have pursued his enemies even unto Dan, a name not bestowed on the city till long after the death of Joshua (Gen. xiv. 14, Judges xviii. 29).

The narrative is prolonged after the death of Moses, for in Exodus xvi.34 we read that "the children of Israel did eat manna forty years until they came to a land inhabited, until they came unto the borders of the land of Canaan." In other words, until the time alluded to in Joshua vi. 12.

So, too, in Genesis xxxvi. 31 it is stated, "These are the kings that reigned in Edom before there reigned any king over the children of Israel. The historian, doubtless, here relates the kings of Idumæa before that territory was conquered by David and garrisoned, as we read in 2 Sam. viii. 14.

From what has been said, it is thus clearer than the sun at noonday that the Pentateuch was not written by Moses, but by someone who lived long after Moses.

Bibliography for Further Reading

Roth, Cecil. *A History of the Marranos,* Jewish Publication Society, 1941

Yerushalmi, Yosef. *From Spanish Court to Italian Ghetto,* Columbia University Press, 1981

Yovel, Yirmiyahu. *Spinoza and Other Heretics,* Princeton University Press, 1989

Unit XIX

East European Jewry

Jewish Origins in Eastern Europe

The earliest references to Jewish settlement in Eastern Europe date from 345 B.C.E., when the Persian monarch Artaxerxes III was reported to have deported 10,000 Jews to the Caspian Sea. This may be related to a revolt by Jews against the Persian Empire, because we also have a report of the destruction of Jericho. If the report is authentic, it may suggest the origins of the "mountain Jews" of Southern Russia. Jews in Kurdistan and Armenia, to be sure, trace their origins to the Ten Lost Tribes. However, these reports cannot be authenticated. Josephus reports that the Armenian king Tigranes, a relative of Herod, settled Jews in Armenia in 10 C.E. Similarly, the Talmud reports a Rabbi Jacob of Armenia. The fact that Jews have survived in these areas into the twentieth century, frequently with widely varying customs and traits, suggests early sustained Jewish settlements in the region.

The earliest organized Jewish presence in Russia occurred in the Khazar kingdom, whose story excited the imaginations of Jews throughout the Middle Ages. Under the impact of Byzantine persecutions in the fourth through seventh centuries, Jews emigrated into Russia. By the eighth century the Khazar King Bulan adopted Judaism and declared his independence of Christianity and Islam. Most likely, this kingdom ceased to be Jewish by the tenth century. Arab historians record it as among the most tolerant of medieval states. The Khazars were ignorant of Talmudic law and offered animal sacrifices at local shrines. They refrained from lighting candles on Shabbat, reflecting Karaite influences.

The significance of the Khazar kingdom politically lay as a buffer zone and safety valve for Jews fleeing persecutions under Islam and Christianity. Psychologically, the existence of the Khazar kingdom stirred the messianic hopes of Jews everywhere. Economically, their kingdom facilitated Jewish trade routes eastward as far as China.

The Mongolian invasion of Genghis Khan destroyed the Khazar kingdom in the thirteenth century. Jews remaining in the area may have joined East European Jewish communities along the Polish-Russian border. By the thirteenth century Jews were being invited to settle in the frontier regions along the Lithuanian-Russian border. Casimir the Great, in 1344, granted a full charter of privileges to Jews to build up the newly-founded Polish state. Lacking a native bourgeoisie, Casimir hoped that Jews would increase the economic capacities of the Polish nation-state. Many towns possessed the privilege of *de non tolerandus Judaeis,* yet most generally allowed Jews to enter on market and fair days.

By contrast, the Russian czars were primarily interested in keeping Jews out of Russia. In 1563 Ivan IV conquered areas in which Jews were settled and forced them to convert to Christianity. In 1579 the area was reconquered by Poland, and Jews were permitted to return there.

Russian xenophobia prevented Jewish presence on Russian lands. Ivan prohibited Jewish merchants from doing business in Russia on the grounds that they marketed "poisonous herbs" and would corrupt the pure faith of native Russians. By the sixteenth century an interesting dichotomy had arisen between Russia and Poland: Jews were welcome to settle in Poland, and a vibrant Jewish community was developing there. Conversely, Russia's concern was to keep the Jews out.

Polish-Jewish Autonomy

Polish Jewry represented the most extensive example of Jewish communal autonomy in the Middle Ages. The Council of Four Lands originated in 1580 primarily as a tax-collecting super-communal Jewish organization. It enjoyed virtually complete autonomy. Jewish rabbinical conferences and synods were convened on a country-wide basis governing Jewish life throughout Poland.

Communal authorities regulated both the inner and outer lives of Polish Jewry. They supervised Jewish diplomacy, taxation, education, and Jewish-Christian relations, and Jewish courts were responsible for handing over Jewish criminals to the Polish police authority.

Consequently, there was widespread perception of strength within Poland and within Polish Jewry. The very name "Polin" became a play on two Hebrew words meaning, "Here we shall sleep," indicating that Jews were in Poland to stay. The Jewish population increased from 30,000 in 1500 to perhaps 500,000 by 1648. Jews had flocked to Poland from Western Europe, in particular from Germany, and Poland became the demographic center of Ashkenazic Jewry. There was some Karaite immigration from the south, but the overwhelming majority of Polish Jews were Rabbanite, and rabbinic authorities enjoyed the widest application of Jewish law to daily life.

Symbolizing this extension of rabbinic authority were the Polish *yeshivot,* the renowned academies of higher Jewish learning. These reached their apex in the sixteenth century, when perhaps more Jews were studying Talmud than at any previous moment in Jewish history. The Polish academies were famed for their contributions to Jewish law—particularly the work of Rabbi Moses Isserles, who composed the definitive commentary on the comprehensive code of Jewish law known as the *Shulhan Arukh* ("The Arranged Table").

To be sure, there were those who criticized the methods of the Polish *yeshivot,* which placed heavy stress on rote learning and memorization. The method known as the *pilpul* referred to logical arguments and counter-arguments on the literal meaning of the texts, with little emphasis placed on the values underlying it. Later Hasidism criticized this trend as lacking religious feeling and experience. Nevertheless, the greatness of Polish Jewry was in many ways tied to the eminence of its *yeshivot.*

Nor was learning restricted to Jewish men. Polish Jewry developed a comprehensive biblical commentary for women known as the *Tsena U'rena* ("Go Out and See"). The commentary was tied to the needs of the prayer book and synagogue, enabling women to follow the weekly services. Although women's learning lagged behind that of men, the development of the *Tsena U'rena* signaled growing recognition of the need for women's Judaic literacy albeit directed differently—toward the moralistic, homiletic, and exhortative rather than the *halacha,* which remained essentially a male preserve.

The extent of communal autonomy was perhaps best captured in the *hezkat hayishuv,* or right of settlement. Jewish immigrants wishing to come to Polish cities had to apply for permission by the communal authorities. These were particularly concerned about the economic capacity of Jewish communities to absorb new immigrants and the number of marriageable men and women. On the surface, this *hezkat hayishuv* was clearly undemocratic. In principle, Jews ought to have enjoyed the right of settlement anywhere. It reflected, however, the power of Jews to regulate their own affairs and, at times, to overrule individual freedoms in the name of communal health and stability.

Generally, anti-Semitism was negligible, and tolerance prevailed in Poland. To be sure, there were some restrictions in Polish cities. The Polish crown, however, intervened regularly on behalf of Jews. University students did occasionally attack Jews for sport. During sectarian controversies within Polish Christianity, Jews were often caught in the middle. The Jesuits, in particular, projected greater anti-Semitism within Polish Christianity. Therefore, one could not speak of anti-Semitism as non-existent. However, Polish tolerance clearly overshadowed traditions of anti-Semitism.

Economically, Jews enjoyed a broad array of occupations in Poland. Jews were found in agriculture, innkeeping, liquor distilling, and rent-collecting (*arendators*). To be sure, these occupations set the stage for conflict between Jews and Polish peasants. Moreover, banking and trading remained important. In 1607, the Council of Four Lands ruled that it was permitted for Jews to take interest, provided they did so as a joint stock corporation or partnership. Interest from individual to individual remained prohibited, but the needs of a credit economy could be met by creating the legal fiction of a joint stock partnership. This *"heter iska,"* or permission granted for business purposes, reflected again rabbinical willingness to reinterpret Jewish law and apply it to new situations. The rabbis preserved the principle of not collecting interest, but de facto transformed it to meet a new economic reality.

Lastly, Jews developed their own guilds regulated by the Council of Four Lands. Medieval guilds functioned as trade associations, regulating prices and providing collegial fellowship among members of the craft, as well as training new people to enter apprenticeships followed by journeyman status. However, the medieval guilds were generally laden with Christian symbolism and often excluded Jews from membership. To function economically, Jews began developing their own guilds to fulfill the identical functions of price-fixing, collegiality, and training. The presence of guilds, to be sure, obviated the presence of a free market, for prices were fixed in accordance with the doctrine of the "just price."

The Cossack Rebellion and the Chmielnicki Pogroms

The Cossacks constituted primarily Ukrainian peasants. They had not been noticeably anti-Semitic, and some Jews had served in the Cossack armies. Earlier the Cossacks had rebelled against their Polish overlords, but without evidence of anti-Semitism and also without success.

In the Cossack rebellion of 1648, anti-Semitism became a critical ingredient in arousing strong feelings of rebellion. Bodgan Chmielnicki, who had earlier employed Jewish generals, now claimed that Jews were persecuting the Greek Orthodox. In effect, Chmielnicki transformed the rebellion into an anti-Jewish crusade in which anti-Semitism served as the ideological-moral justification for the revolt.

The pogroms themselves have been highly exaggerated in number of victims. Estimates range as high as 100,000, but there were at most 50,000 Jews in the Ukraine. Once again, the ideology of martyrdom prevalent in Ashkenazic lands became part and parcel of the Jewish estimate of the pogroms. To be sure, many Jews physically resisted the Cossacks, especially when they received support from the Polish nobility. Most left the Cossack lands for the cities and returned to the Ukraine once the rebellion had subsided. Some were forcibly converted, and these were later permitted to return to Judaism.

The 1649 treaty, however, forbade Jews from the Ukraine. Warfare continued in the area for the next 20 years, culminating in intervention by the Swedish king, for Sweden had long taken an interest in Russian affairs. Jews now were accused of collaborating with the Swedes.

For Jews, the 1648 pogroms represented a fundamental psychological blow. 1648 had been a year of messianic expectations based upon biblical calculations. These expectations, again, were both futile and psychologically discouraging. Secondly, the community was now impoverished, with greater social polarity between rich and poor. Only the wealthy could now afford extensive Talmudic education and thereby rise to the top of the Jewish social ladder. Many indeed left Poland, particularly for Germany, and a decline of Jewish learning occurred as leading rabbis emigrated. Hasidism subsequently protested against the tyranny of the rich, suggesting that the social chasm had broadened, particularly in the aftermath of the 1648 pogroms.

The Council of Four Lands tried to normalize Jewish life. It instituted a fast day to commemorate the tragedy and pressured the monarchy to grant the Jews certain tax reductions. Jewish historian Simon Dubnov claims that a "decline of Polish Jewry occurred after 1650." In practice, the decline was probably more psychological than physical, for the *kehilla* and the Council of Four Lands remained vibrant through the eighteenth century. Generally, Jews had received protection from the Polish crown. By contrast, the pressure for persecution had emanated from the Catholic Church.

Moreover, the *kehilla* continued to function much as it had prior to 1648. The rabbis maintained authority in social and spiritual matters. The power of excommunication insured compliance to the will of the *kehilla.* Even capital punishment could be invoked in extreme cases. The *kehilla* organized all communal institutions ranging from prayer to charity to education to real estate, taxes, cemeteries, and the courts. The super-communal agency, the Council of Four Lands, continued to be responsible for diplomacy, Jewish-Christian relationships, and setting standards of education throughout Poland.

Clearly, atrocities occurred, as recorded in both Jewish and general sources. However, the majority of Jews survived and the community managed to continue. The Cossacks were by no means racially oriented, as were the Nazis, for many Jews survived via temporary conversion to Christianity. However, there is no question that psychologically the name Chmielnicki became associated with the worst atrocities and tragedies of Jewish history. Only the twentieth century experience of Hitler reduced the demonic stature of Chmielnicki.

Moreover, in the eighteenth century the invasions and pogroms recurred. The Haidamak massacres of 1768 signified renewal of the

Cossack pogroms. There was also a rise in blood libels at the time, stemming from rivalry of Catholic and Greek Orthodox clergy. Catholic clergy renewed the blood libels, often as a vehicle to demonstrate greater religious zealousness than their Greek Orthodox colleagues.

At the same time, one could begin to see signs of westernization in Polish Jewish culture. The men of the enlightenment emphasized the importance of secular learning. In particular, they rebelled against the practice of early arranged marriages. They expressed an early voice on behalf of romantic love and the nuclear family, criticizing the prevailing family pattern which often led to personal tragedies when young people were married by communal decision, absent any personal or romantic ties between them. These "enlighteners" also criticized the degree of superstition within Polish-Jewish Kabbalah. As mysticism gained popularity in Poland, it had become much more "practical" or inclined towards magical and superstitious rituals that would affect changes in human life. For example, the well-known *Book of Raziel* was meant to protect homes against fires. The men of the enlightenment, or *maskilim,* pointed to the fact that homes had burned down in any case.

That is not to say that the men of the enlightenment were anti-Orthodox. On the contrary, they wrapped themselves in the mantle of Maimonides and defended the rational Orthodoxy of enlightened circles. They articulated a religion of reason and a rejection of dogma. Many entered into fields of science and medicine. What the Haskalah represented was a movement for internal Jewish change, urging Jews to abandon traditional models of mysticism in favor of more "enlightened" religion and greater secular education. Their critique of the Jewish family amounted to what we would call today a return to the traditional model of family of parents and children living together harmoniously. Significantly, they invoked the image of the Bible, with its focus upon romantic love rather than upon arranged marriages. Lastly, they derided the tendency of very young people to marry on the grounds that they simply were not ready for the serious responsibilities and commitments necessary for marriages to work.

What put an end to Polish Jewry was not the Cossack rebellion nor the aftermath of the Haidamak massacres. Rather, the Polish partitions of the late eighteenth century ended Poland as a state and bequeathed Russia a Jewish population of over 750,000 Jews. Until then, Russia had been relatively *"judenrein,"* although a small Jewish colony had existed in Moscow. Russian policy had clearly been exclusionary. The demise of Poland as a nation-state and the partition of Poland between Russia and Austria created a new Jewish settlement in Russia and significantly raised the question of how Russia would treat her Jews.

Reading: Nathan Hannover, selections in Michael Meyer ed., *Ideas of Jewish History*

Nathan Hannover was born in Poland and traveled extensively through Central Europe. In 1653, he published the volume entitled Yeven Metzula *("Deep Mire") chronicling the Chmielnicki pogroms. His account is very much in the tradition of the "lachrymose conception of Jewish history," relating the 1648 pogroms to a long chain of Jewish persecutions. In general, he ascribes the pogroms to punishment for Jewish sins. In the selection included here, he notes how the entire chain of Jewish persecution was foreseen by David in the* Psalms.

Jewish History as Prophecy Fulfilled

> "I am the man that hath seen affliction by the rod of His wrath" (Lam. 3:1). For the Lord smote His people Israel, His firstborn. From heaven to earth He cast down His glorious and lovely land of Poland, "fair in situation, the joy of the whole earth" (Ps. 48:3) and His ornament. "The Lord hath swallowed up unsparingly the habitations of Jacob" (Lam. 2:2), destroyed His inheritance, "and hath not remembered His footstool on the day of His wrath" (ibid., 2:1) and His anger.
>
> All of this did King David (may he rest in peace) foresee in his prophecy: that Tatars and Greeks would join together to destroy Israel, His chosen, in the year *zot* of His creation. The Greeks said, as is their custom: "Whoever wants to stay alive must change his faith and make a public statement renouncing Israel and its God." But the Jews paid no heed to their words; they stretched out their necks for the slaughter, sanctifying the name of God. These were the land's great scholars and the oth-

er men, women, and children: all of His community. "The Lord is a God of vengeance" (Ps. 94:1). May He wreak His vengeance and return us to His land.

King David (may he rest in peace) forewarns of this [*zot*] persecution in Psalm 32 (vs. 6): "For this [*zot*] let everyone that is godly pray unto Thee in a time when Thou mayest be found [*le'et metzo*] . . ." so that the calamity will not come about. The letters of the words *le'et metzo* have the same numerical value as *yavan vekedar yahdav hubaru* [Greece and Tatary joined together]. Dog and cat joined to uproot the people of Israel, which is compared to a straying lamb. It happened in the year five thousand and *zot* [408] of the Creation.

Psalm 69 (vss. 2-3) also refers to this persecution: "Save me, O God. . . . I am sunk in deep mire . . . and the flood overwhelmeth me" etc. *Tavati biven metzula* [I am sunk in deep mire] possesses the numerical value of *hemil vekedar beyavan yahdav hubaru* [Chmiel and Tatary joined together with Greece], scorpion and wasp. *Shibolet* [the flood] is numerically equivalent to *hemiletzki, bayavan, vekedar* [Chmielnicki, Greece, and Tatary]; thus wrath and anger overwhelmed me. (In the Polish language his name was changed to Chmielecki to indicate his nobility, but in Russian he was called Chmiel.) The great scholar, our teacher R. Jehiel Michel, judge and head of the academy in the holy and precious community of Nemirov, whose soul departed in purity for the santification of God's name, said that *hemil* was an acronym for *havlei masbiah yavi le'olam* [he will bring about the birth pangs of the messiah]; and after him will come the feet of Elijah.

Therefore I have called my book dealing with this incident *Yeven Metzula* ["Deep Mire"] for the Psalmist alludes to the catastrophe and speaks of the enemy nation, Tatars and Greeks, and of the enemy Chmiel (may his name be blotted out; may the Lord send a curse upon him). This book shall preserve the tale for future generations. I have dwelt at length upon the causes which initiated this brutish design: that the Greeks revolted against the kingdom of Poland like a rebellious cow, that Greeks and Tatars joined together although they had always hated each other. I have related all of the battles and persecutions, large and small. Likewise, the dates on which the major persecutions occurred have been recorded so that everyone might be able to note the day on which his father or mother died and to observe the memorial properly. The book will also describe all of the good and just practices of the glorious Jewish community of Poland-all in the pure fear of the Lord. I based these practices upon the six pillars which support the mighty world.

I have written it all in lucid, clear language and printed it upon fine, clean paper. Therefore, buy this book without delay. Do not withhold your money. Thus I will be able also to publish the book *Plant of Delights* containing homilies I have composed on all of the Torah. For this merit, God, fearful and awesome, will preserve you from every anguish and distress. And may He speedily send us the Messiah. Amen; thus may God do, who dwelleth in splendor. These are the words of the author, Nathan Nata, son of our teacher, R. Moses Hannover Ashkenazi (may the memory of the righteous be for a blessing; may the Lord avenge his blood) who lived in the holy community of Zaslav, which is near the large holy community of Ostrog in the province of Volhynia in the great land of Russia.

Bibliography for Further Reading

Biale, David. *Eros and the Jews,* Basic Books, 1992

Dunlop, Douglas. *History of the Jewish Khazars,* Schocken Books, 1967

Weinryb, Bernard. *The Jews of Poland,* Jewish Publication Society, 1973

Unit XX

Sabbetianism and its Aftermath

Lurianic Kabbalism

The background to Sabbetianism lies in the transformation of Jewish mysticism in sixteenth-century Safed in Palestine. Another response to the expulsion of the Jews from Spain, in addition to the economic and social ones described in Unit XVIII, was the renewal of Jewish mysticism in the Holy Land. Under the leadership of Isaac Luria and his primary disciple, Hayyim Vital, who came to Safed in the 1560's, Kabbalism now emphasized tenets that signified renewed interest in Jewish messianism. Particularly salient among Luria's doctrines was the transmigration of souls, or reincarnation. Earlier Jewish mysticism had relegated reincarnation to the periphery—strictly as punishment for crimes of sexual deviancy. In Luria's concept, however, transmigration of souls became central. Every soul had a specific purpose to accomplish in this world. If the body died before that purpose was accomplished, the soul would be reincarnated in yet another figure who would advance the work further.

All individuals, then, possess specific purpose and meaning to their lives in this world. What is the purpose? A second major doctrine of Luria's was that of *tikkun olam,* the repair of the world. This related to a cosmic tragedy that had taken place at the time of creation. During the process of creation, the vessels containing the original emanations of *sefirot* had shattered. In place of the order of creation, there was now chaos. Good and evil were hopelessly intermixed. The task assigned to humanity was to restore that order, to liberate the sparks of good from the shells of evil. The original Adam had virtually accomplished the task in the Garden of Eden. However, the fall of man in partaking of the Tree of Knowledge had set the processes back. The task remained that of repair of the world. But rather than being accomplished on the sixth day of creation, as originally intended, that task had now been given over to the entire course of human history.

Why had the cosmic tragedy occurred originally? Some Kabbalists assigned it to the doctrine of *tzimtzum*, or contraction. The doctrine of contraction asked how the infinite God could have created a finite world. The answer lay in Divine contraction, God's withdrawing from part of the universe, leaving space for this world to come into existence. In so doing, the Infinite remained Infinite (Infinity minus five is still Infinity), yet space was now created where God was not. Allowing that space to come into existence permitted the possibility for a finite universe to be created. However, given that the finite universe was a place where God was not, the possibility for evil being very real and terrible was quite strong.

Yet another theory ascribed the tragedy to Divine will. Had God not permitted the cosmic tragedy to take place, there would have been no purpose to human existence. Divine contraction permitted the possibility for human beings to be free. In being free they possessed the potential for actions that could be angelic or demonic, for real freedom implied the freedom to do evil as well as good. Having that freedom gave purpose, direction, and nobility to human action. But that freedom required a contraction of Divine power, or creating a place where God was not. The cosmic tragedy thus gave purpose and direction to how humanity could utilize its freedom.

Sixteenth-century Kabbalists believed that the processes of *tikkun* were nearly complete. The redemption was imminent, for after a long period of repair, the Divine harmony had once again been nearly restored. It was unclear what the role of the messiah would be except perhaps to declare that *tikkun* was complete and that redemption had arrived. However, redemption was clearly defined as the culmination of *tikkun*. This redemptive spirit impelled the immigration to Palestine and particularly Safed, which was favored over the more difficult conditions in Jerusalem.

The idea of messianism in this Kabbalistic revision was restorative rather than catastrophic, for redemption would culminate a long period of human *tikkun*. The vision of the future was by no means apocalyptic, but rather viewed redemption as gradually evolving from a long period of constructive human endeavor. There was little emphasis, in this view, upon a personal redeemer. Exactly what the messiah himself would do was left quite unclear.

What this view of redemption did accomplish was to infuse new meaning to the exile. The exile was not punishment for sin but rather a further step in the processes of *tikkun*—spreading the Jews out across the world to enable them to advance the process of *tikkun* everywhere. Ironically, this Kabbalistic view to some extent anticipated nineteenth-century Reform and neo-Orthodoxy's concept of a universalist Jewish mission to the gentiles. On a more immediate level, it explained the exile from Spain as one of the last steps in the spreading of *tikkun*.

Sixteenth-century Safed did nurture a Jewish renewal. Moses Cordovero articulated the theoretical Kabbalah in which Kabbalistic theosophy, or knowledge of God, was defined as knowledge of the *sefirot*—the "words" of God, which, from a Divine perspective were part of the Infinite, but from a human perspective could be perceived as independent entities. Cordovero thereby negated the concept of the Kabbalah as being polytheistic. All the *sefirot* were contained within the Infinite. Human beings could perceive them only if they were independent entities.

At this time, Joseph Karo authored the comprehensive code of Jewish law known as the *Shulhan Arukh* ("the arranged table"). This book became the definitive guidebook for the codes of Jewish practices through modern times. Karo himself was a Kabbalist as well as a halachist par excellence.

More generally, Lurianic messianism proclaimed a doctrine of human perfectibility. The entire Jewish people contained within it the mission and the responsibility to redeem the world—to complete the processes of *tikkun*. By doing so, they would create the good society. As Gershom Scholem has noted, this form of Kabbalah approximated more the nineteenth-century idea of progress than did the classical notions of a personal redeemer. By freeing messianism of its apocalyptic elements, Kabbalah infused human activity with Divine and historical purpose. The exile now became a mission to free the sparks of good rather than punishment for sin.

Transmigration of souls would ensure that Divine purpose be continued from generation to generation.

Sabbetai Zvi

Sabbetai Zvi was born in Smyrna in 1628. Gershon Scholem described him as a manic-depressive, performing bizarre acts in high periods of mania and subsequently regretting them in deep periods of depression.

Sabbetai's actions were truly bizarre. He pronounced the Tetragrammaton, the ineffable four-letter name of the Almighty. He told the sun to stop in the heavens. He put a fish in a crib and pronounced over it that the redemption would come by the constellation of Pisces. Twice he married without consummation. A third time he married a prostitute of whom it had been prophesied that she would marry the messiah. Yet a fourth marriage was conducted with a Torah scroll. Sabbetai also changed the calendar, observing the three holidays of Succot, Passover, and Shavout all within the span of one week. He called women to the Torah, reflecting an attempt at liberation of women from the repressive conditions within the Ottoman Empire and promised to free them from the ancient curse of Eve. Lastly, he abolished the historical fasts of the Jews commemorating the destruction of Jerusalem.

All these actions seemed to have redemptive implications. Some of them purported to reflect the redemptive powers of the messiah himself. Others reflected a new messianic era in which the calendar would be changed and aspects of Jewish law altered. Subsequently, Sabbetai regretted these actions during periods of depression.

What transformed Sabbetai from visionary to messianic pretender was Nathan of Gaza, a brilliant Talmudist and Kabbalist, who was said to have received a vision declaring Sabbetai to be the messiah. Nathan believed himself to be a reincarnation of Isaac Luria, and he quickly emerged as the critical ideologian declaring Sabbetai leader of a messianic movement.

Moreover, Sabbetai received considerable support from rabbis of the time. The rabbinate was split on the issue. Initially, the rabbis excommunicated Sabbetai and exiled him from Smyrna. He went to Salonika and subsequently to Constantinople, where he was again excommunicated and beaten by the rabbis.

However, rabbinic opposition to Sabbetai declined in light of the widespread repentance taking place among the Jews in Sabbetai's circles and the absence of Christian opposition. The year 1666 had been calculated as potentially a messianic year both in Jewish and in Christian circles. Moreover, Sabbetai based himself on the Lurianic doctrine that the messianic era would dawn peacefully rather than via great battles or upheavals. As a result, in Egypt and in Palestine Sabbetai received considerable rabbinic support. Opposition to him grew further away from his primary sphere of activity in the Ottoman Empire.

Nathan's theology provided the movement with a belief system. In some respects, this approximated and reflected a number of Christian influences. For example, the test of who was a Jew now became belief in Sabbetai, despite the absence of specific signs that he was the redeemer. Moreover, Nathan argued that at the end of days many of the physical commandments, or *mitzvot,* would be abolished. Once the shells of evil had been removed and cosmic harmony been restored, there was no purpose in continuing with the specific commandments of the Jews. This obviously approximated the Christian doctrine of supersession, namely that the Torah of the Jews had once been purposeful but was no longer salient in the new era of Jesus.

Some rabbis, to be sure, worried whether Sabbetai was only one in a long line of failed messiahs and messianic pretenders. Jacob Saspourtas in Hamburg argued that Sabbetai's failure could have adverse psychological effects, while the antinomian and Christological positions articulated by Nathan signaled positions radically at odds with rabbinic Judaism. Nathan had said that Sabbetai would save the soul of Jesus, and Sabbetai himself was intrigued by the relationship of Jesus to the messiah. Sabbetai was rumored to have counted Jesus as one of the prophets.

The Moslem authorities, too, were concerned about Sabbetianism. Although Sabbetai did not launch a political and military campaign, Moslems were concerned over the disruption of normal life and adverse economic impact within the Ottoman Empire. Therefore they imprisoned Sabbetai, although he continued to hold court while in an Ottoman prison. However, the absence of persecution against him and his followers in some respects strengthened his legitimacy, for usually rebels were put to death quietly. In arresting Sabbetai, the Moslems were apparently encouraged by Jewish authorities who articulated traditional Jewish opposition to messianism. Like the Moslems, they, too, were concerned about the phenomenon of Jews, especially Jewish women, prophesying in the streets of Smyrna.

Ultimately, the Moslems offered Sabbetai the choices of conversion or death. In "taking the turban," or converting to Islam, Sabbetai was said to have saved Ottoman Jewry from a pogrom at the hands of the Turkish authorities. Nathan explained Sabbetai's conversion as an act of redemption. In Nathan's theology the actual function of the messiah was to liberate the last sparks of good. However, these were so closely encapsulated in shells of evil that to fulfill his task the messiah himself had to enter the midst of evil in order to liberate the good. Sabbetai's conversion, in this view, became a hidden act of *tikkun*. Nathan pointed to the precedents of Moses, the original redeemer, living his early life as an Egyptian, and Esther, who saved the Jewish people by becoming a Persian queen. This vision of the messiah as taking on another faith for redemptive purposes had special appeal to the Marrano Jewish population, who also saw their self-image as that of Esther and Moses.

Nathan counseled that no Jews should follow Sabbetai into Islam. Most now abandoned the movement entirely, for a converted messiah was no longer a successful messiah. A tiny minority of Jews followed Sabbetai into Islam. They maintained an underground Jewish existence into the twentieth century, known as the Donmeh.

Nathan did counsel Jews to continue believing in Sabbetai, whose ups and downs were now explained on the basis of the history of his soul as it struggled to attain its appropriate quotient of *tikkun*. Moreover, the movement did not lose complete momentum. There were many rumors of Jewish armies ready to march on Palestine, linking up with the Ten Lost Tribes in the East. Christian chiliasm, in turn, fed upon these rumors, given traditional Christian concern identifying the messiah with the destruction of the Moslem Turks. In fairness, the rumors were not given great credence by Jews, and Nathan himself discouraged belief in miracles. Nathan rejected medieval Jewish political models. He urged the Jews no longer to be dependent upon outside assistance. In the messianic era the Jews would be self-sufficient and self-reliant. In this context Nathan presaged an incipient Jewish modernity—of rebellion against the Jewish status quo and an attempt to shape the

Jewish future in directions shaped by the Jews themselves rather than by relying upon external events.

Sabbetai died in 1676. His apostasy followed by his death produced a crisis in Jewish messianism. Most reverted to traditional Jewish politics, although Scholem has traced a Sabbetian underground persisting even into the nineteenth century—people who openly rejoined the Jewish community, but privately believed in the messiahship of Sabbetai Zvi. The rabbis themselves attempted to restore normalcy, but the damage wrought by the Sabbetian movement was quite considerable. Hysteria persisted among the masses, who felt that Sabbetai's failure had shattered Jewish aspirations and hopes.

The Sabbetians themselves explained Sabbetai's death as part of the greater travails that the messiah himself would undergo to bring the redemption. Some argued that Sabbetai had not really died but had simply ascended to heaven and awaited his return. Nathan himself continued to wander in the Mediterranean preaching the imminent "second coming" of Sabbetai Zvi. Some noted the miracle that the Jews had been saved, for the Turkish authorities had left them alone despite a virtual act of rebellion.

Sabbetai's followers now split into several groups. The Donmeh consisted of about 200 families who felt that Sabbetai had demanded their conversion as well. These led a Marrano-type existence within the Ottoman Empire, avoiding intermarriage with Turks. As a particular subgroup within the Empire, they maintained clandestine relations with rabbis in Salonika. Their estimates varied and clearly never attained numbers greater than 10,000. However, they were a critical element in the Young Turk movement of the early twentieth century, the Committee for Union and Progress, seeking to modernize Turkey as a nation-state. With the 1923 Ataturk Revolution, the CUP and the Donmeh within it felt that their task had been accomplished, and they rapidly assimilated within Turkish society. There were reports, however, of Nazi murders of Donmeh in Greece during World War II.

A more radical expression of Sabbetianism was the Frankist movement led by Jacob Frank. Frank argued for a radical reversal of values, especially sexual values. The last actions of the messiah had indeed been acts of *tikkun*. However, the sparks of good were now so deeply encased in shells of evil that Sabbetai's true followers had to enter the midst of evil in order to liberate the good.

Under these circumstances, the distinctions between good and evil collapsed. The good had become evil, and the evil had become good. As a result, Frank renounced the Talmud and encouraged Polish Catholic bishops to order debates with rabbis to facilitate conversion to Christianity. The disputation resulted in the burning of the Talmud in eighteenth-century Poland. Frank was persecuted by the Polish *kehilla* and sought revenge by testifying on behalf of blood libels against Jews. Ultimately, Frank merged into Catholicism, yet before doing so, he seems to have entertained territorial dreams of personal kingship posing as a Polish noble who imposed rigid discipline upon his followers. He provided official sanction to sexual depravity including wife-swapping and sexual orgies. Also he trained six-year-old children in the martial arts. His conversion provided a measure of relief to the rabbis of the *kehilla.* Frank died in 1791. However, his daughter Eva maintained his court through Napoleonic times. In fact, Frankists were numbered among the supporters of the French Revolution as well as other progressive causes.

The significance of Frankism lay in its transmutation of values. The holy had become profane, and the profane had become sacred. Frank represented reversal of the traditional covenant among the Jews to sanctify the holy and desecrate the profane.

Most Jews, and for that matter most followers of Sabbetai, did not express themselves in so radical a way. However, fairly widespread "moderate Sabbetianism" continued within the Jewish community through the eighteenth century. This moderate Sabbatianism accepted the apostasy and death of Sabbetai as necessary steps, for redemption was a long process, and until its final culmination, Jews must continue to live their lives as Jews. Yet moderate Sabbetianism embroiled the Jewish community in endless controversy over who was a covert Sabbetian. Some rabbis became heresy hunters, trying to ferret out closet Sabbetians among their colleagues. Others conducted clandestine Sabbetian courts in which they taught their followers the secrets of Sabbetai Zvi.

For example, the conflict between two major rabbis, Jacob Emden and Jonathan Eybueschuetz, rocked the Jewish community in the mid-eighteenth century. Emden, although generally sympathetic to Moses Mendelsohnn, (see Unit XXII) was the leading heresy-hunter among the eighteenth-century rabbis. Eybueschuetz was a well-known halachist. On the basis of written evidence,

Emden accused Eybueschuetz of being secretly a Sabbetian heretic. Although the Polish Council of Four Lands ultimately decided in favor of Eybueschuetz, the damage had been done in undermining the cohesiveness of Jewish communal life and respect for the rabbinate as an institution.

What then does one make of Sabbetianism? Clearly it was the most powerful messianic movement affecting Jewish history. Like other messianic movements, it failed and was destructive in its psychological impact upon Jews. The Sabbetian debacle left a residue of sadness and frustration within the Jewish community. To some extent modern Hasidism would be an effort to restore the joy to Jewish life after the Sabbetian catastrophe.

Secondly, Sabbetianism embodied the ethos of Jewish modernism. Although ostensibly a medieval movement rooted in Jewish mysticism, the ethos of Sabbetianism, like the ethos of the Marrano phenomenon, bore a distinctively modern cast. Sabbetianism rebelled from within against Jewish tradition. It challenged the authority of rabbinic leadership. It forecast major changes in Jewish ritual and practice. Although one should not go so far as to link Sabbetianism with the Reform movement of the nineteenth century, it is fair to say that Sabbetianism created a climate within the Jewish community in which religious changes and reform became more legitimate options. The early reformers clearly were not Sabbetians. However, they operated within a context in which the authority of rabbinic leadership had been challenged profoundly.

Lastly, Sabbetianism challenged the basis for medieval Jewish existence. It held out the promise of the Jews forging their own destiny. It would be an overstatement to equate the Sabbetians with modern Zionists. However, modern Zionists operated also within a climate in which Jews perceived alternative possible futures. The legacy of Sabbetianism enabled Jews to consider other directions for Jewish life. In that respect, although destructive as a movement, Sabbetianism laid the foundations for new directions in modern Jewish history.

The fundamental legacy of Sabbetianism, however, was frustration and despair. Like other messianic movements, although far more extensively, Sabbetianism had raised the hopes of Jews, only to see them shattered. As far away as Amsterdam, Spinoza's secretary had written to him inquiring about his opinion concerning this messianic movement. Other reports of Sabbetianism existed as far away as England. The failure of Sabbetianism reflected the folly of placing so many hopes in a would-be redeemer. The glory of Hasidism, as we will see in the next unit, was to restore some of the joy to Jewish living given the Sabbetian failure. Ironically, Hasidim itself would spawn the next major messianic upheaval in modern Jewish history. In the late twentieth century, the followers of the Lubavitcher Rebbe would launch a frenzy of messianic activity identifying the Rebbe with the messiah. Similar lessons, however, are to be learned. The frustrated messianic expectations among the Rebbe's followers, especially in the interval since his death, have bred only disappointment and despair. Traditional rabbinic wisdom of focusing less upon a messianic redeemer and more upon constructing day-to-day Jewish lives is far healthier advice than placing bets on whether a particular individual qualifies as the messiah.

Reading: Moses Maimonides, "Laws Concerning the Installation of Kings"

During the controversy over the messiahship of Sabbetai Zvi, supporters and opponents of Sabbetai alike turned to the writings of Moses Maimonides for validation. Maimonides had been a leading spokesman for the "rational" view of the messiah, downplaying miracles and apocalyptic events. Rather, in this view, the world will continue on its present course with the critical exceptions of the security of Israel among the nations and the rule of peace in international relations. Most importantly, Maimonides had argued that rabbinic tradition was unclear about the particular course of events at the end of days, and therefore people should not exert energies seeking to calculate the messianic time or its details. Ironically, supporters of Sabbetai cited these Maimonidean statements as proof-texts that Sabbetai could still be the messiah even though he had not performed major miracles. The spirit underlying these Maimonidean writings, of course, discouraged active messianic movements.

The Messiah will arise and restore the kingdom of David to its former might. He will rebuild the sanctuary and gather the dispersed of Israel. All the laws will be reinstituted in his days as of old. Sacrifices will be offered and the Sabbatical and Jubilee years will be observed exactly in accordance with the commandments of the Torah. But whoever does not believe in him or does not await his coming denies not only the rest of the prophets, but also the Torah and our teacher Moses.

Do not think that the Messiah needs to perform signs and miracles, bring about a new state of things in the world, revive the dead, and the like. It is not so. . . . Rather it is the case in these matters that the statutes of our Torah are valid forever and eternally. Nothing can be added to them or taken away from them. And if there arise a king from the House of David who meditates on the Torah and practices its commandments like his ancestor David in accordance with the Written and Oral Law, prevails upon all Israel to walk in the ways of the Torah and to repair its breaches [i.e., to eliminate the bad state of affairs resulting from the incomplete observance of the law], and fights the battles of the Lord, then one may properly assume that he is the Messiah. If he is then successful in rebuilding the sanctuary on its site and in gathering the dispersed of Israel, then he has in fact [as a result of his success] proven himself to be the Messiah. He will then arrange the whole world to serve only God, as it is said: "For then I shall create a pure language for the peoples that they may all call upon the name of God and serve him with one accord" (Zeph. 3:9).

Let no one think that in the days of the Messiah anything of the natural course of the world will cease or that any innovation will be introduced into creation. Rather, the world will continue in its accustomed course. The words of Isaiah: "The wolf shall dwell with the lamb and the panther shall lie down with the kid" (Isa. 11:6) are a parable and an allegory which must be understood to mean that Israel will dwell securely even among the wicked of the heathen nations who are compared to a wolf and a panther. For they will all accept the true faith and will no longer rob or destroy. Likewise, all similar scriptural passages dealing with the Messiah must be regarded as figurative. Only in the Days of the Messiah will everyone know what the metaphors mean and to what they refer. The sages said: "The only difference between this world and the Days of the Messiah is the subjection of Israel to the nations."

From the simple meaning of the words of the prophets it appears that at the beginning of the Days of the Messiah the war between Gog and Magog will take place. . . . Concerning all these things and others like them, no one knows how they will come about until they actually happen, since the words of the prophets on these matters are not clear. Even the sages have no tradition regarding them but allow themselves to be guided by the texts. Hence there are differences of opinion on the subject. In any case, the order and details of these events are not religious dogmas. Therefore a person should never occupy himself a great deal with the legendary accounts nor spend much time on the Midrashim dealing with these and similar matters. He should not regard them as of prime importance, since devoting himself to them leads neither to the fear nor to the love of God. . . .

The sages and prophets longed for the days of the Messiah not in order to rule over the world and not to bring heathens under their control, not to be exalted by the nations, or even to eat, drink and rejoice. All they wanted was to have time for the Torah and its wisdom with no one to oppress or disturb them.

In that age there will be neither famine nor war, nor envy nor strife, for there will be an abundance of worldly goods. The whole world will be occupied solely with the knowledge of God. Therefore the Children of Israel will be great sages; they will know hidden things and attain an understanding of their Creator to the extent of human capability, as it is said: "For the earth shall be full of knowledge of God as the waters cover the sea" (Isa. 11:9).

Bibliography for Further Reading

Carlebach, Elisheva. *The Pursuit of Heresy,* Columbia University Press, 1990

Schechter, Solomon. "Safed in the 16th Century," *Studies in Judaism,* Athenaeum, 1970

Scholem, Gershom. "Redemption Through Sin," *The Messianic Idea in Judaism,* Schocken Books, 1971

———. *Sabbetai Sevi,* Princeton University Press, 1973

Unit XXI

Hasidism

Origins

Hasidism originated in eighteenth-century Poland. Its primary founder was Rabbi Israel Baal Shem, who was born approximately 1700 C.E. and appeared to most people to be an ordinary laborer. He was not known for his Talmudic scholarship, the primary symbol of authority in the Jewish community, nor, of course, was he known for possessing wealth.

Rather, the term "*baal shem*" connotes mastery of the Divine Name—the holy Tetragrammaton, which is said to work wonders. Israel became known as a *baal shem* in the sense that he was apparently successful in effecting cures by writing amulets with God's name printed on them. His success might be considered a form of psychosomatic medicine. He also emphasized daily immersions in the *mikvah,* or ritual bath, especially on Fridays in preparation for the Sabbath. Thus, a ritual most usually associated with women's purity after the menstrual period was extended on a daily basis to men.

Doctrines

The key to understanding Hasidism lies not in the biography of its founder, but rather in the specific doctrines Hasidism has embraced. Perhaps the most important of these is the doctrine of joy. Hasidism believes that it is appropriate to worship the

Almighty only in a state of joy, as *Psalms* indicated, "Worship the Lord in joy." (Psalms 100:2) This reflected a state of mind—namely, that the natural mood for humanity ought to be joyous.

One cannot underestimate the historical significance of this doctrine of joy. After the Sabbetian debacle, profound disappointment and sadness settled onto the Jewish world. The Jewish condition remained one of exile and subjugation. The hopes and aspirations of the Jews for restoration had been frustrated. Hasidism served as a natural corrective to the excessive despair of post-Sabbetian Jewish life. To be a Jew meant not lamenting over the tragedies of Jewish history, but rather a statement of joyous celebration in being able to relate to God. Perhaps Hasidim's most profound historical contribution was to restore a language and behavior pattern of joy to Jewish life. For the Hasid, the answers to why be Jewish lay not in the Jews being a persecuted people, but rather in God's closeness to the Jewish people. Therefore the only appropriate stance to take was one of joy in being able to worship God.

To be sure, this doctrine of joy contained excesses. Hasidism believed that external stimulants were a legitimate vehicle of obtaining a state of joy. Liquor, in particular, flowed freely, as Hasidim believed that if one could not work oneself up into a state of joy, other substances could be utilized to raise the individual to a joyous state.

Nevertheless, in assessing this doctrine, one should not confuse the peripheral with the central components. The major significance of the doctrine of joy was its message to the Jewish community concerning the nature of being Jewish and the appropriate attitude of human beings toward their position in the world. The doctrine of joy was counter-cultural in the sense that it flew in the face of the natural Jewish condition. It amounted to a powerful statement on what attitude the Jew should take toward his or her environment. That at times it was abused, or became artificial, is not surprising. What is surprising was the willingness of Hasidism to transform the given condition of the Jews by defining Jewishness as a cause for celebration and not an occasion for sadness.

This doctrine of joy was closely related to Hasidic theology, which Gershom Scholem has characterized as close to but not the same as pantheism. Pantheism identifies God with nature, a position originally articulated by Spinoza and antithetical to classic Jewish theology because it denies creation—i.e., if God is nature,

God cannot have been the creator of nature. Rabbinic Judaism, however, had debated a somewhat different question as to whether God is transcendental or immanent in the universe. Is God as creator above all that exists, or does God's presence permeate reality? Rabbinic sources and classical Jewish philosophy had argued that God is primarily transcendental and only secondarily immanent. Certainly, humanity ought relate to God as if God were transcendental.

Hasidism reversed this analysis. For the Hasidim, again relying on one of David's psalms, "His glory fills every place" (Psalms 72:19), God was primarily immanent and only secondarily transcendental. God's presence permeated all reality, and God could be encountered in every place.

Scholem regards this doctrine of immanence as "panentheism," meaning not pantheism but a variant of it that preserves God's transcendence and role as creator. Theologically, God's immanence carried profound implications. First, it democratized Jewish life in the sense that God was accessible to everyone and at every point. Secondly, if God was accessible to humanity, then the only natural state in which to approach Him would be one of joy. In short, the doctrine of panentheism corroborated the Hasidic doctrine of joy. If God were to be found everywhere, then the only appropriate state of mind for human beings ought be one of joyous celebration of God's presence.

Socially, this clearly meant a magnification of the importance of the lower classes. Clearly not everyone could aspire to intellectual leadership of the Jewish people. The Talmudic elite was a closed circle by no means dissimilar to the "star system" of American universities. Young men were identified as future Talmudic scholars and virtually anointed as the academic stars of the yeshiva world. Hasidism, by contrast, argued that depth of religious feeling was far more significant than intellectual mastery of sources. The message of Hasidism was that the Jewish lower classes, often too poor to afford a Talmudic education, could by virtue of their piety attain religious greatness.

One Hasidic tale aptly documents this perspective. The story was told of the Jewish peasant boy who entered services at the holiest moment of the High Holy Day prayers. At a moment of utter solemnity, he uttered a whistle. Immediately the congregants sought to hush him, for he had disturbed the solemnity of the High

Holy Day services. The Hasidic rabbi, however, quickly quieted the crowd. He announced that this whistle, coming from an ignorant peasant boy, had pierced the walls of heaven because of its sincerity and depth of religious feeling. Rather than be reprimanded, the boy ought be thanked by the congregation for having facilitated the acceptance of its prayers.

Thirdly, for the Hasid, the purpose to human existence was *deveikut* or "clinging" to the Almighty. The idea of humanity following God's ways had deep roots in Jewish theology. Man was created in the image of God, and therefore it was only appropriate for human action to parallel Divine action. Thus, for example, men and women were co-creators with God. The *mitzvot* provided human beings with an opportunity to imitate God's ways.

Hasidism, however, like other mystical movements, aimed at more intimate connection between God and human beings. This was attained through *deveikut*, or clinging to God. The mechanism of clinging was the Hasidic doctrine of joy. The physical embodiment of *deveikut* was the Hasidic rebbe, or *tzaddik*. The legitimacy of the *tzaddik* lay not in his scholarship but in his accessibility to Divine revelation. The *tzaddik* was more than a teacher to his followers. Because he stood so close to God, he possessed mystical insight and clarity of vision. The Hasid would consult with his rebbe concerning day-to-day choices and private matters.

To be sure, this could lead also to abuse. Many, hoping that the *tzaddik* would work wonders for them, would visit the *tzaddik* in the expectation that a blessing from him would grant children. Each week the followers of the *tzaddik* would gather around his table hoping to pick up some of the crumbs of his plate in the belief that this would provide physical closeness and connection to the rebbe. This was the origin of the well-known Hasidic custom of eating the "*shirayim*" or remains of the rebbe's table. Without question, the doctrine of the *tzaddik* possessed the danger of degenerating into a cult of personality.

Most rebbes, however, made no claim to be either miracle men or wonder workers. They were rebbes not because of superstitious beliefs in their powers but rather because, as Jewish leaders, they demonstrated personal interest in the lives of their followers and generally were men of integrity and far-sightedness who could make decisions on both a communal basis and on the basis of individual needs. Although belief in the rebbe could become a cult of personality, as evidenced recently in the Lubavitch Hasidic movement, the idea of a rebbe again signified the tendency of Hasidism toward greater democratization. Through relating to the rebbe, the individual felt he was relating to a Jewish leader who possessed a greater degree of *deveikut,* and through relating to him, the individual could relate to God spiritually. The concept of the rebbe was meant as a vehicle to enhance Jewish spirituality rather than as a political statement of authority within the Jewish community.

Mention should also be made of the Maid of Ludmir, one of the few females to rise to a position of Hasidic leadership. The Maid of Ludmir was, indeed, an exception. She voluntarily undertook the ascetic and celibate life. In that sense, while Christianity had no shortage of saints and virgins, the Maid of Ludmir adopted a lifestyle considered essentially deviant for a Jewish woman. Her nineteenth-century Hasidic court has attracted a great deal of interest and attention because of its colorfulness. However, under no circumstances may she be regarded as a typical example of female Jewish leadership.

Perhaps most controversial was the Hasidic vision of evil as strictly an illusion. A God that was immanent was wholly good, and therefore no evil could exist in the here and now. What exists rather is a hierarchy of good, and what appears to us as evil is simply a lower step in that hierarchy.

Hasidism, in other words, made for an optimistic acceptance of this world. The natural condition of humanity ought be one of ecstasy because this world was totally good and because God was immanent within it. Since God's presence filled up every space, there were no areas of neutrality. Every action human beings took was God-oriented. There was no such thing as absolute evil, nor were there places which were utterly profane.

This optimistic view of the world, however, was problematical. First, if God was everywhere, was there such a thing as profanity? Historically, Judaism had banned Torah from impure or profane places. Would that ban continue? Secondly, the Hasidic emphasis on ecstasy meant the use of music as well as stimulants to reach that state of ecstasy. Hasidim argued, for example, that since it was appropriate to approach God only in a state of joy, it would take periods of lengthy preparation before one would be able to worship. Therefore, Hasidim often prayed at times much later than the stated times for prayer. Although, on the surface, this would appear to be a minor deviation in Jewish practice, it symbolized increased division within the Jewish community between Hasidim and their opponents.

Thirdly, the emphasis upon religious ecstasy connoted a fundamental critique of the Talmudic academy. Hasidim derided the absence of joy from Talmudic learning. They argued that the academies had become centers of intellectual striving but were lacking in religious feeling or in the joy of the study of Torah. Hasidim were arguing for an experiential element in what basically had been an intellectual experience. The deans of the Talmudic academies responded that learning had been primary in Jewish life and had defined what it was to be a Jew—to study, to wrestle with questions and with doubt, and to search for answers. Hasidism, by contrast, seemed to approximate the Christian critique of Judaism as emphasizing intellectual learning rather than the primacy of faith.

Hasidism also suggested a more positive estimate of human nature. Man was harmonious with nature and shared kinship with God. Therefore, for Hasidism, minimal human pride and dignity were necessary in order to undertake religious experience. Ultimately, the Hasid humbled himself before God, but as he ascended the ladder of spiritual experience, the Hasid first had to feel himself at home with God and on a level where he could address God meaningfully. Martin Buber subsequently expanded this idea to the notion of an I—Thou relationship, in which God and man could meet one another in dialogue.

Historically, Hasidism was again addressing some of the feelings of inferiority that permeated Jewish life after the disaster of Sabbetianism. Hasidism turned to the Jewish people and said, "Do not despair that your dreams and aspirations have been frustrated." Rather, as human beings, we have the capacity to relate to God meaningfully. Being a Jew is, then, an incredible opportunity for spiritual enhancement. One need not feel oneself a member of a despised or defeated people. To be sure, Hasidism tended to neutralize the messianic dimension of Jewish life. It possessed little in the way of redemptive content, unlike the concept of *tikkun* that had inspired Lurianic Kabbalism. Rather messianism was replaced by a mystic concept of personal salvation. Although later Hasidic groups would revert to messianism, the apparent neutralization of the messianic dimension was historically appropriate to the efforts of Hasidism to rehabilitate Jewish spirituality in the aftermath of Sabbetai Zvi.

The Controversy over Hasidism

The rabbinic establishment did not greet the emergence of Hasidism benevolently. The Talmudic academies were led by Elijah Gaon, better known as the Vilna Gaon, the dean of Talmudic scholars, and his prize disciple, Rabbi Hayyim of Volozhin. It was Rabbi Hayyim who spearheaded the battle and polemic with Hasidism. The Vilna Gaon feared that Hasidism represented the legacy of Sabbetianism and Frankism. He therefore applied to Hasidism the term "the sect," associating it with those earlier disasters in Jewish life. The rabbinic establishment quickly defined itself in opposition to Hasidism. Hence originated the term "mitnagdim" meaning the opposition or opponents. The tradition of the mitnagidim was the tradition of Talmudic learning, emphasizing not mystical states but intellectual accomplishment as the road to religious salvation.

Philosophically, Rabbi Hayyim took issue with the Hasidic interpretation of the doctrine of immanence. Immanence, in Rabbi Hayyim's view, carried with it the doctrine of moral relativism. If God was found everywhere, then all values were equal. If everything was acceptable, then there was no distinction between good and evil, which had characterized Judaism historically. In other words, Rabbi Hayyim pointed to Jewish law as containing a value pluralism which distinguished between good and bad values as a basic scaffold, underlying how Judaism approached the world around it. The obligation of the Jew lay in performing an act of "*havdalah,*" distinguishing between the holy and the profane, the sacred and the sinful. Therefore, Rabbi Hayyim counseled that human beings can relate to God only as if He were transcendental. God's immanence is a function of the Divine perspective. But if we relate to God as if He were immanent, then values lose their distinction, for God is found everywhere. For example, Rabbi Hayyim pointed to the willingness of the Hasidim to discuss thoughts of Torah in profane places. Superficially, this appeared to be a minor deviation. Philosophically, it reflected the Hasidic emphasis upon immanence in contrast to the mitnagdic emphasis upon transcendence and value pluralism.

The conflict between mitnagdim and Hasidim frequently assumed ugly forms. There were bans and counter-bans of excommunication, as well as physical abuse. Hasidim celebrated the death of the Vilna Gaon. Mitnagdim pointed to the personality cult, which they decried as idolatry, encouraging greed and faith in miracle-working. Mitnagdim also pointed to bizarre activities of Hasidim, including somersaulting, banging and loud shouting during services. Hasidic and mitnagdic leaders informed on one another to the secular authorities, resulting in occasional imprisonment.

These controversies symbolized the break-up of the *kehilla* as an organized Jewish community. In that respect, Hasidism represented an aspect of modernity in rebelling against communal authority from within the Jewish community. The growth of Hasidism was a part of the broader growth of volunteerism within Jewish communal life, as opposed to the principle of compulsory membership that had dominated medieval Jewish communal existence. Secondly, Hasidism challenged the medieval view of man as sinful and thereby represented a modern thrust that emphasized human capacity for perfection. All that human beings do is holy and therefore man is capable of building the good society. To be sure, when Hasidism degenerated into beliefs in superstitions and miracle-working, it was distinctively medieval in outlook. Its overall historical significance, however, lay in rescuing Jewish mysticism from the debacle of Sabbetianism, restoring a sense of joy to Jewish life, and initiating modern concepts of human nature as well as Jewish communal organization.

Moreover, it is important to understand that Hasidism was by no means monolithic. The Bratzlaver Hasidim, for example, did not have a rebbe or leader. Once Rabbi Nachman of Bratzlav died, he was never replaced. Similarly, the Lubavitch Hasidim emphasized Talmudic learning as well as religious ecstasy. The Rebbe of Lubavitch defined himself as a religious teacher rather than as miracle worker. The differences, for example, in America today between Satmar and Lubavitch Hasidim are, in many ways, greater than the differences between Hasidim and mitnagdim. The Satmar Hasidim are best known for their anti-Zionism, while the Lubavitch Hasidim have become identified with opposition to Israel's returning any of the territories on the grounds that it would be a violation of the Divine will.

Hasidim today represent the least American of American Jews. Clearly, they function in ways that are very dissident with mainstream American culture. Within American Jewry, they have been the group least concerned about preserving separation between church and state, arguing for the public displays of religious symbols and prayer in the public schools. Similarly, the Lubavitch engaged in direct intervention in Israeli politics, especially during the "Who is a Jew?" affair in 1988.

Conversely, Hasidim represent a true test of American diversity and multi-culturalism. In many ways the Hasidim challenge the Jewish community as to how serious it is in its commitment to inclusiveness and embracing those who are different. Lubavitch Hasidism, in particular, has sought to reach out to unaffiliated Jews, often in places where the organized Jewish community is not positioned to reach people effectively. How the Jewish community relates to the approximately 60,000 Hasidim in America will be an appropriate test of its capacity to manage diversity and to articulate a true pluralism of different ways of expressing Jewish identity. These tensions became especially pronounced during the anti-Jewish rioting that took place in Crown Heights, New York in the summer of 1991, when the organized Jewish community hesitated before declaring its solidarity with the Hasidic community which had come under attack.

Reading: Lucy Dawidowicz, ed., *The Golden Tradition*

This reading describes the Kotzker Hasidim, whose rebbe was well-known for his wisdom. Note, in particular, the Hasidic emphasis upon service of the Almighty. Personal aggrandizement and benefits were alien to this approach, for the true Hasid dedicated himself to service of God.

"Menahem Mendel's Hasidic Mode" by Pinhas Zelig Gliksman

The following selection has been translated from Gliksman's two-volume work about Menahem Mendel of Kotsk:

> After Bunam's death, his followers parted company. Some became disciples of Rabbi Menahem Mendel of Tomaszow; others remained with Bunam's only son, Abraham Moses. It was said that Menahem Mendel's followers were more religiously learned and more committed than the others. In To-

maszow, Mendel exercised his rabbinic leadership with great spiritual vigor and inspiration. He deepened and broadened Bunam's approach to hasidism, walking humbly, studying Gemara and Tosefot, and concentrating on the Maharal's works.

In 1829, a little more than a year after Bunam's death, Mendel settled in Kotsk, a small town in the province of Lublin, on the highway to Warsaw. According to an 1853 census, Kotsk had 1,652 Jews and 1,270 Gentiles. After Mendel settled there, Kotsk's reputation spread among Jews, and many hasidim made pilgrimages there. In many cities and towns, congregations of disciples of the Kotsker rebbe were organized. Great scholars and magnates attended Kotsk-oriented prayer houses. In Kotsk itself, the rebbe's congregation was enormous; it became a great center which attracted rabbis, scholars, learned men, promising young people, and the aristocratic among the rich. The influence, too, of the rebbe of Ger, the Hiddushe ha-Rim, was significant, for he seized every opportunity to spread the teachings of Kotsk. He brought his influence to bear on the sons of wealthy Warsaw Jews who studied with him, urging them to visit the rebbe of Kotsk, to strive toward purity and sincerity in their thoughts, and to try to approach the true will of the Creator.

The late Wolf Landau of Strykow, one of the most distinguished of Kotsker hasidim, at the Sabbath table once told us:

"I will tell you the first discourse I heard from the rebbe of Kotsk. I had already heard many of his sayings on the Torah, but with this discourse he inflamed my heart. When he sat down Friday night, after blessing the wine, his face became transfigured, disembodied. He stretched out his hands, washed them, and after blessing the bread, said, 'All that the Lord has spoken we will do and obey. In this world there are wise men, scholars, philosophers who study and search for the recognition of God. But what can they comprehend? Only as much as the level of their intelligence permits. But the Jews have instruments, that is, observance of the commandments, which makes them comprehend more than the level of their intelligence would permit, in fact upward to the level of the ministering angels. That is the meaning of "We will do and obey." If we have the instrument for doing—the performance of the commandments, then we may heed, comprehending everything that is on high.'"

A hasid, always absorbed in his business affairs, once told the rebbe of Kotsk he regretted his business allowed him no time for the Torah and hasidism as he had when he lived with his in-laws. To this, the rebbe replied:

"The Mishna says: 'Rabbi Hananya ben Akashya said: "The Holy One—blessed be He!—desired to enlarge Israel's merits. Therefore he multiplied for them Torah and commandments."' At first, this is hard to understand. For if He had given the Jews fewer commandments, it would be easier to fulfill them, whereas the many commandments cannot be fulfilled because of the press of business. But the explanation is different. The Lord interposed commandments in everything that man does and creates. For example, when he builds a house, he is commanded to make for it a parapet on the roof, a mezuza and a *sukka.* When he plows and sows his field or his vineyard, he must observe the negative commandments not to mix seeds, not to reap to the edges of the field, not to gather the gleanings but to leave them for the poor and the stranger, and the positive commandments of offerings and tithes, and, in the seventh year, of observing a Sabbath year of rest. The Torah gave you commandments affecting your business, buying and selling, to give true weights and measures, to abjure falsehood and deceit, to be honest in yea's and nay's, and to avoid looking at women. This is what Rabbi Hananya ben Akashya meant when he said that the Lord multiplied the Torah and commandments for the Jews and gave them every opportunity, in all human activity, always to be able to observe the commandments, at leisure and in the press of business."

The Holy Zohar commented on the biblical verse that in the six hundredth year of Noah's life all the fountains of the great deep were broken up. He said this meant the year 5600 (1840) and that the floodgates and fountains of wisdom would then open. The rebbe of Kotsk said that the fountains of wisdom did indeed open at that time—accounting for the important scientific discoveries and inventions of the time. Because of our sins we were not worthy enough to receive these new sources of wisdom, and so the unbelievers seized and used them for worldly purposes.

It was the Kotsker rebbe's custom to speak short and sharp that his words might reach the heart. Once a Habad hasid visited him. The rebbe asked what he aimed at, as he recited the shema and the Eighteen Benedictions. When the hasid told him, the rebbe snapped, "But what about the guts?" For his approach was, so to speak, to reach a man's core. A hasid of Kotsk once said to another rebbe's hasid "Your rebbe preaches his wisdom to the heavens, but our rebbe speaks to our guts."

The hasidim of Kotsk were deeply concerned that every religious service, a prayer or a physical act, even a groan, be done without ulterior motive, but only sincerely to do God's will. Otherwise, they described it as "service to oneself," a sort of idolatry. For what difference if one worships an idol or oneself? The Kotsker hasidim vigorously combated egoism, which poisons and seduces the soul, intoxicating with its selfishness, preventing the attainment of truth and fulfillment. The rebbe of Kotsk taught that the "I" is a thief in disguise, insinuating itself in man and corrupting him, without his own realization. The one affected does not know that he has been affected.

To resist, one must delve deep into oneself to search out the hidden thief, the "I," using different remedies to pluck it from his heart. This process the Kotsker hasidim called "departure from the domain of self," to be cleansed of every self-interest, even the slightest. Traits of conceit and pride were associated with "non-departure from the domain of self."

The Kotsker hasidim repudiated services too exalted for the person expected to perform them. It is a fraud for a person to do something he is not fit for, a sort of self-delusion based on lies and hypocrisy. The Kotsker hasidim strove therefore after self-perception, each man to know himself and his place in the world. When a man made a promise he did not keep, or gestured or sighed in a way not his own, not authentic and openhearted, the rebbe of Kotsk called that stealing.

The Kotsker rebbe was enormously sensitive in recognizing frivolous words or an insincere gesture. At first glance, he penetrated a person's thoughts and he could tell how much that man's "I" had hurt him, though the man himself was quite unaware of the disease in his soul. But the rebbe's sharp barbs cured that man. A man whose sense of smell is most acute can smell a very faint unpleasant odor to which others are insensitive.

The Kotsker rebbe's hasidim explained their rebbe's recognition of truth in the same way. He had come so close to the truth that he was immediately sensitive to even the slightest inauthentic gesture, so fastidious was his own sense of the truth.

To attain the truth, to eradicate selfishness and ulterior motives, the hasidim of Kotsk strove to walk humbly, to serve God secretly while in public appearing not to. They delved deeper to remove vanity and pride, so that their walking humbly was a walking humbly even for themselves, lest they themselves think they were doing good or were good.

A wise rabbi once joked that hasidim of Kotsk do good in private and act bad in public, while others act bad privately and do good publicly. Yet, he quipped, it was easier to catch one of these others in a bad deed than a Kotsker hasid in a good one.

Bibliography for Further Reading

Buber, Martin. *Tales of the Hasidim*, Schocken, 1947.

———. *Hasidism and Modern Man,* Humanities International Press, 1988

Green, Arthur. *A Tormented Master,* Schocken Books, 1981

Harris, Liz. *Holy Days,* Summit Books, 1985

Mintz, Jerome. *Hasidic People,* Harvard University Press, 1992

Scholem, Gershom. *Major Trends in Jewish Mysticism,* Schocken Books, ch. 9, 1961

Wiesel, Elie. *Four Hasidic Masters,* University of Notre Dame Press, 1978

Unit XXII

Decline of the Medieval Kehilla

Background

Ghetto society had sharply restricted Jewish-gentile contact to the twin realms of politics and economics. The only Jews to enjoy regular contact with the gentile world were communal leaders and businessmen, who perceived gentile society in strictly economic and utilitarian terms. Little if any cultural contact existed between the two realms.

By contrast, the Jewish encounter with modernity meant an extension of contacts with the gentile world. In truth, many felt that once exposed to gentile society, Judaism as a religion would disappear. Such indeed was the view of Voltaire, perhaps the archtypical figure of Enlightenment thinking.

Of course, Judaism did not disappear. However, communal authority and autonomy, which had been the hallmarks of medieval Jewish existence, gradually declined in favor of a modern ethos in which membership in the community was voluntary and Jewish identity far more personal and existential. Communal authority declined because of the confluence of external and internal factors. Externally, the nation-state increasingly was interested in breaking down the corporate nature of Jewish communal existence because the nation-state could not tolerate private groups exercising public authority. Conversely, within the *kehilla*, new voices for change were beginning to advocate reform in areas ranging from education to the role of women in family and social life.

Internal Change

During the seventeenth and eighteenth centuries, the *kehilla* experienced increased polarization between rich and poor. Among the richer Jews, new trends reflected greater secular influence. These ranged from greater interest in contemporary art to greater materialism in housing and personal possessions. Thus, for example, the contemporary ethical literature criticizes wealthy Jews and especially women for excessive clothing and material possessions. Rabbinic legislation reflects concern with new issues that were relatively foreign to the medieval community, such as unwed mothers and adultery. This legislation points to a change in the inner life of the Jew—what historian Jacob Katz has defined in his book by that name as *Tradition and Crisis,* (Schocken) namely the crisis of Jewish identity in an age when tradition is on the decline. Ideologically, these trends later coalesced in the movement known as the *Haskalah* or Jewish Enlightenment. Antedating the *maskilim* (proponents of the Haskalah), however, were social trends already creating facts on the ground that effectively questioned the authority of Jewish tradition in a modern age.

Women were beginning to play new roles in family and society. Women's earning capacity rose creating the unprecedented phenomenon of women traveling alone on business and even staying in gentile homes. Such business trips functioned to break down barriers between Jew and gentile. Selling goods brought Jews into the homes of non-Jews, where a range of matters would be discussed, far beyond the limitations of a specific business deal.

The memoirs of Gluckel of Hameln provide us with an excellent portrait of German Jewry during this age of transition, as well as a social history of Jewish women. Gluckel retains her traditionalist world view. However, she writes of growing secularization, noting that her son has rejected an arranged marriage in favor of seeking out a romantic relationship in Berlin.

Jewish education became the classic battlefield between traditionalists and modernizers. The classical Jewish education of the time consisted of the *heder*—literally, a room—in which teachers or *melamdim* based their curriculum on the needs of the synagogue. For example, the weekly Torah portion was studied, irrespective of content. The caricature of this became teaching five-year-olds about the laws of sacrifices. Generally, the *melamdim* were poorly paid and were enslaved to their jobs—an early example of the slogan, "Those who cannot...teach." Although most Jews were able to follow the services, there was some rate of illiteracy.

The critics of this system attacked both its goals and its methods. The goal of creating a Talmudic scholar meant that little attention was paid to students' individual needs. Some, of course, were more oriented to literature, philosophy, or history. Yet all were given the same Talmud-based curriculum as if, in secular terms, they were all pre-law students.

Thus the *cheder* catered only to the needs of the minority who were well-adapted to the study of Talmud. Moreover, the methods of Talmudic instruction came under heavy attack for their emphasis upon *pilpul,* or logistical debate over the meaning of the text. Teachers frequently conceded that the *pilpul* possessed little practical or personal value beyond sharpening the mind.

Lastly, Talmudic education broadened the chasm between rich and poor, for usually it was only the sons of the wealthy who had the time to devote extended years to Talmudic study. Thus the Talmudic aristocracy became increasingly self-perpetuating, with little room for upward mobility on the social and communal scales.

Previously, Jewish tradition had served as a cohesive factor in the Jewish community. Tradition had served to regulate the day-to-day lives of Jews, and strong communities had been nurtured through preservation of that tradition. Modern Jews faced a new problem: If tradition has been dethroned, what else can hold the Jews together? Jewish modernity, in many ways, consists of a long series of efforts to build new cohesive structures and preservatives of Jewish identity in the modern world. Often, however, the problem of the modern Jew remains that posed by Franz Kafka in his novels: The law no longer tells me exactly what I should do and how I should go about doing it. How do I create order and meaning in this very irrational and, in some ways, dangerous universe?

External Changes

The nation-state itself underwent a variety of economic and political changes which set the groundwork for Jewish emancipation. Economically, capitalism emphasized the importance of the individual, thereby undermining communal organization. By stressing individual growth, the very idea of sacrifice for the sake of the larger good was called into question. Why, for example, should an individual bow to communal decision-making denying him rights to settle in a particular town if he felt that personal economic opportunities were there for him? The ultimate logic of economic individualism meant a decline in attachment to community and society in favor of the individual value of personal fulfillment.

Politically, the tendency of the nation-state toward greater absolutism weakened all of the corporations—the private sub-communities that throughout the medieval period had exercised public authority. For the Jews, that meant increased government interest in court Jews who served as the representatives of their communities. These court Jews would be tied to the absolute monarchs. As their presence grew, the *kehilla* found itself decreasingly capable of representing communal interests. The nation-state in fact encouraged the rise of the court Jew. As court Jews became more powerful, the nation-state could become more centralized by turning to the court Jew as a major force representing the Jewish community, rather than dealing with the more diversified interests of the *kehilla*. Moreover, the authority of the court Jew owed more to his personal and financial standing in the court of the monarch than it did to his reputation and credibility within the Jewish community. The spirit of absolutism, reflecting the growth of the nation-state and the centralization of monarchy, in turn fostered the spirit of the court Jew, who was only loosely connected with the *kehilla*. Lastly, the absolutist state frowned upon inter-communal bodies such as rabbinic synods, for these represented communal bonds independent of the nation-state.

Increasingly the state began usurping powers that had been normally the prerogatives of the *kehilla*. For example, the *kehilla* previously had postponed marriages so as to limit the number of breadwinners in any locality. Now the state argued that only it could provide the appropriate marriage licenses.

That is not to say that the *kehilla* disappeared overnight. It experienced a long period in which increasingly its authority became restricted to tax collecting. Beyond that, communal authority became increasingly voluntary and moral in nature rather than compulsory.

At work here was whether a modern nation-state could permit private corporate bodies to function in their midst—to become states within states. To the extent that the answer to that question was no, Jewish emancipation became a necessity. However, emancipation itself only culminated a lengthier process occurring inside and outside the Jewish community weakening the communal authority of the *kehilla* and transferring it to the public authority of the nation-state. The traditional society did not disappear, but was gradually weakened by these internal and external changes taking place over a span of three centuries.

The Jewish Enlightenment

Spearheading this movement for reform was *Haskalah*, an intellectual movement attempting to "enlighten" the Jews by attacking their economic and spiritual poverty. Educationally, the *maskilim* emphasized the Bible, in effect undermining the *kehilla*'s emphasis on the Talmud. The *Haskalah* contained both conservative and radical wings. It by no means connoted abandonment of Jewish tradition, but rather reformulated Jewish tradition along the lines of modernity and modern culture.

The *maskilim* turned to the figure of Maimonides, rehabilitating him as if he were a medieval *maskil*. Their theory of education was set forth in an important pamphlet by Naftali Herz Wessaly entitled "Worlds of Peace and Truth." Wessaly argued that the Torah of humanity preceded the Torah of the Jews. Prior to the covenant with Abraham, there existed a universal covenant of natural law. Absent natural law, there could be no Torah of the Jews. Therefore, for Wessaly, to become acquainted with secular culture, with the law of nature, connoted a religious good.

Educationally, one should teach morality and values before teaching Talmud. The Torah of humanity prepared one for the higher learning of the Talmud. Wessaly interpreted Jewish chosenness on the grounds that only Abraham had kept the Torah of humanity. Other nations had left it. Because Abraham observed natural law and morality, his people had been chosen to receive the gift of the Torah of God.

Moreover, not everyone could be a Talmudic scholar. It was fitting that they learn other things, e.g. languages, which were economically useful. Wessaly hoped to boost the reforms offered by Joseph II, the Hapsburg king of Austria, in 1781, urging the Jews to enter into secular occupations and absorb secular culture.

But the most typical figure of the *Haskalah* in Germany was Moses Mendelssohn, widely acclaimed as the teacher of German Jewry and hailed as yet a third Moses. Mendelssohn argued that

Judaism was superior to Christianity because the truths of Judaism were truths of reason, whereas the truths of Christianity were dogmas and beyond reason. In other words, Mendelssohn argued that Judaism best approximated the criteria of the religion of reason, for the truths of Judaism were accessible via reason alone. Miracles had occurred in Jewish history, but the truths of Judaism did not depend upon these miracles. By contrast, miracles such as the Resurrection and the Virgin Birth were dogmas of Christianity without which Christianity could not exist.

Moreover, Mendelssohn argued, perhaps following Spinoza, on behalf of separation of church and state. Because of the social contract, man owed duties to the state but not to the church. The state could compel action but could not compel belief. Conversely, the church could engage in moral exhortation but had no compulsive powers.

Therefore, Mendelssohn argued, Jewish communal power of excommunication was an anachronism in the modern world. As the price for Jewish emancipation, the Jews ought best give up the power of excommunication and restrict the power of the synagogue to moral exhortative powers of persuasion rather than police authority.

Theologically, Mendelssohn argued that Judaism knew no dogmas. It consisted entirely of a set of religious commands. Why these commands were given to the Jews alone remains a mystery. In effect, Mendelssohn was arguing that Jew and gentile could meet on neutral grounds of reason. By that criterion, Judaism offered an advantage because it was the ultimate religion of reason. Paradoxically, of course, much of Jewish law contradicted reason. Mendelssohn argued that these laws were obligatory on the Jews alone and ought to be observed strictly on the basis of personal choice. The Jewish church could have no compulsory powers. He hoped that all Jews would observe the law out of free choice as part of the special covenant between God and the Jews.

To the Jews of the time, Mendelssohn emerged as the primary teacher of Judaism. He translated the Torah into German to convey the beauties of both German culture and biblical Hebrew. Mendelssohn was by no means a deist, although deism was becoming increasingly popular—i.e. rejecting revelation in favor of belief in a creator God who served as a watchmaker and now was simply presiding over nature which took its own course. Deism, which ultimately became Unitarianism, expressed a belief in Christianity without the belief of the divinity of Jesus. Deism remained fundamentally antithetical to Judaism, for it saw Judaism as wanting in the categories of morality and reason, a subject to which we shall return in the next unit. Mendelssohn, by contrast, upheld revelation. But he restricted revelation to revelation of law. The truths of religion needed no revelation. Revelation had been real and historical at Mount Sinai, but its content was limited to law. The miracles that were recorded on Sinai were in the realm of physical fact; namely, they did occur, but Jewish religion did not depend upon their veracity.

To the gentile world, Mendelssohn explained the continuing need for Judaism to teach the world justice. Until such time as all men had arrived at true religion, it was necessary that Judaism and the Jewish people continue. Judaism, in Mendelssohn's view, is the primary religion of reason and therefore is best equipped to teach humanity. Until such time as all humanity has arrived at the religion of reason, the Jews ought best preserve their unique treasure of Jewish law and *mitzvot.*

Clearly this is defensive Jewish thinking. Mendelssohn was responding virtually directly to Spinoza's challenge of why remain Jewish in a world that would accept Jews as universal men and women. Mendelssohn responded that Judaism was ahead of the world. It possessed the true religion of reason. Therefore it ought continue as a special faith and people until such time as the rest of the world caught up. Moreover, the gentile world was by no means prepared to accept the Jew as Jew. On the contrary, Mendelssohn was regarded as the "exception Jew" who could translate Judaism to the outside world but was by no means representative of the Jews as a people. For example, although Immanuel Kant had high regard for Mendelssohn and probably read Judaism through Mendelssohnian eyes, he had very little respect for the internal merits of Judaism as a faith. Mendelssohn was challenged to abandon Judaism and join Christianity. He responded, following Gottfried Wilhelm Leibniz, that diversity of faiths was a good in and of itself. It would be harmful to society as a whole for there to be fewer religions in the world.

This type of thinking remains defensive at best and contradictory at worst. Mendelssohn cannot really explain why the Jews are a chosen people, why they are the beneficiary of the special revelation of law. Rather, he wishes to maintain Jewish existence and preserve peoplehood, which he knows cannot be done unless the Jews retain distinctiveness and special mission. Therefore, he does not follow the logic of Spinoza and join the religion of reason. Instead, he argues for continued Jewish existence in order to teach reason to the gentile world. He titled his major work *Jerusalem* as a statement that the physical Jerusalem, the city of the Jews, still symbolized the true worship of God. Although Jerusalem has lost her power and influence, she remains the symbol of the true faith. Mendelssohn spawned the Hebrew *Haskalah,* which tended to be far more cohesive and conservative with respect to Jewish peoplehood. The German *Haskalah* of his follower David Friedlander was more assimilationist, and Friedlander hoped to lead the Jews into German Christianity absent belief in Jesus.

Haskalah accomplished much as a social movement in modern Jewish history. It called for major reforms in Jewish education and the Jewish family. The *Haskalah* advocated the nuclear family model based upon romantic attachments rather than arranged marriages. It urged Jews to become secularly educated and to enter productive labor occupations. By turning to the Hebrew language, *Haskalah* renewed Hebrew as a literary language for Jews, paving the way for it to become again a national language. Although the *maskilim* did not write critical history, preferring to see historical figures as extensions of their self-image, they renewed interest in the Jewish past and its experience.

At the same time, *Haskalah* also undermined aspects of Jewish unity and cohesion. Some members of the *Haskalah* were blatantly assimilationist and wished to substitute German culture for Jewish culture. Of Mendelssohn's own children, all but one converted to Christianity. By defining Judaism in personal rather than collective terms, the *Haskalah* paved the way for a redefinition of Jewish identity that eschewed Jewish peoplehood and the public square for the privacy of the Jewish home.

In short, there are diverse elements in *Haskalah*—conservative and liberal, national and anti-national, preservative and cohesive, yet at the same time divisive. *Haskalah* stands as the primary ideological thrust transforming the Jews into a modern people. The men of *Haskalah* wished to transform fundamentally Jewish status and to regard modern culture as a benefit rather than a threat. The problem with the *Haskalah* became that of how to preserve Judaism in an age of modernity. Having won their victories transforming the medieval ethos to a modern one, the question remained why be Jewish or what is distinctively Jewish about the existence of Jews in the modern world? The slogan popularized by the *Haskalah* in Russia, by the poet Y. L. Gordon, "Be a Jew at home and a man in the street," ultimately connoted the privatizing of Jewish identity. Zionism succeeded in restoring a public focus to Jewish identity. Today, however, we stand probably in greater need of restoring a private focus of Jewishness to our own homes.

Reading: Memoirs of Gluckel of Hameln, Ellen Umansky ed., *Four Centuries of Jewish Women's Spirituality*

Gluckel of Hameln was one of the most remarkable women of the late Middle Ages. Widowed prematurely, she maintained her business while raising her children. Her memoirs are one of the most important examples of pre-modern Jewish women's literature available. They also serve as an example of an ethical will written to guide her children in the musar *teachings she felt most important.*

In my great grief and for my heart's ease I begin this book the year of Creation 5451 [1690–91]—God soon rejoice us and send us His redeemer!

I began writing it, dear children, upon the death of your good father, in the hope of distracting my soul from the burdens laid upon it, and the bitter thought that we have lost our faithful shepherd. In this way I have managed to live through many wakeful nights, and springing from my bed shortened the sleepless hours.

This, dear children, will be no book of morals. Such I could not write, and our sages have already written many. Moreover, we have our holy Torah in which we may find and learn all that we need for our journey through this world to the world to come. It is like a rope which the great and gracious God has thrown to us as we drown in the stormy sea of life, that we may seize hold of it and be saved.

The kernel of the Torah is, Thou shalt love thy neighbor as

thyself. But in our days we seldom find it so, and few are they who love their fellowmen with all their heart—on the contrary, if a man can contrive to ruin his neighbor, nothing pleases him more.

The best thing for you, my children, is to serve God from your heart, without falsehood or sham, not giving out to people that you are one thing while, God forbid, in your heart you are another. Say your prayers with awe and devotion. During the time for prayers, do not stand about and talk of other things. While prayers are being offered to the Creator of the world, hold it a great sin to engage another man in talk about an entirely different matter—shall God Almighty be kept waiting until you have finished your business?

Moreover, put aside a fixed time for the study of the Torah, as best you know how. Then diligently go about your business, for providing your wife and children a decent livelihood is likewise a *mitzvah*—the command of God and the duty of man. We should, I say, put ourselves to great pains for our children, for on this the world is built, yet we must understand that if children did as much for their parents, the children would quickly tire of it.

Above all, my children, be honest in money matters, with both Jews and Gentiles, lest the name of Heaven be profaned. If you have in hand money or goods belonging to other people, give more care to them than if they were your own, so that, please God, you do no one a wrong. The first question put to a man in the next world is, whether he was faithful in his business dealings. Let a man work ever so hard amassing great wealth dishonestly, let him during his lifetime provide his children fat dowries and upon his death a rich heritage-yet woe, I say, and woe again to the wicked who for the sake of enriching his children has lost his share in the world to come! For the fleeting moment he has sold Eternity.

When God sends evil days upon us, we shall do well to remember the remedy contrived by the physician in the story told by Rabbi Abraham ben Sabbatai Levi. A great king, he tells us, once imprisoned his physician, and had him bound hand and foot with chains, and fed on a small dole of barley-bread and water. After months of this treatment, the king dispatched relatives of the physician to visit the prison and learn what the unhappy man had to say. To their astonishment he looked as hale and hearty as the day he entered his cell. He told his relatives he owed his strength and well-being to a brew of seven herbs he had taken the precaution to prepare before he went to prison, and of which he drank a few drops every day. "What magic herbs are these?" they asked; and he answered: "The first is trust in God, the second is hope, and the others are patience, recognition of my sins, joy that in suffering now I shall not suffer in the world to come, contentment that my punishment is not worse, as well it could be, and lastly, knowledge that God who thrust me into prison can, if He will, at any moment set me free."

However, I am not writing this book in order to preach to you, but, as I have already said, to drive away the melancholy that comes with the long nights. So far as my memory and the subject permit, I shall try to tell everything that has happened to me from my youth upward. Not that I wish to put on airs or pose as a good and pious women. No, dear children, I am a sinner. Every day, every hour, and every moment of my life I have sinned, nearly all manner of sins. God grant I may find the means and occasion for repentance. But, alas, the care of providing for my orphaned children, and the ways of the world, have kept me far from that state.

If God wills that I may live to finish them, I shall leave you my Memoirs in seven little books. And so, as it seems best, I shall begin now with my birth. . . .

Bibliography for Further Reading

Katz, Jacob. *Tradition and Crisis,* Schocken Books, 1961

———. *Out of the Ghetto,* Harvard University Press, 1973

Meyer, Michael. *Origins of the Modern Jew,* Wayne State University Press, 1972

Unit XXIII

Jewish Emancipation in France

Background

Jews began returning to southern France in the sixteenth century. Most likely, these were former Marranos emigrating from the Iberian peninsula. For example, the French philosopher Michel de Montaigne descended from a Marrano family, a factor that may have been influential in his religious tolerance accompanied by religious skepticism. Montaigne argued that he was a Christian strictly by accident of birth. Therefore, he had no right to be intolerant of any other faith or religious group.

The bulk of French Jewry, however, lived in Alsace-Lorraine. These were Ashkenazi Jews in what had once been German-held territory and would continue to be a point of contention between France and Germany for hundreds of years. These Ashkenazim were primarily involved in money-lending and were far less acculturated than their Sephardic co-religionists. The French economic minister J. B. Colbert praised their economic productivity, although he felt their religion to be a scandal to the nation-state. Therefore, he urged that no further Jewish settlement be permitted in France, so that existing Jews might disappear without harm to the nation-state.

The economic situation of most Jews was actually quite poor. Only the elite Sephardim could be considered affluent, meaning that virtually all Ashkenazim and the overwhelming majority of Sephardim desired emancipation for economic reasons. It has been estimated that as many as 50 percent of the Sephardic community were living off the dole. Jews had been granted special *lettres patents* during the sixteenth and seventeenth centuries guaranteeing their rights and presence in France. However, the *lettres patents* granted to Ashkenazic Jews retained the older medieval disabilities restricting Jewish residence and movement within France, as well as burdensome taxation requirements to the point that 80 percent of the communal budget went to taxation. For example, in Metz where Jews formed one-eighteenth of the population, they were responsible for one-sixth of the taxation. Therefore, the specter of impoverished Jewish communities spurred the drive to Jewish emancipation.

Internally, secularization rose as religious observance declined. This was perhaps less the case in Alsace-Lorraine, but even the Orthodox had translated the prayer book into French, suggesting that they, too, regarded secularization as part of the social compact of living in France.

Therefore, by 1789 there were two primary Jewish communities in France: Alsace-Lorraine and southern France, centering in Bordeaux and Bayonne. There was a tiny and clandestine Jewish community in Paris, which would ultimately become, of course, the primary center of French Jewry. All told, there were probably 40,000 Jews in France. Although they were seriously divided, culturally and ethnically, they desired universal emancipation as a vehicle of boosting their status and economic opportunities in France.

The Emancipation Debate

The debate over emancipation in France may be summarized in the phrase of Stanislas de Clermont-Tonnere, "To the Jews as individuals everything, to the Jews as a nation, nothing ... otherwise let them be banished from the land." What this quotation suggests is that proponents of Jewish emancipation wished to grant Jews individual rights. They were not prepared to accept the corporate or collective identity of Jews as Jews. Their expectation was that if emancipation were granted to the Jews, the Jew ultimately would become like everyone else. In other words, the expectation of Jewish assimilation accompanied the grant of equal status. Emancipation became a contractual bargain of civil equality to the Jews in exchange for the dissolution of Jewish corporate status. When the

Jew continued to remain part of a distinctive ethnic group, anti-Semitism would return to France in ever more virulent forms.

Therefore, both proponents and opponents of emancipation agreed on the need to regenerate the Jew. The Jew qua Jew was unacceptable. The Jew was acceptable only were he to transform himself into a Frenchman. Proponents of emancipation argued that emancipation become the vehicle for Jewish regeneration. Opponents argued that once the Jew has transformed himself, then emancipation will follow. Over the course of time, proponents of emancipation triumphed in Western Europe, and opponents triumphed in Eastern Europe. However, liberals and conservatives alike agreed on the absence of any internal merit within Judaism or Jewish culture that would be worth preserving. Although the French Revolution did grant emancipation to the Jews, it became readily apparent that emancipation was by no means an unmixed blessing. Rather the bargain of emancipation demanded Jewish assimilation, but also triggered an anti-Semitic backlash once it was discovered that Jews retained corporate identification with other Jews.

The best illustration of this "enlightened" opinion concerning Jews and Judaism emanated from the pen of the leading French *philosophe*, or man of the Enlightenment, Voltaire. Voltaire was classically liberal in arguing against persecution of the Jews. However, his image of Jews and Judaism was unabashedly negative. He spread the canard that Jews continued to engage in human sacrifice. He claimed that Judaism lacked a concept of soul or afterlife, despite extensive Talmudic literature on the subject. Moreover, in his view, the Jews had plagiarized the stories of the ancient Near East, adding nothing original. The Jews of today remained greedy and materialistic. Their heroes, such as King David, were immoral figures, for David was both an adulterer and a murderer. The Jews of today remained the Jews of the past. They were still usurers, obscurantists, and had no leading cultural figures. Judaism represented a debased tradition deficient in rational morality. Therefore, Voltaire advised the Jews "*soyez philosophe*" - meaning "become a philosopher" like me and then we can embrace you as a universal person.

Historians have debated the degree of anti-Semitism in Voltaire's writings. For Peter Gay, Voltaire's biographer, anti-Jewish statements were part of a larger attack upon all organized religion.

Arthur Hertzberg, in his important book *The French Enlightenment and the Jews,* argues that Voltaire expresses a left-wing and secular critique of Jews and Judaism that is reflective of the anti-Semitism of the Enlightenment. First, there is simply too much venom directed against Jews per se to be marginalized as an attack upon organized religion generally. Secondly, within the context of the debate over emancipation, Voltaire is arguing that liberal-minded men and women would never persecute Jews. However, Judaism connotes an irrational tradition that is not worth preserving. The idiom of anti-Semitism here noticeably departs from the medieval idiom of Jew as Christ-killer and is more indebted to the secular and modern idiom of Spinoza that Judaism has become an anachronism in the modern world.

Proponents of Jewish emancipation, therefore, argued that given emancipation, Jews would change. In the meantime, the state required more people and more productive citizens. Therefore, as Salo Baron has suggested, emancipation was a necessity for the nation-state. A modern nation-state required the integration of corporate groups into society. For the men of the Enlightenment, anyone that was educable could become a citizen. One need not be a biological member of the nation-state. The Abbe Gregoire, perhaps the leading proponent of emancipation, went further: With emancipation and Jewish regeneration, the Jews would ultimately become ripe targets for conversionist efforts. If they have rejected conversion until this point, Gregoire argued, it was only because of gentile oppression. Approach the Jews out of love, and then conversion to Christianity will be a real possibility.

The Jewish community recognized that emancipation would exact a toll in dissolving the communal structure of French Jewry. They realized, for example, that the power of excommunication would have to lapse. Nevertheless, they wished the economic benefits of emancipation. Although the Sephardim of Bordeaux were generally more satisfied with the status quo and were actually quite ambivalent about their relations with the Ashkenazim of Alsace-Lorraine, they too fought for emancipation out of a joint sense of communal responsibility.

Several conclusions emanate from this debate over emancipation. First, the French Enlightenment, for all its vaunted liberalism and protection of individual rights, did not permit cultural pluralism. It expected that Frenchmen will owe a singular loyalty to

French society and the nation-state. It held little room for ethnic or religious diversity. Those traditions would be far more representative of England and America then they would be of the European continent.

Secondly, the debate suggests, following Hertzberg, that anti-Semitism is far from being the monopoly of the right. The Enlightenment initiated a secular left-wing tradition of anti-Semitism that may be traced through nineteenth-century socialist thought and has echoes in the twentieth century, e.g. the patrician anti-Semitism of a Henry Adams or, more recently, a Gore Vidal. This tradition of anti-Semitism rarely initiates concrete political activity against Jews. However, it does turn a blind eye to pogroms against Jews and certainly reflects indifference to the Jews' survival as a nation. Jews have often allied with the left out of historical memory that the left brought emancipation and the right opposed emancipation. In so doing, Jews have often ignored or downplayed the reality that anti-Semitism is by no means foreign to left-wing thinking. Although Hertzberg may overstate the case in attempting to link Voltaire with the Nazis, his points are well-taken: Anti-Semitism occurs on all ends of the political spectrum; Enlightenment anti-Semitism reflected an alternative tradition of contempt for Jews and Judaism in secularized idiom; and Voltaire's gratuitous remarks on Jewish usurers should by no means be regarded as accidental to his thinking, but rather form a far more central component in his general outlook, which opposed all organized religion. Voltaire's anti-Semitism was no simple footnote. It reflected an Enlightenment tradition of anti-Semitism that would have serious consequences for Jews, especially when Jews failed to assimilate.

Thirdly, the bargain of emancipation must be understood in terms of its contractual nature. Liberals and conservatives alike agreed that the Jew qua Jew was unacceptable. Emancipation, from its very beginning, did not limit itself to simple extension of human rights to Jews. Rather, it expected the dissolution of Jewish corporate identity. Therefore, something was wrong with emancipation from its opening stages. It did not grant civil and political rights to Jews simply on the basis that Jews as human beings deserved them. It granted these rights on the condition and expectation of Jewish transformation. The resurgence of anti-Semitism in France, e.g. the Dreyfus affair and subsequently Vichy France, reflected the triumph of those who argued that emancipation was not working. Rather than become a Frenchman, they insisted, the Jew had remained a Jew.

The French Revolution

The Revolution brought emancipation in stages. Bordeaux Jewry received emancipation first, in September 1790. Alsatian Jewry followed twelve months later, but remained subject to taking the discriminatory oath of allegiance. Both Ashkenazim and Sephardim, in fact, were excluded from the original Declaration of the Rights of Man of 1789. Jews had to petition directly for emancipation, again pointing to its contractual nature, rather than its being an extension of principle applying to all individuals in France. Moreover, that Ashkenazi Jews had to retain the humiliating *more Judaico,* or special oath of allegiance incumbent upon Jews, signified the continued suspicion and resentment that Jews were not truly Frenchman. Finally, and paradoxically, the National Assembly kept the Jewish community alive by refusing to nationalize the communal debt. For purposes of emancipation, Jews had become individuals. For purposes of owing money, they remained a community.

Moreover, the Jacobin government was quite reluctant to grant Jews emancipation on the grounds that it would result in new uprisings, as the peasants of Alsace-Lorraine were violently anti-Semitic. The real tensions within Alsace-Lorraine did retard emancipation, despite Jacobin ideology and commitment to the principles of the revolution. During the revolution sporadic outbreaks occurred against Jews. Simultaneously, during the Jacobin Reign of Terror against all organized religion, synagogues were converted into "temples of reason," Torah scrolls were burned, and the Sabbath was banned. Jews, however, remained supportive of the revolution, convinced that the right-wing opposed the revolution and remained hopelessly anti-Semitic.

Napoleon and the Jews

Under the influence of his conservative advisers, who argued that emancipation was not working, Napoleon reopened the Jewish question in 1806. He posed twelve questions to an Assembly of Notables, representing French Jewry, implying that if the answers were unsatisfactory, emancipation would be revoked. If the answers were satisfactory, the Notables would be reconstituted along the model of a Grand Sanhedrin, reflecting Napoleon's love for pomp and circumstance. Napoleon proclaimed a one-year moratorium on debts owed to Jews, reflecting resentment over continuing Jewish involvement in credit and usury. Liberals attacked this as corporate treatment of Jews and a return to the *ancien regime*. The decree signaled that emancipation was very much on trial. Its future would be determined by how Jewish leaders would respond to Napoleon's queries. Although much has been made of Napoleon's desire to appeal to East European Jewry via the Sanhedrin and future promises of emancipation, it became very much a domestic French document regulating the future of French Judaism.

Napoleon's questions were targeted to examining the separatistic character of Judaism. In essence, they focused upon four areas: marriage and marriage procedures, the patriotism of Jews, the jurisdiction of the rabbis (i.e., was their authority police jurisdiction or simply moral persuasiveness) and a double standard of Judaism regarding gentiles, particularly with respect to usury legislation. The Sanhedrin had little trouble in proclaiming the patriotism of French Jews and consigning the police jurisdiction of the rabbis to the past by saying that today the rabbis exert only moral persuasiveness, meaning that the power of excommunication had lapsed. They reinterpreted the ban against taking interest from a Jew to mean that usury, or excessive interest, was always forbidden. Inasmuch as Jews now consider Frenchman to be their brethren, there should be no distinction between taking interest from a Jew and taking interest from a Frenchman. Most problematical was the Jewish ban on intermarriage. Here, the members of the Sanhedrin rejected Napoleon's recommendation that Jewry encourage intermarriage. They argued that Judaism opposes mixed-marriage. However, the fact of one's intermarriage would not place one outside the French Jewish community.

Many have criticized these answers as evasive. However, the men of the Sanhedrin did not engage in outright falsehoods. They sought to proclaim the full citizenship of the Jews, historicize the political dimensions of Judaism, and reformulate Judaic principles along lines of eradicating contradictions between being a Jew and being a Frenchman. Underlying the Sanhedrin was the perception of change in the nature of the Jewish community. It had become voluntaristic and therefore would accept adherents from all circles within Jewry, even those who were uncommitted and even those who would intermarry. The answers internalized the emancipation critique of Jewry as needing to become more productive. However, French Jewry was not prepared to accept emancipation if it meant offering a sanction of approval to the phenomenon of intermarriage, which would ultimately have meant the dissolution of French Jewish identity.

Napoleon was generally satisfied with the answers he received and ordered the Sanhedrin to institutionalize them as a constitution for French Judaism. He revoked the moratorium on Jewish debts. However, in 1808, Napoleon returned to the Jewish question with his Infamous Decree restricting Jewish commerce and movement in France and making it far more difficult to collect debts. Jews were compelled to adopt French surnames, and rabbis were expected to become spokesmen for the French government. Jews, however, persuaded Napoleon that they were moving toward the ending of usury and were entering more productive occupations such as artisanry. They claimed to be fulfilling the terms of emancipation. Napoleon accepted the evident desire of French Jews to be French and soon revoked the Infamous Decree.

What was lasting from Napoleonic legislation was the Consistoire for French Jewry, analogous to a similar system created for Protestants. The rabbis now became civil servants. Their salaries were paid by the nation-state. Membership in the Consistoire was compulsory, and thus the Consistoire preserved the unity of French Jewry, while outlawing Jewish sectarianism and even private *minyanim*. The Ecole Rabbinique was created in 1830 to train a French rabbinate who would be French-speaking and loyal to the French government. Conversely, however, rabbis would be prohibited from criticizing state policy, suggesting, as Alexis de Tocqueville noted, that when church and state are united, religion loses its critical role as an independent moral voice and conscience assessing state policy.

In turn, the Consistoire ensured the monopoly of Orthodox Judaism within France. No Reform movement occurred until the twentieth century and only following the separation of church and state. Although French Orthodox rabbis were generally more liberal then their colleagues elsewhere, the alliance of Judaism with the state produced not a vibrant and vital Judaism, but rather religious indifference and apathy. The absence of a Reform movement did not mean greater commitment to Orthodoxy. What it did mean was greater assimilation and religious indifference.

Napoleon, of course, was overthrown by the Battle of Waterloo. The Congress of Vienna, however, in 1815, retained the status of the Jews as emancipated citizens, although emancipation was subsequently revoked in German lands. In France, however, emancipation could no longer be undone. On the contrary, the terms of emancipation would regulate the lives of French Jewry and Judaism into the twentieth century.

Reading: Paul Mendes-Flohr and Jehuda Reinharz, eds., *The Jew in the Modern World*

The questions confronting the Napoleonic Sanhedrin underscore the dilemma of the modern Jew torn between his desires for inclusion in the modern state and the need to assert a separate Jewish identity. The notables who convened to answer Napoleon's questions in effect were defining the terms of Jewish emancipation in France. To be sure, that they were not able to give Napoleon all that he wished to hear. On the contrary, by insisting on continuing to discourage mixed marriage, they were asserting continued Jewish separatism even as they affirmed their membership in the French nation.

> One of the secretaries [proceeded to read the following] questions proposed to the Assembly of the Jews by the Commissioners named by His Majesty the Emperor and King. . . .
>
> 1. Is it lawful for Jews to marry more than one wife?
>
> 2. Is divorce allowed by the Jewish religion? Is divorce valid, when not pronounced by courts of justice, and by virtue of laws in contradiction with the French code?
>
> 3. Can a Jewess marry a Christian, or a Jew a Christian woman? Or has the law ordered that the Jews should only intermarry among themselves?

4. In the eyes of Jews are Frenchmen considered as brethren or as strangers?

5. In either case what conduct does their law prescribe towards Frenchmen not of their religion?

6. Do the Jews born in France, and treated by the law as French citizens, consider France as their country? Are they bound to defend it? Are they bound to obey the laws, and to follow the directions of the civil code?

7. What kind of police-jurisdiction have the Rabbis among the Jews? What judicial power do they exercise among them?

8. Are the forms of the elections of the Rabbis and their police-jurisdiction regulated by the law, or are they only sanctioned by custom?

9. Are there professions from which the Jews are excluded by their law?

10. Does the law forbid the Jews from taking usury from their brethren?

11. Does it forbid or does it allow usury toward strangers?

Bibliography for Further Reading

Gay, Peter. *Voltaire's Politics,* Vintage Books, 1965

Hertzberg, Arthur. *The French Enlightenment and the Jews,* Schocken Books, 1990

Katz, Jacob. *From Prejudice to Destruction,* Harvard University Press, 1982

Unit XXIV

Reform Judaism

Origins

The origins of Reform Judaism may be located in Germany. The Hamburg Temple in 1817 introduced numerous changes in synagogal liturgy, language and use of music in order to enhance decorum. The Brunswick Rabbinical Conference of 1844 sought to break down barriers between Jew and gentile. The Sabbath and dietary laws were abandoned so as to facilitate Jewish-gentile interaction. Lay leaders had been spearheading this movement for over two decades. Brunswick represented an attempt by the German rabbinate to reassert control over the direction of Reform.

The context for this Reform movement lay in the ongoing struggle for Jewish emancipation in Germany. Emancipation had begun in 1807. After the Prussian defeats of Jena and Austerlitz, the Prussian state found itself in disarray. Its Minister of Education, von Humboldt, proclaimed the need to modernize Prussia and to do so by integrating the private corporations, particularly the Jews.

Progress toward emancipation was steady yet protracted. In the 1840's King Frederick William IV attempted to revoke the limited emancipation already granted to Jews. Reform arose as an attempt to reformulate Judaism to approximate the image that proponents of emancipation wished to perceive within the Jewish community.

What exactly were the proponents saying? The dominant figure of German philosophy and perhaps of all German academic life in the nineteenth century was Immanuel Kant. Kant argued that a true morality must be self-legislated and autonomous. Jesus articulated a moral vision that was self-generated rather than externally commanded. Judaic morality, by contrast, appeared heteronomous rather than autonomous.

The medieval philosopher Saadiah Gaon had distinguished between *mitzvot* that we know on the basis of our reason and *mitzvot* that are commanded. However, he cautioned that the only reason for our obeying the rational *mitzvot* was precisely because they are commanded. Maimonides had gone even further, arguing that any gentile who observes natural law will be granted salvation provided the gentile recognizes natural law as commanded by God. Kant was following Mendelssohn's formulation as Judaism lacking in dogma but being a religion of commandment. He argued that the Jew could never be truly moral because the basis for right action emanated from Sinai rather than from personal autonomy.

Georg Hegel, the leading philosopher of history, articulated a different yet no less powerful critique. Hegel argued that the Jews had no sense of history. There had been no development within Judaism since 586 B.C.E. The Jews of today remain the Jews of yesteryear.

Both Hegel and Kant were proponents of Jewish emancipation. Both had badly misread the essence of Judaism, particularly in their ignorance of rabbinic Judaism. Kant had slighted the entire tradition of free will within Judaism, which made morality a matter of free choice even if Jews were exhorted to choose the good. Hegel had similarly ignored rabbinic development within Jewish history. For example, the holiday of Hanukkah represented not a vestige from Judaism in its original form but a response to historical development.

Reform Judaism, however, argued that the strictures of Kant and Hegel applied only to Orthodox Jews. Orthodoxy was a religion of commands. Reform Judaism, by contrast, emphasized the autonomy of human beings in making their own ethical choices. Similarly, while Orthodox Jews claimed that they were observing Judaism precisely as Moses had done, Reform Judaism perceived itself as responding to changing historical needs and conditions.

Issues and Doctrines

Perhaps no issue was more symbolic in the development of Reform Judaism than the place of Hebrew in the liturgy. Hebrew was eliminated from the Reform prayer book as were other references to the national character of Judaism. Reform redefined Jewish identity as being "Germans of the Mosaic persuasion," meaning that Jewish identity consisted of faith without any ties to Jewish peoplehood or dreams for a national restoration.

Not all Reformers were prepared for such a radical redefinition. Zecharias Frankel, an enlightened Jew who desired moderate reforms, protested the Brunswick Rabbinical Conference on the grounds that Hebrew had been the cohesive force of world Jewry. The loss of Frankel was disappointing to the Reformers, because his voice commanded the authority of tradition and history. Frankel had wanted reforms that would enhance rather than detract from Judaism. He understood Jewish identity as positive and historical, meaning a rejection on the one hand of fundamentalism and on the other hand of radical reforms that were dissonant with Jewish history and tradition. For that reason Frankel protested the elimination of Hebrew, for Hebrew had functioned as the historical language of the Jewish people.

Frankel wished reforms that would evolve over historical time. The vehicle of such reforms must be scientific and historical scholarship rather than simply the desire to integrate into German society. For Frankel, there were no parts of Judaism that were accidental. All parts were essential, and one could not lop off parts without doing violence to the whole.

Many Reformers agreed with Frankel in theory, but in practice wished to change much more of historical Jewish observance. They admired Frankel for his rejection of fundamentalism, but found him too wedded to historical Judaism and unwilling to make the changes necessary to modernize it. Frankel followed the founder of modern Jewish historical scholarship, Heinrich Graetz. Graetz's metaphor for Judaism was a tree. It had roots, a trunk, branches, and leaves. Only the very externals could be lost without doing violence to the tree as a whole. Therefore, while some changes were desirable, particularly with respect to the obviously irrational components of Judaism, all changes must evolve historically and naturally and can never be permitted to damage the tree itself.

The Reformers, by contrast, distinguished between essence and accident. They equated the essence of Judaism with ethical monotheism. That remained constant over the centuries. Jewish law, by contrast, was accidental. The law must be evaluated from an autonomous perspective as to whether it enhances the position of the Jew in the modern world or detracts from Jewish presence in modern society. With respect to the Shabbat, for example, the Reformers argued that state service must take precedence over Shabbat. The dietary laws were now regarded as a political institution dividing Jew from gentile that might best be abandoned. Similarly, the Reformers emphasized the need for decorum in the synagogue, for the absence of decorum represented the fundamental irrationality of medieval Judaism. Hence, they advocated the use of music in the synagogue to recapture the dignity of the service. The theology of the Reformers was universalistic in nature. Their major reason for remaining Jews consisted of the mission theory—heavily indebted to the prophets generally and Isaiah in particular—of the Jews serving as "a light onto the gentiles." The mission of the Jews was to teach ethical monotheism. Jews ought remain a distinctive entity until the rest of the world caught up with Judaism.

To be sure, this mission theory was contradictory in nature. It assumed that the Jews were ahead of civilization rather than behind it. Yet the essence of Reform Judaism called for the Jews to catch up to general society. Secondly, the mission theory assumed that Christianity was deficient by comparison with Judaism. The reason for remaining Jewish was that Judaism would do a better job at convincing the general world of the truths of ethical monotheism. Aside from the implicit critique of Christianity, it assumed a general society prepared to accept the Jew as teacher and as ethically superior. Lastly, the logic of the mission theory and Reform Judaism generally was that the Jews are no longer a distinctive people. Jews have more in common with liberal Germans than they would with Orthodox Jews in Eastern Europe. Yet Reformers continued to protest the rights of Jews outside of Germany. The Damascus blood libel of 1860, for example, drew a vigorous response from Abraham Geiger, the leader of Reform Judaism. Such protests were justified on humanitarian grounds. Yet one could not resist questioning whether the passions of Reform Jews would have been as exercised if the victims of pogroms and blood libels had been Armenians or Russian peasants. The logic of Reform dictated that the Jews would have no political program and no special ties to Jews elsewhere. Yet the passions of the Jews as a people remained despite such theological reformulation. Perhaps the best illustration was that circumcision, derided as barbaric and irrational, was never abandoned by the Reform movement. It represented too enduring a historical symbol of the Covenant between God and the Jewish people.

German Reform possessed both radical and moderate wings. The radical wing, represented by Rabbi Samuel Holdheim, called for moving the Sabbath to Sunday, abandoning the dietary laws, and celebrating intermarriage as the ideal marriage between Jew and gentile. Conservative forces within the movement were far more hesitant in declaring radical reforms. For David Einhorn, usually associated with the radical wing, especially in terms of his vigorous crusade for abolishing American slavery, every intermarriage was "another nail in the coffin of Jewish identity." Geiger insisted upon maintaining the dietary laws, as did virtually every Reform rabbi until the late nineteenth century.

This moderation generally triumphed within Germany, for the communal responsibilities of the rabbis caused them to recognize a reservoir of piety among the German masses that could not be so easily abandoned. The German-Jewish *kehillah* survived through the nineteenth century, and all rabbis remained members and therefore unwilling to break their bonds with more traditional Jews.

In America, by contrast, radical Reform triumphed, culminating in the Pittsburgh Platform of 1885. The Pittsburgh Platform denationalized Judaism, abandoning references to God, the Jewish people, and restoration to a national homeland. The Pittsburgh Platform prevailed for half a century. In time, the triumphs of Zionism and the atrocities of Hitler compelled a rethinking of Reform principles. By the Columbus Platform of 1935, Reform signaled a return to Jewish peoplehood and a revaluing of the Jewish homeland.

Reform Judaism Today

In America today, Reform Judaism is probably the largest of the movements, claiming the allegiances of some 38 percent of all American Jews. Its public face has been the voice of social ethics reminding Jews of their obligations to pursue justice in the broader society. More recently, it has experimented with more traditional innovations, such as the growth of Reform day schools and a greater appreciation of ritual and the utilization of Hebrew in the prayer book. Most importantly, it was Reform Judaism that restored the value of conversion to Judaism in the Jewish historical experience. In 1978 the Reform movement announced its program of outreach to spur conversion to Judaism by those who were unchurched. In practice, the outreach program has been designed to reach out to mixed-married couples and encourage the conversion of the non-Jewish partner. The Reform movement correctly stated that conversion had historically always been a component of rabbinic Judaism. In the ancient world Judaism often adopted missionary stances. In the medieval period Jews stopped doing so because of Christian and Islamic persecution. In the modern period, especially following Moses Mendelssohn, Jewish values were translated as abandoning proselytizing activity. Missionizing was left to gentiles. Jews did not look for converts. The Reform movement argued that it was this modern tradition of Judaism that had been deviant. Aggressive search for converts had taken place historically. Jews had even been expelled from ancient Rome for undermining the gentile family structure through conversion to Judaism.

Despite its numeric strength, the Reform movement confronts serious challenges and the prospect of future erosion. Conversion has generally declined since the early 1980's, as intermarriage has become more normative. The effects of mixed marriage as a whole are felt most poignantly within the Reform synagogue. As a number of Reform rabbis have recently lamented, what is the distinction between Jew and gentile in the synagogue, if gentiles have full rights of participation. Unfortunately, the Reform practice of aggressively welcoming mixed-married couples has had the unintended consequences of reducing the incentive for conversion, while blurring the distinction between Jew and gentile.

Secondly, Reform insistence upon autonomy has raised the question of what, if any, are the limits to Reform Jewish practice. For example, can there be Judaism without belief in God as advocated by secular humanistic Judaism, which has a small number of congregations interested in affiliating with the Reform movement? Leo Baeck, the leader of German Jewry during the Holocaust years and a patron figure for the Reform movement, had as early as the beginning of the twentieth century urged that Reform have no embarrassment about commands within Judaism. Yet today the insistence upon autonomy represents one of the critical fault lines within the Reform movement. Insisting, for example, on the rights of rabbis to officiate at mixed marriages constitutes a statement of belief in autonomy. Insisting upon communal responsibility and faithfulness to Judaic principle frequently necessitates a violation of that autonomy, as Reform theologians Emil Fackenheim and Eugene Borowitz have frequently noted.

The most divisive issues separating Reform Judaism from its more traditional counterparts relate to rabbinic officiation at mixed marriages, patrilineal descent, and homosexuality. The Reform rabbinate today is divided between a majority which refuses to perform mixed marriages and a minority which does so. Recent research has indicated that rabbinic officiation accomplishes little in terms of involving the mixed-married couple in Jewish communal practices. Rabbinic officiation certainly communicates the message that intermarriage is now an acceptable option for American Jews. However, the refusal of rabbis to officiate at mixed marriages often places enormous strains between rabbi and congregation. Although there are few Reform rabbis who gladly perform mixed marriages, the numbers of those willing to officiate has risen as intermarriage has become increasingly normative, if not prevalent, within Reform congregations.

In 1983, the Reform movement accepted the patrilineal descent definition of who is a Jew, stating that a child was a Jew if that child had one Jewish parent and both parents committed themselves to the exclusive raising of that child within the Jewish faith through positive affirmations of Judaism, especially rites of passage and Jewish education. In practice, the patrilineal descent decision has been interpreted not as a statement associated with the conditions of child-rearing, but rather as a simple definition that one is a Jew if one has a parent of either gender who is Jewish.

This decision clearly marked a fundamental departure from Jewish history. Although virtually every Reform rabbi in America had practiced patrilineal descent since World War II, the decision signaled a reaffirmation of Reform commitment to continue to make significant changes. Moreover, the decision had a number of unforeseen consequences. It drove a wedge between the Reform and Conservative movements, for Conservative Judaism adhered to the historical definition of Jewish identity through the matrilineal principle. Reform Judaism assumed that Conservative Judaism would follow in short order, but increasingly the Conservative movement has rejected patrilineal descent.

Secondly, the patrilineal descent decision had deleterious consequences upon the relationship of Reform Judaism with Israel. Enormous strides had been made in developing Zionism within the Reform movement. Although in the 1930's and 1940's as many as one- third of Reform rabbis had supported the American Council for Judaism in its opposition to the Jewish State, by 1948 that number had been reduced to a handful and in subsequent years the public posture of the Reform movement had been decidedly Zionist and pro-Israel. For example, in Houston, at the classic Reform temple, Beth Israel, one could not, at a certain time, be a member if one was a Zionist. Today it's gone the other way, and Beth Israel has its own day school. Perhaps the best symbol of Reform Zionism was Rabbi Alexander Schindler's legitimation of Prime Minister Menahem Begin's policies during Schindler's tenure as chairman of the Conference of Presidents of Major Jewish Organizations.

Yet by accepting patrilineal descent, the Reform movement drew a wedge between itself and Israeli society. The Law of Return, passed by the Israeli Knesset and a fundamental bedrock of Zionist principles, had articulated Jewish identity through either the matrilineal line or conversion to Judaism. Although the Reform movement insisted that conversion to Judaism should not be interpreted as strictly Orthodox conversion, it could not insist upon the patrilineal principle without driving a wedge between Israel and the diaspora. As a result, it was no surprise that the Reform movement in Israel opposed the patrilineal descent decision, albeit unsuccessfully.

Nor may one overlook the apparent relationship between acceptance of patrilineality and a decline in conversion to Judaism. No sooner had the Reform movement accepted patrilineal descent publicly than conversion to Judaism seemed to plummet. We have long known that one motivation for conversion to Judaism was the desire to raise Jewish children. Converts were far more frequently found among gentile women than gentile men. By declaring patrilineal descent, the Reform movement had seemingly removed one of the major stimuli toward conversion to Judaism.

Lastly, Reform Judaism has been somewhat ahead of the Jewish community in its acceptance of gay and lesbian synagogues and rabbis. Although most American Jews agree on the need to preserve civil liberties for homosexuals and are not prepared to countenance retreat from that principle, there is much less consensus concerning validation of homosexuality as a communal norm through the presence of avowedly gay rabbis and sanctification of same-sex ceremonies. Interestingly, the Central Conference of American Rabbis recognized this point in accepting gay and lesbian and lesbian rabbis by stating "to the extent that sexuality is a matter of choice, heterosexual marriage represents the only appropriate choice as *kiddushin* (sanctified marriage)." However, public knowledge and awareness of the CCAR resolution has faded in favor of the widespread popular perception that Reform does not distinguish between heterosexual and homosexual behavior.

What then of the future? There are two possible directions for the Reform movement. Some of its advocates proclaim that it will indeed be the movement of the future, as its numbers will grow owing to increased numbers of gentiles intimately related to born Jews. Others forecast continued erosion, for mixed marriage means minimal Jewish identity, with the children of mixed marriages identifying even less and the grandchildren not at all. This scenario, which forecasts considerable erosion over the course of the next two generations, is far more pessimistic about the Reform future.

Considerable evidence exists to sustain both positions. The Reform movement today appears numerically larger than at virtually any point in American Jewish history. Conversely, Reform rabbis have already reported that the presence of large numbers of mixed-marrieds within Reform congregations has made it difficult, if not impossible, to sustain the message of Jewish in-marriage. Reform youth movements find it anomalous to be encouraging teen-agers to date other Jews when mixed marriage is so common among their elders.

Both scenarios emanate from the fluidity of boundaries between Jew and gentile in late twentieth-century America. On the one hand, the fluidity of boundaries opens up the possibility of attracting gentiles to Judaic observance and involvement. On the other hand, it threatens the distinctiveness of Reform Judaism as a religious presence within American culture, suggesting that a bland formulation of "Judeo-Christian" ethics now prevails in American society. The fluidity of boundaries is incredible testimony to how welcoming America has been to Jewish participation—more so than any society in diaspora Jewish history. The problem faced by Reform Judaism, however, is that for a minority to survive in a majority culture, it requires greater distinctiveness and firmer boundaries between itself and that majority culture.

Reading: Gunther Plaut, ed., *The Growth of Reform Judaism*

The Pittsburgh Platform was a statement of classical Reform Judaism. Note, in particular, its emphasis upon rationalism and ethics rather than on peoplehood and God. The emphasis shifts pronouncedly in the Columbus Platform to greater stress on Jewish peoplehood. Even the Columbus Platform, however, fell short of a declaration in favor of Zionism, although it did support rehabilitation of Palestine.

The Pittsburgh Platform

In view of the wide divergence of opinion and of the conflicting ideas prevailing in Judaism today, we, as representatives of Reform Judaism in America, in continuation of the work begun at Philadelphia in 1869, unite upon the following principles:

First—We recognize in every religion an attempt to grasp the Infinite One, and in every mode, source or book of revelation held sacred in any religious system the consciousness of the indwelling of God in man. We hold that Judaism presents the highest conception of the God-idea as taught in our holy Scriptures and developed and spiritualized by the Jewish teachers in accordance with the moral and philosophical progress of their respective ages. We maintain that Judaism preserved and defended amid continual struggles and trials and under enforced isolation this God-idea as the central religious truth for the human race.

Second—We recognize in the Bible the record of the consecration of the Jewish people to its mission as priest of the One God, and value it as the most potent instrument of religious and moral instruction. We hold that the modern discoveries of scientific researches in the domains of nature and history are not antagonistic to the doctrines of Judaism, the Bible reflecting the primitive ideas of its own age and at times clothing its conception of divine providence and justice dealing with man in miraculous narratives.

Third—We recognize in the Mosaic legislation a system of training the Jewish people for its mission during its national life in Palestine, and today we accept as binding only the moral laws and maintain only such ceremonies as elevate and sanctify our lives, but reject all such as are not adapted to the views and habits of modern civilization.

Fourth—We hold that all such Mosaic and Rabbinical laws as regulate diet, priestly purity and dress originated in ages and under the influence of ideas altogether foreign to our present mental and spiritual state. They fail to impress the modern Jew with a spirit of priestly holiness; their observance in our days is apt rather to obstruct than to further modern spiritual elevation.

Fifth—We recognize in the modern era of universal culture of heart and intellect the approach of the realization of Israel's great Messianic hope for the establishment of the kingdom of truth, justice and peace among all men. We consider ourselves no longer a nation but a religious community, and therefore expect neither a return to Palestine, nor a sacrificial worship under the administration of the sons of Aaron, nor the restoration of any of the laws concerning the Jewish state.

Sixth—We recognize in Judaism a progressive religion, ever striving to be in accord with the postulates of reason. We are convinced of the utmost necessity of preserving the historical identity with our great past. Christianity and Islam being daughter-religions of Judaism, we appreciate their mission to aid in the spreading of monotheistic and moral truth. We acknowledge that the spirit of broad humanity of our age is our ally in the fulfillment of our mission, and therefore we extend the hand of fellowship to all who cooperate with us in the establishment of the reign of truth and righteousness among men.

Seventh—We reassert the doctrine of Judaism, that the soul of men is immortal, grounding this belief on the divine nature of the human spirit, which forever finds bliss in righteousness and misery in wickedness. We reject as ideas not rooted in Judaism the belief both in bodily resurrection and in Gehenna and Eden (hell and paradise), as abodes for everlasting punishment or reward.

Eighth—In full accordance with the spirit of Mosaic legislation which strives to regulate the relation between rich and poor, we deem it our duty to participate in the great task of modern times, to solve on the basis of justice and righteousness the problems presented by the contrasts and evils of the present organization of society.

The Columbus Platform

Guiding Principles of Reform Judaism

In view of the changes that have taken place in the modern world and the consequent need of stating anew the teachings of Reform Judaism, the Central Conference of American Rabbis makes the following declaration of principles. It presents them not as a fixed creed but as a guide for the progressive elements of Jewry.

A. Judaism and Its Foundations

1. Nature of Judaism. Judaism is the historical religious experience of the Jewish people. Though growing out of Jewish life, its message is universal, aiming at the union and perfection of mankind under the sovereignty of God. Reform Judaism recognizes the principle of progressive development in religion and consciously applies this principle to spiritual as well as to cultural and social 1ife.

Judaism welcomes all truth, whether written in the pages of scripture or deciphered from the records of nature. The new discoveries of science, while replacing the older scientific views underlying our sacred literature, do not conflict with the essential spirit of religion as manifested in the consecration of man's will, heart and mind to the service of God and or humanity.

2. God. The heart of Judaism and its chief contribution to religion is the doctrine of the One, living God, who rules the world through law and love. In Him all existence has its creative source and mankind its ideal of conduct. Through transcending time and space, He is the indwelling Presence of the world. We worship Him as the Lord of the universe and as our merciful Father.

3. Man. Judaism affirms that man is created in the Divine image. His spirit is immortal. He is an active co-worker with God. As a child of God, he is endowed with moral freedom and is charged with the responsibility of overcoming evil and striving after ideal ends.

4. Torah. God reveals Himself not only in the majesty, beauty and orderliness of nature, but also in the vision and moral striving of the human spirit. Revelation is a continuous process, confined to no one group and to no one age. Yet the people of Israel, through its prophets and sages, achieved unique insight in the realm of religious truth. The Torah, both written and oral, enshrines Israel's ever-growing consciousness of God and of the moral law. It preserves the historical precedents, sanctions and norms of Jewish life, and seeks to mould it in the patterns of goodness and of holiness. Being products of historical processes, certain of its laws have lost their binding force with the passing of the conditions that called them forth. But as a depository of permanent spiritual ideals, the Torah remains the dynamic source of the life of Israel. Each age has the obligation to adapt the teachings of the Torah to its basic needs in consonance with the genius of Judaism.

5. Israel. Judaism is the soul of which Israel is the body. Living in all parts of the world, Israel has been held together by the ties of a common history, and above all, by the heritage of faith. Though we recognize in the group loyalty of Jews who have become estranged from our religious tradition, a bond which still unites them with us, we maintain that it is by its religion and for its religion that the Jewish people has lived. The non-Jew who accepts our faith is welcomed as a full member of the Jewish community.

In all lands where our people live, they assume and seek to share loyally the full duties and responsibilities of citizenship and to create seats of Jewish knowledge and religion. In the rehabilitation of Palestine, the land hallowed by memories and hopes, we behold the promise of renewed life for many of our brethren. We affirm the obligation of all Jewry to aid in its upbuilding as a Jewish homeland by endeavoring to make it not only a haven of refuge for the oppressed but also a center of Jewish culture and spiritual life.

Throughout the ages it has been Israel's mission to witness

to the Divine in the face of every form of paganism and materialism. We regard it as our historic task to cooperate with all men in the establishment of the kingdom of God, of universal brotherhood, justice, truth and peace on earth. This is our Messianic goal.

B. Ethics

6. Ethics and Religion. In Judaism religion and morality blend into an indissoluble unity. Seeking God means to strive after holiness, righteousness and goodness. The love of God is incomplete without the love of one's fellowmen. Judaism emphasizes the kinship of the human race, the sanctity and worth of human life and personality and the right of the individual to freedom and to the pursuit of his chosen vocation. Justice to all, irrespective of race, sect or class is the inalienable right and the inescapable obligation of all. The state and organized government exist in order to further these ends.

7. Social Justice. Judaism seeks the attainment of a just society by the application of its teachings to the economic order, to industry and commerce, and to national and international affairs. It aims at the elimination of man-made misery and suffering, of poverty and degradation, of tyranny and slavery, of social inequality and prejudice, of ill-will and strife. It advocates the promotion of harmonious relations between warring classes on the basis of equity and justice, and the creation of conditions under which human personality may flourish. It pleads for the safeguarding of childhood against exploitation. It champions the cause of all who work and of their right to an adequate standard of living, as prior to the rights of property. Judaism emphasizes the duty of charity, and strives for a social order which will protect men against the material disabilities of old age, sickness and unemployment.

8. Peace. Judaism, from the days of the prophets, has proclaimed to mankind the ideal of universal peace. The spiritual and physical disarmament of all nations has been one of its essential teachings. It abhors all violence and relies upon moral education, love and sympathy to secure human progress. It regards justice as the foundation of the well-being of nations and the condition of enduring peace. It urges organized international action for disarmament, collective security and world peace.

C. Religious Practice

9. The Religious Life. Jewish life is marked by consecration to these ideals of Judaism. It calls for faithful participation in the life of the Jewish community as it finds expression in home, synagogue and school and in all other agencies that enrich Jewish life and promote its welfare.

The Home has been and must continue to be a stronghold of Jewish life, hallowed by the spirit of love and reverence, by moral discipline and religious observance and worship.

The Synagogue is the oldest and most democratic institution in Jewish life. It is the prime communal agency by which Judaism is fostered and preserved. It links the Jews of each community and unites them with all Israel.

The perpetuation of Judaism as a living force depends upon religious knowledge and upon the Education of each new generation in our rich cultural and spiritual heritage.

Prayer is the voice of religion, the language of faith and aspiration. It directs man's heart and mind Godward, voices the needs and hopes of the community, and reaches out after goals which invest life with supreme value. To deepen the spiritual life of our people, we must cultivate the traditional habit of communion with God through prayer in both home and synagogue.

Judaism as a way of life requires in addition to its moral and spiritual demands, the preservation of the Sabbath, festivals and Holy Days, the retention and development of such customs, symbols and ceremonies as possess inspirational value, the cultivation of distinctive forms of religious art and music and the use of Hebrew, together with the vernacular, in our worship and instruction.

These timeless aims and ideals of our faith we present anew to a confused and troubled world. We call upon our fellow Jews to rededicate themselves to them, and, in harmony with all men, hopefully and courageously to continue Israel's eternal quest after God and His kingdom.

Bibliography for Further Reading

Borowitz, Eugene. *Reform Judaism Today: How We Live,* Behrman House, 1983

Fackenheim, Emil. *Encounters Between Judaism and Modern Philosophy,* Jewish Publication Society, 1983

Glazer, Nathan. *American Judaism,* University of Chicago Press, [1957] rep. 1988

Mayer, Egon. *Intermarriage and Rabbinic Officiation,* American Jewish Committee, 1987

Meyer, Michael. *Response to Modernity: A History of the Reform Movement in Judaism,* Oxford, 1990

Silberman, Charles. *A Certain People,* Summit Books, 1986

Silverstein, Alan. *Alternatives to Assimilation,* Brandeis University Press, 1994

Wertheimer, Jack. *A People Divided,* Basic Books, 1993

Unit XXV

Neo-Orthodoxy

"Old" Orthodoxy

Any discussion of neo-Orthodoxy in nineteenth-century Germany must begin with the Orthodoxy that was subject to revision—what is today known as ultra-Orthodoxy or "old Orthodoxy." The leader of the old Orthodox was Rabbi Moses Sofer, better known as the *Hatam Sofer.* Sofer rejected emancipation on principle. He saw little that was beneficial in the promise of emancipation. Most likely the old Orthodox represented a majority of German and certainly Hungarian Jewry in the mid-nineteenth century.

For the old Orthodox, secular learning was legitimate only for vocational purposes. This utilitarian approach to secular learning presupposed that there were no values in secular culture per se worth discussing. If one required certain skills to make a living, secular learning was an appropriate vehicle of attaining those skills. However, under no circumstances could there be any "art for art's sake" or turning to secular culture as a source of ideas and values.

The old Orthodox stressed the national components of Judaism, such as Hebrew and Palestinian settlement. Although they would later reject political Zionism, they did not question Jewish peoplehood and the dream of natural restoration.

Lastly, the old Orthodox argued that Jewish custom was as sacrosanct as Jewish law. There could be no evolution in history or departure from previous custom. Thus they opposed changes in the liturgy, even in marginal areas such as liturgical poetry. Sofer's slogan became, "Whatever is new is forbidden from the Torah," a phrase alluding to the prohibition on first fruits in the Land of Israel, but which was now applied to prohibition of the new currents of Western culture and enlightenment. To say the least, Reform Judaism fell under this ban of "whatever is new."

Moses Sofer and the partisans of old-Orthodoxy believed that they must protect the walls of tradition against breaches wrought by modern culture. As a result, they sought to "build a fence around the law." By erecting such fences, usually defined as additional regulations and prohibitions, they would preserve the inner core of Judaism against the challenges of modernity. For that reason, Jewish customs could not be uprooted. On the contrary, the old-Orthodox abolished the distinction between custom and law.

Similarly, Sofer and his colleagues opposed recourse to philosophic reason as a vehicle for understanding the truths of Judaism. Specifically, they opposed the efforts by Mendelssohn and other men of enlightenment to determine the reasons underlying Jewish laws. They feared that if one emphasized the reasons for the law, and those reasons were no longer applicable or salient, observance of the law itself would fade. By similar logic, they opposed translation of the Torah into the German language, for translation, they felt, would ultimately undermine Torah and relativize its values.

Samson Raphael Hirsch and Neo-Orthodoxy

Samson Raphael Hirsch marked a departure from the position of the *Hatam Sofer* and the old Orthodox. Hirsch had no fear of emancipation. His *Nineteen Letters,* which were meant as an introduction to his defense of Jewish law, *Horeb,* were addressed to a student and argued for full acceptance of emancipation as an enormous opportunity for Jews and Judaism.

Hirsch's ideological defense of Judaism provided a mirror image to that of German Reform. His theory of religious humanism, known as "man-Israelite," argued for another version of the mission concept of "light onto the gentiles." For Hirsch, to be a Jew meant serving humanity. Jews ought to survive to spread their message to the gentile world.

Moreover, like his Reform colleagues, Hirsch turned away from efforts to resettle Palestine. For the Jews to return to their homeland would amount to abandonment of humanity. He noted that the Torah had been given in the wilderness, meaning that territory was not important to its observance. He defined Israel as a people rather than a nation, meaning that it was bound together by Torah and not by land. The exile for Hirsch meant a summons to the Jews to go forth onto the nations. For Hirsch, the lesson of the fast day of Gedaliah, commemorating the assassination of a Jewish governor who successfully accommodated to Babylonian rule, meant that Jews should refrain from molding their own destiny and taking history into their own hands. Redemption will come, but in its own time.

For these reasons, Hirsch shunned the life of seclusion and private study of Torah so favored by the old Orthodox. He saw in emancipation an enormous opportunity for Jewish ideas to impact upon general society. Hirsch's universalism matched that of the Reformers. Both Reform and neo-Orthodoxy agreed on the mission theory of Jews to general society, and both were committed to embracing the new opportunities provided by emancipation.

Moreover, Hirsch was also in agreement with Reform on the need to revise the Judaism of the Middle Ages. He protested the emphasis upon *pilpul* and the exclusive study of the Talmud, noting: "Study became the end instead of the means, while the actual subject of the investigation became a matter of indifference. People studied Judaism but forgot to search for principles in the pages of Scripture. That method, however, is not truly Jewish. Our great masters always protested against it." As a result, Hirsch turned to writing an extensive commentary on the Torah. He sided with the practitioners of *Haskalah* in attacking the models, methods, and even personnel responsible for Jewish education.

Perhaps most importantly, he embraced secular learning as valuable not strictly for utilitarian purposes but as part of God's Divine creation. His motto, "*Torah im Derekh Eretz*" meant that to be a Jew was to be acquainted with "the ways of the world"—meaning science, history, philosophy, and literature.

To be sure, he explicitly opposed the view of Maimonides that secular study would be valuable in interpreting Torah. Hirsch desired only enlightenment from secular learning. He did not desire a value system that would shape his understanding of Torah. The motto of "*Torah im Derekh Eretz*" did not connote that the two value systems were co-equal. Rather Torah was primary, and secular learning was ancillary. Secular learning would enlighten and deepen our understanding of God's ways. It could not serve as a resource for the understanding of Torah, as Maimonides had tried to construct centuries earlier.

This view of secular learning brought Hirsch into conflict with both Reform Judaism and the new historical scholarship pioneered by Frankel and Graetz. Hirsch argued that no non-Jewish criteria ought be utilized for the study of Judaism. Hence lay his critique of Maimonides, whom he regarded as having erred profoundly in harnessing Aristotelian philosophy for the understanding of Judaism. At times, Hirsch utilized romantic etymologies in his understanding of words in Scripture, but never did he utilize secular content as a vehicle of interpreting Jewish text.

In terms of history, Hirsch argued that Jewish law was not subject to historical development. He differed from the old Orthodox in conceding that custom had undergone historical evolution and therefore could be changed today. However, no changes were possible in the realm of law.

Graetz, in fact, had studied with Hirsch for three years, but grew disenchanted with Hirsch's insensitivity to history and historical development. As a result of the break between them, however, Hirsch would have nothing to do with the father of modern Jewish historiography. When Graetz enrolled Jewish communal leaders in a fund-raising campaign to build a Jewish orphanage in Jerusalem, Hirsch insisted that Orthodox leaders have nothing to do with the project. Graetz became paradigmatic of the new historical scholarship, which Hirsch regarded as a fundamental threat to contemporary Orthodoxy. Not only would scientific historical scholarship contradict many of the inherited truths concerning Jewish texts, but it would serve as a license and mandate for expansive changes in the application of Jewish law to contemporary times.

Hirsch also believed that a separate Jewish school system was necessary to promote the new concept of "*Torah im Derekh Eretz.*" He insisted on the necessity of having secular subjects taught to Jewish children under the auspices of Orthodox instructors committed to the new ideology. In Frankfurt, he set up Jewish elementary and secondary systems, paving the way for the contemporary day school system which strives to incorporate both secular and Jewish learning under one roof. That is not to say, however, that Hirsch favored a synthesis between the two models of learning. He desired co-existence of secular and Jewish learning rather than integration between the two. The efforts to integrate Jewish and general history common in leading modern Orthodox day schools today represent a significant departure from Hirsch's ideology.

In general, in areas that were external to the realm of Jewish law, Hirsch was prepared to countenance significant change and accommodation to modernity. He insisted, for example, on the use of German in his sermons and writings, translating the Torah and the prayer book into the German language. In accepting emancipation, he abandoned traditional rabbinic jurisdiction, particularly the ban of excommunication or *herem*. At one point, he went so far as to attempt to abolish the *Kol Nidre* prayer inaugurating the Yom Kippur holiday on the grounds that it had no standing in Jewish law and, if taken literally, suggested to the gentile society that the word of the Jew was by no means obligatory. Hirsch discovered, however, that the *Kol Nidre* prayer had become so symbolic of the Yom Kippur experience that efforts to abolish it would automatically fail, for the prayer evoked much in Jewish historical memory.

By the 1870's, the new and united German state established by Bismarck had witnessed the triumph of Reform Judaism in Germany. Hirsch led the fight to secede from the *Gemeinde*, or German-Jewish *kehilla*. He did so on the grounds of freedom of conscience. In fact, the *Austrittsgesetz*, or Law of Separation, granted the right of withdrawal to individuals and communities on the liberal grounds of the freedom to choose.

But Hirsch's withdrawal meant a weakening of the Jewish community and communal unity. Reform leaders bitterly criticized his secession, saying that it would allow for the exit from the community of indifferent Jews who did not wish to pay communal taxes. They offered Hirsch exclusive supervision over dietary laws. Hirsch countered that while his community had many non-observant Jews, he was unprepared to legitimize Reform leadership as an alternative expression of Judaism. The Hirschian view embraced diversity among Jews, but did not extend to religious pluralism.

What Hirsch did signify was the search for neutral ground on which Jew and modern men and women could meet as equals. He granted Jewish law its domain but limited it, allowing room for freedom of conscience in matters such as secular education, dress, politics, and other areas on which Jewish law was silent. Unlike the old Orthodox, who argued that Jewish law applies to every realm of human activity, Hirsch was carving out territory on which freedom of conscience could prevail. In this respect, he wrestled with precisely the same dilemmas of Reform Judaism and of modern Jewish thought generally—namely, to find a place where Judaism and modernity would stand as one. In many respects the position of Moses Sofer and the old-Orthodox was more consistent. They argued that modernity fundamentally contradicted Jewish tradition, and therefore modernity ought be dismissed entirely or relegated to strictly utilitarian purposes. Hirsch was not prepared for this rejection of modernity, nor did he see that as an effective prescription for preserving Jewish life. Rather he looked at modern culture and searched for neutral grounds on which the Jew could internalize and imbibe that modern culture without doing violence to Jewish law and tradition.

Hirsch was by no means the sole representative of neo-Orthodoxy in Germany. His colleague Azriel Hildesheimer established a rival wing of neo-Orthodoxy. In Hildesheimer's rabbinical seminary, room was found for limited use of scientific scholarship in the study of Talmud. He remained concerned with and offered support for settlement in Palestine. Lastly, he argued for selective cooperation with non-Orthodox groupings on behalf of common Jewish causes.

Hildesheimer and his followership gradually evolved into *Mizrachi,* which was founded in 1902 as a religious Zionist group dedicated to cooperation with the non-Orthodox in the building of a Jewish state. Chief Rabbi Abraham Isaac Kook articulated its finest expression, viewing "all Israel as holy," meaning that all Jews ought cooperate together in the mission of Zionist renewal. Hirsch and his followers gradually evolved into Agudath Israel, a secessionist Orthodox group that avoided cooperation with the non-Orthodox and never joined the religious Zionist groupings.

These divisions suggest the diversity within Orthodoxy itself. To some extent, they reflect differing estimates of secular learning—whether it be legitimate for strictly utilitarian purposes, legitimate as God's creation, or legitimate as vehicles in understanding Jewish texts. In other respects, they reflect differing attitudes toward the non-Orthodox movements and Orthodox responsibilities to and relations with them. Lastly, they reflect differing perspectives upon exile and homeland. The diversity suggests the need to avoid stereotyping or categorizing all Orthodox Jews as cut from one cloth. Orthodoxy is united on the primacy of Jewish law within Jewish life. It is divided over a host of social and political questions concerning relations with Israel, with non-Orthodox bodies, and with secular culture.

Orthodox Judaism Today

In America today, Orthodox Judaism has refuted the predictions of its demise so current in the 1950's. Orthodox numbers today are probably not very great, approximately six to seven percent of American Jewry, or 350–400,000. However, Orthodoxy does represent 10 percent of Jews under age 25, suggesting that the Orthodox have succeeded in retaining their young and hold the promise of future growth, inasmuch as they are the only grouping within American Judaism to enjoy a positive birth-rate of more than two children per family.

There are many reasons for Orthodox renewal and resurgence. Survivors of the Holocaust, dedicated to preserving Judaism on the new shores in America, refocused their energies upon Orthodox renewal in the postwar world. Perhaps the greatest fruit of their efforts has been the network of Jewish day schools, pioneered by the Orthodox but now emulated as well within the Conservative and Reform movements. At one time the day school movement was regarded entirely as an option for a marginal Orthodox minority. Today it has become a mainstream option, enrolling over 168,000 Jewish students or 37 percent of all Jewish children receiving any form of Jewish education today. Moreover, the day school has demonstrated repeatedly that it has become the most effective vehicle for intensive Jewish education and ensuring Jewish continuity. Thirdly, the strength of the Orthodox Jewish family should not be underestimated. The Orthodox are the sole group to enjoy a positive birth-rate, generally have stronger marriages, for Jewish religion does cement marriage, and provide a model of family life of parents, children, and grandparents participating together in Jewish communal endeavors. The image of the Orthodox synagogue today is not that of an elderly generation nostalgic for a world that is lost. Its contemporary image is that of a bustling institution in which Jews of different generations celebrate the joys of being Jewish.

These strengths of Orthodoxy today reflect the power and force of Orthodox commitment to Jewish preservation. The Orthodox have built the strongest communities, which, in turn, are able to speak a language of norms, values, expectations, and commitments to their members. The Orthodox message to contemporary Jewry is that Jewish continuity can come only at the price of personal sacrifice and dedication on behalf of tradition and community.

That is not to say that Orthodoxy is without problems. It confesses intellectual weakness with respect to the role of modern science and scholarship in the understanding of Jewish tradition and text. For example, the most popular Bible commentary today in Orthodox circles is the Artscroll Mesorah series, a commentary which pretends that historical scholarship simply does not exist. This ahistoricism, which Graetz protested to Hirsch, continues to afflict Orthodox education. It is a trait of intellectual weakness that Orthodoxy is unable to confront legitimate claims of modern science and scholarship.

Secondly, Orthodoxy has experienced considerable protest from Jewish women and leaders of the feminist movement. This has generally taken on two forms: protest against apparent disabilities imposed upon women in the context of divorce law, which has led to personal tragedies in the case of the *agunah,* a woman prevented from remarrying because her husband is either missing or has refused to provide her with a bill of divorce or *get;* and protest against the secondary role of women in the synagogue and in Jewish public life. These protests remain unresolved. Orthodox leaders generally recognize the necessity of addressing the human tragedies involved in divorce legislation. They are divided over how best to address the complaints of women against their incapacity of participation in public prayer.

Thirdly, Orthodoxy has faced internal strains over the issues of pluralism in Jewish life. The general Orthodox drift to the right, symbolized by the collapse in 1994 of the Synagogue Council of America, the umbrella body bridging the three primary religious movements, has raised serious questions of how Orthodoxy can cooperate with the broader Jewish community on issues of external protection, support for Israel, and internal Jewish continuity. The growing power of Orthodox isolationism has led to decreased numbers of Orthodox rabbis participating in joint rabbinical bodies and a withdrawal of Orthodox leaders from general communal initiatives and undertakings.

This isolationism, of course, leads to further "Orthodox-bashing" and raises levels of hostility between Orthodox and non-Orthodox Jews. The Baruch Goldstein affair, or the massacre in Hebron in February 1994, evoked a widespread backlash against Orthodoxy and Orthodox Jews, as did the "Who is a Jew?" controversy in 1988. All too often Orthodox Jews are equated either with the views of Baruch Goldstein and Meir Kahane or with the views of the Lubavitcher Rebbe, who desired a change in the Law of Return. The assassination of Prime Minister Yitzhak Rabin in 1995 by Yigal Amir, who proudly claimed "I've been studying Talmud all my life," aggravated these tensions. Orthodox leaders pointed out, to little avail, that 4,000 years of Jewish history produced only one Goldstein and one Amir, and that groups such as the Rabbinical Council of America have opposed changes in the Law of Return. Yet the current drift within contemporary Orthodoxy points to the growth of old Orthodoxy and the relative decline of Modern Orthodoxy.

The model of the old Orthodox has become "Listen to your rabbis, even if they tell you that right is left and left is right"—that is, a call for rabbinic supremacy and the authority of Talmudic scholars. The Modern Orthodox note that rabbinic authorities have often been wrong in the modern period—particularly on questions of Zionism, immigration to the United States, and the role of secular learning in Jewish life. Yet the Modern Orthodox have become a beleaguered group within Orthodoxy under challenge from both right and left.

Modern Orthodoxy today stands for the critical engagement with Western culture—internalizing its positive values and critiquing and transforming values it finds negative. That requires a serious commitment to live in two worlds—to engage in Western culture in a critical yet informed spirit.

The Modern Orthodox have demonstrated that they are prepared to pay the price for Jewish continuity. Twelve years of Jewish day school has become normative, ensuring a rich Jewish education culminated by a year spent in Israel after high school in an Israeli institution of higher learning. In that respect, the Orthodox success story has been the reflection of its dedication to preserving Jewish heritage and tradition, a success story that in many ways is paradigmatic for the non-Orthodox community. How Orthodoxy will relate to that non-Orthodox community, whether with openness and inclusion or isolation and rejection, remains very much a question for the future.

Reading: Samson Raphael Hirsch, *The Nineteen Letters, Sixteenth Letter*

The Nineteen Letters *of Samson Raphael Hirsch, ostensibly letters to a student named Benjamin who is attracted by the new currents of modern culture, stands as a classic document of Modern Orthodoxy. Note Hirsch's criticism of efforts to return to Palestine and his disdain for the life of seclusion in isolation from social action. He calls for Jewish immersion in the modern world out of the quest to build a better society. Modern Orthodoxy took its cue from Hirsch in seeking to constructively engage modernity rather than reject it.*

The Sixteenth Letter: Emancipation

You ask my opinion about emancipation, the problem which at present so greatly agitates many minds. You ask me whether, in the spirit of Judaism, I consider emancipation possible and desirable, and whether I think that we ought to strive for it. As for yourself, dear Benjamin, you write that, according to your newly-won conception of Judaism, you do not know what to make of it. You now doubt whether striving for emancipation is in keeping with the spirit of Judaism, because it means joining something alien and breaking away from Yisrael's destiny. You doubt whether it is desirable, for Yisrael's uniqueness could easily be obliterated by too much closeness to the non-Jewish world.

I will respect your scruples and will tell you my view. Is emancipation in harmony with the spirit of Judaism?

When Yisrael began its great pilgrimage through the ages and nations, Yirmeyah proclaimed its duty to

> Build houses and dwell therein; plant gardens and eat their fruit; take wives unto yourselves, and beget sons and daughters; and take wives for your sons, and give your daughters in marriage that they bear sons and daughters,

> and that you multiply *there,* and diminish not. *And seek the peace of the city whither I have exiled you, and pray for it to the Lord, for in its peace there will be peace unto you.*

It follows that rejection and confinement to a narrow way of life are not essential conditions of the *galus.* Rather, it is our duty to ally ourselves as closely as possible with the state, wherever we may find ourselves, without harm to the spirit of Judaism. After all, our former independent statehood did not represent the essence or the purpose of Yisrael's national existence but merely a means to the fulfillment of its spiritual task. The bond of Yisrael's unity was at no time land and soil but only the common task of keeping the Torah. In consequence, Yisrael still today constitutes one entity even though it is far from its land and, in exile, is joined to other nations. (You may use the Hebrew terms *am* and *goy* for this entity, if the word "people" necessarily connotes, to you, a group living together in a common territory.) One day God will again reunite the Jews outwardly too, as a people gathered on its soil, and the Torah will again form the constitution of a state, serving as a model and a manifestation of God and the human mission. This is the future which we have been promised and which forms the goal of the *galus*—we should long for it, but we must not actively work to bring it about. We are still being educated for this future, so that we will then exemplify "Yisrael" in prosperity more truly than we did in the past. This future will go hand in hand with the elevation of all of humanity to universal brotherhood under God, the One Alone.

Bibliography for Further Reading

Ellenson, David. *Rabbi Azriel Hildesheimer and the Creation of a Modern Jewish Orthodoxy,* University of Alabama Press, 1991

Heilman, Samuel. *Defenders of the Faith,* Schocken Books, 1992

———, and Cohen, Steven M. *Cosmopolitans and Parochials,* University of Chicago Press, 1989

Lamm, Norman. *Torah U'Mada,* Jason Aronson, 1990

Liberles, Robert. *Religious Conflict in Social Context,* Greenwood, 1985

Rosenbloom, Noah. *Tradition in an Age of Reform,* Jewish Publication Society, 1976

Wertheimer, Jack. *A People Divided,* Basic Books, 1993

Unit XXVI

Modern Anti-Semitism

Origins

Modern anti-Semitism resurged in Europe in the closing decades of the nineteenth century. It appeared as a continental phenomenon—pogroms in Russia, blood libels in Eastern and Central Europe, anti-Semitic political parties in Germany and Austria, the Dreyfus affair in France, and agitation for immigration restriction in England and America. The background for this resurgence of anti-Semitic activity lay partly in the bargain for emancipation. Once that bargain had appeared to be a failure—namely, the Jews had retained their corporate identity and had failed to assimilate into European society—anti-Semitism returned in ever more crude and virulent forms. In other respects, it represented a residue of the medieval past coupled with new currents of the modern ethos that were exclusionary in nature toward the Jews.

The language of anti-Semitism clearly changed in the modern context. No longer was it exclusively an idiom of religion and religious faith. The Jew was no longer condemned as Christ killer or infidel. Rather, the idiom assumed new forms—economic, political, social, and even racial. Religious anti-Semitism continued, but was now embedded in a broader context in which the Jew was often criticized as being a stranger, or as one who has corrupted the values of European society.

Secondly, modern anti-Semitism attached undue significance to Jewish influence and power. The mind of the modern anti-Semite exaggerated the problem of the Jews as being the key to solving all of society's issues and problems. The modern anti-Semite maintained that the Jew has enormous leverage over the future course of history. In so exaggerating the parameters of the Jewish question, the modern anti-Semite raised the stakes on the solution to the Jewish question.

Lastly, modern anti-Semitism lacked the theological constraints of medieval anti-Semitism. No Doctrine of the Witness insisted that the Jews must be preserved to the end of days as witnesses to the validity of Christianity. Modern anti-Semitism could envision a world without Jews. There are no built-in protections against a "final solution" that would mark the unprecedented genocide of a people. Because the stakes were so much higher and the fury of modern anti-Semitism was not necessarily tempered by theological constraints, the need for effective Jewish responses was all the greater.

Richard Wagner

A good illustration of the mind of a modern anti-Semitic personality may be found in the writings and music of Richard Wagner, a critical figure in European Romantic musicology. Wagner in 1850 published an essay entitled "Judaism in Music," in which he argued that Jews were capable strictly of imitative music. They were unable to arouse emotion. In Wagner's view, it was art that restored values to people and provided them with their esthetics. Art held the capacity for regenerating society, but the Jews were incapable of true art.

The modern world, for Wagner, symbolized a breakdown of the Greek synthesis of art and politics. Art had become far too rational and artificial, out of touch with the folk values of the Germans as a people. Wagner hoped to recreate the classic Greek synthesis of art and politics. Yet the Jews stood as corrupter of German culture. Ironically, it was now the Jews who were the agents of philistinism, corrupting society through bourgeois materialism. The influence of the Jews was quite considerable, for the Jews dominated not only the musical establishment but also media reports on music and culture. For example, the Bayreuth Festival, an annual musical event at which Wagner's compositions were featured, always received negative treatment at the hands of the Jewishly controlled media.

Wagner's racism received fullest treatment in his magnum opus, *Parsifal,* a Wagnerian adaptation of the legend of the Holy Grail. Medieval treatments of the Grail had suggested that only a pure hero can obtain the salvation of the Grail. Thus Lancelot was ineligible, for he had committed adultery with Guinevere. Gawain was far too murderous a knight. Only the innocent and pure knight Galahad, or in some versions Percival, could obtain the Grail. Wagner, however, gave this legend a new twist. The purity of Parsifal consisted in his racial purity. What prevented Germany from attaining her rightful place in Europe was the corruption of the German race which the Jews have engineered. Purify the race by eliminating the Jews, and Germany will finally be able to ascend the heights of greatness.

Wagner reflects many of the features of modern anti-Semitism. The language is now that of cultural and racial criticism rather than religious hatred. The role of the Jew and his influence have been exaggerated beyond proportion. The Jew controls cultural opinion through manipulation of the media and pollutes the German race through excessive intermarriage. Lastly, the issue of the Jews transcends Jewish-German relations and relates to the entire dilemma of Germany in European culture. Solve the Jewish question, and all problems will naturally be resolved.

To be sure, Wagner stopped short of forecasting a Final Solution. Most likely, he wanted only limitations placed upon the Jews, especially on their immigration into Germany. The racial ideology was developed in far greater depth by Wagner's son-in-law, Houston Stuart Chamberlain, but it would not be capable of translation into an ideology of a final solution until wedded to the conspiratorial thinking of the *Protocols of the Elders of Zion.* Nor was modern anti-Semitism the monopoly of the right. Socialist ideology identified the Jews as conspicuous among those who dominate the economy and who threaten to unemploy large sections of the middle class. For Karl Marx, a born Jew converted in childhood, in his virulently anti-Semitic essay, "On the Jewish Question," the Jew embodied the spirit of the French Revolution of egoism and of individual property rights. The state needs to be emancipated from such egoism. Yet the Jew is a fundamental obstacle, for money is central in the life of the Jew and the liberal individualism whose spirit the Jew embodies prevents his allying with members of his social class. Marx's call for an internationalization of the working classes leaves very little room for private affiliation, much less the ties of ethnic brotherhood. Marx seems to lack all empathy with the Jews as a people, although he did express some sympathy for poor Jews living in Palestine. Otherwise, Marx employs a plethora of anti-Semitic stereotypes in varying references to Jews throughout his writings. To be sure, his daughter, who lived among impoverished Jews of East London, expressed considerable support for Jews as victims of pogroms. Marx himself, however, internalized some of the primary features of anti-Semitic rhetoric and sentiment of the Western society which he was seeking to overthrow.

Nor was his anti-Semitism without influence. The French socialists, in particular, reiterated the worst forms of Marxist anti-Semitism. Although for German socialists, anti-Semitism remained "the socialism of fools"—meaning asking the right questions but proposing the wrong solutions—French socialists such as Charles Fourier and Pierre Joseph Proudhon became notoriously anti-Semitic. This anti-Semitism goes far to explain the silence of the French socialists until very late in the Dreyfus affair.

Missing from Wagner's conservative or romantic anti-Semitism and from Marx's left-wing socialist anti-Semitism was the conspiracy theory of history. This was expressed in the *Protocols of the Elders of Zion,* a forged document purporting to be the minutes of meetings of Jewish leaders plotting to take over the world. The *Protocols* appear to have originated in Czarist Russia as a vehicle for blackening the Russian revolutionary left by declaring it to be part of a Jewish plot to take over the world.

For the authors of the *Protocols,* a unity of world Jewry connected Zionists, Jewish liberals, and Jewish revolutionaries in a calculated conspiracy to enshrine the chosen people through world domination. For the *Protocols,* the Jew only posed as liberal or as revolutionary. Through their control of the newspapers, which in Germany were, in fact, owned mostly by Jews, the Jews dominated the communications industry and formed public opinion in ways that would advance their cause. Zionism was merely a public manifestation of this international plot. The Jewish money power, epitomized by the Rothchilds, the international Jewish banking family, threatened to strangle the money markets of Europe and the Western hemisphere.

Surprisingly, the *Protocols* were very well-received in the aftermath of World War I. They were distributed among the troops during the war and subsequently received very favorable press attention in England and the United States. In America, Henry Ford published the *Protocols* in his influential weekly, *The Dearborn Independent.* Although Ford subsequently apologized, the damage had been done, given the prestige of the Ford name. The positive reception accorded the *Protocols* can be explained only by the growing hysteria concerning Communism in the wake of the success of the Bolshevik revolution. Vladimir Lenin and Leon Trotsky had proclaimed that their aim was "permanent revolution" or spreading Bolshevism beyond the boundaries of national countries and ultimately creating a worker's paradise. The fear of Bolshevism as Jewish-inspired, coupled with the relative success of Zionism in the immediate aftermath of World War I, suggested to many that the *Protocols* contained the key to understanding international events. Nazi ideology would wed the conspiratorial world-view of the *Protocols* to the racial world-view of Wagner and Chamberlain, creating what one historian has termed a "warrant for genocide" against the Jews.

The Dreyfus Affair

Paradigmatic of this new anti-Semitism was the Dreyfus Affair in France in the 1890's, stretching into the early twentieth century. The forces who argued that the French Revolution and Jewish emancipation were fundamentally wrong now arrayed against Captain Alfred Dreyfus—the Army, the monarchists, and the clergy. Dreyfus became a test of democracy in France. Which France would prevail—the France of enlightenment and liberalism or the France of the *Ancien Regime*?

To be sure, French democracy did survive. Although the Dreyfus Affair lasted a decade and greatly agitated French Jewry both in France and Algeria, Dreyfus was finally exonerated, and the Third Republic remained intact. Yet clearly the Dreyfus Affair exposed the reality of anti-democratic and anti-Semitic forces within France. It shattered many of the illusions Jews had placed in democracy and education as preventives of anti-Semitism. Moreover, many of the forces opposed to Dreyfus would attain power under Vichy France during World War II.

Dreyfus had been the first Jew to enter into the upper echelons of the French military. He desperately wished to be accepted as French. It was inconceivable that he could have been guilty of selling military secrets to the Germans. As Theodor Herzl reported in covering the Dreyfus affair, if Dreyfus were not Dreyfus, he would have been anti-Dreyfus.

Yet Dreyfus was convicted because he was a Jew. His family had lived in Alsace-Lorraine and was suspected, therefore, of German leanings, although the family had left Alsace-Lorraine after it had been conquered by Germany in 1870. Dreyfus was the victim of a conspiracy within the French military to betray France and then blame a Jewish captain for the deed. Although Dreyfus subsequently was pardoned, he initially was found guilty on the basis of flimsy evidence and on the suspicion that, as a Jew, he had never become a true Frenchman. The bargain of emancipation had failed, and the Jews continued to remain a nation set apart.

French Jewish reaction, with some notable exceptions, trusted in French justice to prevail and refused to perceive the Dreyfus Affair as a Jewish issue. The evidence of anti-Semitism was consistently underestimated by French Jewish leadership. Inspired by the Dreyfus family, which eschewed any specifically Jewish representation on behalf of Dreyfus, French Jewry opted for a low profile during this difficult period. Although Dreyfus was accused of being a Judas and was linked with Golden Calf imagery as being willing to sell his loyalty for money, Jews continued to insist that anti-Semitism was alien to France. At most, anti-Semitism could be only a German import. These denials occurred precisely when anti-Semitism sustained the affair for a ten-year period, and anti-Semitic riots occurred intermittently in France and Algeria. For the Catholic clergy, anti-Semitism became a vehicle to express anti-republican sentiment.

Although anti-Dreyfus sentiment was found primarily on the right, the French left was not without blemish. The socialists initially viewed Dreyfus as a Jewish capitalist. Only very late in the affair, after Emile Zola's famous "*J'Accuse*" and eloquent defense of republican principles, did socialists begin moving to Dreyfus's side.

Although Dreyfus was ultimately acquitted and pardoned, marking the triumph of republicanism, Jews suffered enormously during the affair. Jews were subject to regular assaults in the streets. Jewish stores and synagogues were frequently torched. A number of deaths ensued, and Jewish businesses suffered from persistent boycott. Yet the Dreyfus Affair did not shatter Jewish confidence in France. Jews continued to identify with France and with French traditions of liberalism and democracy. As noted, the Dreyfus family preferred quiet, behind-the-scenes intercession to public protests on behalf of Dreyfus. This perspective clearly underestimated the degree of anti-Semitism in France. Ultimately, the fears of renewed anti-Semitism in France would prove all too prophetic during the Vichy regime, which marked the final triumph of the anti-Dreyfusards.

Jewish Reactions

How did Jews respond to the emergence of anti-Semitism as a continental phenomenon? The most instinctual response was in many ways the most effective—mass immigration of Jews from Eastern Europe to Western Europe and North America. New Jewish communities were built in Canada, the United States, Latin America, South Africa, and even Australia. Western Jewry, to be sure, often tried to discourage immigration as it would undermine the position of the native Jewish communities. For example, in France, the Alliance Israelite Universelle withheld assistance from immigrants, so as to make new places of residence appear unattractive. The ideology of the Alliance was to spread emancipation to areas where it had not as yet arrived, again reflecting Jewish faith in enlightenment and education to end anti-Semitism.

Despite some ambivalence, Western Jewry did absorb large numbers of immigrants. The Jewish population of England, for example, rose from 60,000 to 300,000 between 1880 and 1914. In the United States, on average over 100,000 Jews per year entered American shores between 1900 and 1914. This immigration was not strictly a response to persecution. Certainly, in the United States, immigration antedated the arrival of persecutions and had more to do with the image of America as a booming and developing country providing numerous opportunities to those willing to risk their future. The primary motive behind Jewish immigration was not persecution but rather economic opportunities. Persecution, of course, provided an added spur and stimulus to Jewish migration patterns.

Interestingly, the presence of new immigrant communities also stimulated the development of ethnic historical societies. The American Jewish Historical Society and the Jewish Historical Society of England undertook projects to prove the antiquity of Jewish settlement in their respective countries. Such historical scholarship demonstrating the role of the Jew in local and national life was meant for defensive purposes. If one could prove, for example, that the Jew had participated in the American Revolution, the claim that the Jew was a foreigner and a drain on native resources was considerably undermined.

Most immigrants did not conform to Orthodox patterns of observance. The rabbis of Eastern Europe had discouraged immigration to the West. For them, America could not sustain Jewish observance. Therefore, those Jews most willing to obey rabbinic authority were least likely to come to the United States. Those most likely to immigrate were the ones least deferential to the wisdom of the rabbis. The standards of religious observance were actually quite low within the immigrant community. The immigrants tended to be young, were generally more willing to undertake risks, and often had larger families because they placed their hopes and aspirations in the future success of their children.

Jewish organizations, of course, placed their hopes in spreading Jewish rights to lands of oppression. For example, at the Congress of Berlin in 1878, Jewish representatives pressured for guarantees of Jewish equality in Romania in exchange for her independence, as granted by the Great Powers at the Congress. The demand was accepted, but was ultimately undermined by Romanian authorities. The national Jewish organizations sought to combat anti-Semitism through the legal system and through the power of public opinion. They assumed that a society based upon law and a positive educational system could not harbor anti-Semitism. Unfortunately, their experience varied. England contained much anti-Semitic opinion, but with little impact or effect upon the position of Jews in British society. In Germany, by contrast, German Jewish leadership waged a battle in the courts and in the media against anti-Semitism, yet frequently discovered that well-known anti-Semites would go unpunished or be dismissed with relatively light sentences, as Hitler himself discovered after the Beer Hall Putsch.

In Eastern Europe, the alternatives to immigration lay either in Zionism or in supporting revolutionary movements. Among the leadership of Russian Communism, for example, 16 percent were Jews in 1917. These were best represented by Leon Trotsky, who had no Jewish consciousness, although he was identified as a Jew by Czarist and Stalinist elements alike. Trotsky, like other Jews in the upper echelons of the Bolshevik movement, did not turn to Communism out of any specifically Jewish roots. He had little if any knowledge of Jewish tradition and little concern with the condition of the Jews as a people. He arrived at Communism by virtue of the force of its own ideology and principles.

Among the Jewish masses, however, given the growing pressure on the right, Jews drifted to the revolutionary left. The Jewish condition by no means dictated an alliance with the Bolshevik forces. The masses of Jews in Eastern Europe were heavily represented in the middle classes, those most hurt by the Russian Revolution. Moreover, Jews feared the internationalism of the revolution.

Nevertheless, given the growing anti-Semitism among the forces of the Czar, Jews naturally supported the Bolsheviks. The Bund, in particular, attempted to organize Jewish workers in support of the revolution. Lenin had initially opposed the separatism of the Bund. Ultimately, he co-opted them into the revolutionary forces and permitted them to revitalize the Yiddish language as a vehicle to bring the revolution to the Jewish street.

The Bund's program was that of cultural autonomy for Jews, hoping to attain Jewish national rights in countries of diaspora existence—a revitalization of the older model of Jewish autonomy or *kehilla*, granting the Jews the right to their own political representatives and to their own educational institutions.

By 1905, virtually all groups in Russia supported the program of cultural autonomy, best identified with the Jewish historian Simon Dubnov. American Jewish leaders, as well, argued that autonomy was necessary, for Jewish emancipation was by no means an immediate solution. The minority rights treaties achieved at Versailles in the aftermath of World War I granted Jews minority rights in the nation-states in Eastern Europe created by Versailles. Although these did not apply either to Communist Russia or to Weimar Germany, they did extend to the Jewish communities of Poland, Romania, and numerous other states created by Versailles. All too often, however, these treaties went unenforced, and the League of Nations was in no position to compel obedience to them.

The minority rights or autonomy solution was tried by history but failed to solve the Jewish question. Zionism remained the most successful of efforts by Jews to join the modern world and, at the same time, provide a refuge for endangered Jewry. Minority rights treaties, like Jewish revolutionary activity, would prove illusory at best.

Karl Marx, "On the Jewish Question"

Karl Marx wrote "On the Jewish Question" as a critique of Bruno Bauer, who opposed Jewish emancipation because the spirit of Judaism contradicted the spirit of humanity. Marx responded that Bauer had posed fundamentally wrong questions. The problem was not the emancipation of the Jews, which Marx by no means opposed. The problem was the definition of true emancipation. Granting the Jews civil rights, i.e. political emancipation, would accomplish little by itself. Rather what was necessary was the emancipation of society from the hold of religion generally, and of Judaism, in particular. Marx by no means shrank from vivid expressions of anti-Semitism, perceiving within Jewry the overriding spirit of "mammon" or materialism. Marx's legacy of socialist anti-Semitism recurred frequently on the left throughout the nineteenth and twentieth centuries.

The chimerical nationality of the Jew is the nationality of the trader, and above all of the financier.

The law, without basis or reason, of the Jew, is only the religious caricature of morality and right in general, without basis or reason; the purely formal rites with which the world of self-interest encircles itself.

Here again the supreme condition of man is his legal status, his relationship to laws which are valid for him, not because they are the laws of his own will and nature, but because they are dominant and any infraction of them will be avenged.

Jewish Jesuitism, the same practical Jesuitism which Bauer discovers in the Talmud, is the relationship of the world of self-interest to the laws which govern this world, laws which the world devotes its principal arts to circumventing.

Indeed, the operation of this world within its framework of laws is impossible without the continual supersession of law.

Judaism could not develop further as a religion, in a theoretical form, because the world view of practical need is, by its very nature, circumscribed, and the delineation of its characteristics soon completed.

The religion of practical need could not, by its very nature, find its consummation in theory, but only in practice, just because practice is its truth.

Judaism could not create a new world. It could only bring the new creations and conditions of the world within its own sphere of activity, because practical need, the spirit of which is self-interest, is always passive, cannot expand at will, but finds itself extended as a result of the continued development of society.

Judaism attains its apogee with the perfection of civil society; but civil society only reaches perfection in the Christian world. Only under the sway of Christianity, which objectifies all national, natural, moral and theoretical relationships, could civil society separate itself completely from the life of the state, sever all the species-bonds of man, establish egoism and selfish need in their place, and dissolve the human world into a world of atomistic, antagonistic individuals.

Christianity issued from Judaism. It has now been re-absorbed into Judaism.

From the beginning, the Christian was the theorizing Jew; consequently, the Jew is the practical Christian. And the practical Christian has become a Jew again.

It was only in appearance that Christianity overcame real Judaism. It was too refined, too spiritual to eliminate the crudeness of practical need except by raising it into the ethereal realm.

Christianity is the sublime thought of Judaism; Judaism is the vulgar practical application of Christianity. But this practical application could only become universal when Christianity as perfected religion had accomplished, in a theoretical fashion, the alienation of man from himself and from nature.

It was only then that Judaism could attain universal domination and could turn alienated man and alienated nature into alienable, saleable objects, in thrall to egoistic need and huckstering.

Objectification is the practice of alienation. Just as man, so long as he is engrossed in religion, can only objectify his essence by an alien and fantastic being; so under the sway of egoistic need, he can only affirm himself and produce objects in practice by subordinating his products and his own activity to the domination of an alien entity, and by attributing to them the significance of an alien entity, namely money.

In its perfected practice the spiritual egoism of Christianity necessarily becomes the material egoism of the Jew, celestial need is transmuted into terrestrial need, subjectivism into self-interest. The tenacity of the Jew is to be explained, not by his religion, but rather by the human basis of his religion—practical need and egoism.

It is because the essence of the Jew was universally realized and secularized in civil society, that civil society could not convince the Jew of the unreality of his religious essence, which is precisely the ideal representation of practical need. It is not only, therefore, in the Pentateuch and the Talmud, but also in contemporary society, that we find the essence of the present-day Jew; not as an abstract essence, but as one which is supremely empirical, not only as a limitation of the Jew, but as the Jewish narrowness of society.

As soon as society succeeds in abolishing the empirical essence of Judaism—huckstering and its conditions—the Jew becomes impossible, because his consciousness no longer has an object. The subjective basis of Judaism—practical need—assumes a human form, and the conflict between the individual, sensuous existence of man and his species-existence, is abolished.

The social emancipation of the Jew is the emancipation of society from Judaism.

Reading: Hans Kohn ed., *Nationalism*

In 1850 Richard Wagner published an article, "Judaism in Music" anonymously. For Wagner, art and culture lay at the center of national identity and ethos. The Jews, however, were incapable of true art. They could only imitate that which was done by others. German culture, in short, had become philistine precisely because it was dominated by Jews.

The Jew remained irretrievably alien, and Jewish prominence in the media and in culture therefore prevented Germany from assuming her rightful place among the nations.

If emancipation from the yoke of Judaism appears to us the greatest of necessities, we must above all prove our forces for this war of liberation. Now we shall never win these forces from an abstract definition of the phenomenon *per se*, but only from an accurate acquaintance with the nature of our involuntary feeling of an instinctive repugnance against the Jew's essential character. Through it, through this unconquerable feeling—if we avow it quite without ado—must there become plain to us what we hate in that essence; nay, through his very laying bare, may we even hope to rout the demon from the field, whereon he has only been able to maintain his stand beneath the shelter of a twilight darkness—a darkness we good-natured humanitarians ourselves have cast upon him, to make his look less loathsome.

The Jew—who, as everyone knows, has a God all to himself—in ordinary life strikes us primarily by his outward appearance, which, no matter to what European nationality we belong, has something disagreeably foreign to that nationality: instinctively we wish to have nothing in common with a man who looks like that. By far more weighty, nay, of quite decisive weight for our inquiry, is the effect the Jew produces on us through his speech; and this is the essential point about the Jewish influence upon music. The Jew speaks the language of the nation in whose midst he dwells from generation to generation, but he speaks it always as an alien. . . . Our whole European art and civilization, however, have remained to the Jew as a foreign tongue; for, just as he has taken no part in the evolution of the one, so has he taken none in that of the other; but at most the homeless night has been a cold, nay more, a hostile onlooker. In this speech, this art, the Jew can only after-speak and after-patch—not truly make a poem of his words, an art-works of his doings. . . .

Alien and apathetic stand the educated Jew in the midst of a society he does not understand, with whose tastes and aspirations he does not sympathise, whose history and evolution have always been indifferent to him . . .

Now, our modern arts had likewise become a portion of this culture, and among them more particularly that art which is just the very easiest to learn—the art of music, and indeed that music which, severed from her sister arts, had been lifted by the force and stress of grandest geniuses to a stage in her universal faculty of expression where either, in new conjunction with the other arts, she might speak aloud the most sublime, or, in persistent separation from them, she could also speak at will the deepest *bathos* of the trivial. Naturally, what the cultured Jew had to say, in his situation, could be nothing but the trivial and indifferent, because his whole artistic bent was, in sooth, a mere luxurious and needless thing. At present no art affords such plentiful possibility of talking in it without saying any real thing, as that of music, since the greatest geniuses have already said whatever there was to say in it as an absolute separate-art. After this there was nothing left but to babble after; and indeed with quite distressing accuracy and deceptive likeness, just as parrots reel off human words and phrases, but also with just as little real feeling and expression as these foolish birds. Only in the case of our Jewish music-makers this mimicked speech present one marked peculiarity—that of the Jewish style of talk in general, which we have more minutely characterised above. . . .

Bibliography for Further Reading

Holmes, Colin. *Anti-Semitism in British Society,* Holmes and Meier, 1979

Katz, Jacob. *From Prejudice to Destruction: Anti-Semitism 1700–1933,* Harvard University Press, 1982

———. *The Darker Side of Genius,* Brandeis University Press, 1986

Marrus, Michael. *The Politics of Assimilation,* Clarendon Press, 1971

Schorsch, Ismar. *Jewish Reactions to German Anti-Semitism,* Columbia University Press, 1972

Wistrich, Robert. *Revolutionary Jews from Marx to Trotsky,* Barnes and Noble, 1976

Unit XXVII

Reaction in Eastern Europe

Background

The Polish partitions at the end of the eighteenth century not only meant the end of Poland as an independent nation-state, but also bequeathed Russia with approximately 750,000 Jews after 1791. Where previously the Russian czars had sought to keep Jews out of Russia, Russia now had to deal with precisely the same questions of emancipation and integration that Western European countries were addressing at the time of the French Revolution. The difference lay in the answers. In Russia, the conservative forces triumphed, arguing that the Jews must prove themselves to be Russians first, and then emancipation will follow—in contrast to the bargain of emancipation that prevailed in Western Europe.

Initially, in 1776, Catherine II proclaimed equality for Jews. Subsequently, however, in 1791 she established the Pale of Settlement, concentrating Jews in White Russia and excluding them from cities and ports. This measure was initiated partly in reaction to the French Revolution. In larger degree, it reflected Catherine's growing sense that Russia's significant Jewish population would prove to be a problem and should best be concentrated in a particular area of Russia.

In 1794 taxes were doubled on Jewish merchants and burghers. In the villages Jews increasingly went into lease-holding, innkeeping, and the sale of liquor. These professions, of course, insured greater conflict between Jews and Russian peasants. An 1812 commission discovered that Jews were not guilty of exploiting the peasantry via the sale of liquor. Drunkenness among the Russian peasantry, the commission found, was more the fault of Russian proprietors than of Jews who functioned as their agents. Implied in the commission's report, however, was the dangerous reality that Jews were beginning to serve as diversionary function for the Russian government, deflecting attention away from the real plight of the Russian peasantry.

Isolation of the Jews and their concentration in the Pale of Settlement was also coupled with efforts at assimilation. Jews were offered inducements to attend public school in Russia. Jewish schools were compelled to teach European languages. Other tax inducements were intended to stimulate Jewish settlement in the Crimea, near the border with the Ottoman Empire, an area Russia was interested in developing. Nevertheless, the isolation of the Jews led to their economic strangulation. Long before the actual onset of pogroms at the end of the nineteenth century, Jews had already begun emigrating westward.

Czar Nicholas I

Czar Nicholas I was probably the most important ruler in nineteenth-century Russia. His tenure lasted over 30 years from the 1820's to the 1850's. Nicholas also followed the dual policy of isolation and assimilation of Jews. In 1840, he established the Crown School System to bring enlightened culture to Russian Jewry. Quickly it became apparent that the Crown School System was conversionist in intent. Nicholas generally had been opposed to secular education and had barred peasants from the Russian public schools. However, he hoped that exposure to enlightenment would make the Jews ripe for Christianity. Although the system had been initially endorsed by several leading Russian *maskilim,* or Jewish men of enlightenment, these quickly recognized its conversionist program and resigned from the project.

Although the Crown School System proved to be a failure, Nicholas's policies did accomplish the long-term weakening of Russian Jewish communal existence. The *kehilla* increasingly became a tool of the government. Its powers were reduced primarily to tax collecting. The *kehilla* was officially abolished in 1844, although Jews remained collectively responsible for taxes and for service in the Russian army.

Military service was perhaps the most notorious of Nicholas's measures to insure Jewish assimilation. Previously Jews had been exempted from service in the army through payment of a special tax. In 1827, however, the *kehilla* was directed to provide a special Jewish quota of recruits. "Good Jews" were exempted. These categories included merchants, graduate students, artisans, farmers, and public school students. The "undesirable" Jews now turned to hiding in the forests and mutilating their bodies so as to avoid service in the army, which meant virtually automatic assimilation and apostasy from Judaism. Most notorious, of course, was juvenile conscription, for youthful recruits found it impossible to retain any vestige of Judaism over the course of their 30-year conscription responsibility.

Salo Baron has estimated that over the course of Nicholas's tenure, some 60,000 Jews were recruited into the Russian army. The process turned Jew against Jew and weakened the authority of the *kehilla.* In order to fulfill the quota, the *kehilla* employed *khappers* or kidnappers who would find those Jews, usually from the lower classes, who might make good soldiers. The *khappers* quickly discovered that the business was quite lucrative, for they could exempt children whose parents were prepared to pay ransom fees. Widespread riots took place against the *kehilla* and the *khappers,* in turn weakening communal cohesion and unity. Although only Jews ages 12–25 were to have been conscripted, the *khappers* frequently took children who were even younger in order to fill their quotas. Generally, they found it easier to draft children than married adults. Once drafted, children almost invariably were lost to Judaism. Jewish ritualistic objects, such as phylacteries, were removed forcibly. Conscripts were compelled to attend Christian sermons and participate in Christian rituals. Baptism was virtually a prerequisite to any promotions within the army. The Crimean War (1853–1856) was especially hard on conscripts, as Jews had to fill larger quotas to meet the requirements of the Russian military. It has been estimated that half of those conscripted in fact were baptized into Christianity.

Alexander II abolished juvenile conscription shortly after Nicholas II's death. The policy had, in fact, demoralized the army, which had demonstrated its weaknesses during the Crimean War. Alexander II even permitted Jews to settle in new areas, including Moscow. This incipient enlightenment, however, was quickly followed by reaction, and subsequently by pogroms. Although Alexander II abandoned the extreme policies of his predecessor, he, too, continued the dual policy of "isolation and assimilation."

During this period Jews began turning to the revolutionary movements. Until the 1870's, the *maskilim,* or Jewish men of enlightenment, had generally sided with the Russian government. They hoped for its internal reform and for liberalizing its policies toward the Jews. Now they began speaking of fundamental revolution in Russian society. Some would even join the violent and anti-Semitic Russian revolutionary movement known as the *Narodniks,* who were responsible for the assassination of Alexander II in 1881, thereby contributing to the subsequent cycle of anti-Jewish violence and pogroms.

Western European Jewry now began agitating on behalf of emancipation for their Russian co-religionists. For example, Sir Moses Montefiore, long the leader of the Jewish community of England, undertook a diplomatic mission to the Czar in 1840 requesting alleviation of Russian Jewish disabilities. These diplomatic campaigns would continue to 1914, albeit with minimal successes. Leading Jews in liberal societies invoked governmental support on behalf of Jews living in Russia. For example, the American Jewish Committee mounted a successful campaign in 1911 to abrogate the Russian-American commerce treaty. However, these liberal governments lacked sufficient leverage with the Russian government to effect any significant improvement in the condition of Russian Jewry. Significantly, however, a tradition of protest concerning persecuted Jews abroad developed in liberal Jewish societies. That tradition of diplomatic protest unfortunately lapsed during the more difficult decades of the 1930's and 1940's.

The Russian Pogroms

The pogroms began in 1881. In approximately 160 cities and towns, anti-Jewish outbreaks occurred. Generally these were not instigated by the authorities. The authorities appeared indifferent to these outbreaks, and the Russian police often frustrated efforts by the Jews at self-defense. Previously the authorities had been quick to act. Now, however, they tended to blame the Jews for their misfortunes. Governmental spokesmen explained the pogroms by the theory of Jewish exploitation of the peasantry. Unfortunately, this theory was given wide credibility in Western circles ordinarily sympathetic to Jews.

The official response was to restrict further the Pale of Settlement. Jews were expelled from Russian cities, particularly Kiev. The effect of these restrictions would lead to the economic collapse of Russian Jewry. The welfare rolls, for example, increased by 25 percent between 1894 and 1898. By 1891 virtually all Jews were expelled from Moscow. There is no evidence, however, for governmental complicity in the pogroms. The main forces driving the pogroms emanated from below rather than from above. Jews correctly charged that the Russian government bore responsibility, given that it possessed authority within the area of the pogroms. However, contrary to widespread popular myth, the government itself did not participate in the initial round of pogroms of 1881–1883. This was not the case in the second round of pogroms beginning in 1903.

A second myth of the pogroms relates to their effects and impact. Contrary to popular myth, there was not widespread loss of life. The number of Jews who were killed in the pogroms numbered less than 1,000. Although we can number over 100 anti-Jewish outbreaks in the Pale of Settlement, the actual loss of life was comparatively light. The effects of the pogrom were psychological, in that the coupling of violent outbreaks against Jews with destruction of Jewish property and further restrictions threw the community profoundly out of balance. To be sure, the actual loss of life can never be minimized. However, the pogroms cannot be seen as a dress rehearsal for the much larger massacres of Jews that took place during the Russian revolution and its accompanying civil war.

Lastly, the pogroms exposed the failure of enlightenment and emancipation theory. Of particular dismay to Jews was the relative silence of the intellectuals within Russian society. Most Russian intellectuals knew very little of Jews. In Russian novels, Jews appear primarily as prisoners, spies, and traitors. Fyodor Dostoevsky recommended Jewish emancipation, but only if the Jew could be kept under control. As a Russian nationalist and Slavophile, Dostoevsky opposed Jews as a Western element and as foreigners. Although he personally denied anti-Semitism, Dostoevsky followed the lead of Karl Marx in identifying Jews with gold and the principle of money. In his novels, Dostoevsky portrayed Jews either as nihilist revolutionaries or as capitalist exploiters of Russia and Russians via usury. When asked about the infamous blood libel, Dostoevsky's response was "I don't know." Yet more damaging and disappointing than these negative portraits of Jews and Judaism was the silence of Russian intellectuals at the outbreak of the pogroms in 1881. The emancipation theory had always proclaimed that with greater education anti-Semitism would naturally decline. The failure of intellectuals to condemn the pogroms shattered that assumption. The participation of Russian university students among the pogromists was even more disappointing. Some of the revolutionaries argued that the pogroms were actually progressive because they focused the attention of the peasantry upon their problems in society.

The second round of outbreaks was symbolized by the infamous Kishinev pogrom of 1903. This pogrom, and the others that followed it, were organized by the government in an attempt to defame the left-wing revolutionary movements as a Jewish phenomenon. Leo Tolstoy now spoke out vigorously and forcefully. Kishinev represented significant loss of life. Over 50 Jews were killed. Psychologically, it was damaging to Jews because it exposed the Jewish failure to resist. The poet laureate of the Zionist movement, Chaim Nachman Bialik, in his famous poem "In the City of Slaughter," not only decried Kishinev, but also called for a fundamental transformation in Jewish life in which Jews would resist their oppressors. To be sure, Kishinev was unique, for in other pogroms resistance did occur.

The background to these pogroms lay in the Russo-Japanese war of 1904–1905 and the growth of a Russian revolutionary movement. There were many rumors of an alliance between Jews and Japanese during the war. The American Jewish financier Jacob Schiff had floated a loan to the Japanese—something he had resisted doing for the czars. In October 1905, the Black Hundreds mounted a series of anti-Jewish pogroms aimed at blackening the revolutionary forces by calling attention to their Jewish leaders. Although the government disliked the unruliness of the Black Hundreds, it tolerated the pogroms, especially in the context of the unexpected Russian defeat at the hands of the Japanese.

The 1905 Russian Revolution marked an improvement in the condition of the Russian peasantry but a worsening of the condition of Jews. Russian Minister of the Interior Peter Stolypin initiated a number of agrarian reforms, but also implemented an anti-Semitic program involving the expulsion of the Jews from Kiev in 1910 and strict enforcement of the *numerus clausus,* a Jewish quota, at high schools, and the Russian bar. This Stolypin reaction culminated in the infamous Mendel Beilis case of 1913, a blood libel which acted virtually as a substitute for the pogroms.

During the elections to the Russian Duma, or Parliament, in 1905, Jews naturally supported those groups interested in liberalizing Russia and transforming her into a parliamentary state. Jews were found primarily among the Constitutional Democrats. However, the struggle for Jewish emancipation remained futile. The Czars dismissed the Duma and reverted to tyrannical rule. The 1913 Beilis case secured broad international attention for the plight of Russian Jewry. However, little could be done, especially in light of the Triple Entente of England, France, and Russia, in the years prior to World War I. Although the liberal democracies generally sympathized with the plight of Russian Jewry and provided an open-door policy of welcoming Russian Jewish immigrants and refugees, they were not prepared to intervene in the internal conditions of Russia. Some disliked Russia's internal policies, but felt that they had to respect the right of the government, especially a major power, to regulate its own internal affairs. Others felt the Jews were partly to blame for their situation. In a stupefying editorial, the *London Times* argued that Jewish emancipation would only worsen matters in Russia, for it would expose the enormous gulf between Jews and the Russian peasantry. Even in the case of Beilis in 1913, although the majority of opinion in the West remained pro-Beilis, it was remarkable how many felt that the blood libel must have some credibility. If Beilis himself was innocent, many felt that the crime related to ritual practices among the Jews of Eastern Europe. To be sure, this represented at most an extreme viewpoint. Dominant sentiment assumed Beilis's innocence and blamed Russian authorities for the trial and the blood libel.

However, liberal opinion in the West clearly had been relatively tolerant of Russian anti-Semitism. Some, particularly in England, had been appalled by the atrocities committed by the Ottoman Empire against the Bulgarians in the 1870's and the Armenians in the 1890's. These people pointed to Russia's more positive record when compared to the treatment of minorities within the Ottoman Empire. Benjamin Disraeli, the British Prime Minister, had supported the Ottoman Empire during the Bulgarian atrocities. His enemies argued that perhaps underlying his support for the Ottomans was his Jewish ancestry, for Jews had traditionally aligned themselves with Ottoman policies protecting Jews. Conversely, of course, Jews detested Russia and its Czarist government. Disraeli had been a Conservative Prime Minister. His Liberal opponents cultivated the alliance with Russia. The growing entente between Russia and the liberal powers in the West made it increasingly difficult for Jewish protests against Russian policies to be effective. Although notables such as Charles Darwin and the Archbishop of Canterbury had participated in protests against the Russian pogroms in the 1880's, that tradition appeared increasingly peripheral to the Anglo-Russian Entente.

The outbreak of World War I in August 1914 necessitated placing the Jewish question on the back burner. Although Jewish leaders were told repeatedly that after the war the Allies would return to the question of Russian Jewry, little could be said or done now that the Allies were engaged formally in war alongside Russian armies. Jews perceived the German armies in Eastern Europe as liberators and the Russian armies as oppressors. Wherever the German army marched in Eastern Europe, it generally offered protection to Jews. The Russian army, by contrast, carried the stigma of Czarist oppression.

The Russian Revolution, of course, fundamentally transformed this situation. Jews greeted the Revolution as liberation from a long record of tyranny. Over the course of time, however, Jews discovered that the totalitarian society of the Soviets was far more destructive than the tyrannical society of the Czars.

Reading: Hayyim Nachman Bialik, "The City of Slaughter"

As noted in the text, Hayyim Nachman Bialik served as poet laureate of Zionism. His poem, "The City of Slaughter," described the notorious Kishinev pogrom, which led to the establishment of the American Jewish Committee as a defense agency. Note, in particular, his ironic critique that Jewish failure to resist connoted shame and desecration rather than sanctification of God's name. His poem blasts both the viciousness of the aggressors and the passivity of the Jews.

The City of Slaughter (from Songs of Wrath)

Arise and go now to the city of slaughter;
Into its courtyard wind thy way.
There with thine own hand touch, and with the eyes of thine head
Behold on tree, on stone, on fence, on mural clay,
The spattered blood and dried brains of the dead.
Proceed then to the ruins, the split walls reach,
Where wider grows the hollow and greater grows the breach;

Pass over the shattered hearth, attain the broken wall
Whose burnt and barren brick, whose charred stones reveal
The open mouths of such wounds, that no mending
Shall ever mend, nor healing ever heal.

Descend then to the cellars of the town,
There where the virgin daughters of thy folk were fouled,
Where seven heathen flung a woman down,
The daughter in the presence of her mother,

The mother in the presence of her daughter,
Before slaughter, during slaughter and after slaughter!
Touch with thy hand the cushion stained; touch
The pillow incarnadined:
This is the place the wild ones of the wood, the beasts of the field
With bloody axes in their paws compelled thy daughters to yield:
Beasted and swined!

Note also, do not fail to note,
In that dark corner and behind that cask
Crouched husbands, bridegrooms, brothers, peering from the
cracks,
Watching the martyred bodies struggling underneath
The bestial breath,
Stifled in filth, and swallowing their blood.
Watching from the darkness and its mesh
The lecherous rabble portioning for booty
Their kindred and their flesh.

Crushed in their shame, they saw it all;
They did not stir or move;
They did not pluck their eyes out, they

Beat not their brains against the wall,
Perhaps, perhaps, each watcher had it in his heart to pray,
A miracle, O Lord, and spare my skin this day!

Those who survived this foulness, who from their blood awoke,
Beheld their life polluted, the light of their world gone out—
How did their menfolk bear it, how did they bear this yoke?

They crawled forth from their holes and fled to the house of the
 Lord,
They offered thanks to Him, the sweet benedictory word.
The *Cohanim* sallied forth, to the Rabbi's house they flitted:
Tell me, O Rabbi, tell, is my own wife permitted?
And thus the matter ends, and nothing more;
And all is as it was before.

Come, now, and I will bring thee to their lairs
The privies, jakes and pigpens where the heirs
Of Hasmoneans lay, with trembling knees
Concealed and cowering,—the sons of the Maccabees!
The seed of saints, the scions of the lions . .
Who, crammed by scores in all the sanctuaries of their shame,
So sanctified My name!

Your deaths are without reason; your lives are without cause.
What says the Shekhinah? In the clouds it hides
In shame, in agony alone abides;
I, too, at night, will venture on the tombs,
Regard the dead and weigh their secret shame,
But never shed a tear, I swear it in My name.
For great is the anguish, great the shame on the brow;
But which is greater, son of man, say thou—
Or liefer keep thy silence, bear witness in My name
To the hour of my sorrow, the moment of My shame.

And when thou dost return
Bring thou the blot of My disgrace upon thy people's head,
And from my suffering do not part,
But set it like a stone within their heart.

Bibliography for further reading

Baron, Salo. *The Russian Jews under Tsars and Soviets,* Schocken, 1987

Greenberg, Louis. *The Jews in Russia: The Struggle for Emancipation,* Schocken, 1974

Lederhendler, Eli. *The Road to Modern Jewish Politics: Political Tradition and Political Reconstruction in the Jewish Community of Tzarist Russia,* Oxford University Press, 1989

Stanislawski, Michael. *Tsar Nicholas I and the Jews,* Jewish Publication Society, 1983

Zipperstein, Steven. *The Jews of Odessa: A Cultural History, 1794–1881,* Stanford University Press, 1985

Unit XXVIII

Modern Zionism

Background

The reality of emancipation blurred Jewish perceptions of exile. The distinctions between homeland and homelessness were not nearly as demarcated as they had been in the medieval period. The very language shifted from a language of exile to a language of diaspora.

Modern anti-Semitism reawakened the sense of exile. Zionism marked a return to traditional Jewish models of self-understanding. The Jew had lost his homeland and was currently experiencing the abnormal state of exile and homelessness. Zionism represented an effort by the Jews to normalize their situation. It constituted a rebellion against the failure of emancipation to solve the Jewish question, coupled with a desire for a return to homeland, i.e. Palestine, the historical land of the Jews.

Therefore Zionism synthesized both modern and traditionalist elements. The language of modern nationalism, of normalizing the Jews as a nation, and of modernizing the Jewish spirit through an ethos of self-determination—all these represented components of modernity that Zionism sought to internalize. As Arthur Hertzberg argues in *The Zionist Idea,* Zionism represents the last in a long series of efforts by the Jews to join modernity. Conversely, the return to Jewish history and homeland represents traditionalist themes within Zionism. Zionism found itself in a paradox—evoking both a modern ethos of nationalism and self-determination and a classically Jewish ethos of exile and return to homeland.

This contradiction within Zionism ultimately became central to the very definition of a Jewish state. If the homeland consists of nothing more than a safe space for Jews to live in, then there is no question concerning content. The content ought consist of the best of modern culture—democracy, liberalism, and pluralism. However, if the ethos of Zionism also signifies a reconnection with Jewish heritage and tradition, then the question of the content of a Jewish state becomes both far more significant and far more divisive. Does a Jewish state recognize or lend significance to the *sancta* of Judaism? Does a Jewish state arrogate a specific role to Jewish religion? The very singing of *Ha-tikvah* as the national anthem of the Jewish state presupposes a specifically Jewish claim rooted in Jewish heritage and tradition. It is these contradictions between a modern and a classically Jewish ethos that neither Zionism nor the State of Israel has resolved completely. The Zionist experience has lived with these paradoxes and contradictions—a compromise which satisfies no one, but permits both liberals and traditionalists to support and endorse the Zionist endeavor.

Moreover, the constituency for Zionism reflected this division between modernists and traditionalists. The leadership of the movement was generally Western in orientation. It came to Zionism via emancipation and its failures. Its primary concerns were that of rescuing Jews.

Conversely, the constituency for Zionism, its rank and file, was far more traditionally Jewish. Their roots lay in Eastern Europe where the sense of exile was far stronger. They could foresee no Jewish homeland save the historical land of the Jews, i.e. Israel. When the British Empire offered East Africa as a Jewish homeland, Zionist leaders wished to accept, partly on the grounds that an offer from Britain could not be rejected, and partly because East Africa (actually Kenya, but known as the Uganda project because of the presence of the Uganda Railway) would offer a temporary refuge for Jews fleeing pogroms. Rank-and-file Zionists, led by Chaim Weizmann, argued that there could be no homeland but Palestine. They argued that Zionist leadership had lost touch with the ethos and folkways of the Jewish people if they could even consider the idea of an alternative to the historical Jewish land.

Zionist Ideology

Although Theodor Herzl is regarded as the founder of modern Zionism, many of his ideas were already articulated by Leon Pinsker in 1882 (a dozen years before Herzl's Zionist awakening during the Dreyfus trial) in an important pamphlet entitled "Auto-Emancipation." Pinsker had been a proponent of Jewish enlightenment. His hopes for a liberal Russia, however, had been shattered by the Russian pogroms. In particular, the silence of the intellectuals had troubled him, for the underlying assumption behind emancipation ideology had been that the best educated elements of society were the least likely to be anti-Semitic. Therefore, Pinsker turned to a new analysis of anti-Semitism. He argued that anti-Semitism was xenophobia. No one likes a stranger. The problem of the Jews is that they are a ghost people, everywhere a stranger and nowhere at home.

This had been the classic failure of emancipation. Jews had hoped emancipation would solve the Jewish question. They had discovered, however, the folly of relying upon others. Pinsker's solution lay now in auto-emancipation, or self-determination. The Jews must become like all other nations. The trappings of nationalism—a land and language of their own—must be recovered by the Jews. Nor could the Jews rely on other parties. Pessimistically, Pinsker concluded, if the Jews are to normalize themselves, they will have to do the job alone.

Theodor Herzl was a Viennese journalist who, in covering the Dreyfus trial, became convinced of Dreyfus's innocence. The only reason that Dreyfus was in the dock, Herzl argued, was the reality of anti-Semitism. Emancipation clearly had failed in that Dreyfus himself represented the dream of emancipation theory—a Jew who had arrived at the pinnacle of the French military, yet the Jew remained a foreigner. He was under suspicion of selling military secrets to the Germans, not because he had done so but because of his Jewishness.

Therefore Herzl concluded that the Jews must normalize themselves. His pamphlet "The Jewish State" articulated a theory of Jewish nationalism along lines similar to those of Pinsker. The Jews must take on the trappings of normalcy and become a normal nation. They must obtain a land and language of their own. Neither Herzl nor Pinsker insisted upon Palestine as the Jewish homeland. They were primarily concerned with solving the problem of anti-Semitism. Any land would do, although clearly Palestine was preferable. Neither evoked the sense of Jewish history and power of Jewish tradition. Their vision of the content of a Jewish homeland was that of a liberal democracy absent any preferred or special position of Judaism or Judaic culture.

One difference between Herzl and Pinsker lay in their assessment of the gentile world. Pinsker, as noted, was quite pessimistic. The Jews had to become self-reliant and would receive no assistance from gentile powers. Herzl, by contrast, was quite optimistic concerning gentile society. Anti-Semitism connoted a problem for the gentile world as well. The nation-state would suffer from Jewish revolutionary activity until such time as the Jewish question was solved. Therefore Herzl optimistically anticipated the help and support of gentile powers in realizing his vision. He conducted himself as an international Jewish diplomat, negotiating from government to government searching for assistance and allies.

This Herzlian vision was crowned at the first Zionist Congress in Basle, Switzerland, in 1897. The Congress declared the goal of the Zionist program to be to secure the rights to a Jewish homeland guaranteed by international law. This was Zionism from the top down. Herzl and his followers were interested in building a coalition of political leaders, particularly among gentile governments, to give a homeland to the Jews. Pinsker, by contrast, was far closer to the *Chovevei Tzion*, the Jewish settlers in Palestine trying to build Zionism from the bottom up. Their vision lay in creating facts on the ground that later on would be recognized by the broader Jewish community and the international arena of nation-states.

The optimistic vision of Herzl translates into Labor Zionism today. Herzl's successors, Chaim Weizmann, David Ben-Gurion, and, in latter days, Shimon Peres and Yitzhak Rabin, consistently looked outward to friendly gentile assistance in the realization of their vision. Weizmann placed his trust initially in England. Ben-Gurion and his lieutenant Peres turned initially to France for primary assistance. In latter years, they increasingly focused upon the United States.

The pessimistic Zionism of Pinsker has consistently articulated a far more self-reliant theme in Zionist history. Pinsker, followed by Vladimir Jabotinsky, Menahem Begin, and, in more recent years,

Yitzhak Shamir, remained pessimistic of how much assistance Jews could really receive from the gentile world. None were prepared to cut their ties with outside powers. Jabotinsky admired the British Empire and continued to hope that Britain would facilitate the Zionist dream. However, it was the isolationist Zionists who maintained that ultimately the Jew remained alone and had to become self-reliant.

There is much to sustain both visions of Zionism. Clearly, Israel fought every major war to victory together with the cooperation of friendly gentile powers—Russia and Czechoslovakia in 1948, Britain and France in 1956, and the United States in 1967 and 1973. The Balfour Declaration of 1917 represented the triumph of Herzlian Zionism, with its dictum that "His Majesty's government views with favour the establishment in Palestine of a national home for the Jewish people." Israel itself was created by a United Nations vote in which over two-thirds of the U.N. members supported the Zionist dream of a Jewish state. Unprecedentedly, and some would say miraculously, the creation of Israel was virtually the only chapter in the early history of the Cold War in which both the United States and the Soviet Union were in agreement.

Yet the isolationist side of Zionism can also be sustained. It was Begin who recognized that Britain would never fulfill its obligations in the Jewish national home and proclaimed "the revolt" against the British Empire. The "Zionism is racism" resolution at the United Nations in the mid-1970's signaled the isolation of Israel and her delegitimization in the family of nation-states.

Therefore the debate continues between optimists and pessimists. The greatest victories of Zionism were diplomatic victories. These entailed fulfillment of the Herzlian vision that, rather than stand alone, the Jews must seek out friendly allies and supporters. Perhaps the finest moment in all of Israel's history was when the pessimistic school of Zionism, i.e. Begin and the Likud, adopted the program of optimistic Zionism in the Camp David accords in September 1978. Conversely, perhaps the lowest moments in Israel's history lie in the triumph of the isolationist world view—as when Begin maintained he was resisting Hitler in fighting the Palestine Liberation Organization in Lebanon in 1982.

Conversely, Herzl erred in predicting, even favoring, future Jewish assimilation. Herzl envisioned that those Jews who wished to be Jewish would emigrate to the Jewish homeland. That would at long last permit those Jews who wished to assimilate to disappear into gentile society. Herzl was wrong on both counts. Zionism would not solve the problem of anti-Semitism. On the contrary, anti-Semitism would increase exponentially via anti-Zionist sentiment within the Third World. Similarly, he erred profoundly in predicting future Jewish assimilation. Zionism would restore a greater focus upon Jewish identity and would constantly remind Jews of their Jewishness. Rather than facilitate assimilation, Zionism would become a critical bulwark in preserving Jewish continuity.

Implementing Zionism

The most critical difference between Herzl and Pinsker was that Pinsker was strictly a visionary and intellectual leader whereas Herzl built an organization and implemented a program. Perhaps Herzl's most lasting contribution lay in his organizational skills. He built the World Zionist Organization by providing it with annual Zionist Congresses, beginning in Basle in 1897, which would serve to rally the troops; a specific program and goal in terms of an internationally guaranteed charter of Jewish settlement; and a communication organ entitled *Die Welt*. Significantly, the language of communication was German. This again reflected the absence of empathy with historical tradition and the national culture of the Jews. Lastly, he provided Zionism with stable financial institutions—a bank to raise money by selling shares to Jews everywhere and a fundraising arm, the Keren Kayemet, to raise money for Jews in Palestine.

This was Zionism from the top down. Herzl opposed the *Chovevei Tzion*, who favored piecemeal infiltration and colonization of Palestine. Such colonies, Herzl argued, would only alienate the nationalist Arab population. This vision of Arabs, in turn, constituted yet another fundamental flaw in Herzl's analysis. He assumed the Jews would raise the standard of living for the neighboring Arabs, who would welcome them with open arms. He badly underestimated the degree of Arab national attachment to Palestine.

The practical Zionists opposed the Herzlian program. Asher Ginzberg, better known under his pen name Ahad Ha'am (meaning "One of the People"), criticized Herzl's vision for its absence of Jewish content. Arthur Hertzberg has described Ahad Ha'am as the "agnostic rabbi," meaning one who lacked faith in revelation yet acknowledged its compelling power.

Ahad Ha'am argued in favor of practical work in Palestine. He urged that Zionism address not the problem of the Jews but rather the problem of Judaism—the question of Jewish assimilation—and provide a compelling reason for continued Jewish identity in the modern world. The answer to the problem of Judaism, Ahad Ha'am argued, lay in the development of a spiritual center in the Jewish national home that would strengthen Jewish identity everywhere in the diaspora. Ahad Ha'am took as his model the Second Jewish Commonwealth, wherein a majority of Jews lived in the diaspora yet received spiritual and cultural sustenance and leadership from the Jewish homeland in Israel. Such a homeland could exist only in the historical land of the Jews—namely, the land of Israel. In the homeland the Jews would develop a rich national culture that would sustain Jewishness and Jewish identity everywhere in the diaspora.

Significantly, Herzl opposed the emphasis upon national culture. He feared that cultural questions were too divisive and would awaken all of the old battles about the role of Jewish law and religion in contemporary Jewish life. Ahad Ha'am countered there was no point to a Jewish homeland if its content was strictly political. Political Zionism would never guarantee the survival of Judaism as a cultural entity. Zionism could never content itself with providing a refuge for Jews. It must address the problem of Judaism: Is there a salient Jewish message in the modern world?

Both the Reform movement and Orthodoxy had failed in Ahad Ha'am's view. Reform Judaism had proclaimed that Judaism can survive by spreading its message to the gentile world. Its focus, however, had been to anchor it in a Jewish future and had lost its roots in the Jewish past. Orthodoxy, by contrast, was too locked into historical models and had little sense of where the Jewish future was heading in a secularized world. It was Zionism, however, that could provide a synthesis of past and present. Zionism occupied a middle ground precisely because, on the one hand, it was modern and liberal, while on the other hand, it was classical and traditional. However, Zionism could never succeed if its program was strictly political. Only a Jewish national renewal involving aspects of Jewish culture and religion would enable the Jews to play their rightful part in modern society. Like Herzl, Ahad Ha'am both succeeded and failed at the same time. He clearly underestimated the force of modern anti-Semitism. The problem of the Jews, at least in the short run, was far greater than the problem of Judaism. For all Jewish leaders, the Holocaust was unprecedented and unexpected. None predicted the scale of Hitler's war against the Jews.

However, Ahad Ha'am correctly perceived the problem of Jewish continuity in the modern world. The problem of Judaism lay in Jewish assimilation: Why continue to be Jewish in a modern context? His answer, that a Jewish homeland would serve to inspire the condition of Jews everywhere in the diaspora, lies at the root of many Jewish continuity initiatives today that are Israel-centered. Ultimately, secular Zionism would never be able to sustain a distinctive culture of Jewishness and Jewish identity. It would require the "rabbi" side of Ahad Ha'am—namely, greater anchoring in Jewish history, tradition, culture, and religion.

The Balfour Declaration clearly represented the triumph of Herzlianism. In 1917 Great Britain issued a foreign office statement that England "views with favour the establishment in Palestine of a national home for the Jewish people." England's motivations in doing so were quite complex. She hoped to rally American Jewry into bringing America more quickly into the war. Strategically, she hoped to prevent French troops from taking over the Suez Canal by creating a buffer between Syria and Egypt. She overestimated the potential of Russian Jewry to keep Russia in the war. Last, and by no means least, Britain feared that Germany would issue a similar statement and wished to do so first. Clearly, there were a number of false assumptions underlying Britain's motivations. She badly overestimated the capacity of American Jewry and Russian Jewry to influence the policies of their respective governments. She misunderstood that Germany's alliance with the Ottoman Empire would prevent issuing any similar statement. Lastly, Britain failed to recognize that the Declaration itself provided contradictory promises—a national homeland for Jews, but without undermining the rights of those non-Jews already resident in Palestine.

Ninety percent of Palestine's population remained Arab. Britain's Balfour Declaration, together with its military occupation in Palestine, did lay claim to awarding Britain a League of Nations mandate to implement the Balfour Declaration in Palestine. This San Remo Declaration of 1922, to which the Balfour Declaration formed a preamble, represented the high tide of Zionism. Britain's mandate to be in Palestine lay in fulfilling the dream of a Jewish national home. However, the mandate, in essence, involved two contradictory promises. Britain could not satisfy the aspirations of the Jews without doing violence to the aspirations of Palestinian Arabs. Nor could England protect Arab national rights without doing violence to the dreams of a Jewish national home. Until 1939 Britain did her best to "muddle through." However, it remained most doubtful that both parties could co-exist on the same piece of land.

In 1939, under growing pressure from the prospect of war with Nazi Germany, Britain moved to pacify the Palestinian Arabs. The White Paper of 1939 sharply limited Jewish immigration at the worst moment in Jewish history, and promised a unitary Arab state within 10 years. Morally, the White Paper was bankrupt. Britain's only claim to be in Palestine was to fulfill the terms of the Balfour Declaration rather than to retreat from it. The Permanent Mandates Commission of the League of Nations, in fact, condemned Britain for the White Paper. For the Jews, it was an unmitigated tragedy because it closed off the primary point of refuge for Jews fleeing Hitler. From the perspective of *realpolitik,* Britain's actions appear understandable. The Jews would support Britain in a war effort regardless. Conversely, one could not guarantee Arab neutrality much less support for Britain's struggle with Hitler.

Nor did Britain's position change after World War II. Although successive British governments condemned the White Paper, they continued to implement it through 1948. The Arab-Zionist conflict suggested that there were two competing claims to a single piece of land. British national policy, however, after 1939, favored one claim to the exclusion of the other.

Conclusion

Zionism also marked a fundamental transformation in Jewish self-perception and collective identity. Emancipation and enlightenment had placed great focus on the privacy of Jewish identity. The model of the Jewish enlightenment was, "Be a Jew at home and a man in the street." Emancipation theory had essentially privatized Jewishness. What Zionism did was restore a public focus to Jewish identity. Zionism's message was to root Jewish identity in Jewish peoplehood and collective national endeavor. This provided a very important corrective to the earlier focus upon private and individual behavior.

To be a Jew today suggests participation in Jewish collective endeavors and membership in the Jewish people. The weakness in Jewish life has again become the absence of Jewishness in the home. In the public square, Jews feel incredibly self-confident about asserting their political positions and their ties to Israel. In the privacy of their own home, they find themselves unable to articulate compelling reasons as to why their children should lead a Jewish life.

Reading: Arthur Hertzberg, *The Zionist Idea*

Leon Pinsker wrote the pamphlet "Auto-emancipation" in the aftermath of the Russian pogroms of 1881. In many ways he anticipated Herzl's arguments although he clearly is far more pessimistic about the cooperation of the gentile world, hence the title "Auto-emancipation." Note, in particular, Pinsker's definition of anti-Semitism as xenophobia and his quest for normalization of the Jews as a people.

> No people, generally speaking, has any predilection for foreigners. This fact has its ethnological basis and cannot be brought as a reproach against any people. Now, is the Jew subject to *this* general law only to the same extent as the other nationalities? Not at all! The aversion which meets the foreigner in a strange land can be repaid in equal coin in his home country. The non-Jew pursues his own interest in a foreign country openly and without giving offence. It is everywhere considered natural that he should fight for these interests, alone or in conjunction with others. The foreigner has no need to *be,* or to *seem* to *be,* a patriot. But as for the Jew, he is not a native in his own home country, but he is also not a foreigner; he is, in very truth, the stranger par excellence. He is regarded as neither friend nor foe, but as an alien, of whom the only thing known is that he has no home. People do not care to *confide* in the foreigner, or to trust the Jew. The foreigner claims hospitality, which he can repay in the same coin in his own country. The Jew can make no such return; consequently he can make no claim to hospitality. He is not a guest, much less a welcome guest. He is more like a beggar; and what beggar is welcome? He is rather a refugee; and where is the refugee to whom a ref-

uge may not be refused? The Jews are aliens who can have no representatives because they have no fatherland. Because they have none, because their home has no boundaries behind which they can entrench themselves, their misery also has no hounds. The *general law* does not apply to the Jews, as strangers in the true sense of the word. On the other hand, there are everywhere *laws for the Jews,* and if the general law is to apply to them, this fact must first be determined by a special *law.* Like the Negroes, like women, and unlike all free peoples, they must be *emancipated.* It is all the worse for them if, unlike the Negroes, they belong to an advanced race, and if, unlike women, they can show not only women of distinction, but also men, even great men.

Since the Jew is nowhere at home, nowhere regarded as a native, he remains an alien everywhere. That he himself and his forefathers as well were born in the country does not alter this fact in the least. Generally, he is treated as an adopted child whose rights may be questioned; *never* is he considered a legitimate child of the fatherland. 'The German, proud of his Teutonic character, the Slav, the Celt—not one of them admits that the Semitic Jew is his equal by birth; and even if he be ready, as a man of culture, to admit him to all civil rights, he will never go as far as to forget the Jew in this, his fellow citizen. The *legal emancipation* of the Jews is the crowning achievement of our century. But *legal emancipation* is not *social* emancipation, and with the proclamation of the former the Jews are still far from being emancipated from their exceptional *social position.*

The emancipation of the Jews naturally finds its justification in the fact that it will always be considered to have been a postulate of *logic,* of *law,* and of *enlightened self-interest.* It can never be regarded as a spontaneous expression of human *feeling.* Far from owing its origin to the spontaneous *feeling* of the peoples, it is *never a matter of course;* and it has never yet taken such deep root that discussion of it becomes unnecessary. In any event, whether emancipation was undertaken from spontaneous impulse or from conscious motives, it remains a rich gift, splendid alms, willingly or unwillingly flung to the poor, humble beggars whom no one, however, cares to shelter, because a homeless, wandering beggar wins confidence or sympathy from none. The Jew is not permitted to forget that the daily bread of civil rights must be given to him. The stigma attached to this people, which forces it into an unenviable isolation among the nations, cannot be removed by any sort of official emancipation, as long as it is the nature of this people to produce vagrant nomads, as long as it cannot give a satisfactory account of whence it comes and whither it goes, as long as the Jews themselves prefer not to speak in Aryan society of their Semitic descent and prefer not to be reminded of it—as long as they are persecuted, tolerated, protected, emancipated.

This degrading dependence of the eternally alien Jew upon the non-Jew is reinforced by another factor, making a fusion of the Jews with the original inhabitants of a land absolutely impossible. In the great struggle for existence, civilized peoples readily submit to laws which help to give this struggle the worthy form of a peaceful competition. Even in this case the peoples usually make a distinction between the native and the foreigner, the first, of course, always being given the preference. Now, if this distinction is drawn even against the foreigner of equal birth, how harshly is it insisted upon with reference to the eternally alien Jew! How great must be the irritation at the beggar who dares to cast longing glances upon a land not his own—as upon a beloved woman guarded by distrustful relatives! And if he nevertheless prosper and succeed in plucking a flower here and there from its soil, woe to the ill-fated man! Let him not complain if he experiences what the Jews in Spain and Russia have experienced.

The Jews, moreover, do not suffer only when they achieve distinguished success. Wherever they are congregated in large masses, they must, by their very *numbers,* have a certain advantage in competition with the non-Jewish population. In the western provinces of Russia we behold the Jews herded together, leading a wretched existence in the most dreadful destitution. Nevertheless, there are unceasing complaints of the exploitation practiced by the Jews.

To sum up what has been said: For the living, the Jew is a dead man; for the natives, an alien and a vagrant; for property holders, a beggar; for the poor, an exploiter and a millionaire; for patriots, a man without a country; for all classes, a hated rival.

Summary

The Jews are not a living nation; they are everywhere aliens; therefore they are despised.

The civil and political emancipation of the Jews is not sufficient to raise them in the estimation of the peoples.

The proper and the only remedy would be the creation of a Jewish nationality, of a people living upon its own soil, the auto-emancipation of the Jews; their emancipation as a nation among nations by the acquisition of a home of their own.

We should not persuade ourselves that humanity and enlightenment will ever be radical remedies for the malady of our people.

The lack of national self-respect and self-confidence, of political initiative and of unity, are the enemies of our national renaissance.

In order that we may not be constrained to wander from one exile to another, we must have an extensive and productive place of refuge, a gathering place which is our own.

The present moment is more favorable than any other for realizing the plan here unfolded.

The international Jewish question must receive a national solution. Of course, our national regeneration can only proceed slowly. *We* must take the first step. Our *descendants* must follow us with a measured and unhurried pace.

A way must be opened for the national regeneration of the Jews by a congress of Jewish notables.

No sacrifice would be too great in order to reach the goal which will assure our people's future, everywhere endangered.

The financial accomplishment of the undertaking can, in the nature of the situation, encounter no insuperable difficulties.

Help yourselves, and God will help you!

Reading: *The Balfour Declaration*

The 1917 Balfour Declaration represented fulfillment of the Herzlian program of an internationally recognized charter of the Jews to a homeland in Palestine. Note, however, the inherent contradiction of providing the Jews with a "National Home" in Palestine without infringing upon the rights of non-Jews already there. This contradiction within Zionism has plagued Arab-Jewish relations to this day.

Dear Lord Rothschild,

I have much pleasure in conveying to you, on behalf of His Majesty's Government, the following declaration of sympathy with Jewish Zionist aspirations which has been submitted to, and approved by, the Cabinet:—

"His Majesty's Government view with favour the establishment in Palestine of a national home for the Jewish people, and will use their best endeavours to facilitate the achievement of this object, it being clearly understood that nothing shall be done which may prejudice the civil and religious rights of existing non-Jewish communities in Palestine, or the rights and political status enjoyed by Jews in any other country."

I should be grateful if you would bring this declaration to the knowledge of the Zionist Federation.

Yours Sincerely,
Arthur James Balfour

Bibliography for Further Reading

Avineri, Shlomo. *The Making of Modern Zionism,* Basic Books, 1984

Hertzberg, Arthur. *The Zionist Idea,* Atheneum, 1969

Lacqueur, Walter. *A History of Zionism,* Holt, Reinhardt and Winston, 1989

Unit XXIX

Jewish Settlement in America

The earliest Jewish communal settlement in North America dated from 1654, when 23 Jews, fleeing the fall of Recife from Dutch to Portuguese hands, left South America and landed in New Amsterdam. The Dutch Governor, Peter Stuyvesant, initially opposed their entry, but he was overruled by the Dutch West India Company, which desired to increase the tax base of the New Amsterdam colony. Much to Stuyvesant's chagrin, Jews immediately campaigned for their rights as colonists. Asser Levy, in particular, led the struggle to secure Jews the right of military service—an important symbol of Jewish equality in the struggle for emancipation.

The British conquest of the Dutch colonies in 1665 brought a general grant of religious freedom. More significantly, the model of Jewish emancipation at work in the British colonies was a far more complete model than that available to Jews on the European continent. In the colonies, no general debate took place over whether the Jews were worthy of emancipation. Emancipation was granted in virtually all the colonies on the basis that Jews were human beings and deserved their full equal rights. This difference between the model of emancipation in North America and on the continent of Europe had significant implications for modern Jewish history. There was no bargain of emancipation in North America. Jews were not expected to transform themselves into American citizens. On the contrary, the model of emancipation left significant room for a collective Jewish ethos in which Jews would not be considered less American if they remained committed to Jewish community and continuity. Although some restrictions remained throughout the British colonies, these were generally ignored. To be sure, Sunday blue laws characterized America as a Christian land. However, Jews did not feel that they were second-class citizens in colonial America.

For example, Jewish opinion was divided during the American revolution. Some Jews generally supported Britain. Other Jews supported the revolutionaries. Although the role of Haym Solomon in financing the revolutionary army has been exaggerated, his actions did signify how closely some Jews were tied to the revolutionary cause and how attracted they were to the various colonial bills of rights guaranteeing Jewish equality in the new American nation. The very idea of building a new nation in which Jews would be equals solidified Jewish support for the revolution.

More generally, colonial Jewry was characterized by great stability. Little change occurred in the Jewish condition until waves of Jewish immigration began arriving, initially from Central Europe and subsequently from Eastern Europe. Colonial Jews had no indigenous religious leaders. Rabbis had to be imported from abroad. This situation signified their real problem—that of assimilation rather than of anti-Semitism. Colonial Jewry lacked an ethos of Jewish learning and religious identification. This situation foreshadowed a larger theme of American Jewish history: Protecting Jews against their enemies would not be as great a problem as ensuring Jewish continuity. The story of American Jewry would be a success story of Jewish integration in America. The weakness of American Jewry would be in defining its self-identity as Jews.

German Jewry in America

German Jews joined a broader German immigration to America in the 1830's and 1840's. The motive for this immigration was primarily economic opportunity, coupled with a desire to flee anti-Jewish legislation. In America German Jews entered the peddling trades, which in turn led to retailing and wholesaling businesses. Coupled with upward economic mobility was decreased religiosity, for spending increased time away from home and hearth meant less time devoted to religious practices.

Under the impact of German immigration, the Jewish

community became both larger and more fragmented. New theological currents challenged the public Orthodoxy of the earlier American Jewish community. To some extent, the growth of Reform Judaism in America formed part of the broader pattern of German immigration and emulation of German cultural and intellectual currents.

Perhaps no dispute divided the Jewish community more sharply than slavery. Two of the leading rabbis of the time, Morris Raphall of New York City and David Einhorn of Baltimore debated the issue publicly. Raphall claimed that the Bible had sanctioned slavery, citing the curse of Noah upon his son Ham. Einhorn argued that to be a Jew meant opposition to the subjugation of one human being by another. Both advocates, to be sure, were being somewhat disingenuous. The curse of Ham applied very specifically not to Africans but rather to Canaanites, an early reference to Jewish justifications for invading the land of Canaan. Conversely, while biblical Judaism and rabbinic Judaism placed significant restrictions upon slavery in an effort to preserve the human rights of slaves, there was no specific prohibition upon slavery per se. Jews had divided loyalties during the American debate concerning slavery. Most Jews in the South probably supported slavery as an institution. Conversely, Jews in the North found Einhorn's opposition to slavery more congenial.

Reform Judaism obtained its fullest expression on American shores. The Pittsburgh Platform of 1885 became the core document of Reform Judaism in America. It generally reflected the views of the German-speaking rabbinate within the United States. The platform itself was clearly a radical document. Its philosophical spirit was that of unrestrained rationalism omitting any reference to God. Progress was inevitable, reflecting the optimism of nineteenth-century liberalism. The essence of Judaism was defined as ethics and the emphasis upon the pursuit of social justice as the only fit occupation for a Jew. Lastly, the Pittsburgh Platform denied any references to Jewish peoplehood, national homeland, or future restoration.

Significantly, the radicalism embodied in the spirit of the Pittsburgh Platform never took root in Germany itself. There the presence of a communal framework necessitated that the Sabbath be observed on Saturday and that due respect be given for the dietary laws. By contrast, in America the spirit of greater individualism and the absence of any overarching communal framework permitted more radical voices to triumph. For example, at an early commencement of the Hebrew Union College, the Reform rabbinical school, shrimp was served despite the presence of leading traditionalist rabbis, who felt it necessary to leave the dinner. Regrettably, no apology was forthcoming. Some Reform rabbis found their way to Unitarianism, arguing that the logic of Reform Judaism ultimately meant the celebration of a single universal faith. Felix Adler, in fact, developed the Ethical Culture movement, which maintained that it made no sense to remain within the particularistic confines, broad as they were, of Reform Judaism. Significantly, there were virtually no Orthodox rabbis in this German immigration. Reform Judaism became a movement of ideologically committed rabbis who, absent the restraints of the *kehilla,* implemented the program of the Pittsburgh Platform.

The Reform movement quickly became institutionally strong. A lay congregational body known as the Union of American Hebrew Congregations was created in 1873, a rabbinical school based in Cincinnati, the Hebrew Union College, in 1875, and a rabbinical organization, the Central Conference of American Rabbis, in 1889. Among the Jewish religious movements, Reform quickly became the best organized institutional body. Although its ideology would often appear out of touch with the mass base of American Jewry, it represented the leading voices within Jewish communal leadership until at least the First World War.

Russian Jewish immigration, however, would alter the profile of American Judaism. By 1905, even so radical a Reform rabbi as Kaufman Kohler would retreat from observance of the Sabbath on Sunday. By 1937, especially given the significance of modern Zionism and the force of Nazi anti-Semitism, Reform would retreat completely from the Pittsburgh Platform. The 1937 Columbus Platform endorsed Jewish peoplehood and a return to religious ritual. In taking steps toward Zionism and restoration of the Jewish homeland, Reform Judaism recognized that its extreme universalism had failed to capture the minds and hearts of Jewish Americans.

During the Civil War itself, as noted, Jews could be found on both the Union and Confederate sides. The leading Jew of the Confederacy was probably Judah P. Benjamin, who was particularly close to Jefferson Davis and rose to become Minister of War within the Confederacy. Before the war Benjamin had served in the United States Senate. His abolitionist opponents, in turn, made him suffer for his Jewishness. Personally he regarded Judaism as a burden and a restraint upon his success. After the war he retreated to Paris and London.

Abraham Lincoln acted quickly to quell any apparent anti-Semitism within governmental policies. Responding to perhaps the first example of organized Jewish lobbying in Washington, Lincoln supported legislation that Jewish chaplains be appointed for the troops in the Union Army. More importantly, he revoked the infamous Order No. 11 of General Ulysses S. Grant in the Mississippi valley expelling all Jewish traders from the area. Grant had issued the order in the context of war profiteering. He did not perceive himself as prejudiced against Jews. On the contrary, he appointed Jews to office and pressured the Romanian government over her treatment of Jews during his tenure as President. In later years he claimed the order was issued without reflection. Nevertheless, the order signaled the presence of anti-Semitism in America, for a public institution such as the military had discriminated directly against Jews.

East European Immigration

After the Civil War immigration of Jews from Eastern Europe increased exponentially to America. By 1900, an average of 100,000 Jews were settling each year in the United States. The Jewish community grew from 250,000 in 1880 to over 3,000,000 in 1914.

There were many reasons for this immigration. The postwar American economy signaled significant growth and the opportunity to build better lives in the United States. The presence of a native American Jewry insured that Jews coming to settle in the United States would find already established institutions and communal frameworks. Native Jewish traditions of charity and social welfare provided some assistance to new immigrants. Conversely, the dominant images of Eastern Europe left Jews with few incentives to stay. Pogroms only exacerbated an already existing immigration. Most Jews who came to America were looking to build new lives for their families. Economic reasons outweighed the reasons of pogroms.

The immigrant process remained difficult, one raising serious social problems. Considerable concern related to Jewish involvement in the white slavery traffic. More pervasive was juvenile delinquency, as immigrant parents found it increasingly difficult to communicate with adolescent American children. Organized crime was particularly vexing to American Jewry. The names of Jewish racketeers and mobsters drew particularly unfavorable comment. Arnold Rothstein became perhaps America's most notorious Jewish criminal. The mere use of his name enticed a number of Chicago White Sox baseball players into fixing the 1919 World Series, that most hallowed of American institutions. Significantly, Rothstein refused any involvement in the plan to throw the World Series. So widespread was his reputation, however, that the ball players involved immediately believed that Rothstein's money would guarantee their payments if they successfully "lost" the World Series.

Jewish leaders tried to address the problems raised by the new immigration. Most probably would have preferred for Jewish problems to be solved in Eastern Europe rather than bring them to the United States. However, unlike Jewish leaders in England, for example, they did not try to discourage Jewish immigration to America. Certainly they did not withhold charitable donations in order to discourage immigrants from coming here. They did try, unsuccessfully, to disperse the immigrants away from the major metropolitan centers. For example, the Galveston project was an unsuccessful venture to channel immigrant Jews into Texas and disperse them throughout the Mississippi valley. They also moved to counter Jewish criminality and juvenile delinquency, although only upward mobility and acculturation to America would put an end to these sorry trends. They fought immigration restrictions to America consistently, although the battle would be lost in the years immediately after World War I, when immigrant exclusion and quotas would become the hallmark of immigration policy—precisely at a time when Jews would need places to which they could flee.

Native Jews were particularly concerned about the economic plight of the immigrants. They wished it known that Jews would care for their own and immigrants would never become a public charge. Their actions constituted some of the finest pages in American philanthropy. In 1896 the first Jewish Federation was created in Boston. Federated philanthropy would prove to be a model subsequently imitated by organizations such as the United Way—

namely, centralizing fundraising within communities and then dispersing it to direct-service agencies on the basis of need and priority. Although staffed by professionals, these Federations would be governed by volunteers, and part of the distinctive Jewish contribution to America was underscoring the role of volunteer oversight and management in non-profit agencies.

Not surprisingly, immigrant Jews tended to support liberal rather than conservative political candidates. In national elections, they supported the Republican Party of Lincoln—a pattern that would be broken only by Alfred Smith and subsequently by Franklin Roosevelt's New Deal. Locally, they supported the Democrats as the party of labor and the cities. Jews were especially involved in the labor union movements, many of which retained Jewish leaders long after they had ceased to have Jewish constituents.

Of greatest concern, naturally, was the battle against anti-Semitism. In the 1870's, anti-Semitism became social discrimination against Jews. Jews seemed to represent a threat to the upper-middle class status of wealthier Americans, such as those who patronized the Grand Hotel in Saratoga, New York, which refused to allow the very distinguished Joseph Seligman to stay there. The major third-party movement of the period, the Populist Party, criticized Jewish wealth and plutocrats such as the Rothchild family. Although the anti-Semitism of the Populists had little real impact upon American Jewry, it did pave the way for the conspiratorial mind-set of the *Protocols of the Elders of Zion.*

There were also concrete instances of violence directed against Jews. In 1902, following the mass funeral of Chief Rabbi Jacob Joseph, Jewish mourners were attacked by Irish workers while police looked on. Subsequently, to be sure, the public report of the incident blamed the New York City police force, and a number of key officers were dismissed.

The Leo Frank case of 1913 resulted in an anti-Jewish lynching. Leo Frank was a northern Jewish businessman resident in Atlanta who was charged with raping and then murdering a Southern teenager. Although the evidence against Frank was flimsy, he was found guilty. The Governor of Georgia virtually ruined his own career by commuting Frank's sentence, and an angry mob lynched Frank. Atlanta Jewry suffered grievously during the affair. Southern cries of carpetbagger, fanned with anti-Semitic resentment, resulted in Frank's conviction. The Jew remained a foreigner in the South and was frequently perceived as a Shylock-type character.

Perhaps most damaging was the patrician anti-Semitism restricting the presence of Jews at elite universities. No less an intellectual than Henry Adams had argued that the Jew was corrupting America, undermining her ethos and spirit, for the Jew could never join the WASP elite. Because universities served as a training ground for America's future leaders, restrictionist advocates argued that the role of the Jew must be limited, lest the Jews as parvenus take all the good places in American society. Columbia University declined from 40 percent Jewish enrollment to 20 percent. Similar quotas pervaded the rest of the Ivy League.

Ideological anti-Semitism, to be sure, remained rare. Tom Watson, a leading Populist, played a critical role during the Frank affair. However, the anti-Semitism of the Populist Party had little effect. America remained a liberal country with pluralistic traditions. Church-state separation guaranteed that the Jew would not feel an outsider in America. Conversely, the presence of other targets made American anti-Semitism considerably less vigorous or vociferous.

Immigrant restrictionism did affect Jews negatively. The National Origins Act of 1921 established firm quotas by country of national origin, discriminating severely against those countries from which Jews wished to immigrate. In 1924 this act fixed the quotas according to the American population census of 1890, meaning that, while there was no official Jewish quota, the proportion of Jews entering the country reflected the ratios from an early point in American immigration history rather than the proportions existing after World War I. Underlying this xenophobia was, of course, the fear of Bolshevism, particularly after the Russian Revolution and the publishing of the *Protocols of the Elders of Zion*.

Jews were by no means the sole target of immigrant restrictionism. Japanese and Italians also frequently encountered hostility and exclusionist sentiment. The American Legion and the Daughters of the American Revolution urged that America combat the dangers posed by immigrant radicalism. Leading politicians such as Henry Cabot Lodge and Robert LaFollette, despite their liberal inclinations, perceived the Jews as distinctively un-American.

Rather than establish a single national Jewish defense organization, American Jews established a variety of human relations agencies. The American Jewish Committee originated in 1906 as a diplomatic representation to the American government to alleviate the condition of Russian Jewry in the aftermath of the Kishinev pogrom. The Anti-Defamation League in 1913 developed from a public relations effort to free Leo Frank. Although these efforts at organization and defense failed, they set the precedent and pattern for American Jews engaging in the democratic processes of America on behalf of specifically Jewish interests. American pluralism granted Jewry considerable leeway for collective Jewish politics, including the right to utilize democratic means to advance Jewish interests. Public education, political lobbying, diplomatic representation, and even mass demonstrations would become the vehicles of American Jewish minority politics in the twentieth century.

The major defense organizations, the American Jewish Committee, the American Jewish Congress, and the Anti-Defamation League, would not always be in agreement. They would labor, in different ways, to advance the domestic and international position of the Jewish people. The multiplicity of Jewish organizations meant that there was no single voice speaking on behalf of the Jewish community. However, that multiplicity also enabled different groups of Jews to reach different target constituencies within American society. Jews were able to fight anti-Semitism freely, finding allies in other ethnic and religious sectors of American society.

Reading: *A Bintel Brief*

"A Bintel Brief" refers to the advice columns in the Yiddish press, specifically the Jewish Daily Forward in early twentieth-century America. Immigrant Jews wrote daily asking for advice on various facets of their acculturation to America. In the selections printed here, note the difficulties immigrants faced economically, in family conflicts, and religiously and theologically.

1910

Dear Editor,

Since I do not want my conscience to bother me, I ask you to decide whether a married woman has the right to go to school two evenings a week. My husband thinks I have no right to do this.

I admit that I cannot be satisfied to be just a wife and mother. I am still young and I want to learn and enjoy life. My children and my house are not neglected, but I go to evening high school twice a week. My husband is not pleased and when I come home at night and ring the bell, he lets me stand outside a long time intentionally, and doesn't hurry to open the door.

Now he has announced a new decision. Because I send out the laundry to be done, it seems to him that I have too much time for myself, even enough to go to school. So from now on he will count out every penny for anything I have to buy for the house, so I will not be able to send out the laundry any more. And when I have to do the work myself there won't be any time left for such "foolishness" as going to school. I told him that I'm willing to do my own washing but that I would still be able to find time for study.

When I am alone with my thoughts, I feel I may not be right. Perhaps I should not go to school. I want to say that my husband is an intelligent man and he wanted to marry a woman who was educated. The fact that he is intelligent makes me more annoyed with him. He is in favor of the emancipation of women, yet in real life he acts contrary to his beliefs.

Awaiting your opinion on this, I remain,

Your reader,
The Discontented Wife

Answer

Since this man is intelligent and an adherent of the women's emancipation movement, he is scolded severely in the answer for wanting to keep his wife so enslaved. Also the opinion is expressed that the wife absolutely has the right to go to school two evenings a week.

1910

Dear Editor,

I am an operator on ladies' waists for the past four years and I earn good wages. I work steady but haven't saved money, because I have a sick wife. I had to put her in the hospital where she lay for four weeks, and then I had to bring her home.

Just after I brought her home, the General Strike began and I could see that I was in trouble. I had to go to the union to beg them not to let me down in my situation. I just asked for some money to have a little soup for my sick wife, but they answered that there wasn't any money. I struggled along with my wife for four weeks, and when I saw that I might lose her I had to go back to work at the shop where we were striking. Now my conscience bothers me because I am a scab.

I am working now, I bring home fifteen, sometimes sixteen dollars a week. But I am not happy, because I was a scab and left the union. I want to state here that I was always a good union man.

Dear Editor, how can I now go back in the union and salve my conscience? I am ready to swear that I will remain a loyal union man forever.

Your reader,
F.H.

Answer

Neither the operator nor the union is guilty. During the strike, thousands upon thousands of workers complained that they were in need, but at the beginning of the strike there really was no money.

It is now the duty of the union to investigate the case, and if it is shown that circumstances were as the operator describes, they will certainly forgive him and he can again become a good union man.

1913

Dear Editor,

I come from Europe, where I was brought up by a father who was a *Talmud* scholar and a cantor. I took after my father both in learning and voice, and when I became a *Bar Mitzvah* my leading the congregation in prayer impressed everyone. My name became known in many cities and people came to hear me conduct the services.

When I turned eighteen a respected man from a town near Kovne took me as a son-in-law, gave me four hundred rubles and five years of room and board. I married his pretty sixteen-year-old daughter, moved into my father-in-law's house, ate, drank and devoted myself to the study of *Torah*. Once in a while, on a special Sabbath or a holiday, I led the prayers in *shul*, but I took no money for that.

After the five years I was left with a pretty young wife, two children and my dowry money. My father-in-law then established for me, or I should say for my wife, a small grocery and told me, "You will continue to study *Torah* and your wife will make a living for you." But my wife wasn't very good at business and the money went fast. Meanwhile, my father-in-law died, my mother-in-law went to her son in Kovne, and we were left alone.

I began to talk to my wife about going to America and after long deliberation we left home. When we came to this country, our *landsleit* helped us a little to get settled and when the High Holy Days came, I earned a hundred and eighty dollars as a cantor leading the *Musaph* prayers. I began to make a living as a cantor, and people hired me for weddings, funerals and other affairs.

As time went on my horizons broadened. I read all kinds of books, I accumulated worldly knowledge and I began to look at life quite differently.

In short, I can't reconcile myself to continue making a living as a cantor, because I am no longer religious. I can't act against my conscience, and the right thing to do is to give up my present livelihood. I want to learn a trade now, perhaps become a peddler or find another means of earning a living that has nothing to do with religion.

My wife, who held onto her old beliefs and is still fanatical, doesn't even want to hear of my plans. She argues that serving as a cantor is honorable. It is also questionable whether I can earn enough to support a family from working in a shop or from peddling.

Now there are arguments about this between me, my wife and our close friends, and we all decided to place the question in your hands. I want to hear what you have to say about it.

Your reader,
The Progressive Cantor

Answer

Freethinkers as well as religious people will answer this question in the same way. Even the rabbi will say that, according to Jewish law, only a pious Jew may be a cantor. His wife and his religious friends who are trying to convince him to remain a cantor are really committing the worst sin according to their beliefs.

For a non-believer to be a cantor for an Orthodox congregation is without a doubt a shameful hypocrisy.

Bibliography for Further Reading

Cohen, Naomi. *Encounter with Emancipation,* Jewish Publication Society, 1984

———. *Not Free to Desist,* Jewish Publication Society, 1972

Dinnerstein, Leonard. *The Leo Frank Case,* University of Georgia Press, 1987

Evans, Eli. *Judah P. Benjamin,* The Free Press, 1989

Hertzberg, Arthur. *The Jews in America,* Simon and Schuster, 1989

Howe, Irving. *World of Our Fathers,* Simon and Schuster, 1976

Joselit, Jenna. *Our Gang,* Indiana University Press, 1983

Kraut, Benny. *From Reform Judaism to Ethical Culture: The Religious Evolution of Felix Adler,* Hebrew Union College Press, 1979

Sachar, Howard. *A History of the Jews in America,* Knopf, 1992

Unit XXX

Conservative Judaism and Reconstructionism

Conservative Judaism

The most distinctly American expression of Judaism and Jewish religious thought became known as Conservative Judaism. To be sure, Conservative Judaism did claim roots in nineteenth-century Germany, particularly in the "historical school" of Zechariah Frankel. At the Breslau Jewish Theological Seminary Frankel insisted upon the utilization of scientific scholarship in the study of rabbinic Judaism. Judaism, for Frankel, had evolved historically over time, and some changes in Jewish law were both desirable and necessary, so long as they were evolutionary rather than revolutionary. Moreover, Frankel emphasized Jewry as a people and nationality, arguing that Reform Judaism had robbed Judaism of its essence by denying Jewish peoplehood.

However, despite some similarities in curriculum between the Jewish Theological Seminary of Breslau and the Jewish Theological Seminary of America, Conservative Judaism evolved essentially as an American religious movement. The American value of pluralism suggested that there was more than one version of Jewish tradition, and that religious change can occur within the framework of tradition. Advocates for Conservative Judaism, such as Solomon Schechter, a scholar and rabbi who was brought over from England in 1902 to head the American Jewish Theological Seminary, argued that history and community remained critical authorities for determining what is Jewishly legitimate and acceptable. Religious change could not be permitted to do violence to the record of Jewish history. Conversely, no change was acceptable unless it was acceptable to "catholic Israel," meaning the Jewish community at large in its universal and historical senses. For example, rather than eliminate references to sacrifices from the liturgy, as was done in Reform Judaism, Conservative Judaism historicized the sacrificial rite. Prayers related to sacrifices noted that these were performed in the historical past. We remember that time, but we do not pray for the restoration of sacrifices.

Clearly, Conservative Judaism was not Orthodoxy. It was not prepared to accept the binding authority of tradition on every matter. Nor, however, could Conservative Judaism accept the liberalism of Reform Judaism. It continued to define itself as a religious movement governed in accordance with Jewish law. Even in the limited areas where change in Jewish law was regarded as desirable—permitting individuals to drive to and from the synagogue on Shabbat, or eating cooked dairy foods in non-kosher restaurants—these changes were justified on the grounds of necessary historical accommodations. They did not suggest that Conservative Judaism revered the authority of *halacha* any less than did the Orthodox.

In theory, then, Conservative Judaism was meant to appeal to those Jews who desired to govern their lives in accordance with *halacha* but were also open to the critical study of the Bible and Talmud and were prepared for limited modifications in Jewish law in light of historical scholarship. In practice, however, Conservative Judaism never became this "left" side of Orthodoxy. It failed to create a core of committed *halachic* Jews who governed their lives in accordance with Jewish law, as the Orthodox had done. Rather Conservative Judaism appealed to acculturated American Jews who desired the survival of their ethnic group and wished to associate with other Jews, but who were not prepared to accept the binding authority of Jewish law. These middle-class suburban Jews found Reform Judaism to be too upper-class socially and too removed spiritually from the concerns of Jewish peoplehood. They desired a movement that was more ethnically Jewish, committed to the principles of Zionism, and conducive to a wholly Jewish atmosphere for the raising of their children. For these Jews, the intellectual questions of Jewish scholarship and its implications for *halacha* were far less important than finding appropriate institutions and vehicles that would permit them to express their identification with the collective Jewish people. Therefore, the intellectual and ideological dimensions of the movement were far more salient for the Conservative rabbinate and for the Jewish Theological Seminary than they ever became for the Conservative laity. The end result was a wide gap in religious observance between Conservative rabbis committed to *halacha* and a middle-class laity desiring more an ethnic church than a body of responsa or *halachic* guidelines.

Conservative Judaism, therefore, became a middle way between Reform and Orthodoxy. Culturally, Conservative Jews were far removed both from the German upper classes that dominated Reform and the religiously observant Orthodox Jews. Conservative Jews were generally of East European background. They accepted and welcomed incorporation of American patterns. They had generally left the initial area of settlement in major cities and were now moving toward the suburbs. They feared that growing Americanization might well mean the assimilation and intermarriage of their progeny. They turned to Conservative Judaism, not to provide *halacha* but a stronger sense of *Yiddishkeit*. For that reason, Zionism did not pose a problem for Conservative Jews. They did not want Zionism as a refuge for themselves, because they felt that America, indeed, was different. However, Zionism did provide them a stronger sense of peoplehood and Jewish identity. This type of cultural Zionism would strengthen the traditions of pluralism out of which Conservative Judaism had sprung and, in turn, strengthen commitments to Jewish peoplehood and identity.

The ideological problems of Conservative Judaism were apparent from its beginnings. The very concept of "catholic Israel" was paradoxical. Schechter invoked "catholic Israel" so that change should occur only in accordance with the expressed will of the Jewish people and community over the ages. For example, the holiday of Purim may lack historical foundation. However, Jews ought to continue to observe it because it represents the inherited body of Jewish practices over the centuries. Whether Purim was historical fact or fiction was not really the issue. What mattered was that Jews had believed in Purim as a redemptive holiday for over 2,000 years. The history of the celebration of Purim for over two millennia outweighs doubts concerning its historicity.

The paradox of the concept of "catholic Israel" ought to be readily apparent. A majority of Jews today do not govern their lives in accordance with *halacha.* To ask, therefore, what Jews have done would, by definition, define catholic Israel as breaking with the authority of Jewish law. Or, to press the example further, most Jews today simply do not observe Purim at all. The logic of catholic Israel would mean the dismantling of Jewish law as irrelevant to the lives of Jews today. Efforts by Conservative Jews to find guidance in Jewish law would make far more sense within Orthodoxy than within Conservative Judaism. For example, Conservative Judaism rejected patrilineal descent as a violation of Jewish history and Jewish law. Yet if the overwhelming majority of Jews today in America accept patrilineality, would not the concept of catholic Israel necessitate such a change?

Conservative leaders were sensitive to this paradox. They redefined the doctrine of catholic Israel to mean the community of Jews committed to Jewish law. Unfortunately, the redefinition does not resolve the paradox. The community of Jews today committed to *halacha* is far too small to define itself as "catholic Israel."

The contradiction remains between the ideology of Conservative Judaism and the practices of its adherents. Conservative Judaism today is largely split between those who proclaim it a movement governed by Jewish law and those who argue that its future direction must be "post-halachic" in nature. Those who advocate the continued salience of Jewish law and the binding authority of *halacha* note that Conservative Judaism can never relativize *halacha.* Constraints against patrilineal descent, for example, or homosexuals in the rabbinate must continue because these behaviors are proscribed by *halacha.* To be sure, they acknowledge that significant changes were made, particularly in granting women full opportunities at participation in public liturgy. However, they caution that egalitarianism with respect to women does not connote widespread change in the nature of Jewish law. The critical document for these traditionalists within the movement is the current statement of principles, *Emet V'emunah,* a doctrinal statement adopted in the mid-1980's defining Conservative Judaism as a *halachic* movement, despite the inclusion of women in the rabbinate and granting women full opportunities to participate equally with men in the liturgical services. *Emet V'emunah* defined the Conservative Jew as a questing Jew, constantly looking to Jewish sources and heritage for guidance in confronting day-to-day decision-making.

Liberals within the movement, who argue for a "post-halachic" stance, evoke a far more radical concept of religious pluralism. They argue that once one has broken with a fundamentalist reading of Jewish text, all norms are subject to revision and reevaluation. If we do not believe that the snake spoke to Eve in the Garden of Eden, then we are not bound to accept literally virtually any of the laws in Scripture or Talmud. All are subject to review and reevaluation. To be sure, liberal-minded Conservative Jews argue that most of Jewish law and tradition remains salient. However, they are far more willing to revise Jewish law in accordance with contemporary times. If all of Torah constitutes an extended *midrash,* portions of it may legitimately be abandoned if the *midrash* no longer possesses salience. Thus advocates of this vision of Conservative Judaism, such as Rabbi Neil Gillman, a professor of Jewish theology at Jewish Theological Seminary, argue vigorously that strictures against homosexuality in Jewish tradition represent only outmoded myths or taboos. If this *midrash,* for example, no longer possesses salience, there ought be no bars to inclusion of homosexuals as rabbis or clergy. Opponents argue that Jewish tradition and law remain binding, and therefore Judaism cannot attach the status of "sanctified marriage" to homosexual relationships, much less sponsor gay synagogues or clergy.

Therefore the debate continues. *Emet V'emunah* represents a triumph for the traditionalists. The document affirms Conservative Judaism as normative, albeit open to limited changes. It calls upon Conservative Jews to study seriously Jewish tradition and to become literate in their heritage. It promotes gender equality, but that is the primary arena in which contemporary change occurs. In most other respects, the Conservative Jew is enjoined to conduct his or her lifestyle in accordance with the norms of traditional Jewish law. Lastly, *Emet V'emunah* affirms Jewish chosenness. The Jews remain a unique and distinctive people, and no apology is necessary for affirming chosenness. On the contrary, the doctrine of the chosen people retains its power to bestow the Jewish people with a special and particular mission distinguishing them from gentiles.

How then do we evaluate Conservative Judaism? Conservative Judaism retains the largest number of affiliated (as opposed to self-defined) Jews today. More Jews are affiliated with Conservative synagogues than with any other religious movement. In addition to numbers, Conservative Judaism boasts several institutional and educational accomplishments. The network of Solomon Schechter Day Schools provides quality forms of Jewish education in non-Orthodox settings to Jews across the country. The Ramah Camps have proven to be among the most effective forms of informal education, creating viable Conservative communities. The Jewish Theological Seminary has not only trained rabbis but has also served as a first-rate center of Judaic scholarship. Similarly, the inclusion of women in the rabbinate provided a major new resource for enhancing Jewish communal life.

Yet the weaknesses within the movement remain apparent. The movement suffers from an ongoing gap of observance between laity and the rabbinate. Perhaps most tellingly, there are very few Conservative communities in America today. The Ramah camps are an exception, but they build self-contained communities only for three months during the year. In contrast to Orthodoxy, which has built vibrant communities, Conservative Jewry has strengthened itself institutionally even while the human ties within those institutions remain relatively weak. Certainly, the movement has never created communities of committed *halachic* Jews sharing the Jewish calendar and life-cycle together. Informal communities such as the *havurot*, while important, are far too small to define the movement.

Defining the movement today are synagogues that create an address for young Jewish families anxious to raise Jewish children. They wish an authentically Jewish environment to assist them in strengthening their families. Seen from the top down, Conservative Judaism is failing to sustain Jews committed to Jewish law. Seen from the bottom up, however, it is succeeding in strengthening Jews as Jews, committed to the Jewish people, to raising Jewish children, and to looking to the synagogue as resource and buffer in an often unfriendly universe.

In many ways the future of American Jewry will be determined by the winds of change within the Conservative movement. To the extent that the movement creates strong Jewish families committed to Jewish continuity, it holds the potential to secure the future of American Jewry. To the extent it is unable to sustain Jews as Jews, it raises the prospect of a declining American Jewry that will continue to suffer serious losses via erosion and assimilation.

Reconstructionism

The founder of Reconstructionist Judaism was Mordecai Kaplan, who, in his 1934 book, *Judaism as a Civilization,* argued that all the religious movements were flawed and that Judaism required fundamental reconstruction upon the principle of being a unique civilization. For Kaplan, modern Jews could no longer believe in the doctrine of a chosen people and Divine revelation. He redefined God as the principal life force behind the universe, rather than a God of history and revelation. The Jews were not chosen but rather formed a distinctive civilization with unique heritage, customs, folkways, and culture. The synagogue, in Kaplan's view, ought be reconstructed as a "synagogue center" for the Jewish people, encompassing all forms of the Jewish civilization including art, music, and dance. American Jews, Kaplan argued, live in two civilizations—the American and the Jewish. Both must be preserved, and any expression of Judaism that requires denial of that American civilization will be doomed to failure. *Halacha,* for Kaplan, possessed a voice rather than a veto. Jews ought consult tradition for guidance and inspiration, but tradition did not possess compelling authority. Jews today must ask whether their tradition speaks persuasively to modern conditions. They can never be content with the simple answer that tradition commands it.

Kaplan did not anticipate a new religious movement. He had been ordained and practiced as an Orthodox rabbi and served as a faculty member at the Conservative Jewish Theological Seminary. He hoped that all of the movements would accept the principles of Reconstructionism. Because of his close ties with JTS, he was most reluctant to establish a fourth religious movement.

Therefore, the number of practicing Reconstructionist Jews and existing Reconstructionist synagogues has remained small. Only in the latter part of Kaplan's life did Reconstructionism begin to obtain the institutional trappings of a religious movement. A rabbinical school, the Reconstructionist Rabbinical College, was established in Philadelphia in 1968. Today there are approximately 70 affiliated Reconstructionist congregations and approximately 120 ordained Reconstructionist rabbis.

Kaplan's successes, however, go far beyond the institutional trappings of Reconstructionism as a religious movement. In many ways he captured the "folk theology" of today's American Jews.

They wish to be Jewish and to associate with other Jews. Kaplan's Zionism expresses their identification with Israel as a Jewish state, despite their lack of motivation to settle there. Zionism, for Kaplan, became a critical component of the Jewish civilization and an expression of how Jews perceive themselves in American society. Lastly, American Jews do live in two civilizations. They wish to preserve both components of their identity.

Similarly, Kaplan has had a significant impact upon the institutional fabric of Jewish communal life. Synagogues in all the movements have been created in Kaplan's image as centers of the Jewish people rather than simply houses of worship. To be sure, Kaplan would decry the materialism and absence of serious culture within today's Jewish institutions. However, the notion of a synagogue serving the needs of the entire Jewish family rather than catering strictly to liturgical needs has been widely adopted within each of the movements.

What then can one say of the Reconstructionist movement itself? Reconstructionism today has gone far beyond Kaplan in its theology. Reconstructionism harbors a number of contrasting and often conflicting theological currents. Some Reconstructionists have rediscovered Jewish mysticism and Hasidism—trends pronouncedly in contrast to Kaplan's rationalism. Reconstructionism today builds upon the human existential need to know there is a God to whom one can meaningfully relate. The movement is far more spiritual and "New Age" in its theology and religiosity than in Kaplan's day. For many Jews unconnected with Jewish communal life, Reconstructionism provides a significant point of entry and affiliation.

Aside from obvious institutional weaknesses in terms of numbers and Reconstructionist settings, Reconstructionism suffers ideologically from the issue of the limits, if any, to religious pluralism. It is unclear to many whether Reconstructionism will say no to virtually anything that Jews happen to do. For example, alone among the religious movements, Reconstructionism approves of rabbis participating in civil services of mixed-marriages. Perhaps even more controversial have been Reconstructionist attitudes toward homosexuality. Alone of rabbinical seminaries, the Reconstructionist Rabbinical College admits students without reference to sexual orientation. Specifically, Reform Judaism believes that the community should include gays and lesbians, including granting them clergy status, but it states clearly that heterosexuality must be the preferred norm for Jews. By contrast, Reconstructionism sees no distinctions Judaically between heterosexual and homosexual relationships.

Opponents argue that in refusing to establish any preferred sanctified status, Reconstructionism has adopted a religious relativism in which there are no boundaries to what Jews may do. Reconstructionism itself states there are clear demands, expectations, and norms for Reconstructionist Jews. Insistence upon absolute gender equality is one such norm. Concern for preserving the environment constitutes a second category of expectations and commitments for Reconstructionist Jews. In that sense, Reconstructionist Judaism perceives itself as preserving the best of the religious movements—Orthodox intensity of community, Conservative emphasis upon study, and Reform commitment to social action. Only time will tell whether these initiatives will sustain Jewish continuity. Kaplan's legacy today constitutes a dual challenge: Reach out to alienated groups and, at the same time, define the parameters and boundaries of Jewish civilization.

Reading: *Emet V'emunah*

Emet V'emunah *is a 1988 doctrinal statement of Conservative Judaism. It generally emphasizes continued commitment to* halacha, *or Jewish law, but within an egalitarian context. Conservative Judaism, therefore, remains faithful to its grounding in Jewish law, but the statement argues that changes must be made to ensure gender equality. Note, in particular, the conclusion of the document that the Conservative Jew remains striving to enhance observance and knowledge of Judaic tradition.*

The Ideal Conservative Jew

> Throughout most of its history, Jewish life was an organic unity of home and community, synagogue and law. Since the Emancipation, however, Judaism has been marked by increasing fragmentation. Not only do we find Jewish groups pitted against one another, but the ways in which we apprehend Judaism itself have become separate and distinct. That unified

platform upon which a holistic Jewish life was lived has been shattered. Participating in a majority culture whose patterns and rhythms often undermine our own, we are forced to live in two worlds, replacing whole and organic Judaism with fragments: ritual observance or Zionism, philanthropy or group defense; each necessary, none sufficient in itself.

Facing this reality, Conservative Judaism came into being to create a new synthesis in Jewish life. Rather than advocate assimilation, or yearn for the isolation of a new ghetto, Conservative Judaism is a creative force through which modernity and tradition inform and reshape each other.

During the last century and a half, we have built a host of institutions to formulate and express and embody our quest. As important as these are, they in themselves cannot create the new Jewish wholeness that we seek. In spite of the condition of modern life, we must labor zealously to cultivate wholeness in Jewish personalities.

Three characteristics mark the ideal Conservative Jew. First, he or she is a *willing* Jew, whose life echoes the dictum, "Nothing human or Jewish is alien to me." This willingness involves not only a commitment to observe the *mitzvot* and to advance Jewish concerns, but to refract all aspects of life through the prism of one's own Jewishness. That person's life pulsates with the rhythms of daily worship and Shabbat and *Yom Tov.* The moral imperatives of our tradition impel that individual to universal concern and deeds of social justice. The content of that person's professional dealings and communal involvements is shaped by the values of our faith and conditioned by the observance of *kashrut,* of Shabbat and the holidays. That person's home is filled with Jewish books, art, music and ritual objects. Particularly in view of the increasing instability of the modern family, the Jewish home must be sustained and guided by the ethical insights of our heritage.

The second mark of the ideal Conservative Jew is that he or she is a *learning* Jew. One who cannot read Hebrew is denied the full exaltation of our Jewish worship and literary heritage. One who is ignorant of our classics cannot be affected by their message. One who is not acquainted with contemporary Jewish thought and events will be blind to the challenges and opportunities which lie before us. Jewish learning is a lifelong quest through which we integrate Jewish and general knowledge for the sake of personal enrichment, group creativity and world transformation.

Finally, the ideal Conservative Jew is a *striving* Jew. No matter the level at which one starts, no matter the heights of piety and knowledge one attains, no one can perform all 613 *mitzvot* or acquire all Jewish knowledge. What is needed is an openness to those observances one has yet to perform and the desire to grapple with those issues and texts one has yet to confront. Complacency is the mother of stagnation and the antithesis of Conservative Judaism.

Given our changing world, finality and certainty are illusory at best, destructive at worst. Rather than claiming to have found a goal at the end of the road, the ideal Conservative Jew is a traveler walking purposefully towards "God's holy mountain."

Bibliography for Further Reading

Gillman, Neil. *Conservative Judaism,* Behrman Books, 1993

———. *Sacred Fragments,* Jewish Publication Society, 1990

Green, Arthur. "Spirituality" in *Contemporary Jewish Religious Thought,* ed. by Arthur A. Cohen and Paul Mendes-Flohr, Scribners, 1987

Hauptman, Judith. "Women and the Conservative Synagogue" in *Daughters of the King: Women and the Synagogue,* ed. by Susan Grossman and Rivka Haut, Jewish Publication Society, 1992

Kaplan, Mordecai M. *Judaism as a Civilization,* Jewish Publication Society/Reconstructionist Press, 1981

Liebman, Charles. "Reconstructionism in American Jewish Life," in Jacob Neusner ed., *Understanding American Judaism,* Volume II, KTAV, n.d.

Schorsch, Ismar. "Zachariah Frankel and the European Origins of Conservative Judaism," *From Text to Context,* Brandeis University Press, 1994

Sklare, Marshall. *Conservative Judaism,* Schocken, 1985

Wertheimer, Jack. *A People Divided,* Basic Books, 1993

Unit XXXI

Jewry and the Soviet Union

The Russian Revolution

During World War I, the Allies promised their Jewish communities that after their victory over Germany they would raise the question of the treatment of Jews within Czarist Russia. Conditions, however, within Russia quickly deteriorated. Over 100,000 Jews died during the war because of expulsions and starvation. In 1915 Germany conquered the Pale of Settlement. Conditions within the Pale became progressively more desperate, and 70,000 Jews were forcibly transferred from Russia to Germany.

Jews initially supported the Kerensky Revolution and subsequently the Bolshevik Revolution of November 1917. In theory, the Bolsheviks brought emancipation to Russian Jewry and outlawed anti-Semitism. In practice, Vladimir Lenin waged "war Communism" against Judaism, as he did against organized religion generally. The *kehillah* was dissolved. Synagogues were closed, as were *mikvaot*, or ritual baths. Similarly ritual slaughter, circumcision, and Hebrew education all were forced to go underground.

In their place, Lenin created Yiddish schools to disseminate the Communist ideology. The *Yevsektsia*, or Jewish Sections of the Communist Party, suppressed Jewish organizational life. Yiddish itself remained a national language of Russia. As late as 1959, the Russian census indicated that 18 percent of Russian Jews listed Yiddish as their mother tongue. This, of course, was down from 97 percent in the 1897 census.

During the Russian Civil War, Jews suffered enormously from

the anti-Semitism of the Russian White Army trying to effect a counter-revolution. Similarly, the Ukrainian National Army, commanded by Simon Petlyura, committed massive pogroms against Jews in the Ukraine. The Bolsheviks themselves launched quick moves to counter anti-Semitism within their own armies. Jews, however, were caught between the Ukrainian National Army and the counter-revolutionary forces. Only the failure of the Ukrainian independence movement brought some measure of security to Jews. It is estimated that over 200,000 Jews were killed during the Civil War, which lasted four years, featuring regular pogroms against Jews. Seven hundred fifty thousand were made homeless by the Civil War, and 28 percent of Jewish houses were burned. Although the Red Army committed its own share of excesses, it did succeed in bringing anti-Semitism to a halt.

The Bund itself initially had high hopes for the Kerensky regime. As a result, the Bund campaigned for the Constituent Assembly, whose non-Bolshevik majority was forcibly disbanded by the Bolsheviks in January 1918. By 1919 the Bund had accepted the Soviet Government. Under the leadership of Esther Frumkin, who had earlier urged Jews to light Sabbath candles on Friday night in order to bring the message of the revolution to the Jewish street, the Bund offered to join the Communist Party. The Bolsheviks denied the request of the Bund to preserve its autonomy, and the Bundists were able to join only as individuals. By 1921 the Communist Party ordered the Bund disbanded.

The Bolsheviks hoped that emancipation would lead to the quick assimilation of Soviet Jewry. They assumed that Lenin's New Economic Program would bring benefits to Jews economically. The Jewish Sections were charged with suppressing Jewish organizations and combatting Russian Zionism. Ex-Bundists, such as Esther Frumkin, were prominent within the leadership of the Jewish Sections. She hoped that Socialism would transform the Jews into a proletariat element. Therefore she agreed to direct the Jewish Sections' anti-religious campaign. Were the Jewish sections not led by Jews, their policies would clearly have labeled them as anti-Semitic.

The New Economic Program did attempt to bring Jews into agriculture. A 1924 Commission on Jewish Labor recommended that Jews be brought into farming occupations. One-half million Jews were therefore transferred to the Ukraine and the Crimea.

Efforts to regenerate Jewry there floundered, however, and were subsequently abandoned because of local anti-Semitism.

Stalin and the Jews

Leonid Trotsky was the best-known Jew within the revolutionary leadership. His father had insisted upon his receiving a minimal Jewish education. Trotsky was obsessed with anti-Jewish pogroms and was convinced that the "Jewish question" would be solved only via the revolution of the working classes. He clashed with the Bund over the question of Jewish cultural autonomy and denied the Jews were a people. He feared that domestic anti-Semitism would increase in the Soviet Union and therefore refused to direct the Bureau of Internal Affairs, for fear of inciting further anti-Semitism. Without question, Trotsky acted quickly to check pogroms within the Russian Army. He also opposed the forcible assimilation policy of the Jewish Sections. More generally, Trotsky lacked the bitter Jewish self-hatred that his colleague Rosa Luxemberg expressed in Germany.

Yet we should by no means romanticize Trotsky. He believed in "permanent revolution," hoping that Bolshevism would spread from country to country. Like Luxemberg, he argued that nationalism by definition was retrograde. He typified what Isaac Deutscher referred to as "the non-Jewish Jew." His very change of name from Bronstein to Trotsky expressed his feelings of alienation from Jewish heritage and peoplehood. He refused the request of a Leningrad rabbi to raise the Jewish question within the Bolshevik Party. He continued to defend the Soviet Union, even after the Nazi-Soviet pact and after the invasion of Finland. Rabbi Stephen Wise, in his obituary, probably captured his alienation best: "He knew not Israel, and Israel mourns not his grave."

Yet Trotsky's defeat at the hands of Stalin clearly marked a setback for the position of Jewry within the Soviet Union. Jews were generally not found in Stalin's following. They repudiated the narrowness of his vision of "Socialism in one country," preferring the permanent revolution advocated by Trotsky. Stalin did launch the ill-fated Birobidzhan venture in 1928 to proclaim an autonomous Jewish republic in Siberia. Most likely his motives were to deflect attention from Zionism, restratify Jewry out of the middle class, and create a buffer against potential Chinese and Japanese expansion.

By 1937 some 18,000 Jews had settled in Birobidzhan. However, the experiment clearly was a failure. Conditions were not ripe for Jewish settlement, and the Jews who went there were poorly trained and received inadequate support. Although Birobidzhan would continue through the postwar years, it did more to raise the hopes of Jews abroad than improve the conditions domestically of Soviet Jewry.

Moreover, Stalin's purges in the 1930's eliminated Jewry from leadership positions within the Communist Party. Within the senior ranks of the Communist Party, Lazar Kagonovitch, Stalin's trusted henchman, remained the sole Jew in a position of power and influence. Kagonovitch enjoyed family relationships with Stalin, and, coupled with his personal loyalty, was able to escape all of the Stalinist purges. In 1930, the Jewish Sections themselves were disbanded, charged with Trotskyite leanings. Esther Frumkin herself was imprisoned during these purges.

The cultural stagnation of Soviet Jewry continued. Very few were able to maintain a traditional life-style although, through the efforts of Lubavitch, a modicum of Jewish observance persisted. The Soviet government attacked Jewish culture as a nationalist deviation. Zionism was outlawed, and Hebrew books were suppressed. Circumcision or attendance at synagogues would generally lead to banishment from the party and the loss of employment. The mass base of Russian Jewry remained uncircumcised and uneducated Jewishly. As a transitional agency, the *Yevsektsia* had succeeded in destroying the Jewish community and bringing the revolution to the Jewish street. Subsequently, it too was betrayed by Stalin.

In the mountain areas, blood libels and pogroms resurged in the 1920's. Mountain Jews appealed to the central Moscow government against local officials who revived medieval anti-Semitic imagery. By the 1930's the Stalinist government itself had abandoned the earlier campaign against anti-Semitism and permitted the revival of anti-Semitic stereotypes and prejudices. Convicted anti-Semites received at most light sentences. The purges themselves required anti-Semitic targets in order to focus their hatreds and resentments. This is probably the origin of the "Goldstein" character in George Orwell's novel *1984*.

The 1939 Nazi-Soviet Pact brought unintended consequences for Soviet Jewry. As Poland was again partitioned between Germany and Russia, Russia absorbed an additional 2,000,000 Jewish citizens. These Jews had not been exposed to two decades of Bolshevik assimilation, and most vigorously adhered to their Jewishness and Jewish identity.

The non-aggression pact between Russia and Nazi Germany also silenced Jewish protests against Hitler. Previously, Soviet propaganda had protested Hitler's anti-Semitism. Maxim Litvinov, the Jewish foreign minister, was removed from office, signaling sensitivity to Hitler's racialism.

Operation Barbarossa, or Hitler's attack upon the Soviet Union in June 1941, brought terrible effects upon Soviet Jewry. The *Einsatzgruppen,* or mobile killing units, accompanied the German army rounding up Jews in areas where the German army had conquered, forcing them to dig large pits outside of the town and then shooting them into the pits. Approximately 1,500,000 Jews died through the *Einsatzgruppen* massacres. The best-known of these massacres occurred at Babi Yar in the Ukraine.

Particularly dismaying to Jews was the role of Ukrainian bystanders. Some delighted in collaborating with Hitler in revenge against the Soviet Union for denying Ukrainian independence and as vengeance for the assassination of the Ukrainian national hero Simon Petluria by a Jew in Paris in 1926. The Nazis, in fact, utilized anti-Semitism to curry favor with the local Ukrainian populace. The Ukrainian partisan movement was infamous for killing Jews, Soviet prisoners of war, and Poles. Ukrainian collaborationists blamed Jewish Communists such as Maxim Litinov and Lazar Kaganovitch for starting the war. The Babi Yar massacre was based on the libel that Jews had desecrated Kiev and burned houses.

The Soviet Government did little to avert the Final Solution. It did create the Jewish Anti-Fascist Committee to publicize and condemn Nazi atrocities. The Anti-Fascist Committee was headed by Ilya Ehrenburg, the leading Soviet Jew in the arts and letters. It documented Nazi atrocities through the so-called "Black Book," which was publicized in the West, as part of the committee's efforts to renew Jewish culture. Stalin hoped that the Jewish Anti-Fascist Committee would rally the support of world Jewry against Hitler. Again, this was an example of what some might call "constructive anti-Semitism," namely exaggerating the influence of the Jews out of all proportion to reality.

In the initial postwar years, Stalin continued his relatively benign policy of permitting Jewish culture to flourish. Solomon Mikhoels led the revival of the Yiddish theater. Additional support was given to Birobidzhan, which witnessed an influx of an additional 10,000 Jews. Most significant, of course, was Stalin's support for the creation of Israel. This was probably an effort to diminish British influence in the Middle East, in the hope that a Jewish state would be more likely to be sympathetic to Soviet interests. Zionism, however, remained officially outlawed within the Soviet Union. By contrast, in the Soviet satellites, all Jews were free to emigrate to Palestine.

The years following 1948 have commonly been known as the "black years" of Soviet Jewry. Once again purges were launched against Jews in public life. Jews were barred from the foreign service, from the general staff, and from the Politburo. The Anti-Fascist Committee was suppressed, and Jewish culture again went underground. Stalin now identified the Jews as cosmopolitan nationalists, claiming that Jews looked abroad to America and to Israel. Ehrenburg, for example, was warned against his ties with Jews elsewhere.

The reception accorded Golda Meir as first Israeli Ambassador to Moscow by the Soviet Jewish community typified this cosmopolitanism. Jews demonstrated their heart-felt attachment to the Jewish people and the Jewish state through support for Golda Meir. To Stalin, this symbolized continued Jewish internationalism and cosmopolitanism and a deficiency in Soviet patriotism.

The black years extended to the Soviet satellites. In Czechoslovakia, the infamous Slansky trials occurred, with Jewish Communists charged with Zionist sympathies. Rudolf Slansky himself was bitterly hostile to Zionism. Nevertheless, he and his associates were charged with betraying Communist interests on behalf of international Zionist concerns. In one of the most incredible ironies of Cold War history, Jean-Paul Sartre and other French leftists declared that the Rosenbergs (Julius and Ethel) in America were being tried only because of anti-Semitic sentiment, while the Slansky trials were regarded as fair and just. In later years, Sartre regretted his excessive sympathy for the left and hostility to Zionism and Israel. However, his protest against the Rosenberg trial, when placed alongside his silence during the Slansky trials, reflects an incredible lack of judgment and a double standard.

The culmination of the black years was the "Doctors' Plot" of

1953. Stalin charged that a group of leading Soviet Jewish physicians were planning to poison Soviet leaders. The plot apparently served as a pretext for further purges and deportations, although these were opposed by Stalin's lieutenants Nikita Khrushchev and Lazar Kagonovitch. Stalin died before the full implications of the Doctors' Plot could be implemented.

The black years were limited to attacks upon secular Jewish culture. Religious culture was left relatively untouched. Perhaps Stalin feared the pressure of world reaction. He did enlist rabbis to praise the virtues of the Soviet regime. He also may have felt that religion was doomed in any case. Conversely, he worried about Zionism and Jewish peoplehood. For example, the wife of Stalin's Foreign Minister, Vyacheslav Mikhailovich Molotov, a Jewish woman, was exiled on account of her friendship with Golda Meir.

Soviet Jewry after Stalin

Khrushchev revoked the Doctors' Plot and charged Stalin with anti-Semitism, among a litany of other crimes. However, Khrushchev completed Stalin's work in eliminating Jews from key positions within Soviet leadership. He also reinstated the anti-religious campaign, closing rabbinical schools and banning the production of *matzot* for the Passover holiday. In Poland, Khrushchev urged Polish Communists to emulate the Soviet Union by purging Jews from leadership positions. Similarly, he blamed Jews for fomenting the 1956 Hungarian Revolution. In the early 1960's, Khrushchev charged Jews with economic crimes, such as black marketeering within the Soviet Union. While all Communist countries had underground economies because of rigid socialist legislation, the USSR singled out Jews for undermining socialism. Of the 250 individuals executed for economic crimes, 50 percent were Jewish.

The Leonid Brezhnev years witnessed the rise of a Soviet Jewish dissident movement and the pressure for the right of emigration from the Soviet Union. The 1966 Soviet census revealed that there were still 2,675,000 Jews within the USSR. These had many reasons for wanting to leave. Some were ideologically convinced of the bankruptcy of the Soviet system and desired to lead their lives in the Jewish homeland. Natan Sharansky became a symbol of these prisoners of Zion. Others became convinced that economic opportunities were simply not available for Jews within the Soviet

Union, where an unofficial quota system limited Jewish presence in many professions. A small minority wished to recover their Jewish religious roots. The holiday of Simchat Torah became a symbol of an outpouring of Soviet Jewish sentiment. Although intermarriage was quite high within the Soviet Union and Soviet Jewish identity seemed sustained primarily by the pressure of anti-Semitism, Simchat Torah signaled a reservoir of Jewishness among Soviet Jews waiting to be reunited with the Jewish people.

Soviet Jewish emigration remained very much a function of Cold War politics. The Soviet Government could not countenance unrestricted Jewish emigration. For Jews to leave meant not only a loss of talent but also communicated to the subject minorities of the Soviet empire that the Soviet Union was anything but a workers' paradise. Conversely, a liberalized emigration policy brought the Soviet Union into closer relations with the United States. The Jackson-Vanik Amendment conditioned the granting of most-favored-nation status to the Soviet Union, exempting her from trade tariffs, upon liberalized immigration policies. Psychologically, the Jackson-Vanik Amendment symbolized the solidarity of American Jewry with Soviet Jewry and the centrality of human rights to America's policies. Unfortunately, the Soviet Union did not accept the terms of the Jackson-Vanik Amendment. Jewish emigration declined after the Soviet invasion of Afghanistan to fewer than 1,000 individuals per year.

Glasnost and Beyond

Glasnost brought fundamental changes to Soviet Jewry. Soviet President Mikhail Gorbachev was most interested in improving the image of the Soviet Union abroad and in restructuring the Soviet economy. He made overtures to Israel and permitted the expression of Jewish culture within the Soviet Union. Most importantly, he opened the doors to Jewish emigration.

To be sure, Jewish emigration was at most a partial solution to Soviet Jewry. By the early 1990's hundreds of thousands of Soviet Jews were emigrating to Israel, which would face the enormous task of absorbing and acculturating them. Within the former Soviet Union at least 1,000,000 Jews remained although some estimates have placed the figure as high as 10,000,000. Their future remained unclear. Many feared the renewal of anti-Semitic sentiment and pogroms, augured by the resurgence of right-wing nationalist organizations such as Pamyat and the rantings of extremist politicians such as Zhirinovsky.

The Soviet satellites had been far from monolithic, even during the heyday of the Soviet empire. Poland had virtually eliminated her Jews, as forced emigration had taken place in 1968 leaving at most several thousand Jews. Hungary, by contrast, had been relatively tolerant toward her Jews, and over 85,000 remained after the collapse of Hungarian Communism in the late 1980's. In Romania, Chief Rabbi Moshe Rosen had presided over the conscious policy of "winding down" the Jewish community through emigration to Israel. Through close ties with the Romanian government, Rosen facilitated the emigration of over 400,000 Jews in the decades after World War II. In Yugoslavia, Marshall Tito enjoyed friendly relations with the 15,000 surviving Jews. After the collapse of Yugoslavia, the remaining Jews would agonize greatly over the resurgence of national sentiments and hatreds within the former Yugoslav state.

The Jewish experience under Communism has not been happy. Although far too many Jews were dazzled by Communist dreams of internationalism and peaceful solidarity, the legacy of the Jewish encounter with Communism represented the incompatibility of Judaism with the totalitarian state. For Judaism to foster continued Jewish group and familial loyalties was anathema to the totalitarian mentality that insisted the state was above the rights of any individual or collective group. Those who protested the tyranny of Soviet totalitarianism found natural allies among the Jews. That Jews retained loyalties to Israel and Jews abroad signaled the failure of the totalitarian mind-set to capture the complete subordination of the individual. Although the numbers of Jewish Communists were always disproportionate to the Jewish percentage of the Soviet population, the real legacy of Soviet Communism was hostility to Jewish concepts of family loyalty, personal freedom, and religious faith.

Reading: Arie Eliav, *Between Hammer and Sickle*

Arie Eliav's Between Hammer and Sickle *describes Soviet Jewry and the Soviet Jewry movement in the early 1970's. The emphasis upon the* Simchat Torah *celebration in Moscow suggests that Soviet Jews, while by no means necessarily religious, cherished the opportunity to express themselves publicly as Jews. The Soviet Jewry movement came to mean that the Jews of silence would be silent no more.*

Simchat Torah: the greatest of festivals

The month-long period of the High Holidays ends with the festival of Simchat Torah. Unlike the Jewish New Year and Yom Kippur, which are solemn and grave, Simchat Torah is a gay festival, perhaps the gayest of Jewish holidays. This is the time when Jews dance joyously with the Scroll of the Law, when one may imbibe wine or liquor so as to sing all the better. And the songs are not the usual melancholy supplications, but jolly hasidic tunes, or Jewish variations on non-Jewish secular and folk songs. This festival, more than any other, has endeared itself to the Jews of the Soviet Union. They have invested it with most of their desires, yearnings, longings, and feelings of identification. It is the only festival which can be compared to a "popular concert," in which children may also participate. It brings some measure of happiness—a thing so often lacking during the year. It is also an occasion for dancing what is akin to a Jewish snake dance. Thus Simchat Torah has become the greatest of the Jewish festivals in the Soviet Union, one with a character all its own.

The things that take place on the night of Simchat Torah in the synagogues of the Soviet Union shed a powerful light on Jewish life in Russia.

This is what I heard from the head of an Israeli family who was present at the great synagogue of Moscow on the night of Simchat Torah:

"We dressed our children in their holiday clothes and gave them the traditional colored flag topped by an apple, with a candle in the apple. The whole family went to the Moscow synagogue. When we got there, it was already hemmed in by thousands of people who filled the street from end to end. Everyone made way for us, as our children were the only ones who carried flags, and you could hear Jews whispering to one another, '*Amolige kinder*' (children of the past).

"The interior of the synagogue seemed to be luminous with

a light which came not only from the chandeliers but also from thousands of shining eyes and from the bright face of the crowd, which now did not comprise only the aged.

"I glanced around and saw young people here and there. I noticed the dark, smiling, curious eyes of a charming girl, who came close to the pulpit. (On Simchat Torah the traditional separation of the sexes inside the synagogue is overlooked, and the women mingle with the men.) There were new faces all around. Had I met any of those people on the street, I would never have associated them—on account of their age, dress, and expression—with a synagogue or a Jewish holiday. They were the kind of people one meets at the Bolshoi, in Gorki Park, at an exhibition in the Pushkin Museum, in the Lenin Stadium, or at a lecture in Dom Kulturi.

"Where were they from? What were they doing here? Was it merely the curiosity of the young that drove them to come and see how their fathers and ancestors had celebrated their festivals? Or were they drawn by a longing for an unknown past?

"The Torah processionals began. The old rabbi and the *gabbaim* of the synagogue took out dozens of Torah Scrolls from the Ark, well-cared-for ancient rolls of parchment that were wrapped in colored velvet embroidered in golden Hebrew letters. The Scrolls were crowned with filigreed decorations, jeweled flowers, and bells. The old, bent Jews, in dark, faded, and worn-out clothes, seemed to be swallowed up in the colorful procession, and it was as though the splendid and ornamental Scrolls marched on unsupported.

"The old rabbi and the *gabbaim* were followed by a few Israeli children carrying miniature Scrolls of the Law and flags. A little five-year-old girl was lifted up by the young people and carried on their shoulders. They joined the procession of the Scrolls. We saw smiling faces everywhere, a rare and wonderful sight in this old and sad synagogue.

"When the first processional was completed, the cantor, accompanied by some of the regular worshipers, began to sing some happy songs. The microphone near the cantor was grabbed by a number of people who boldly sang into it Jewish folk songs and hasidic tunes. Many of the people in the crowd joined in. The processions continued at a faster and gayer pace. The Scrolls were no longer carried by old people or by the regular worshipers. The snaking 'rondo' of the Scrolls swirled through the packed crowd, reaching almost outside the walls of the synagogue and the open area before the synagogue, where thousands more stood crowded together.

"Then some people started dancing. A circle was formed. Everybody danced, old men and women, boys and girls. The circle widened as a second, third, and fourth circle formed within. Then dozens of people were dancing, their arms linked as they moved to the tune of *'Vetaher Libenu.'* Someone started to sing 'David King of Israel lives on forever,' and the dance immediately changed to the more fervent pace of a *hora.*

"As we watched, the dance grew in warmth and ecstasy; the old, worn, and heavy-footed dropped out, and their places in the circle were taken by the young. In the end the circle was made up almost entirely of young people. The dancers, who appeared to be mostly university students, were not adept at the *hora,* but they soon grasped the basic nature of the dance and the words of the song."

I have asked myself: Who were these young people who danced with such great enthusiasm? Was this an isolated event in their lives, a casual occurrence? Are they like the many young Russians who fill the great churches on the eve of Christmas to listen with curiosity to the choir of old women?

I am told that the same thing happens in the synagogue of Leningrad on the night of Simchat Torah, but on a more massive scale. Perhaps this is because the Leningrad synagogue is larger than the one in Moscow, or because a more Western atmosphere prevails in Leningrad. The fact remains that a still larger number of students and Jewish youth assemble there, and the building, the area outside, and the street are filled with thousands of people. And when one hears of similar events occurring in other towns, one begins to wonder whether it is possible that the intense interest the young people show in that evening is not just casual but has very deep roots.

This is how my friend, who described the Simchat Torah celebration in Moscow, put it: "It is difficult to talk to them. When the evening is over, they scatter into the night. And you don't see them, or the likes of them, until the following year.. . ."

The High Holidays are over and Simchat Torah has passed. Once again the synagogue sinks into the grayness of the Russian winter. Once again a few oldsters gather there on weekdays and Sabbaths. Once again arguments, disputes, and schisms arise. Once again they must deliver reports to the authorities. But deep in their hearts, these synagogue Jews know that they, old and degraded as they are, are the ones who guard the embers of the ancient Jewish tradition, which blazes into flame for a brief moment a few times a year.

Bibliography for Further Reading

Gilboa, Eytan. *The Black Years of Soviet Jewry,* Little, Brown, 1971

Gitelman, Zvi. *Jewish Nationality and Soviet Politics,* Princeton University Press, 1972

Hoffman, Charles. *Gray Dawn,* HarperCollins, 1992

Korey, William. *The Soviet Cage,* Viking Books, 1973

Rappoport, Louis. *Stalin's War Against the Jews,* The Free Press, 1990

Sharansky, Natan. *Fear No Evil,* Random House, 1988

Unit XXXII

The Holocaust

The Nazis

The Nazi "war against the Jews" was unique in the annals of human crimes. Never before did one people set out ideologically to exterminate another people or group. To be sure, there have been many examples of atrocities in human history. Some even occurred on a scale inviting comparison with the Nazi Final Solution. Never before, however, had there been an ideological commitment to the extermination of a people. In this sense, the Nazi crime of the Final Solution was both unprecedented and unique.

There was very little that was new in Nazi ideology. Nazi anti-Semitism synthesized the racial theory of history of Houston Stuart Chamberlain with the conspiratorial worldview inherent in the *Protocols of the Elders of Zion.* Like other modern anti-Semites, the Nazis exaggerated the role of the Jew in European society and world history. But if Hitler did not innovate ideologically, he utilized these themes as a "warrant for genocide." Because the Jews were seen as racial vermin and as conspiring to thwart human development, the only solution must be the elimination of world Jewry.

Although Hitler articulated these themes as early as *Mein Kampf,* he did not move to implement the Final Solution immediately. The road to Auschwitz has been called "the twisted road," meaning that there were many changes in Nazi anti-Jewish policy. In the first year of Nazi rule, 1933, some 42 anti-Jewish laws were passed.

The next three years, 1934–1936, witnessed a relative relaxation in the treatment of Germany's Jews. The height of this "moderation" lay in the Berlin Olympics of 1936, for which Berlin was transformed into a city showcasing general tolerance. After the Olympics the treatment of Jews deteriorated. The Kristallnacht of November 10, 1938, constituted a veritable pogrom, followed by large-scale roundups of Jews under suspicion of anti-Nazi activity. Following the pogrom the Nazis turned to encouraging Jewish emigration from Germany.

Historian Karl Schleunes has explained these twists and turns in Nazi policy as the result of a struggle within the Nazi hierarchy between ideological purists, who wished to implement a Final Solution, and economic realists, who argued that the Jew was too important internationally and too central to Germany's welfare to be eliminated immediately. Hitler balanced the claims of these respective groups. Kristallnacht represented the triumph of the ideological purists, but was quickly followed by the ascendancy of the economic realists. With the outbreak of World War II, and more particularly, the attack against the Soviet Union in June 1941, Hitler moved toward the Final Solution.

The consequences of this "twisted road" were significant. First, for many German Jews, it meant that Hitler was an anti-Semite, even a madman, but not really worse than any other dictator. The policy of alternating moderate with extreme treatment lulled German Jewry into believing that the Final Solution was by no means inevitable, despite Hitler's earlier writings. This view, articulated by no less a personage than Rabbi Leo Baeck, leader of Reform Jewry in Germany, was echoed by many outside Germany. The dominant feeling in the West was that Hitler's anti-Semitism clearly was regrettable, even shameful. However, he was by no means intolerable, and many preferred him to the Bolshevik threat of Soviet Russia. In England, Winston Churchill stood virtually alone in arguing that Western civilization could not accommodate itself to the threat of Hitler. In contrast, the American Ambassador to the Court of St. James, Joseph P. Kennedy, argued that there was no necessary conflict between America and Germany. In Kennedy's view, only American Jewry had an interest in provoking a confrontation. Prime Minister Neville Chamberlain echoed this perspective. His response to Kristallnacht was particularly instructive: "No doubt Jews aren't a lovable people; I don't care about them myself; but that is not sufficient to explain the pogrom."

The initial Nazi legislation revoked Jewish emancipation. As noted, the burst of legislative activity in 1933 removed Jews from prominent positions in German society and thereby encouraged their emigration. The Nuremberg legislation of 1936 defined a Jew as anyone who had at least one Jewish grandparent and who considered himself a member of the Jewish religious community. The definition was by no means exclusively racial, but partly racial and partly religious. Defining the Jews served to dehumanize them—to exclude them as a specific category. Definition was particularly necessary in the case of assimilated Jews who regarded themselves as completely German, and it divided the Jewish community by enabling some to think that they could escape via definitional loopholes, e.g. Jews who had worn the Iron Cross. Finally, definition deflected potential Christian opposition to anti-Jewish legislation by focusing attention upon Jewish converts to Christianity. The churches now had to worry about the safety of converts rather than focus primary concern on the treatment of German Jews.

After the Kristallnacht pogrom, the expropriation and Aryanization of Jewish businesses proceeded. In time, expropriation would become the basis for Jewish material claims for reparations by Nazi Germany. In the short run, it served to impoverish German Jewry and to compel Jewish emigration.

With the outbreak of the war, the Nazis moved to ghettoize Jews in areas that they had conquered. To some extent, ghettoization was a control measure to isolate Jews from Germans and to concentrate them within a relatively restricted area. Conditions, however, within the ghetto were so abysmal that the process of decimating the Jewish community through starvation, hard work, and unsanitary conditions already began with ghettoization. Historian Isaiah Trunk has estimated that if the Nazis had done nothing in the way of a Final Solution, ghettoization alone would have destroyed the Jewish community within a decade.

In June 1941, Operation Barbarossa signalled the German attack upon the Soviet Union and the launching of the Final Solution of European Jewry. As the German army marched, the *Einsatzgruppen*, or mobile killing units, accompanied the troops. After an area was conquered, the *Einsatzgruppen* ordered all the Jews in town to be gathered in a single place, stripped them of their belongings, marched them out of town to a secluded area, and then had them dig their own graves. It has been estimated that over 1,500,000 Jews died due to Nazi shootings. The process, however, was by no means foolproof. There were too many witnesses to the event, striking considerable fear among the conquered populations that they would be next. The personalized nature of the killings caused problems for the *Einsatzgruppen,* who had generally been recruited from the professional classes of Germany. In its final stages, the *Einsatzgruppen* utilized death vans to kill Jews by releasing poison gas. In general, however, the *Einsatzgruppen* were too slow for Hitler's plan in implementing the Final Solution.

An even more diabolical plan was necessary to accomplish the total elimination of Jewry. Therefore, the Nazis created six death camps, the most infamous of which was Auschwitz-Birkenau. Jews throughout the conquered territories were deported to these six killing centers. They should not be confused with transit camps or labor camps. Conditions in these transit camps, such as Drancy or Bergen-Belsen, were terrible, and many people died because of illness, starvation, or extreme labor conditions. Dachau, a transit camp, was notorious. However, it was not a killing center as was Auschwitz, Treblinka, or Maidanek. Holocaust deniers acknowledged that undoubtedly many people died, given the severity of the conditions in the camps. They maliciously denied, however, that six camps were created for the express purpose of exterminating Jews.

Nazism connoted a radical evil. Hitler did not simply commit atrocities against Jews. His "war against the Jews" represented a unique attempt at physical genocide of Jewry. As Elie Wiesel has put it well, "not all victims were Jews, but all Jews were victims."

Victims

The most difficult and perhaps most explosive question in understanding the Holocaust concerns the failure of the Jews to resist their oppressors. Although some armed resistance did occur, the overwhelming majority of Jews did not physically resist Nazi tormenters. The armed resistance that did occur was generally unsuccessful. Even the most famous example of resistance, the Warsaw Ghetto revolt, took place only after 90 percent of Warsaw's Jewry had been deported. For the diarists of the Warsaw Ghetto, the question was not why did we resist, but why did we let them go?

Yet the absence of physical resistance must be explained and understood rather than condemned. First, Soviet prisoners of war, militarily trained men, did not resist in any greater capacity than did Jews. The Nazis succeeded in terrorizing their victims and debilitating them, even if they were well-versed in the martial arts. And the Jews lacked both military training and arms.

Secondly, Jews did not enjoy the friendly support of the surrounding population to facilitate armed resistance. Where the Jews were well-integrated into the resistance forces, e.g. Yugoslavia, they participated in disproportionate numbers relative to their population size. In Poland, however, where the bulk of European Jewry resided, the resistance movement did not welcome them. As a result, the purpose of Jewish resistance could not be the defeat of the Nazis. Instead resistance symbolized death with dignity.

Many Jews felt, under these circumstances, that there were other ways of dying with dignity—whether it be teaching Torah at the gravesite or displaying a tenacity to retain Jewish identity, life, and values, even in the face of the Nazi terror. These forms of spiritual resistance were at least as important as the physical armed resistance that did occur. The metaphor of the Jews going like "sheep to the slaughter," although widely used, constitutes an injustice against the victims. Sheep go mindlessly without thought. The victims of Nazism realized they could not defeat the Nazis physically, but existentially they could remain Jews. In this sense, resistance connoted a will to live, the creation of Jewish cultural institutions, and, lastly, the drive to communicate the story of Nazism and the Final Solution to a future court of history that would hold the Nazis accountable. When Warsaw Jews took to writing Holocaust diaries and memoirs, they were articulating a classic Jewish model in the face of oppression—to defy the present reality by insisting upon an alternative future reality, a world in which the Jews would not be victims and the Nazis would be judged as executioners.

What about Jewish leadership in this age of extremity? Every ghetto was organized by a Jewish communal council, a *judenrat,* which the Nazis created to facilitate administration of the area. A Jewish police force insured the preservation of order within the ghetto. To be sure, there was great resentment toward the leadership of the Jewish communal councils and the Jewish police force. Many Jews felt that Jewish leaders were worse than the Nazis, for they were doing the Nazis' bidding. After the war, many charged that if the Jews had not complied with the Nazi orders, the Final Solution could never have assumed the parameters it did. No less a personality than Mahatma Gandhi argued that the Jews should have committed civil disobedience.

Such judgments ignore the reality of Nazism. For Gandhi to evoke the model of non-violent resistance in India against the British government in the context of the Nazi terror is sheer blasphemy. Unlike the British, the Nazis would not have shirked from mass shootings and executions. The men who occupied positions on the communal councils or the *judenrate* indeed hoped to preserve Jewish life rather than end it. Their policy was two-fold: Make the Jews indispensable to the Nazi war effort through economic productivity, and preserve Jewish life on as normal a basis as possible under extreme conditions. Moreover, one cannot generalize about the *judenrate* as a whole. In only a tiny minority of cases, the men of the *judenrat* seemed to have hoped that they could ingratiate themselves with the Nazis and conducted themselves in ways that evoked charges of collaboration and treason. In some cases, the *judenrat* tried to support resistance forces outside the ghetto. In most cases, they hoped to hang on as long as possible until the war would be over and Jewish life could be reconstituted. Pending that day, they tried to maintain normalcy, especially with respect to education of the young and preserving family and social ties within the ghetto.

To be sure, the *judenrat* generally opposed Jewish armed revolt on the grounds that it would be futile, result in the death of innocents, and polarize the Jewish community. The Warsaw Ghetto, for example, remained divided on the question of revolt down to its last days.

Clearly, the *judenrat* erred in believing that it could withstand the Final Solution. *Judenrat* members derived no personal benefit, for 80 percent were killed albeit somewhat later than most other Jews. Rather the failure of the *judenrat* exposed the vulnerability, isolation, and powerlessness of the Jews. The *judenrat*'s policy of "survival through work" could not deflect the Final Solution. For what made the Final Solution possible was the dedicated commitment of the Nazis to its implementation and the absence of a similar commitment among the Allies to the rescue of Jews.

The Bystanders

Nor can one generalize concerning the bystanders. In some places collaboration was the rule. Most shockingly, this was true in France, where, under Vichy rule, a new order was implemented to restore France to traditions of exclusion that rejected liberalism and democracy. The France of Marshall Petain was by no means the France of the Revolution. In this France, Dreyfus was considered guilty and the Jews ought best be relegated to second-class status. Significantly, Vichy France collaborated in the deportation of foreign Jews within France.

Rescue took place in areas where the bystanders did not distinguish between Jew and countrymen. This was most significant in Denmark, where the Danish king set a personal example for the rescue of Danish Jewry. In Hungary, the Swedish diplomat Raoul Wallenberg personally rescued thousands of Jews. In Bulgaria, the deportations of Jews were halted due to the combined pressure exerted by the monarchy, the Greek Orthodox Church, and the papal delegate, Cardinal Roncalli, the future Pope John XXIII. Rescue did occur, but, unfortunately, the efforts mounted on behalf of rescue by no means matched the Nazi efforts at destruction.

The most difficult questions concerning rescue relate to the Western democracies—America, the United Kingdom, and their respective Jewish communities. For America, the critical question has been the image of Franklin D. Roosevelt, long idolized by Jews as the President who had done the most to integrate Jews into American society. Beginning in 1967, with the publication of Arthur Morse's *While Six Million Died,* a spate of books attacked Roosevelt for his failure to act on behalf of Jews. These books indicted the American administration for failing to change American immigration laws, failing to bomb the death camps, and for waiting 14 months after news of the Final Solution was known before creating the War Refugee Board in January 1944. The most extensive of these indictments was authored by David Wyman, *The Abandonment of the Jews.* Wyman argued that Roosevelt knew the truth of the Final Solution in November 1942, but acted to create the War Refugee Board only in January 1944.

Although this indictment of Roosevelt and the American government remains quite popular in Jewish circles, it ignores the political context in which Roosevelt functioned. America in the

1930's remained an isolationist country. The dominant perspectives were articulated by men such as Henry Ford, Charles Lindbergh, and Joseph P. Kennedy—all to the effect that America had no necessary conflict with Nazi Germany. Only the Jews had a necessary conflict. Lindbergh went so far as to warn Jews not to embroil America in a war with Nazi Germany.

Roosevelt, as President, aimed to change that prevailing wisdom. He, like Churchill, was convinced that the Western democracies could not live alongside Hitler. He was determined to bring America into war with Nazi Germany. Rescue activities on behalf of Jews, however, would have abetted the argument made by Roosevelt's opponents that it was only the power of international Jewry that embroiled America into confrontation with Nazi Germany. No support in America existed for changing the immigration laws. The Kristallnacht of November 1938 evoked an outpouring of pro-Jewish opinion, yet, when asked whether sympathy for Jews should be translated into permitting Jewish refugees to enter America, groups as disparate as the American Legion and the American Federation of Labor united in opposing further Jewish immigration. Roosevelt can be evaluated only in the context of his moving America from an isolationist to an interventionist stance. In doing so, he made possible the defeat of Hitler. Although one may criticize specifics of his policy, such as the failure to admit the *St. Louis* ship bearing Jewish refugees, the wholesale indictments against Roosevelt of Wyman and Morse are unfounded. Even Wyman's charge, that Roosevelt should have established a War Refugee Board as early as November 1942, ignores the reality that in 1942 the war was far from won. Rescue activity was feasible only once the course of the war was no longer in doubt. Significantly, the high tide of anti-Semitism during wartime occurred in 1944–1945, precisely the time when the Government actually undertook a rescue initiative. Anti-Semitism did not hinder the reaction of the Government, contrary to the allegations of Morse and Wyman, nearly as much as did the pressing nature of the war effort itself.

The Western democracies' failure to rescue may be partially understood as the failure of the liberal imagination to comprehend the radical evil that Hitler represented. Liberals, as children of the enlightenment, believed that human beings were naturally good and could not fathom that Hitler was truly committed to the Final

Solution of the Jews as a people. All too frequently, liberals in the West tended to rationalize anti-Semitism, blaming the victim by suggesting that anti-Semitism at least partly resulted from the misdeeds of the Jews. More specifically, liberals opposed emphasizing the particular nature of Jewish identity and the "Jewish question." As we have seen, the left frequently desired the assimilation of the Jews. H.G. Wells, the British intellectual, went so far as to argue that the failure of the Jews to assimilate had resulted in their current plight. As a result, liberal values of universalism to some extent conflicted with mounting a specific campaign on behalf of rescue of the Jews. One should not describe this as anti-Semitism or even indifference to anti-Semitism. Rather, liberal ambivalence concerning Jews appears to have been one factor in the failure to rescue.

Also lacking was the moral voice exerted by the Christian churches generally and, most importantly, by Pope Pius XII. Only in his Christmas 1942 message did the Pope condemn Nazi atrocities and even at that point failed to mention Jews. This omission was of great importance. First, the moral voice of the Vatican might well have energized European Catholics to resist Hitler. Secondly, the Vatican had access to some of the best sources of information throughout Europe. Merely publicizing the news of the Final Solution would have given it credibility and made it impossible to dismiss the stories of Nazi atrocities as mere rumors or propaganda. Pope Pius XII had served as a Cardinal in Berlin under his predecessor, Pius XI, and was influenced by considerable Germanophilism. He clearly feared losing the loyalties of German Catholics, and regarded Bolshevism as a greater threat than Nazism. Perhaps most importantly, the Pope regarded it as futile to protest Nazi actions. When 3,000 priests were killed, not a word of protest emanated from the Vatican. To be sure, the Pope did engage in some limited rescue, particularly within the Vatican itself. He also apparently encouraged local bishops to protest the treatment of Jews. Yet the ambivalence of Pope Pius XII is perhaps best represented in the tragic story of Kurt Gerstein, a Catholic member of the SS who tried, unsuccessfully, to report the news of the Final Solution to the Pope. Ultimately, in frustration, Gerstein committed suicide.

The question of American Jewry and its leadership is perhaps both more painful and more controversial. Clearly, American Jewry was disunited. The Zionists, the Orthodox, the American

Jewish Congress, the American Jewish Committee, Reform leadership—all had differing visions as to what should be done on behalf of Jews abroad. The absence of unity did not determine whether the American government would act. However, it did permit the dismissal of Jewish requests on the grounds that one could not satisfy the Jews in any case.

Particularly illustrative was the failure of the campaign to boycott German-made goods. The boycott was the brainchild of Rabbi Stephen Wise and the American Jewish Congress. The hope was to garner gentile support and thereby damage German trade abroad. However, the boycott evoked a polarized response within the Jewish community. The American Jewish Committee felt that a public boycott of German-made goods would abet the conspiracy myth of a Jewish plot to take over the world. In addition, Jewish leadership in Germany opposed the boycott, and the American Jewish Committee, largely comprised of Jews of German ancestry, naturally turned to their brethren in Germany for instruction and guidance. Lastly, the Zionist Organization also opposed the boycott because it was engaging in the transfer of German Jews to Palestine by providing Germany with a market for its goods in Palestine. Whether the boycott would have worked or not is questionable. Clearly, the controversy over the boycott demonstrated how fragmented American Jewry was and its inability to mount a sustained campaign on behalf of rescue. To be sure, one must understand that American Jewry constituted in the 1930's a relatively new community, unsure of itself, fearful of domestic anti-Semitism, and struggling to meet its own needs during the Great Depression. Most importantly, Jewish leaders regarded Roosevelt as their primary friend and feared actions that might undermine Roosevelt or play into the hands of his domestic enemies, many of whom were openly anti-Semitic.

In addition, some mistakes clearly were made. The most renowned leader of American Jewry at the time, Rabbi Stephen Wise, believed that he was the appropriate messenger to the Roosevelt administration. In fact, Wise lacked sufficient leverage and influence with the President. Had he tried to reach the Jews in Roosevelt's inner circle—the Bernard Baruchs, the Felix Frankfurters, the Sam Rosenmans, and the Ben Cohens—he might have been more effective. In fact, that was how the War Refugee Board was created—namely Roosevelt's Secretary of the Treasury, Henry

Morgenthau, was energized by gentile attorneys on his staff to advocate that more be done to rescue Jews.

But the critical lessons of Jewish political activity relate neither to Jewish disunity nor to errors of judgment. The most critical lesson relates to Jewish powerlessness. American Jewry in the 1930's lacked allies. They were isolated in a period of unprecedented organized American anti-Semitism. Similarly in England, their counterparts lacked the capacity to mount effective protests against England's policies limiting immigration to Palestine, which was the only realistic refuge for European Jewry. In Palestine itself, Moshe Shertok (later Sharett) was unable even to obtain a visa to engage in diplomatic representation with an emissary from the Jewish ghetto in Budapest, Joel Brand.

In this sense, Israeli historian Yehuda Bauer has argued that the real lessons of the Holocaust do not lie in "never again." The slogan "never again" presupposes that man's inhumanity to man can never be permitted to triumph. Certainly it is a pious slogan, but it is one that we cannot guarantee. If the Holocaust happened once, there can be no promises that a Holocaust will never recur. Therefore, Bauer argues, the real lesson lies not in "never again," but rather in "never again should Jews be so isolated." The Holocaust years coincided with significant decline in Jewish political influence and power and the absence of friendly allies and coalition partners who shared Jewish aims and objectives. Where the Jews were able to find friendly, supportive populations, such as Bulgaria or even Italy, their survival rates and their integration into the general resistance were suprisingly high. Where the Jews remained isolated, as in Poland, the Final Solution proceeded unchecked.

Conclusion

Since the end of World War II, these questions of Holocaust uniqueness, resistance, and rescue have been debated extensively by historians and philosophers. Hannah Arendt was generally regarded as uncharitable in her view of the victims by suggesting that the banality of evil that characterized Adolf Eichmann extended to his victims as well—namely, that when evil became commonplace, everyone lacked the will to resist it. Many of these debates have a political context. Those who have argued that the Holocaust must be relativized are, on the one hand, rehabilitating

German history by arguing that the Holocaust was an atrocity, but no worse than many other atrocities in the twentieth century. These German historians, led by Ernest Nolte, are generally partisans of the German right, seeking to rehabilitate German nationalism and conservative traditions. Ironically, in America, their counterparts lie on the left. American attempts at relativization seek to equate the Holocaust with the treatment of the American Indian, or with Black slavery.

Both positions are extreme and, rightfully, ought be repudiated. The United States Holocaust Memorial Museum in Washington recognizes that there have been other atrocities in history, and that Jews were by no means the only victims of Nazism. However, the primary message of the Holocaust Museum is one of Holocaust uniqueness. Ideologically, the Nazis were committed to perpetrating the Final Solution and the total elimination of the Jews. That fact remains historically unprecedented. For that reason, the uniqueness of the Holocaust must be remembered as the single greatest crime in human history.

Reading: Jacob Glatstein ed., *Anthology of Holocaust Literature*

Elie Wiesel has been the spokesman of this generation for the Holocaust. No writer has so succeeded in telling the story of the Shoah *as has Wiesel through his remarkable progression of novels. Note, in particular, Wiesel's pathos in describing the conflict between father and son concerning a piece of bread in the nightmare of the death train.*

Elie Wiesel, The Death Train
Translated from the Yiddish by Moshe Spiegel

Indescribable confusion reigned.

Parents searched for their children, children for their parents, and lonely captives for their friends. The people were beset by loneliness. Everyone feared that the outcome of the journey would be tragic and would claim its toll of lives. And so one yearned to have the companionship of someone who would stand by with a word, with a loving glance.

Afterward, an ominous silence fell upon us. We squatted on the soft snow that covered the floor of the railroad car like a carpet, and tried to keep warm by drawing closer to our neighbors.

When the train started to move, no one paid any attention to it. Careworn and burdened with conflicting thoughts, each of us wondered if he was wise to continue on the journey. But in our weariness, whether one died today, tomorrow, a week or a generation later, hardly seemed to matter.

The night dragged on interminably, as though it were to go on to the end of time. When the gray dawn appeared in the east, I felt as though I had spent a night in a tomb haunted by evil spirits. Human beings, defeated and broken, sat like dusty tombstones in the dim light of early dawn. I looked about the subdued throng and tried to distinguish one from another. And, indeed, perhaps there was no distinction.

My gaze fell on one who stared blankly ahead. A wry smile seemed to play on his ice-encrusted face. Those glazed eyes, whether living or dead, seemed to ensnare my gaze. A hundred and twenty captives, shadows of human lives, extinguished flames of burned-out candles lit on the anniversaries of the deaths of their loved ones. Wrapped in a drenched blanket, his black cap pulled down over his ears, a layer of snow on his shoulders, my father sat beside me. Could it be that he, too, was dead? The thought flashed across my mind. I tried to talk to him. I wanted to shout, but all I could do was mutter. He did not reply, he did not utter a sound. I was certain that from then on I was to be all alone, all alone. Then I was filled with a numbing sense of indifference to everyone and to myself. Well, the Lord giveth and the Lord taketh away. The struggle was over. There was nothing and no one for whom to fight now.

The train ground to an abrupt halt in a snow-covered field. Awakened by the jolt, a few curious captives struggled to their feet to look out. The scene was reminiscent of cattle staring stupidly from a livestock car.

German S.S. guards surrounded the human cargo, shouting, "All the dead are to be thrown out! All the dead are to be thrown out!"

The living were pleased; there would be more space. It would not be as crowded now.

Strong men appeared and examined each one who could not stand up, and rapped out, "Here's one! Get hold of him!"

Whereupon two men would pick the corpse by the shoulders and feet and fling it out of the car like a sack of flour.

From various parts of the car came such cries as, "Here's another—my neighbor! He doesn't move. Help me get rid of him!"

Two deportees stepped forward and tried to lift a form beside me. It was only then that I was aroused from my stupor, and realized the seriousness of the situation. And to this day I cannot understand how I summoned the strength and courage to save my father from the lurking death. I kneeled over him, tearing at his clothes, slapping his face, kissing him and screaming, "Daddy, Daddy—wake up! Get up, Daddy! Don't let them throw you out of the car."

As he failed to respond, the two men said to me, "There's no use your screaming, little fellow. He's dead! Your father is dead, do you understand?"

"No! He is not dead! He's not dead!" I wailed, repeating the words over and over indefinitely. For some reason, I seemed to fear the death of my father more than my own. I tried again and again to release him from the embrace of the angels of death, and I succeeded at last.

My father opened his glazed, ice-encrusted eyes, and regarded me in a dazed way, unable to understand what I was trying to convey to him or the commotion that was being made over him.

"See for yourselves, you murderers. He's alive, he's living!"

The two men eyed my father for a moment, then shrugged their shoulders and muttered, "Not for long," and turned to other silent forms.

There were some twenty-odd dead in our one car, and after they were stripped of their clothes, which the living snatched up, they were flung out of the car.

This task took several hours. Then the train chugged along, and as icy gusts shrieked about it, it seemed that through the accursed world about us could be heard the far-away, muffled wail of the naked bodies that had been abandoned on Polish snow-covered fields.

The journey was insufferable; and every one who lived through it later questioned the natural laws that their survival seemed to disprove.

We were deprived of even bread and water, and snow was our only source of water. Cramped for space and thoroughly chilled, we were very weak by the third day of the journey. Days were turned into nights, and the nights cast a shadow of doom over our very souls.

The train plodded along for what seemed countless days, and the snow fell, fell, fell incessantly. And the exhausted, travel-weary unfortunates lay huddled for days on end, without uttering a word, eyes closed, waiting for one thing only—the next station, where the new yield of corpses would be got rid of. That was what we looked forward to.

The journey lasted ten interminable days and nights. Each day claimed its toll of victims and each night paid its homage to the Angel of Death.

We passed through German settlements, generally in the early morning hours, only in a few instances. Sometimes men on their way to work would halt in their tracks to glare at us as though we were animals in a kind of demonic circus. Once a German hurled a chunk of bread into our car and caused pandemonium to break out as scores of famished men fought each other in an effort to pounce upon it. And the German workers eyed the spectacle with sneering amusement.

Unfortunately, the Torah does not relate how the children of Israel received the first manna in the wilderness. Did they fight over it, and were there any casualties? And did scenes like the one in our car take place there? The German workers tarried a while, gazing at the amusing spectacle, and perhaps assuaging their conscience at the same time with the thought of their benevolence in giving bread to the hungry.

All the other German workers soon followed the example of their kindhearted townsmen. Pieces of bread were cast into all the cars. Bread and victims. And they—the good, gallant Germans—were pleased with themselves and smiled.

Strange, even while jotting down these words, the event seems incredible to me. I seem to be writing a horror novel—a novel that should not be read at night. It is hard to believe that what I set down in writing is really true, has actually happened to me.

And—only ten years ago!

I think to myself: if all that is alive in my memory, and that is seething in my heart, is really true, how am I able to sleep at night? How can I eat my food in peace?

I can still see the scenes I experienced that early morning when the bits of bread fell from heaven.

Unfortunately, the bread also fell into our car. Though I was very hungry, my exhaustion was stronger. So I didn't budge from my spot, refusing to take part in what was going on. Let bread drop down—even from heaven. I would not risk my life to get it. I lacked the strength not only to fight for the hard crusts, but even to eat them. So I squatted in my corner, watching how human beings turned into animals as they attempted to snatch the morsels of food from each others' mouths.

A piece of the heavenly bread fell in a corner of the car; the next moment another corner was emptied of its occupants. Not far from me a young lad bit the ear of someone standing in front of him, in order to get to the priceless bread first. The injured person, bent only upon reaching the bread, was oblivious to the pain. I suddenly beheld a frail, elderly Jew crawling along the floor, one hand clutching his chest. At first I thought that he had been hurt in the fight. But then I saw him take a handful of crumbs from his bosom and devour them almost with ecstasy.

A sly smile played upon his deathly pale face for a moment, and disappeared. Then someone pounced on the old man like a phantom, and the two engaged in a death struggle, clawing, biting, trampling, kicking one another. The old man managed to raise his head, a glint of joy in his bloodshot eyes.

"Little Meyer! Meyer, my son," the graybeard mumbled, "Didn't you recognize me? You have hurt me so much. . . ."

Meyer still struggled to retrieve a piece of bread from his father's bosom. Then the dying old man groaned, "Meyer, you're beating your own father . . . I brought bread for you, too. I had risked my life . . . and you're hitting, beating my—your old father. . . ."

The old man seemed on the verge of death, he no longer made any sound. Meyer had triumphed; his right hand clutched the small piece of bread, and his left wiped the blood trickling from one of his eyes. The old man held a piece of bread in his clenched fist and tried to bring it up to his mouth—to die with the taste of food in his mouth. His eyes were alert now; he was clearly aware of the situation. He was at the portals of death—a condition in which one comprehends all that goes on about him. As he brought the hand with the bread closer to his half-opened mouth, his face glowed with lust for the bread. . . . It seemed as though the old man was holding back the bread intentionally, so that the pleasure of the anticipated feast should last longer. The eyes seemed about to burst from their sockets. And as the old man was about to bite into the bread with his darkened, broken teeth, Meyer once more pounced upon him and snatched the bread from him.

The old man muttered, "What? A last will and testament?" But, except for me, neither his son nor anyone else heard him. At last he breathed his last; and his orphaned son ate the bread. He was sprawled on the floor of the car, his right hand stretched out as though protesting to God, who had transformed Meyer into a murderer.

I could not bear to look at the old man for long. The son soon found himself engaged in a new struggle. Catching sight of the bread in his hand, others then pounced upon him. He tried to defend himself, but the furious throng, thirsting for blood in their frenzy, killed him. And so the two of them, father and son, victims of the struggle for bread, were trampled upon. Both perished starved and alone.

Suddenly, I had the feeling that someone was laughing behind me, and I wondered who it was. But I was afraid to look around for fear of learning that the laughter was not coming from behind me, but from myself. I was fifteen years old then. Do you understand fifteen? Is it any wonder that I, along with my generation, do not believe either in God or in man; in the feelings of a son, in the love of a father. Is it any wonder that I cannot realize that I myself experienced this thing, that my childish eyes had witnessed it?

Meir Katz, a robust, energetic Jew with a thundering voice, an old friend of my father, was with us in the car. He worked as a gardener in Buna. He conducted himself gallantly, both physically and morally. He was placed in command of the human cargo in our car because of his strength. It was thanks to him that I finally arrived alive in the Buchenwald concentration camp.

It was during the third night of our journey—or was it some other?—we lost track of time. We squatted, trying to doze off, when I was suddenly awakened by someone choking me. With superhuman effort, I managed to shout one word—"Father!" That was all I managed to get out, as the unknown attacker was choking off my breath. Fortunately, my father awakened and tried to free me from the stranglehold. Unable to do so, however, he appealed to Meir Katz for help, whereupon the latter came to my rescue.

I didn't know the strangler or the reason for his violent act. After all, I had carried no bread with me. It may have been a sudden fit of insanity, or—just a case of mistaken identity.

Meir Katz also died during that journey. A few days before we reached Buchenwald, he said to my father, "Shloime, I'm on my way out. I can't stand it any longer."

"Meir, don't give up!" my father tried to hearten him. "Bear up! You've got to! Try to have courage!"

"Shloime, it's no use—I'm washed-out," Meir muttered. "I can't go on."

Then the sturdy Meir Katz broke down and sobbed, mourning his son, who was killed in the early days of the Hitler terror.

On the last day of the journey, bitter cold, accompanied by a heavy snowfall, aggravated the situation even more. The end seemed to be near. Then someone warned, "Fellow Jews, in such weather, we've got to move about; we must not sit motionless—or we'll all freeze to death!"

So we all got up—even those who seemed to be dying—and wrapped our drenched blankets about our bodies. The scene was reminiscent of a congregation wrapped in prayer shawls, swaying to and fro in prayer. The snow, the car, even the sky (heaven?)—everything and everybody seemed to be swaying, worshipping, communing with God, uttering the prayer of life, the prayer of death. The sword of the Angel of Death was suspended above. A congregation of corpses at prayer.

A shout, an outcry like that of a wounded animal, suddenly rent the air in the car. The effect was terrifying and some of the people could not endure it silently, and themselves began to scream. Their outcries seemed to come from another world. Soon the rest of us joined in the uproar; screaming and shrieking filled the air. The deafening roar rode the gusts of wind and amid the swirling snow soared to heaven, but, echoing from the closed gates there, reverberated back to earth.

Before long, twenty-five cars crowded with deportees joined us in the hysterical song of death. Everyone had reached the breaking point. The end was drawing near. The train was struggling up the hill of the Thyring forest. The divine tragicomedy was approaching its finale. There were no longer any illusions about surviving; the thousands of deportees were aware of their doom.

"Why don't they mow us down on the spot?" Meir Katz asked through tears. "We could at least be spared further agony."

"Reb Meir, we'll soon arrive at our destination," I tried to comfort him. But the wind drowned out my words. We stood in the open car, under the falling snow, screaming hysterically.

We arrived at the Buchenwald concentration camp late at night. "Security police" of the camp came forward to unload the human cargo. The dead were left in the cars. Only those who were able to drag their feet got out. Meir Katz was left in the car; like so many others, he had frozen to death a short time before we reached our destination. The journey itself was the worst part of the ordeal. About forty of the deportees were claimed by death on that one day alone. Our car had originally started out with a hundred and twenty souls; twelve—among them my father and I—had survived the ordeal.

Bibliography for Further Reading

Cohn, Norman. *Warrant for Genocide,* Harper Torch, 1967

Dawidowicz, Lucy. *The War Against the Jews,* Holt, Rinehart & Winston, 1975

Epstein, Helen. *Children of the Holocaust,* Putnam, 1979

Frankl, Victor. *Man's Search for Meaning,* Pocket Books, 1985

Friedlander, Saul. *When Memory Comes,* Avon Books, 1979

Katz, Steven. *The Holocaust in Historical Context,* Oxford, 1994

Kushner, Tony. *The Holocaust and the Liberal Imagination,* Blackwell, 1994

Lipstadt, Deborah. *Denying the Holocaust,* The Free Press, 1994

———. *Beyond Belief: The American Press and the Coming of the Holocaust,* Free Press, 1986

Miller, Judith. *One by One by One: Facing the Holocaust,* Simon and Schuster, 1990

Wasserstein, Bernard. *Britain and the Jews of Europe, 1939–1945,* Oxford University Press, 1979

Wiesel, Elie. *Gates of the Forest,* Avon, 1966

———. *Night,* Bantam, 1982

Wyman, David. *The Abandonment of the Jews,* Pantheon Books, 1984

Unit XXXIII

Israel and World Jewry

The Refugee Crisis

The aftermath of the Holocaust created an immediate need for refugee absorption. Hundreds of thousands of Jews lived in displaced persons camps. Most had no desire to stay in Europe. The obvious alternatives were either Palestine or America, yet the gates to both remained restricted. The British White Paper continued to be operative. Thus immigration to Palestine was unofficial and, by and large, illegal. In America, the quota system limited Jewish immigration by their countries of national origin.

Everyone recognized that something needed to be done. Many recommended immediate immigration of 100,000 Jews to Palestine. The British Government refused the request, continuing its pre-war policy of appeasing the local Arab population. In December 1945 President Harry Truman, by executive order, gave preferential treatment to displaced persons within the immigration quotas. Jews were allotted two-thirds of the places under the immigration laws. Significantly, Jewish organizations campaigned against this "affirmative action" for Jewish refugees, preferring changes in American immigration laws generally. Organizations such as the Daughters of the American Revolution, the Veterans of Foreign Wars, and the American Legion went much further, advocating a general ban on immigration for the next decade. Nor was this view limited to the extreme right. George Kennan, a liberal Democrat and senior State Department architect of the policy of containment against Communism, also opposed Jewish immigration on the grounds that Jews were prone to Communism. Not surprisingly, Kennan similarly opposed the creation of the State of Israel as detrimental to American interests in the Moslem world.

Within Palestine, British rule was rapidly deteriorating. Officially, immigration remained in accordance with the British White Paper policy. In 1946 there were 18,000 immigrants, only 9,000 officially authorized. Quietly the British government began lifting the restrictions of the White Paper, allowing official Jewish immigration to reach 15,000. However, the pressure of Jews desiring to enter Palestine was much greater. The British began establishing detention camps in Cyprus, preventing Holocaust survivors from immigrating to Palestine. Although conditions in the detention camps were far preferable to anything Jews had experienced under the Nazi terror, the symbolism of the detention camps to the Holocaust survivors suggested the insensitivity and amorality of British Palestinian policy.

Moreover, the refugee crisis itself was severely aggravated by the Kielce pogrom on July 4, 1946, in Poland. Although the war had been over barely a year and the news of the Final Solution was uppermost in people's minds, Kielce witnessed yet another blood libel. A Polish boy reported that he had been kidnapped and abused by Jews and, while kidnapped, that he had seen the bodies of other Christian children. The story was blatantly false. However, the mob quickly retaliated against Jews. Forty-two Jews were murdered and scores more injured. There is some evidence of Soviet provocation, possibly to defame Poland in the eyes of the West. The Soviets were clearly concerned about Western sympathy for Poland as a captive nation soon to be victimized again by Soviet hegemony. Calling attention to Polish anti-Semitism could well deprive Poland of liberal support in the West. The instigator of the pogrom was only nine years old at the time. He remains alive but claims lapses of memory on critical details.

Perhaps even more shocking was the insensitivity of the Polish Catholic Church. The Primate of Poland, Cardinal Hlond, in an interview with foreign journalists a week after the pogrom, agreed that anti-Semitism and the pogrom were regrettable, but that the Jews had been far too prominent in imposing a Stalinist regime upon Poland. Bishop Wyzynski of Lublin repeated the opinion that anti-Semitic expression was a result of the Jews being too active within the Communist Party. Shockingly, however, he went further, declaring, "The Germans murdered the Jewish nation because the Jews were the propagators of Communism," and referred to the classic blood libel against the Jews as a matter that had been "never completely clarified."

To be sure, these were by no means the only reactions from within the Church. The Bishop of Czestochowa firmly condemned the blood libel, and individual priests, such as Father Cwerynski in Cracow, sought to counteract anti-Semitic propaganda. However, for most Jews, the message was clear: Jews were not wanted in postwar Poland, and the moral authority of the Polish Catholic Church could by no means be relied upon to defend Jews against Polish anti-Semitism. By contrast, in New York City, Francis Cardinal Spellman called for the immediate admission of Jewish refugees into the United States.

Polish Jewry, with no place to turn, was now on the move. The presence of a large refugee population in Eastern Europe and in the occupied sectors of Germany increased the pressure on Britain to solve the Palestine problem.

Britain, however, was in no mood to act quickly and decisively. In London, significant protests ensued against British expenditures in Palestine, resulting in anti-Jewish outbreaks in the difficult winter of 1947. British Prime Minister Ernest Bevin warned Jews not to press their case too heavily, lest they ensure an anti-Semitic backlash. The Palestinian Yishuv, however, was not prepared to remain silent. Yishuv leaders, particularly David Ben-Gurion and Moshe Sharrett, now refused all cooperation with the British government. The Jewish underground, the Irgun, led by Menachem Begin, declared a revolt against British installations in Palestine. An explosion at the King David Hotel, headquarters of the British military in Jerusalem, shocked world opinion. Over 90 people were killed, including Jews, British officials, and Arabs.

The action clearly undermined the moral high ground the Yishuv had captured both before and after World War II. Ben-Gurion quickly disassociated himself from the action and urged cooperation with the British authorities in arresting Irgun leaders. The Irgun, for its part, staged kidnappings and reprisals for the British arrests. Most notorious was the affair of two British sergeants hung by the Irgun, one of whom was subsequently found to have had a Jewish mother in England.

The Mandate itself had been inherently unworkable because of the conflicting claims of Jews and Arabs to the same piece of land. The "Exodus" affair, involving a broken-down, overloaded ship bearing illegal refugees to Palestine, symbolized the bankruptcy of continued British rule. In the full light of world opinion, the "Exodus" was denied entry to Palestine. Few events could have made the case better for the necessity of Jewish independence, despite the ambivalence and even outrage over Jewish actions of violence against British installations in the Holy Land.

The Birth of Israel

The debate over the creation of Israel at the United Nations came at perhaps one of the most propitious moments in Cold War history. The United Nations Special Commission on Palestine recommended partition of Palestine into two states, one Arab and one Jewish, with Jerusalem subject to international control. As had been the pattern previously, the Yishuv accepted the attempt at compromise; the Arabs rejected it. In November 1947, the partition plan was brought before a United Nations vote at the General Assembly. United Nations procedure mandated that a resolution on partition would be binding only if it secured a two-thirds majority. Negative votes and all abstentions would be counted in the votes needed to secure the two-thirds majority (in effect making an abstention a negative vote).

Significantly, Russia and the United States agreed to support the partition plan. Russia was motivated primarily by a desire to weaken Britain's influence in the Middle East. The Soviets also anticipated that the conservative Moslem states would be inhospitable to Communist influence, whereas a socialist-led Israel might indeed become far more friendly to Soviet interests.

In the United States public opinion was overwhelmingly pro-Zionist. The State Department, by contrast, bitterly opposed the partition resolution. To Truman's great credit, he overrode the objections of his own foreign policy advisers in favor of both supporting the partition resolution and subsequently adhering to its implementation. The U.N. vote in favor of a partition resolution represented unprecedented Soviet-American agreement on a major international issue during the Cold War.

Nor was Soviet assistance limited to the diplomatic sphere. During the subsequent War for Independence, the Soviet Union generously supplied Israel with arms via Czechoslovakia. To be sure, this Soviet pro-Zionism was short-lived. Although the speeches at the U.N. of then-Soviet Ambassador Andrei Gromyko can be read as some of the finest documents in Zionist and Jewish history, Soviet support for Zionism very soon shifted to a hostile anti-Israel stance. The Zhdanov Doctrine proclaimed that all who were not pro-Soviet are hostile to Soviet interests. By this reasoning, Israel's ties to American Jewry struck Stalin as ingratitude for Soviet efforts and assistance in the creation of Israel.

The problem with the partition agreement was that it was inherently untenable. It created two independent states each divided into multiple zones. The hope was that the economically weaker Arab state of Palestine would be assisted by the Jewish state. Aside from the economic inviability of the Arab state and indefensible borders, implacable Arab hostility doomed the partition plan to failure. The Arab masses remained bitterly anti-Zionist, and mob warfare erupted even before the declaration of Israel's independence on May 15, 1948. During the final months of the British Mandate, the British army did little except disarm the combatants, mostly at the expense of the Israel Defense Forces, the Haganah. Significantly, during this period the United States also maintained an arms embargo on the Middle East. By contrast, the Czechoslovak military trade with Israel was of great importance for the looming struggle.

Indeed, no sooner was Israel declared an independent nation than did the combined forces of seven Arab armies launch their attack. The consequences of this War for Independence were multifold: First, in place of two independent states, what was to have been the new State of Palestine now became annexed to Jordan (the West Bank) and Egypt (the Gaza Strip). Jerusalem became divided between Arab and Jewish sectors. The armistice agreement guaranteed freedom of worship to Jews wishing to pray at the holy places in the Old City of Jerusalem. Sadly, this was never implemented. On the contrary, Jordanian occupation of the Old City meant the desecration of numerous Jewish holy places. Thirdly, the new State of Israel now became a contiguous state extending from the Lebanese border in the north to Eilat on the Red Sea in the south. The Jewish state soon moved its capital and major offices to Jerusalem, despite the fact that the division of Jerusalem was rejected by all major powers, who maintained their embassies in Tel Aviv.

Fourthly, the war created a mass refugee problem. To this day, there is considerable dispute as to the causes of the refugee plight. Arab propaganda blamed Israeli aggression and incitement of Arabs to leave their homes. They particularly cited the massacre at Deir Yassin, perpetrated by the Irgun against Arab civilians. Israeli sources argued that Arab governments expected a quick victory and encouraged local Arab populations to leave the scene of battle pending their return at an early date in the future. Moreover, Israeli sources noted that 500,000 Jewish refugees fled Arab lands in the immediate aftermath of the 1948 War. The Jewish communities of Iraq, Egypt, Yemen, among others, were virtually transplanted to Israel, effecting what many called a transfer of populations.

There is some truth in both of these claims. However, most refugee flight was spontaneous. People were simply terrified by the reality of war and quickly fled. Certainly, in the early stages of the war, most Israeli officials wanted the Arab population to stay, for their remaining in Israel would mean de facto acceptance of the partition plan. Clearly, by the latter stages, as leading Israeli officials have conceded in their memoirs, there was considerable gratification that the local Arabs had chosen to flee. Israel did offer to pay some reparations and facilitate refugee resettlement in other Arab lands. Arab governments, however, utilized the refugee issue for propagandistic purposes. Only Jordan made efforts to absorb refugees within the Jordanian state. Lastly, it should be noted that Jews were also expelled, particularly from the Jewish Quarter of the Old City of Jerusalem.

Finally, the war exposed what many have called the root cause of the Arab-Israeli conflict—namely, the failure of Arab nations to recognize the reality of the Jewish state. Arab extremism dictated that rather than try to contain Israel within very modest boundaries, Arabs were bent on eliminating Israel entirely as a nation-state. Only the Sadat initiative of 1977 marked a fundamental break with that extremism and led to the first peace treaty between Israel and an Arab nation. The test of the current peace process, of course, remains whether the Arabs remain committed to the extremist policy of eliminating Israel entirely or are willing to compromise with Middle East realities.

Israel and World Jewry

The birth of Israel also signified new patterns within existing world Jewry. For the first time in many centuries, Jews had regained sovereignty and independence. Psychologically, this was of great importance to a people that was only now awakening to the horrors of the Holocaust. Israeli intellectuals debated whether Israel was creating a new Jewish nation or was building upon links with diaspora Jewry. Diaspora Jews asked, conversely, to what extent Israel had the primary responsibility for representing Jewish interests world-wide.

The initial question concerned who would speak on behalf of world Jewry. The 1950 Ben-Gurion-Blaustein Agreement established the principle of non-interference in the affairs of one another. That Ben-Gurion turned to the American Jewish Committee rather than to the traditional Zionist organizations signaled Israel's willingness to relate to American Jewry as a whole, which could now be defined as "pro-Israel" generally, rather than underscore the traditional divisions between Zionist, non-Zionist, and anti-Zionist Jewish organizations. Although the principle of non-interference was often breached, acceptance of the principle meant that Israel recognized the legitimacy of opposition to its claims for global Jewish representation. For example, during negotiations with West Germany over reparations to Holocaust survivors, Israel undertook negotiations on behalf of her citizens, while other Jewish organizations negotiated on behalf of Jewish survivors in the diaspora.

Moreover, Israel's reality as a nation-state meant a new public focus upon Jewish identity and signaled the interdependence of Jewish communities everywhere. This was especially the case after the 1967 and 1973 wars, which demonstrated that events relating to Israel affected the lives of Jews everywhere. The wars also underlined the importance of diaspora Jewry as a supporting voice for Israel before national governments and public opinion. The Conference of Presidents of Major Jewish Organizations was established in the 1950's to provide a unified voice of American Jewry on foreign affairs, particularly as they related to Israel and the Middle East. Similarly, the American Israel Public Affairs Committee (AIPAC) was created in the 1950's to monitor legislation affecting Israel on Capitol Hill, particularly with respect to U.S. foreign aid. The emergence of these organizations signaled the growing pro-Israel consensus among American Jews. The American Jewish Committee joined that consensus, as evidenced by the Ben-Gurion-Blaustein Agreement. The once-powerful and anti-Zionist American Council for Judaism, which at its height represented over one-third of the Reform rabbinate, now became marginalized and inconsequential. Support for Israel became virtually a litmus test for the assertion of Jewish identity and commitment in the diaspora. Conversely, membership in the Jewish people defined the content and meaning of being Jewish for both Israel and diaspora Jews. The resettlement of Soviet Jewish and Ethiopian refugees at the end of the twentieth century, undertaken together by Israel and diaspora Jewry, symbolized the extent of Jewish interdependence and peoplehood.

War and Diplomacy

The most critical foreign affairs question concerned the ongoing war between Israel and the surrounding Arab States. Efforts in the 1950's to reach a peace agreement between Israel and Egypt floundered. The discovery of a plan to blow-up American installations in Egypt so as to drive a wedge between the government of Gamal Nasser and the Eisenhower administration resulted in a major political scandal within Israel. The "Lavon Affair" concerned whether the Defense Ministry, headed by Pinchas Lavon, bore responsibility for the fiasco. During these years, David Ben-Gurion had temporarily retired from politics, and Moshe Sharrett, his long-time Foreign Minister, was serving as Prime Minister. Sharrett's government was further rattled by the sensational public trial of Rudolph Kastner, a Foreign Ministry official who was accused of collaborating with the Nazis while serving as head of the Jewish Communal Council in Budapest during World War II. Although a government inquiry cleared Kastner of the charges, he was subsequently assassinated by Jewish extremists. To this day, controversy continues over the assessment of his role in Budapest in the context of larger questions concerning Jewish leadership in the latter years of World War II.

The controversies over Lavon and Kastner rocked the Sharrett administration. Sharrett had opposed retaliation raids against fedayeen guerrillas infiltrating from the Gaza Strip. However, Ben-Gurion returned to the government in June 1956, and subsequently demoted Sharrett. Ben-Gurion adopted a confrontational stance toward Nasser in place of Sharrett's aborted efforts at securing a peace treaty.

Ben-Gurion now collaborated with the governments of Britain and France to overthrow Nasser. Nasser had nationalized the Suez Canal. For Britain and France, once predominant powers in the Middle East, the 1956 Suez War represented their last effort at reasserting their influence and predominance. Their plan was for Israel to attack in the Sinai peninsula and for Britain and France to intervene under the pretext of maintaining peace in the area.

The operation was a military success but a diplomatic defeat. The United States firmly opposed Britain, France, and Israel in what was considered the first break in the postwar Western alliance. At the height of the Cold War, the Eisenhower administration had consistently claimed moral superiority over the Soviet bloc. The United States would not collude in an effort to defend the overt imperialism of Britain and France.

In going to war, Israel hoped to realize the concrete objectives of crushing the fedayeen in Gaza, opening up the Gulf of Aqaba to Israeli shipping via the port of Eilat, and toppling Nasser and forcing Egypt to make peace. In opposing Britain and France, the United States also opposed the Israeli action. Eisenhower insisted that Israel withdraw from the Sinai, even resorting to the threat that tax deductions for American Jewish donations to the United Jewish Appeal would be forfeited. To be sure, Israel accepted the guarantees of a United Nations buffer force in the Sinai coupled with a guarantee for the right of passage of Israeli shipping in the Gulf of Aqaba. These guarantees, however, bore the seeds for the next war. Egypt continued to refer to the Gulf of Aqaba as an "Arab lake." A U.N. force of 3,000 soldiers remained in Egypt only at the sufferance of the Egyptian government. Most importantly, no movement ensued on the question of Arab recognition for Israel as one of the legitimate states in the region. Israel's overall image suffered, as she was now perceived as an agent of two Western imperialist powers. In terms of Israel-United States relations, the Suez War clearly represented the low point in the American-Israeli relationship.

As noted, the resolution of the Sinai campaign laid the seeds for the 1967 Six-Day War. In retrospect, the Soviet Union appears to have incited the Arab states with false reports of Israeli troop concentrations along the Syrian border. In all likelihood, both the Soviet Union and Egypt desired a propaganda coup rather than military action. However, by again closing the Gulf of Aqaba and sending 100,000 Egyptian troops into the Sinai while evicting the token U.N. troops, Egypt effectively made war with Israel inevitable.

In the month of May 1967, Israel felt threatened by diplomatic isolation. France, under Charles de Gaulle, had already begun her search for new allies in the Middle East. De Gaulle warned Israel explicitly that France would not support her if she took military action. The Soviets, as mentioned, vigorously supported Nasser's actions. Most observers maintained that the United States was too preoccupied with the Vietnam War to offer Israel concrete assistance. President Lyndon Johnson asked Israel to refrain from taking action until he had mounted an international consortium that would open up the Gulf of Aqaba to Israeli shipping. However, it became quickly evident that Johnson's international efforts would gain little support. The memory of Jewish isolation during the Holocaust years evoked powerful chords among American Jews during the anxious days of May 1967. Once again, it was feared that Israel and the Jewish people stood alone.

In deciding to go to war on June 5, 1967, Israel sought to break the blockade of Eilat and the diplomatic stranglehold it faced via the Egyptian-Jordanian-Syrian alliance. The result was an overwhelming military victory leaving Israel in possession of the Sinai peninsula, the strategic Golan Heights, the West Bank, and the Gaza Strip. Moreover, a divided Jerusalem, which had symbolized both the aspirations and the frustrations of the Jewish State, was now a united city in Israeli hands. At the United Nations, the United States representatives firmly supported Israel. By November 1967 the United States had succeeded in securing passage of U.N. Resolution 242, calling for Israeli withdrawals but insisting upon recognition of Israel by all parties as a legitimate nation-state within the region. U.N. Resolution 242 served as the basis for subsequent peace initiatives to end the conflict.

Israel as a Jewish State

From its beginnings, Zionism encountered a contradiction between its aspirations for normalcy, of becoming a state like all other nations, and its aspirations to establish a specifically Jewish homeland. In the former view, Israel consisted of a Jewish majority, but its content would be determined by the norms of liberal democracy. In the latter view, of a specifically Jewish State, it was assumed that Israel made sense only in the context of a particular relationship to Judaic heritage, history, and tradition. This debate—over history, religion, and the public symbols of society—has colored much of Israel's brief history. For example, the very Law of Return granting every Jew the right of immediate citizenship upon entry to Israel signaled the importance of Israel to diaspora Jewry and its unique place in Jewish history. Moving the Israeli capital from Tel Aviv to Jerusalem in 1950 and subsequently declaring that Jerusalem's status as the united capital of Israel was nonnegotiable in the aftermath of the Six-Day War also signaled that Israel was not simply another Western democracy, but rather a uniquely Jewish State with particular ties to Jewish history and tradition.

Governing this debate has been what has commonly been referred to as the "religious status quo." Successive Israeli governments have pledged not to alter the particular relationship between Judaism and the Jewish State. In that context, the Orthodox Chief Rabbinate has maintained its monopoly on questions affecting laws of personal status, i.e. "Who is a Jew?" Similarly, the compromises in place in 1948 concerning the use of public transportation on the Shabbat remain in force, allowing buses to be banned from Jerusalem on Shabbat, but permitted in Haifa.

Like most compromises, the religious status quo satisfies neither camp. Approximately 20 percent of Israel's population classify themselves as religious. Most of this group sees the Jewish State as a unique opportunity to apply Jewish law to modern conditions. Secular Israelis, by contrast, approximately 50 percent of Israel's population, desire an American-style democracy in which the coercive powers of the state not be invoked to enforce religious behaviors. Many in this group, however, would agree that Judaism ought to continue to enjoy some preferred status, particularly in education and in the public symbols of the nation-state. An additional 30 percent of the population, who classify themselves as traditionalists, are especially outspoken in urging that Israel remain a fully Jewish State, although they too oppose invoking state powers to enforce religion. Only a tiny minority of "post-Zionists" have argued that Israel's future lies in her integration into the Middle

East and that her links to Judaism and to diaspora Jewry obstruct that full integration.

War and Peace

The aftermath of the Six-Day War left Israel in control of significant territories, but the dream of a peace treaty between Israel and the warring Arab states remained unfulfilled. Israeli policy, as formulated by Levi Eshkol, Golda Meir, and Moshe Dayan, underscored the negotiability of all of the territories with the exception of Jerusalem, but awaited the proverbial phone call from Arab partners to begin the process of negotiations. The Khartoum formula of 1969, however, summarized the Arab response as a series of noes—to recognition, to peace, and to negotiations.

The War of Attrition across the Suez Canal lasted for close to a year. On a virtually daily basis Israeli and Egyptian encampments across the canal bombarded one another. The cease-fire, engineered by Secretary of State William Rogers in the summer of 1970, effectively ended the War of Attrition but promised no further movement on securing peace between Israel and Egypt.

The death of President Nasser and the ascent of his successor, President Anwar Sadat, changed the map of Middle East politics. Although initially dismissed as a lightweight and as a former supporter of Hitler, Sadat altered the course of Israel-Arab relations. In the summer of 1972, he expelled Soviet advisors from Egypt. Most strikingly, in October 1973, he, together with Syria, launched the Yom Kippur War against Israel. The war lasted over three weeks and was clearly the costliest war in Israel's history since the War for Independence in 1948. Although the war concluded with significant Israeli victories, the political culture in the Arab world was fundamentally changed. Sadat had demonstrated that Israel was vulnerable and that combined Arab military power could alter the course of events. The use of economic power, namely an oil boycott, only enhanced the prestige and status of Arab leaders in the Third World. Once again, the identification of Israel with Western-style imperialism, in this case the United States, solidified Israel's isolation in the Third World, culminating in the passage of the infamous Zionism = Racism Resolution in 1975.

America had indeed come to Israel's rescue during the darkest days of the 1973 war. President Richard Nixon undertook significant rearming of Israel and bluntly warned the Soviets to refrain from active intervention in the area. Clearly America, however, did not desire a repeat of the massive Israeli victory of 1967. Rather Nixon, together with Secretary of State Henry Kissinger, undertook to assure Israel's capacity to defend herself but at the same time to preserve Arab self-dignity. For example, American intervention prevented Israel from destroying the Egyptian Third Army that had successfully crossed the Suez Canal into the Sinai peninsula. Kissinger assumed that another Israeli victory would result only in continuation of the status quo. Permitting Egypt, in particular, to claim a partial stalemate and significant successes would, in turn, enable Egyptian leaders to break the diplomatic stalemate and move toward recognition of Israel as part of the region.

The Kissinger vision ultimately was realized, albeit not immediately. Kissinger succeeded, via shuttle diplomacy, to secure disengagement agreements between Israel and Egypt and Israel and Syria. His failure to reach a disengagement accord on the Jordanian border left open the vexing question of the Palestinians and Jewish settlements on the West Bank. Israeli Prime Minister Yitzhak Rabin cooperated with Kissinger's diplomacy offering a "piece of peace for a piece of land." As a result, Israel withdrew partially from the Sinai peninsula and disengaged from confrontation with Syrian forces in the Golan Heights. Kissinger had succeeded in isolating Soviet influence from the region and establishing the United States as an "honest broker" between Israel and the Arab States.

Although Kissinger had laid the groundwork for breaking the diplomatic logjam in the Middle East, it was President Sadat who effected the first real breakthrough in Israel-Arab relations. By visiting Jerusalem and declaring his willingness to sign a full peace treaty in exchange for a complete Israeli withdrawal from the Sinai, Sadat altered the endless cycle of war between Israel and her Arab neighbors. Israeli Prime Minister Menachem Begin, to the consternation of many of his ideological supporters (and even some opponents), agreed to full Israeli withdrawal from the Sinai and even the dismantling of Israeli settlements there. The Camp David Accords, signed by Begin and Sadat in September 1978, for the first time recognized the legitimate rights of the Palestinians. Israel was promised a full peace treaty with Egypt, and hope prevailed that other Arab nations would follow Egypt in reaching peace with Israel. Following the signing of the treaty, in April 1979, the autonomy talks on the future of the occupied territories were unable to advance. The peace with Egypt held, but no additional Arab states were forthcoming in their willingness to advance the Camp David Accords, and tensions remained strong on both the West Bank and the Lebanon border.

As a result, yet another war broke out in 1982 between Israel and the PLO forces stationed in Lebanon. This war began as "Operation Peace for Galilee," meaning an Israeli effort to safeguard the towns of the Galilee from PLO shelling across the Lebanon border. In practice, Minister of Defense Ariel Sharon harbored a much grander desire to destroy the PLO's military domination of Lebanon and install a new Lebanese government that would be prepared to sign a peace treaty with Israel. These broader war aims embroiled Israeli troops in a siege of Beirut, incurred widespread international condemnation, including the disapproval of the United States, and stimulated unprecedented anti-war dissent within Israel itself. The war ended with the expulsion of the PLO from Beirut, but the Israelis had clearly placed too much trust in the Gemayel family as partners in the effort to rebuild Lebanon. Bashir Gemayel was assassinated, Lebanese Christians perpetrated a frightful massacre of Palestinians in the refugee camps of Sabra and Shatilla, and Israel quickly discovered that interventions into the quagmire of Lebanese politics were fruitless at best, destructive at worst. The Kahan Commission, investigating the massacres at Sabra and Shatilla, held Israel indirectly accountable for the atrocities given that Israel bore overall responsibility for preserving order in the area. The Lebanese debacle ultimately signaled the end to Prime Minster Begin's career. A national unity government, headed by his rival Shimon Peres, successfully negotiated Israeli withdrawal from Lebanon.

Two additional conflicts in the late 1980's and early 1990's further altered the Middle East equation. Beginning in December 1987, Israel was compelled to struggle with the Palestinian Intifada on the West Bank and Gaza Strip. The Intifada modeled itself on the Jewish uprising of 1946–1947 against the British Empire. Many Israelis became convinced that occupation was no longer worth the cost—morally, humanly, or economically.

The Gulf War, pitting a U.S.-led coalition against Saddam Hussein of Iraq, further altered the status quo. The war demonstrated that America now remained the sole super-power, and that Arab states could no longer look to the Soviet Union for assistance. The coalition embodied the common interests of Egypt, Saudi Arabia, and Syria in halting a militant Islam, represented by Saddam Hussein. Moreover, the Scud missile attacks upon Israel brought home to many Israelis the dangers of sophisticated weaponry and the capacity of Israel's enemies to inflict damage upon the Israeli psyche and morale, even if Israel's existence as a nation was not at all endangered by the war.

As a result, in the aftermath of the Gulf War, new efforts at Middle East peace were launched. Prime Minister Yitzhak Shamir agreed to attend the Madrid Conference, symbolizing Israeli willingness to negotiate with Palestinian representatives. His successor, Prime Minister Rabin, went considerably further, officially recognizing Yasser Arafat and the Palestine Liberation Organization as the primary partner in securing a peace between Israel and the Palestinians. As a direct result of the Oslo Accords, signed in September 1993, Israel was able to sign a complete peace treaty with Jordan, realizing one of the long unfulfilled ambitions of Israel's military victory in the Six-Day War. The Oslo I and Oslo II Accords represented major steps toward Israeli withdrawal from the West Bank and Gaza Strip, although major issues such as peace with Syria, the final status of Jewish settlements on the West Bank, and the future of Jerusalem all remained as outstanding issues for Israeli foreign policy.

Reading: David Ben-Gurion and Moshe Pearlman, ed., *Ben-Gurion Looks Back*

The following reading is David Ben-Gurion's recollections of the birth of Israel in 1948. Note his conviction that the state must be declared despite the overwhelming military odds and the active discouragement of the legendary soldier and American Secretary of State General George C. Marshall. Lastly, note Ben-Gurion's analogy to the American Declaration of Independence and Revolutionary War, fought by George Washington. This image of Israel as a new and noble democracy, almost a "little America," a David versus Goliath imagery, would pervade many of the early years of Israel's history and of the Israel-American "special relationship."

Reflections on Independence Day

Moshe Pearlman: Ben Gurion, your greatest moment must have been your declaration of Israel's independence on the 14th of May 1948, and I don't suppose there is anything about that day you can ever forget. What were your thoughts at this historic ceremony?

Ben Gurion: I do not know that I can recapture all the thoughts that crowded into my mind on that occasion, but I can remember the core of my thinking, for it was something I had dreamed of and fought for the whole of my life, as had most of the Jews in Israel and many many Jews outside: I thought, now at last we are responsible for our own destiny. It is ours to shape. We had been a minority element in scores of lands for almost two thousand years, our fate determined by others. Sometimes, and in some lands, we enjoyed kind treatment, there was tolerance and the opportunity to develop. At other times, we were restricted, hounded, persecuted, murdered. We had just lost six million of our people, slaughtered by the Nazis. For centuries we had been like flowers in a wood, some plucked by friendly hands, given water and nurtured, others trampled underfoot and crushed. At no time could we be ourselves, enjoy independence, with the freedom to live a normal national life on our own soil, making our own decisions affecting our destiny. Now the hour had struck. We were independent once again. These reflections were uppermost in my mind.

Coupled with them was the knowledge that while I was reading the Declaration of Independence the armies of the neighbouring Arab States were massing on our borders, ready to march across.

When, some hours later, I went to inspect the damage done by the Egyptian bombing which marked the opening of the Arab war on the new State, I remember thinking that if we were now responsible for our destiny, the rational question might well be whether in a few days or a few weeks we would have a destiny to shape. For we had no planes to match their planes, no artillery, no tanks. Yet none of us at the time had any doubt about the outcome.

A few days earlier, I had received an urgent message from General George Marshall. He was United States Secretary of State at the time, and he urged me desperately not to go ahead with my declared intention of proclaiming independence. I had had similar messages from several other governments and distinguished individuals, some friends, some not so friendly. Marshall was a friend, a true friend, and he tried to discourage me not because he was opposed to a Jewish State but because he thought we would be quickly destroyed by the overwhelmingly superior forces of the Arab States. He thought they would attack us if we declared our statehood, and our small, poorly armed forces would be overrun. He begged me to wait for a more favourable political climate and in the meantime international arrangements might be made whereby the United Nations Partition Resolution could be implemented in some form.

Here, then, was the counsel of a friend and the military appreciation of our situation by one of the world's outstanding soldiers. On the face of it, such advice was not to be dismissed lightly. Yet it could not deflect us from our chosen course. For Marshall could not know what we knew—what we felt in our very bones: that this was our historic hour; if we did not live up to it, through fear or weakness of spirit, it might be generations or even centuries before our people were given another historic opportunity—if indeed we would be alive as a national group. However grave might be the repercussions of the decision to declare our independence, I knew that the future would be infinitely worse for my people if we did *not* do so. We decided to go ahead and proclaim our independence as planned. Let me add that there was absolute unanimity among all my colleagues in the 13-member National Administration [the body which became the Provisional Government of Israel the moment the Proclamation had been read and signed].

I remember that these thoughts were in my mind when, on my way home from the late-afternoon Independence ceremony, I watched the people dancing in the streets, celebrating the historic act to which we had all put our hand. I did not dance with them, though I felt with them the emotion of the moment. It was something to see—the sheer joy in their faces, the light in their eyes, the exuberance of their movements, all caught in a surge of ecstasy. They were right to dance, I thought, even though I was all too aware—as many of the dancers must have been aware—of the dangers that faced us and the sacrifice we would suffer in defending the statehood we had just gained.

As a matter of fact, on the night of Independence I was also awakened—twice. The first time was to hear the news of President Truman's declaration recognizing the new State of Israel. The second was to be persuaded to make an Independence broadcast to the world—it was about four o'clock in the morning, so that with the time difference it reached New York listeners in the evening. While I was broadcasting, listeners heard the crump of bombs landing near the improvised Tel-Aviv studio from an Egyptian bomber.

As soon as I had finished my broadcast, I went to inspect the bomb damage, and the plea and warning of General Marshall came back to me. Would he prove right? I did not think so, though I knew his fears were well grounded. I knew equally well in my heart that no one outside Israel could possibly feel as we did, that we *had* to seize the historic moment and that despite the odds we would win. It is probably Clausewitz who talked of the conflict of wills in warfare: the stronger of the two wills wins. I knew, with Marshall, that we would be vastly outnumbered, and that we would face an enormous superiority of arms. But I also knew, what Marshall did not know, that our will would prove stronger—not because we were more militaristic than the Arabs but because we would be fighting for a cause and also because defeat for us would mean national destruction. For the armies of the neighbouring Arab States, it was largely a battle for spoils. Failure for them would not mean the loss of their countries, nor an end to their existence as national entities.

It is also true, as Marshall indicated, that we had only a partisan force to fling against the regular armies of the Arab States. These armies, fully-fledged military machines, had been trained for the kind of warfare that would soon be upon us. They were equipped with the standard weapons appropriate to a regular army, and were organized in the standard formations suitable for large-scale warfare—corps, divisions, brigades. We had the Haganah, an underground defence force with all the limitations of a force that had had to train and operate in secrecy and conceal its weapons from the Mandatory authorities—no heavy weapons, small formations, an emphasis on local defence, much of it static. As a matter of fact it was only two months earlier, in March 1948, that for the first time we had undertaken engagements in which we committed a force as large as a brigade—and a very small brigade at that.

But I had read my Washington, as Marshall had also certainly done, though no doubt with different eyes. What struck me so deeply was the nature of Washington's Army—they were underfed, underarmed, with no proper clothing and meagre transport. They could have been called a rabble. Yet they had the stronger will—and they were victorious. I don't say there is not a limit to the odds that can be faced and overcome. I do say, however, that the will of a people and the spirit and morale of its army are immeasurably powerful factors in war and can be decisive. I knew they would be decisive in our war of independence.

Bibliography for Further Reading

Dinnerstein, Leonard. *America and the Survivors of the Holocaust,* Columbia University Press, 1982

Eban, Abba. *Personal Witness,* Putnam, 1992

Hartman, David. *Conflicting Visions: Spiritual Possibilities of Modern Israel,* Schocken Books, 1990

O'Brien, Conor Cruise. *The Siege,* Simon and Schuster, 1986

Sachar, Howard. *A History of Israel,* Volumes I-II, Oxford University Press, 1979–1987

Segev, Tom. *The Seventh Million,* Hill and Wang, 1993

Shipler, David. *Arab and Jew: Wounded Spirits in a Promised Land,* Penguin, 1987

Unit XXXIV

Where Are We?

American Jewry

The most remarkable feature of American Jewish history since the end of World War II has been the steady decline of anti-Semitism in this country. Opinion polls have consistently demonstrated high appreciation for Jews and lower levels of intolerance. Perhaps the best barometer of the decline in anti-Semitism has been the increased willingness of Americans to intermarry with Jews. By the early 1980's almost four-fifths of American citizens expressed benign approval of the possible marriage of one of their sons or daughters to a Jew.

Perhaps more pointedly, phenomena that historically had featured anti-Semitism were now noticeably lacking in significant anti-Semitic expression. The Rosenberg case of the early 1950's concerning an espionage ring spying on behalf of the Soviet Union centered around the treason of Julius Rosenberg. Rosenberg's guilt has been corroborated by diverse sources, including Nikita Khruschev, who noted Rosenberg's usefulness to the Soviet atomic weaponry program. In that sense, his crimes were serious, given the Cold War Soviet-American rivalry and the overall fear of a third world war involving nuclear weaponry.

In short, Rosenberg appeared to be a test case of the classic Jew = Communist imagery. Moreover, Jews were involved in the Rosenberg case on multiple levels: Rosenberg's accuser, some of his accomplices, the attorneys associated with the case, and Justice Irving Kaufman were all Jews.

Yet what is most remarkable in the case was the relative absence of anti-Semitism. Ironically, Jean-Paul Sartre, a spokesman of the French Left, denounced the execution of Rosenberg as a "legal lynching," while the Communist historian Herbert Aptheker raised charges of anti-Semitism in the case. By contrast, Jewish organizations, including the American Jewish Committee, anxious to prove their own anti-Communist *bona fides*, and perhaps fearful of increased anti-Semitism in America, opposed clemency for the Rosenbergs and upheld their conviction.

Yet one could not miss the contrast between the Rosenberg case in America and the Slansky trials in Prague which took place at the same time. Julius Rosenberg was guilty. He may not have merited the death penalty, but he did betray his country at the height of the Cold War. Rudolph Slansky and the other members of the Prague 13 were all fiercely loyal Communists. Associating Slansky with Zionism was ludicrous, for Slansky's Jewish identity was virtually non-existent and he opposed Zionism as a bourgeois reaction. Yet Slansky and his associates were executed as part of Stalin's anti-Semitic crackdown. Sartre and his associates in the French Left could not bring themselves to denounce Stalin for this miscarriage of justice. Yet they charged anti-Semitism in the Rosenberg case, despite the considerable evidence that Rosenberg was indeed guilty.

Similarly, the Joseph P. McCarthy phenomenon of the early 1950's embodied all the features usually accompanied by anti-Semitism—conspiracy theory, anti-Communist hysteria, and resentment against the Eastern Establishment. The George Wallace phenomenon in the late 1960's also embodied all of these currents. Yet both Wallace and McCarthy deliberately eschewed any expression of anti-Semitism. McCarthy went out of his way to demonstrate his freedom from anti-Semitism by pointing to his two Jewish attorneys, Roy Cohn and David Schine. Wallace too, despite his racism, did not turn against Jews. Both apparently recognized that anti-Semitism had no place in the American political culture of the postwar era.

Finally, perhaps the most notable test case for anti-Semitism was the 1973 oil boycott. Gas prices skyrocketed while oil shortages prevailed. It would have been quite easy to blame America's oil crisis on the unnatural alliance of America with Israel, the enemy of the Middle Eastern oil-producing states. Yet despite a few bumper stickers, widely reported but very rarely actually sighted, the 1973 oil boycott witnessed no anti-Jewish backlash. Most Americans accepted the need to conserve oil and, if anything, blamed the exploitation of the oil-producing states rather than Israel and her American allies.

To be sure, the taboo on anti-Semitic expression in the political arena was broken in the 1980's. On the left, Jesse Jackson's two presidential campaigns, in 1984 and in 1988, unfortunately gave expression to anti-Jewish resentment, particularly as expressed by Jackson's "surrogate," Louis Farrakhan, leader of the Nation of Islam. Similarly Pat Buchanan's 1992 Presidential campaign demonstrated that the taboo on anti-Semitism had been breached. Whether these represented a temporary blip on an overall screen of Jewish acceptance in American society, or whether they portended long-term threats to Jewish presence in America, remains to be seen. Blacks and Jews experienced considerable intergroup conflict in the latter half of the twentieth century, epitomized by the Crown Heights "pogrom" of 1991, three days of anti-Jewish rioting including a murder of a visiting Australian Jew. These tensions, however, albeit real, by no means eclipsed the overall portrait of America as the society in diaspora Jewish history that has been most fully welcoming of Jewish participation.

Indeed, by the close of the twentieth century, American Jews enjoyed unprecedented influence, power, and access to American society. Although Jews were but 2.5 percent of the population, they formed 5 percent of the undergraduate student bodies on college campuses, 10 percent of university faculties, and 20 percent of elite university faculties. Jews were twice as likely to receive a college education and three times as likely to receive post-graduate education than the American Caucasian population generally. In American politics, no less than 10 percent of the United States Senate in the 1980's consisted of Jews. Senator Joseph Lieberman, an influential Democratic Senator from Connecticut, proudly identified as an Orthodox Jew.

Moreover, the opportunities for leading an intensive Jewish life were probably greater in America than in any diaspora Jewish community. Jewish day schools, functioning in virtually every American city, provided an excellent opportunity for immersion in

Jewish heritage. By 1990 almost 40 percent of Jewish students receiving any form of Jewish education were enrolled in Jewish day schools, a model of Jewish education pioneered by American Orthodoxy but now adopted within the Conservative and Reform movements as well. On college campuses, where in the 1950's one could barely find a program of academic Jewish studies, by the 1990's intensive course offerings on Judaic heritage were to be found at most institutions of higher learning. The entry of the academic study of Judaism into the American university culture signaled the acceptance and legitimacy of Jewish presence in contemporary American culture.

Yet the picture remains complicated. As Jews have succeeded in American society, it became unclear how Jewish they would remain. The total numbers of Jews did not increase between 1950 and 1990. At the beginning of the baby-boom years, American Jews numbered 5.4 million. By 1990, their numbers did not exceed 5.5 million—at a time when the American population increased from 150 to 260 million. Intermarriage symbolized the high level of Jewish assimilation. By 1990 half of American Jews were marrying out of the faith, and of these, little more than one-quarter even claimed to be raising their children as Jews.

The American Jewish condition, therefore, appeared to be a double-edged sword. In some respects, Jews were the envy of other ethnic and other religious groupings. For the core of committed Jews, Jewish life had never been so intense, passionate, and active. For example, more quality books of Jewish interest were being published than ever before. However, as the core became more intensively involved, the periphery drifted into American society. The great question for the future of American Jewry consisted of the fate of the "middles" of Jewish life—those who wanted Jewish continuity, symbolized by Jewish grandchildren, yet who lacked the wherewithal and the knowledge to ensure that continuity. American Jews insisted upon the highest levels of excellence in their secular education, but failed to apply the same standards to their Jewish educational attainments. In the public square, Jews appeared to be incredibly self-confident and assertive in representing Jewish interests to American centers of power. Yet in the privacy of their own homes, they lacked a language to explain to their own children why leading a Jewish life was important.

For much of the postwar generation, American Jewry persisted on the dual image of Holocaust and rebirth. Leading a Jewish life was important, in Emil Fackenheim's memorable phrase, "not to grant posthumous victories to Hitler." The Zionist dream, as realized in the creation of Israel, validated the Jewish enterprise. However, at the close of the twentieth century, these two images seemingly receded in importance. The Holocaust remained the dominant event of the twentieth century, yet increasingly Jews questioned whether memories of destruction constituted a sufficient base on which to reconstruct Jewish life. Conversely, American Jews, born after the birth of Israel in 1948, increasingly found themselves as at most "distant relatives" to Israelis, given their significant differences of language, culture, and religious practice.

American Orthodoxy constituted an exception to these trends. Orthodox education underscored the joy and celebration of leading a Jewish life. Observers noted the power of the Orthodox community both to retain members and attract newcomers. The challenge for the non-Orthodox movements at the close of the twentieth century lay in whether they could provide their members with community and personal meaning, the model of Orthodox success in this country.

Despite the predictions of the demise of Orthodoxy that had been so prevalent in the 1950's, by the 1990's Orthodoxy's capacity for self-preservation had been demonstrated. Yet clearly Orthodoxy cannot become a model for American Jews generally. Ninety-four percent of American Jewry do not identify with Orthodoxy. The overwhelming majority belong to the Conservative and Reform movements. These movements also looked to Jewish education to provide a sustained basis for Jewish continuity. They agreed that the Holocaust and Israel would not suffice to preserve Jewish life. They searched for alternative bases, including the power of Jewish texts, Jewish peoplehood, and the quest for spiritual meaning. Their degree of success in these endeavors will map out the future course of American Jewish history.

American Jewry, in short, contained two parallel trends occurring simultaneously. The story of Jewish renewal was real. In every community, one found individuals who were far more Jewishly engaged than their parents and grandparents had ever envisioned. Their numbers were far more evident in the Conservative and Reform movements than within Orthodoxy—although public discussion tended to glorify the successes of Orthodoxy as the most dramatic. Yet parallel to this movement of Jewish renewal ran the story of Jewish assimilation. Too many American Jews had simply stopped paying attention to anything the Jewish community was doing. For these individuals, being Jewish had become an irrelevance. For every convert to Judaism, a born-Jew had converted to another faith. Additionally, over a million Jews defined themselves as non-practicing members of the Jewish faith.

For this latter group, the dangers of internal erosion were real. American Jewry had maintained its numbers for a full generation only by virtue of a short-term baby boom and limited immigration from the Soviet Union. As the birth-rate declined to below replacement level, and immigration from abroad ceased, observers feared that the trends toward assimilation could well overwhelm the trends toward renewal. Yet most observers agreed that only by reconnecting with Judaic heritage could American Jewry hope to ensure its future continuity and enhance its quality of Jewish life.

Are There Distinctive Jewish Ideas?

Our journey through Jewish history has taken us from the tales of Genesis to the rebirth of a Jewish state. What, exactly, have we learned? Are there distinctive Jewish teachings, and can these serve as the basis for perpetuating Jewish life into the twenty-first century?

I wish to close this volume with five distinct themes that, I believe, have remained ever-present in Jewish history and will continue to serve as the foundations for future Jewish existence.

One theme consists of the territorial imperative. For major periods of Jewish life, the Land of Israel has served as the focal point of Jewish settlement. Even during periods of relative Jewish absence from the Land of Israel, although there was no period that Israel was literally *judenrein,* the aspiration for return to Israel remained paramount. Every day, Jews turned to Jerusalem and expressed their desire for a Jewish restoration. The rebirth of a Jewish State, the return to Zion, and the flourishing of Israel as the center of Jewish energies signaled the ongoing nature of the Jewish enterprise. Although contemporary Zionism is far removed from the "return to the soil" favored by early Zionist thinkers, the reality of Israel today means that Jewish life the world over is tightly bound up with events and developments that take place in the historic Jewish homeland.

Yet the importance of the territorial imperative does not overshadow the significance of a second continuing theme—the relationship of Israel to a strong diaspora. The diaspora has been a constant in Jewish life since the destruction of the kingdom of Samaria and the Assyrian exile in 722 B.C.E. The challenge throughout history has been to nurture ties between Jews living across geographical boundaries and cultural and linguistic divides. The Zionist debate over the viability of the diaspora continues. Yet our study of history demonstrates that Jews have flourished best when relations between Israel and the diaspora have been mutually enriching and synergistic. At present, the two major Jewish communities of the world are in Israel and the United States. Smaller communities exist elsewhere, particularly in Europe and, to a lesser extent, in South America, South Africa, and Australia. Given the challenges assimilation poses to these diaspora Jewish communities, it is probably fatuous to speak of bicentralism between Israel and the diaspora. In this sense, the Zionist argument for the centrality of Israel has been corroborated. Yet these diverse communities need one another. The interdependence of Jewish life, especially in an age of global communications, necessitates the constant exchange and interplay of energies between Israel and diaspora Jewish communities.

Within these diaspora communities, the historical question has been the relationship of the Jew to the majority culture. Assimilation, to be sure, has often taken its toll. Equally if not more problematical has been the often hostile reception Jews have received in diaspora countries. Still, other examples suggest a "third way" between assimilation to the surrounding culture and isolation from it. That third way lies in accommodation to the host culture in the diaspora—approving its best features, coexisting with it politically, and availing ourselves of the opportunities provided for cultural growth. What unites a Mordecai Kaplan with a Moses Maimonides is their willingness to live in two civilizations. Both were well-acquainted with the twin threats of anti-Semitism and assimilation. Yet both rejected isolation from gentile culture. Conversely, both advocated continuation of uniquely Jewish ideals and a Jewish presence within gentile society. Lastly, neither abandoned historical Jewish aspirations for returning to the Jewish homeland.

In other words, despite enormous differences of theology, Kaplan and Maimonides are united by a common quest—the development of a new synthesis between Judaism and general culture. That challenge remains no less pressing in America of the 1990's than for Egyptian Jewry in the Middle Ages. Certainly the importance of Jewish community in preserving the fabric of Jewish life must be underscored. Jewish institutions throughout history have served not only to provide services to Jews and to represent the community to gentile audiences, but also to propel the machinery energizing Jewish life. The fact that Jewish communities were autonomous throughout the Middle Ages signaled the power of Jews to sustain their enterprise in diaspora societies. In modern times, the communities have been organized upon voluntary principles. That volunteerism, in some respects, provided a model in America for other ethnic and religious groupings. Today we have a Jewish community that is institutionally strong, but whose future strength will depend upon the willingness of Jews to commit their time and resources to the Jewish enterprise. Salo Baron, the preeminent Jewish historian, correctly identified Jewish communal institutions as primary pillars of Jewish existence. Future Jewish history will test the continued salience of Baron's thesis.

Lastly, Jews have persevered as the People of the Book. What that meant historically was the importance of Jewish literacy generally and continued study of *the* Book—the Torah. Judaism began as a religion of law. While Jews as a people are divided in their attitude toward and observance of the law, Jews are united in their common possession of Torah as heritage. We differ in our particular relationship to that heritage. That all Jews have a share in that heritage has been both an ideological and historical principle of Judaism from ancient through modern times.

Conclusion—A Look at the Future

At the close of the twentieth century, a number of critical questions confronted the Jewish people and posed challenges for the future directions of Jewish history:

1. Israel was undertaking a sustained peace process with the Palestinians and the surrounding Arab nations. The future course of that peace process will determine not only Israel's history but also the agenda of diaspora Jewry.

2. Diaspora Jews were concerned about their future continuity—whether their children and grandchildren would continue to identify as Jews. The problems of assimilation and intermarriage were

particularly salient in the United States, the largest Jewish community in history.

3. Demographic patterns were clearly changing. For the past 2,600 years, a majority of Jews had resided in the diaspora. Yet by the close of the twentieth century Israel was the only Jewish community growing demographically. Most forecasts suggested a demographic ascendancy of Israel over the diaspora by the middle of the twenty-first century.

4. Israeli society was asking questions of itself in terms of the symbols of Zionist history and the Jewishness of the Jewish State. A cultural battle, for example, ensued over assessment of the *Altalena*—a ship bearing arms for Irgun soldiers in 1948, which Ben- Gurion ordered disarmed. When Menachem Begin failed to comply with the order, Ben-Gurion's lieutenants fired upon the ship, resulting in significant loss of life. Was this incident part of Israel's growing pains and a necessary step to avert civil war? Or did it reflect a lapse in judgment on the part of Israel's founding fathers? Historical debates of this nature pointed to fundamental cleavages within Israeli society. The meaning of a Jewish state would remain a divisive issue for Israel to define.

The changes these currents suggested pointed to a Jewish world undergoing transformation. Clearly new challenges awaited the Jewish people and their survival in the twenty-first century. Yet if Jewish history has shown anything at all, it has consistently pointed to the incredible capacity of the Jews to defy reality, to continue against all odds. The details doubtless will vary, but the story will continue.

Bibliography for Further Reading

Hartman, David. *Conflicting Visions,* Schocken Books, 1990
Fein, Leonard. *Where Are We?,* Harper and Row, 1988
Hertzberg, Arthur. *The Jews in America,* Simon and Schuster, 1989

Index

Abarbanel, Isaac, 192–93
Abraham Ibn Daud, 177
Abraham ben Ezra, 178
Abraham ben Zimori of Asfi-Safi, 208, 210
Adams, Henry, 273, 353
Adler, Elkan, *Jewish Travelers in the Middle Ages*, 208–11
Adler, Felix, 349
Ahad Ha'am (Asher Ginzberg), 4, 37–39
Albo, Joseph, 191
Alexander the Great, blending cultures of Greece and the Near East, 50–52
Al-Roy, David, 144
America, Jewish settlement in, 346–58
 anti-Semitism, 352
 Bintel Briefs in Jewish press, 354–58
 Columbus Platform, 349
 East European immigration, 350–54
 Ethical Culture movement, 349
 German Jewry, 347–50
 Hebrew Union College, 349
 immigration quotas, 353
 Jewish chaplaincies in Civil War, 350
 social problems, 350–51
American Jewry and Hasidism, 252
Anti-Defamation League, 354
Antiochus III, commending Jews to live within the laws of their ancestors, 53
Anti-Semitism in modern times
 Anti-Defamation League, 354
 early American Jewish settlement, 352
 the Dreyfus Case, 311–12
 Haidamak massacres, 228–29
 Henry Ford, *The Dearborn Independent*, 311
 Holocaust, the Nazi "war against the Jews," 383–401
 immigration as Jewish response to, 313–16
 Joseph Seligman and Grand Hotel at Saratoga, 352
 Leo Frank, 352–54
 in modern culture, 217–19
 in medieval Europe, 170–71
 mourners at funeral of Jacob Joseph, 352
 origins of, 307–8
 Protocols of the Elders of Zion. 310–11, 352–53, 383
 in Reformation, 202
 Richard Wagner, composer, 308–11
 in Soviet Union, 371, 373–74
Aptheker, Herbert, 423
Arendt, Hannah, 393
Aristotle and Jewish philosophy, 156

Assimilation
conversion of Ruth, 43
exile of Israelites, 35–49
Marranos and American Jews, 217–18
model of Jewish life, 37
Augustine
City of God, 119, 123–25
envisioning conversion of Jews, 164
Azariah dei Rossi, 200–1

Babylonian conquest and destruction of Jerusalem, 47–49
revolt of Israelites, 36–37
Baeck, Leo, 284
Balaam, prophet among gentiles, 24
Balfour Declaration, 336, 339–40, 344
Bar-Kokhba revolt, 140
failed messiah, 93–97
wartime treatment of Christians, 108
Baron, Salo, 130–31, 178, 323, 429
Bathsheba, adulterous relationship with King David, 16
Bauer, Yehuda, 393
Bialik, Hayyim Nachman, "The City of Slaughter," 326, 328–30
Begin, Menahem, 335–36
Ben David, Anan, founder of Karaism, 145–46
Ben-Gurion, 335, and Moshe Pearlman, (ed.) *Ben-Gurion Looks Back* 417–21
Benjamin, Judah P., 349–50
Berger, David, 141
Borowitz, Eugene, 285
Brand, Joel, 393
Brezhnev, Leonid, 376
Buber, Martin, 4, 250; Protestant Reformation and Jews, 202
Buchanan, Pat, 424

Canaan and Canaanites
conquest of, 13–15, 18–19
in Hittite empire, 13
loss of land following sexual abominations, 3
as promised land, 1
Rephaites, early settlers in, 15
Twelve tribes in loose alliance, 14
Chamberlain, Houston Stuart, 309, 311, 383
Chanukah. holiday inaugurated, 54, 57
Chazan, Robert, *European Jewry and the First Crusade,* 171–73
Chinese Jewry, 204
Chmielnicki, Bodgan, anti-Semitic atrocities, 227–28, 230–31
Christiani, Pablo, disputation and dialogue with Nachmanides on messianism, 189, 195–97
Christianity
ascendancy of, 118–20
church and Jews, 115–24
crucifixion superceding covenant with Jews, 2–14
duality of flesh and spirit as basis of break between Judaism and Christianity, 109
hostility to a daughter faith, 107–8
intermarriage, 108
Jewish Christianity, 106–10
Judaism a competitive religion, 115–18
origins of, 103–14
Peter's denial of Jesus, 110–11
translating Scriptures into Latin, 116
see also Jesus Christ, Crusades
Circumcision, covenant to abstain from sexual abominations, 3
Cleopatra, Queen of Egypt, safeguarding Jewish life in Palestine, 56
Clermont-Tonnere, Stanislas de, 270
Coexistence, Islamic and Jewish culture in Spanish Golden Age, 176–87
Cohen, Mark R., 132
Çohn, Roy, 423
Colbert, Jean-Baptiste, 269

Columbus Platform, 283, 286, 290–93
Communal life. *see* America, Jewish settlement in
Communism, Soviet Union and Jewry, 370–82
Conservative Judaism, 359–64
  Emet V'emunah, principles of, 362–63, 367–69
  theological curriculum, 359
  and Zionism, 360–61
Constantine, *Confessions.* Christianity as official religion, 115
Cordelia, Joseph, 210
Cordovero, Moses, 235
Council of Antioch, defining Jewish-Christian relationships, 116
Council of Toledo, conversion or expulsion of Jews, 188
Council of Trent, prohibitions against Jews, 202
Covenants
  binding until the end of days, 6
  circumcision, abstaining from sexual abominations, 3
  Holocaust in light of covenant with God, 6–7
  human responsibilities for destiny and history, 7
  and Israelites in exile, 35–49
  law yielding to covenant of grace, for all humanity, 6
  monotheism and religious intolerance, 5
  Pact of 'Umar, 137–38
  questioning divine omnipotence and reality of evil, 39–41
  rainbow as symbol God will refrain from overwhelming humanity as with the flood, 3, 5
  redemption, promise of, 7
Crescas, Hasdai, 191
Crusades, violence against Jews, 165–68
Cyrus I, Persian king, returning Jews to their homeland, 41
Darwin, Charles, 328
David, Israelite king,
  adulterous relation with Bathsheba and insured death of her husband, 16, 19–20
  founding line of Jewish monarchy, 16, 19–20, and moral laws, 16
  unification of the tribes, 16, 19–20
Dawidowicz, Lucy, *The Golden Tradition,* 253–57
Dead Sea sect, self-exile as "Children of light," 68–69
Deuteronomic reform, 29–30; articulated in diaspora, 38
Deutscher, Isaac, 372
Diaspora
  Elephantine colony, 43
  instituting self-government, 37
  Israelite autonomy in, 35–49
  Jewish literature of, 38–41
  Jews from Russia settling in China, 204
  letter of Jeremiah to exiles, 44–45
  policy of accommodation, 37
  readmission, to England, 206–7
  return to homeland, 41–43
Disraeli, Benjamin, 144, 327–28
"Doctrine of the Witness," 120; claiming Jewry testifies to triumph of Christianity, 164–65
Dreyfus, Alfred, 273; celebrated case of anti-Semitism, 311–12
Dubnov, Simon, 228, 315

Eastern European reaction to Jews
  Alexander II, 323–24
  anti-Semitism and Russian pogroms, 324–28
  Catherine II establishing Pale of settlement, 321
  enlightenment and Russian Crown School System, 322
  history of, 321–22
  military service, 323

Eastern European reaction
to Jews *con't.*
Nicholas I, Czar, 322–24
Russian policy of isolation and assimilation, 321–22, and pogroms, 324–28
Eastern European Jews
Ashkenazic Jewry, 225
Cossack rebellion and Chmielnicki pogroms, 227–28
deportation by Persian rulers, 23
development of guilds, 226
Hasidism, 225
Nathan Hannover, history a prophecy fulfilled, 230–32
Polish-Jewish autonomy and rabbinic authority, 224–27
Russia, settlement in Khazar kingdom, 223–24
Soviet Union and Jewry, 370–82
Ukraine communities, and anti-Semitism, 227
Yeshivot learning for women, 225
Ecclesiastes, ethical code for society, 52, 57–59
Ehrenburg, Ilya, 374–75
Einhorn, David, 283, 348
Eleazar exhorting Jews at Masada to suicide to avoid slavery, 81–88
Eliav, Arie, *Between Hammer and Sickle,* 378–82
Elijah Gaon, 251
Elvira Council restricting Jewish and Christian contacts, 108
Emancipation and enlightenment change in Jewish life, 259–62
France and Jewish emancipation, 269–78
individualism stressed, 261
Moses Mendelsohn and Baruch Spinoza debating dogma and reason, 262–65
nation-state development and decline of medieval Kehilla, 258–66
Sixteenth Letter of Samson Raphael Hirsch, 304–5
Emden, Jacob, 240
Emet V'emunah, doctrine of Conservative Judaism, 362–63, 367–69
Enoch, Book of, and dualism, 69
Erasmus, 199
Eschatology
tikkun olam, repair of the world, 233
Essenes
Jewish sectarianism, 67, 71–72
marriage, view of, 67
political nationalism, 67
sharing community property, 67, 72
Esther, book of as guide to Jewish life, 45–47
Ethical Culture movement, 340
Ethiopia, Jewish community in, 204–5
Eusebius, Christian record of Bar-Kokhba revolt, 101–2

Fackenheim, Emil, 285, 426
Farrakhan, Louis, 424
Flood, Sumerian Epic of Gilgamesh and the Great Flood, 3
Ford, Henry,
The Dearborn Independent and anti-Semitism, 311
Nazi "war against Jews," 390
Fourier, Charles, 310
France, Jewish emancipation, 269–78
see also Jewish Emancipation
Frank, Jacob, Frankist movement, sexual depravity and orgies, 239–40
Frankel, Zecharias, 281, 298, 359
Friedlander, David, 265
Frumkin, Esther, Bund leader, 371, 373

Gandhi, Mahatma, 388
Gay, Peter, 271
Geiger, Abraham, 282–83
Genocide, Holocaust, the Nazi "war against the Jews," 383–401

Gershom of Mainz (Rabbi), 165
Gersonides, contradiction between foreknowledge and free will, 158
Gerstein, Kurt, 391
Gillman, Neil, 363
Ginzberg, Asher (Ahad Ha'am), 4, 37–39
Ginzberg, Louis, 141
Gittin tractate urging Jewish rebuilding unity with a common sense of peoplehood, 97–101
Gliksman, Pinhas, "Menahem Mendel's Hasidic Mode," 253–57
Gluckel of Hameln, 259, 266–68
Gnosticism as anti-Judaism, 122–23
Gorbachev, Mikhail, 377
Gordon, Y. L., 266
Graetz, Heinrich, 281, 298, 302
Grayzel, Solomon, Church and the Jews in 13th-century, 174–75
Great Revolt 66–73 C.E., 78–88
Greece.*see* Hellenistic culture
Greenberg, Irving, 7, 40–41
Gregory the Great, Pope, offering tax benefits for converted Jews, 165

Halevi, Judah, 212
Hananya ben Akashya, 255
Hannover, Nathan, Chmielnicki pogrom
and fulfillment of prophecy, 230–32
Hartman, David, 7
Hasdai Crescas, 191
Hasdai Ibn Shaprut, 179
Hasidism, 242, 245–57
accessibility to Divine revelation, 248
and American culture, 252
anti-Zionism, 252
availability of God to everyone, 247
concept of salvation, 250
humanity following God's ways, 248
intimate connection with God, 248
kinship with God, 250
Kotzker Hasidism, 253–57
Lubavitch Hasidism, 252–53
Maid of Ludmir, 249
optimistic view of world, 249
origins, 245
as psychosomatic medicine, 235
ritual bath, 245
Satmar Hasidim, 252
worship in state of joy, 245, 250
Hayyim of Volozhin, 251
Hegel, Georg, 280
Hellenistic culture
homosexuality, 53
philosophies of Athens and Jerusalem, 50–62
Septuagint translated into Greek, 51
Herod the Great, Israelites and Herodian governance, 74–88
Hertzberg, Arthur, 220
The French Enlightenment and the Jews, 272
The Zionist Idea, 332, 334, 341–44
Herzl, Theodor, 312, 335–38
"Auto-Emancipation," 334
"The Jewish State," 334
Herzog, Isaac Halevi, 206
Hildesheimer, Azriel, 300
Hillel, scholarship and Pharisaic thought, 76
Hirsch, Samson Raphael
emancipation and Orthodoxy, 304
and Neo-Orthodoxy, 296–301
The Nineteen Letters, Sixteenth Letter, 304–5
Hasdai Ibn Isaac Ibn Shaprut, Letter to the king of the Khazars, 186–87
Holdheim, Samuel, 283
Holocaust
The Abandonment of the Jews (Wyman), 389

Holocaust *con't.*
Anthology of Holocaust Literature (Glatstein ed.), 394–401
bystanders, 389–90
The Death Train (Wiesel), 394–401
isolationism and silence of Western democracies, 389–90
John XXIII, Pope, 389
in light of covenant with God, 6–7
national concerns of Western democracies, 389–90
Nazi "war against the Jews," 383–86
Franklin D. Roosevelt, 389
St. Louis, refugee ship, 390
United States immigration law, 390
victims, 386–88
Warsaw Ghetto revolt, 386–88
While Six Million Died (Morse), 389

Innocent IV, censorship of the Talmud, 170
Innocent III, 173, Edict in Favor of the Jews, 174
Intermarriage, Solomon and marriage to daughter of Pharoah, 17
Isaiah, prophecy for ethical conduct, 31–34
Islam
Arabian Peninsula off-limits to Jews and Christians, 128
basic freedoms for Jews, 130–31
Christianity and Judaism, influences on, 126–58
conflict over territory, 128
Donmeh, secret practice of Judaism in Islam, 28–39
Jewish communal organization, 133–34
Jewish culture in Spanish Golden Age, 176–87
Jewry and the Islamic Empire, 129–33
second-class status, 130
Koran references to Judaic and Christian materials, 134–336
Mohammed's regard for Jesus, 127
oral traditions, importance of, 126
Pact of 'Umar, 137–38
respect of monotheistic faiths, 127–28
rituals of, 127
Spanish Golden Age and Jewish culture, 176–87
tensions and animosity increasing with economic decline, 132
Israel
anti-Semitism, 404
Arab hostility, 406–8
Bar-Kokhba revolt, 93–97
Begin, Menachem, 405, 415–16
Ben-Gurion-Blaustein Agreement, 409–10
Ben-Gurion, David, 405, 410–11
Bevin, Ernest, 405
Book of Esther as guide to Jewish life, 45–47
British policy and the Jewish question, 403–5
Capture of Jerusalem and exile, 35–49
chosen people, mission and national purpose, 4
civil war, splitting of tribes, 17
entry into Canaan, 1
exodus to promised land, 12–13
expelling natives from Canaan, 14
Dayan, Moshe, 414
diaspora Jews and statehood issue, 409–10
Eisenhower, Dwight D., 411
Eshkol, Levi, 414
Gemayel, Bashir, 416
the Great Revolt, 78–88
Gromyko, Andrei 407

Israel *con't.*
Jewish nationalism and messianic hope under Roman rule, 77
Johnson, Lyndon B., 412
Kastner, Rudolph, 410
Kennan, George 403–4
Kingships in land of Canaan, 15–16, 18
Kissinger, Henry, 415
Lavon, Pinchas, 410
Law of Return, 413
Meir, Golda, 4414
messianism and homeland, 140–45
Nixon, Richard, 414–15
Peres, Shimon, 416
and Philistines, 13
Rameses II(1290–1224 B.C.E.), oppression of Israel, 12–13
refugee crisis, 403–4, 406, 408
resurgence of paganism
Rogers, William, 414
Rome and Israelites in time of Herod the Great, 74–88
Shamir, Yitzhak, 417
Sharon, Ariel, 416
Sharrett, Moshe, 410
Six Day War, 41
slavery in Egypt, 12–13
Soviet Russia and Zionism, 406–7
Francis Cardinal Spellman, 405
Stalin, Joseph, 407
State of Israel: birth of, 406–8; and statehood established, 412–17
Suez Canal, War of Attrition, 411, 414
Ten Commandments for moral order, 13
Ten Plagues in history of, 13
Truman, Harry, 403, 406
United Nations, 405, 411
war and diplomacy, 410–12; war and peace, 414–17
and world Jewry, 403–21
Wyzynski of Lubin, Bishop, 404
see also Jewish sectarianism
Israel Baal Shem Tov, 245
Isserles, Moses, Rabbi, 225

Jabotinsky, Vladimir, 335–36
Jackson, Jesse, 424
Jacob of Armenia, 223
Jesus Christ
counted as one of the prophets, 108, 237
crucifixion and resurrection, 10–12
life of, 103–6
and Pharisees, 103
teaching Jewish doctrines, 103
Jewish Emancipation in France
anti-Semitism and Jewish emancipation in France, 273
background to, 269–70
constitution for French Judaism, 276
debated, 270–74
and French Revolution, 274
Napoleon and the Jews, 274–77
rabbis compensated by the nation-state, 276
Voltaire, 271–72, and anti-Semitism, 273
Jewish enlightenment, 258–66
Mendelsohn-Spinoza debate on dogma and reason, 262–65
women, role in family and social life, 258–59
Jewish messianism, and sectarianism, 140–50
Jewish mysticism, 33–4
Jewish sectarianism
Dead Sea sect, 68–69
Essenes, 67, 71–72
Pharisees, 63–66, 71
Sadducees, 66–67, 71–72
Zealots, 67–68

Jewry
Crusades, selecting martyrdom rather than conversion, 165–68, 171–73
Holocaust, the Nazi "war against the Jews," 383–401
Islam and Jewish culture in Spanish Golden Age, 176–87
Marranos and conversion, 212–13
Medieval rulers issuing charters of protection for Jews, 168–71
persecution of Jews, 1888–97
see also Eastern European reaction to
see also America, Jewish settlement in
see also Modernity and the American Jew
see also Soviet Union and Jewry
Jochanan Ben Zakkai
advocating accommodation with Rome, 79
Pharisaic leadership after destruction of Second Temple, 90
John Hyrcanus, 55
Joseph II, KIng of Austria, 262
Josephus,
Antiquities, 71–73
citing Jesus as "the Christ," 108
Jewish War, 80–88
Judah the Patriarch and accommodation with Roman rulers, 95–97
committing oral law to writing, 64, 95–96
Judaism
Marrano Judaism, 212–29
reconstructing faith after destruction of the Second Temple, 89–93
Reconstructionism, 365–67
see also Conservative Judaism, Jewish sectarianism

Kabbalah
Lurianic mysticism and messianism, 233–34
and Renaissance humanism, 198–99
Kaganovitch, Lazar, 373–74, 376
Kahane, Meir, 303
Kant, Immanuel, 264, 280
Kaplan, Mordecai, 428–29; *Judaism as a Civilization*, 365
Karaism
disputing authority, 145–49
"Mourners of Zion," 146–47
denying Jewish blood to evade Nazi destruction, 148
Karo, Joseph, *Shulhan Arukh*, 235
Katz, Jacob, *Tradition and Crisis*, 259
Kaufman, Irving, 423
Kehilla, decline with Jewish emancipation and enlightenment, 258–66
Kennedy, Joseph P., 384, 390
Khazar kingdom, Russia and Jewry, 223–24
Khrushchev, Nikita, 376
Kohler, Kaufman, 349
Kohn, Hans (ed.), *Nationalism*, 318–21
Kook, Abraham I., 144, 206, 300
Kook, Zvi Yehuda, 144
Kotzker Hasidism, 253–57

LaFollette, Robert, 353
Leibniz, Gottfried Wilhelm, 264
Lenin, Vladimir, 311, 315, 370–71
Levy, Asser, 346
Lieberman, Joseph, 424
Lindbergh, Charles, 390
Lithuanian settlements, 224
Litvinov, Maxim, 374
Lodge, Henry Cabot, Sr., 353
Lost Tribes, return to Jewish body politic, 28–29
Lubavitcher Rebbe, 242, 303
Lull, Raymond, 198
Luria, Isaac, and Lurianic Kabbalism, 233–35, 237
Luther, Martin, 201–2

Luxemberg, Rosa, 372

Maccabean Revolt, 53–57, 59–62
McCarthy, Joseph P., 423
Machiavelli, 198
Maimonides, Moses, 156–57, 280, 428–29
on Jewish messianism, 143, 145, 180
Epistle on Martyrdom 145, 179, 181, 184–185
Epistle to Yemen, 149
Essay on Resurrection, 181–182
The Guide for the Perplexed, 156, 180, 183
Islamic Jewish culture in Spanish Golden Age, 126–877
on Jewish modernity, 212
Mishneh Torah, 180, 182
messianism and laws on installation of kings, 180, 242–44
and Orthodoxy, 297
rating Christianity, 170
Manasseh ben Israel, 206
Manifest Destiny
Israel as chosen people with mission and national purpose, 4
Marcus, Jacob, *The Jew in the Medieval World*. 186–87
Mark, Gospel of, account of crucifixion and resurrection, 110–12
Marranos
identification of, 213–19
influence and the diaspora, 213–19
Jewish tradition and gentile society, 216
role in economics and world of capitalism, 214
Marriageability
Reconstructionist Judaism, 366
Karaites and Rabbanites, 147–49
Marshall, George C., 417, 419–21
Martyrdom
Jewry electing rather conversion, 165–68, 171–73
Marx, Karl, "On the Jewish Question," 309, 316–18
Masada suicides, 79–88
Meir, Golda, 375
Menahem Meiri (Rabbi), 170, 183–84
Mendelsohn, Moses, 240, 280, 284, 296
argument with Baruch Spinoza on dogma and reason, 262–65
Mendes-Flohr, Paul and Jehuda Reinharz (eds.) *The Jew in the Modern World*, 277
Messianism
disputation and dialogue of Nachmanides and Pablo Christiani, 189, 195–97
expectations of Israelites under Parthian rule, 74
Jewish messianism 140–45
Josephus citing Jesus as "the Christ," 108
of Lubavitch Hasidism, 144–45
Maimonides "Epistle to Yemen," 149
Sabbetianism, 233, 235–37
and "second coming," 238–39
tikkun olam, repair of the world, 233–35, 238–39
Mideast land rights claimed by Arabs and Israelites, 15
Mikhoels, Solomon, 375
Moabite Stone, 21–22
Modernity and the American Jew
anti-Semitism, decline in, 423–25
diaspora and the culture of the majority, 428
distinctive Jewish ideas, 427–30
intermarriage, 422, 429–30
Molcho, Solomon, 193
Moloch, Phoenician deity and child sacrifices, 14
Molotov, Vyacheslav Mikhailovich, 376
Monotheism and religious intolerance, 5
Montaigne, Michel de, 269
Montefiore, Moses, 324

Morgenthau, Henry, 392–93
Morse, Arthur, 390; *While Six Million Died*, 389
Moses of Crete, messianic hope, promise of parting Mediterranean waters, 144
Moses Maimonides, *see* Maimonides, Moses
Mysticism and Jewish philosophy, 158–60
    intimate union of the human soul and God, 158
Kabbala, providing a level of reality, 159–60
Nachmanides, disputation and dialogue with Pablo Christiani on messianism, 189, 195–97
Nachman of Bratzlav, 252
Napoleon and the Jews, 274–77
Nasi, Gracia, 214
Nasi, Joseph, 214
Nathan of Gaza, 36–39
Nemoy, Leon
    Karaites and Sabbath observance, 150–51

Oriental Jewry and Islam, 203
Orthodox Judaism
    Neo-Orthodoxy and Samson Raphael Hirsch, 296–301
    "Old" Orthodoxy, 295–96, and secular culture, 295
    Orthodox Judaism today, 301–4
Paganism
    creation story as struggle of deities for supremacy, 2
    nature governing human actions, 2
    tolerance of the deities of others, 5–6
Palestine
    Land rights claimed in ancient and contemporary times, 15
Papacy, relations with Jews, 169–70
Parthia
    Israel expecting redemption, 74
Paul the Apostle
    and Jewish Christianity, 106–10
    Letter to the Romans, a doctrine of Christian supersessionism, 113
Paul IV (Pope), ghettoizing Jews, 202
Pearlman, Moshe (ed.) with David Ben-Gurion. *Ben-Gurion Looks Back*, 417–21
Peres, Shimon, 335
Peter, denial of Jesus, 110–11
Petlyura, Simon, 371, 374
Pharisees
    and the Great Revolt, 79–88
    Oral Law of Judaism, 65–66
    leadership during Roman rule, 92–93
    punishment, in kind, 65
    resentment of establishment, 69–70
Philo,
    creating Jewish philosophy, 152–55
Philosophy
    divine providence and human freedom, 155–57
    medieval Jewish philosophy, 152–58
    scripture and reason in Jewish philosophy, 152
Pico della Mirandola, 198–99
Pinsker, Leon, 334, 337, 341
Pittsburgh Platform, 283, 288–90, 348–49
Pius XII, Pope, 391
Plagues, Ten Plagues in history of Israel, 13
Plaut, Gunther (ed.), *The Growth of Reform Judaism*, 288–93
Poland, invitation for Jewish settlers, 169
Pritchard, James, 20–21
Prophets and prophecy
    Balaam among gentiles, 24

Prophets and prophecy *con't.*
exhorting peoples on moral conduct, 25
Jeremiah's letter to exiles, 44–45
Nathan rebuking King David, 25
rejecting theory on death and resurrection, 25
Sabbetai counting Jesus as one of the prophets, 237
Protocols of the Elders of Zion, 310–11, 352–53
Proudhon, Pierre Joseph, 310
Ptolemy I, invasion of Palestine and exile of Jews to Egypt, 50–51

Rabbinic Judaism
formation from Talmuds, 64
Ethics of the Fathers, 70
reconstruction of Judaism after destruction of the Second Temple, 89–102
relationship with Christianity, 109
Rabin, Yitzhak, 335
Rainbow, symbol of covenant that God will never again overwhelm humanity as did the Great Flood, 3, 5
Raphall, Morris, 348
Rashi (Solomon Itzhaki), 171
Reconstructionism,
on homosexuality, 366–67
mixed marriages, 366
Zionism of, 366
Redemption
promise of, surviving reality of the Holocaust, 7
Reform Judaism
Columbus Platform, 288, 290–93
in early America, 347–49
homosexuality, 287
intermarriage, 283–85, 287
issues and doctrines, 281–83
Jewishness from patrilineal descent, 285–86
origins, 279–80
Pittsburgh Platform, 288–90
Reform Judaism today, 283–88
social ethics, 283–84
Zionism and law of return, 286–88
Religion and Deuteronomic Reform, 29–30
Renaissance and Reformation,
diaspora Jews, 203–6
England, readmission to, 206–7
ethical conduct, 198
Jewish travelers of Middle Ages, 208–11
Protestant Reformation, 201–3
Reubeni, David, 193, 203, 208
Reuchlin, Johannes, 199
Rome and religion
Constantine establishing Christianity as official religion, 115
Israelites in time of Herod the Great, 74–88
minimizing contacts between Jews and Christians, 115–117
Rosen, Moshe, 378
Rosenbergs, Julius and Ethel, 375, 422–23
Roth, Cecil, 200
Rothstein, Arnold, 351
Russia, Early Jewish settlements in, 223–24
Ruth, conversion of, 43

Saadiah Gaon, 280; messianism, and *Book of Doctrines and Beliefs*, 160–61
Sabbath observance, Karaite-Rabbanite debate, 150–51
Sabbetai Zvi, 236–42
Sabbetianism, 233–44, Jewish modernism and religious changes, 241
Sadducees Jewish sectarianism, 66–67, 71–772
Salome Alexandra, Hasmonean queen, 57
Samaritans and political development, 26–28

Saspourtas, Jacob, 237
Satre, Jean-Paul, 375, 423
Schechter, Solomon, 359, 361, 364
Schiff, Jacob, 325
Schindler, Alexander, 286
Schneersohn, Menachem Mendel, 145
Scholem, Gershom, 122, 199, 235–36, 239, on Hasidism, 246–47
    the *Zohar*, The Book of Splendor, 161–63
Second Commonwealth times,
    ethical conduct in *Ethics of the Fathers*, 70
    Jewish sectarianism, 63–71
    rift among classes of Israelites, 63–73
Sectarianism
    Jewish sectarianism and messianism, 145–49
    Karaism, anti-establishment, 145–49
    "Mourners of Zion," 146–47
Sefirot symbolizing human role as co-creators with God, 159
Seligman, Joseph, 352
Sharansky, Natan, 376
Shamir, Yitchak, 336
Shertok, Moshe, 393
Schine, David, 423
Slansky, Rudolph, 423, 375
Sofer, Moses, 218
    on emancipation, 295
Solomon, Haym, 347
Solomon Ibn Gabirol, 178
Solomon Ibn Verga, 193–95
The Rod of Judah, 194
Solomon Itzhaki (Rashi), 171
Solomon, Israelite king,
    expansion of Jewish state, 16–17
    intermarriage and marriage to daughter of Pharaoh, 17
    unified religious practices of Israelites, 16
Sombart, Werner, 214
Soviet Union and Jewry, 370–82
    Between Hammer and Sickle (Eliav), 378–82
    Birobidzhan venture, Siberian Jewish republic, 372–73, 375
    Einsatzgruppen massacres, 374
    Glasnost, 377–78
    intermarriage, 377
    Jewish emigration, 377
    Pale of Settlement in Russia, 370
    Russian Zionism, 71, 373
    Simchat Torah, rejoicing in the law, 377, 379–82
    Stalin and the Jews, 372–77
    support of State of Israel, 375
    Ukrainian Jews and pogroms, 371
Spanish Golden Age
    Inquisition, conversion or expulsion, 188–97
    Islamic Jewish culture in, 176–87
    Jewish and Christian experiences, 188–97
    Karaites and Law of Return to Zion, 148
    reconquest of Christianity, 189–91
Spanish Inquisition
    expulsion, Marranos and Jewish role in modernity, 212–13
Spinoza, Benedict
    arguments with Moses Mendelsohn on dogma and reason, 262–65
    on modern Jewish identity, 212–13, 216, 218–19
    Theological-Political Treatise. 218, 220–22
Stolypin, Peter, 326–27
Stuyvesant, Peter, 346
Sumerians
    Epic of Gilgamesh, and the Great Flood, 3
    legal code for social order, 1

Talmage, Frank (ed.), *Disputation and Dialogue* on messianism in Christian Spain, 195–97

Temple at Jerusalem
destruction and exile of Israelites, 35–49
aftermath to destruction, 89–03
Julian I, rebuilding Jerusalem Temple, 117–18
Ten Plagues in history of Israel, 13
Thirteenth-Century Europe
economics, growth of capitalism and emigration from Western Europe, 169
Thomas Aquinas, 169
Tocqueville, Alexis de, 276
Tolstoy, Leo, 326
Torah
constitution of Israelites, 43
Oral Law in Pharisaic Judaism, 65–66
religious and legal code, 1
Torquemada, Tomas de, 192
Trotsky, Leon, 311, 314–15
Trunk, Isaiah, 385

Uriah, husband of Bathsheba, 16

Vashti, Persian Queen defying King Ahasuerus, 45–47
Vidal, Gore, 273
Vital, Hayyim, 233
Voltaire, 258

Wagner, Richard, anti-Semitism, 308–11
"Judaism in Music," 318
Wallace, George, 423
Wallenberg, Raoul, 389
Watson, Tom, 353
Weber, Max, 25
Weizmann, Chaim, 333, 335
Wells, H. G., 391
Wessaly, Naftali Herz, "Worlds of Peace and Truth," 262
Wiesel, Elie, 4, 7, 386
Wise, Stephen, 372, 392
Wolf Landau of Strykow, 254
Wolfson, Harry, 152–155
Women and Orthodox Judaism, 302
World to come, *tikkun olam*, repair of the world, 233–35, 238–39
World Zionist Organization, 337
Wyman, David, 390; *The Abandonment of the Jews*, 389

Yerushalmi, Yosef, 177

Zealots
rejecting Roman rule and taxation, 67–68, and the Great Revolt, 78–88
Zionism
of Conservative Judaism, 360–61
historical background, 332–37
ideology of, 334–37
implementation of, 337–40
and Jewish messianism, 140–45
and Orthodox Judaism, 303
the San Remo Declaration(1922), 339
The Zionist Idea (Hertzberg), 332, 334, 341–44
Zohar, mystical text, 159, 161–63
Zola, Emil, "J'Accuse" and the Dreyfus Case, 312